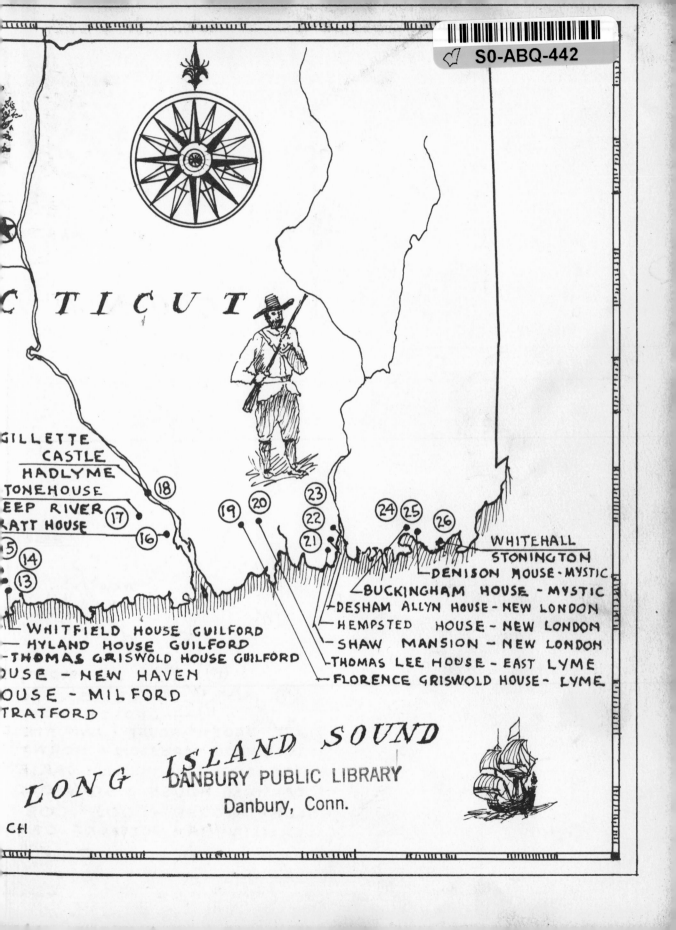

CTICUT

GILLETTE
CASTLE
HADLYME
TONEHOUSE
EEP RIVER
RATT HOUSE

18

17

16

5

14

13

19

20

23

22

21

24 25

26

WHITEHALL
STONINGTON
DENISON HOUSE - MYSTIC
BUCKINGHAM HOUSE - MYSTIC
DESHAM ALLYN HOUSE - NEW LONDON
HEMPSTED HOUSE - NEW LONDON
SHAW MANSION - NEW LONDON
THOMAS LEE HOUSE - EAST LYME
FLORENCE GRISWOLD HOUSE - LYME

WHITFIELD HOUSE GUILFORD
HYLAND HOUSE GUILFORD
THOMAS GRISWOLD HOUSE GUILFORD
OUSE - NEW HAVEN
OUSE - MILFORD
TRATFORD

LONG ISLAND SOUND

CH

Historic Houses and Interiors
in Southern Connecticut

OVERLEAF: Whitehall, Stonington
Florence Griswold House, Old Lyme.

HISTORIC HOUSES
AND INTERIORS IN
Southern Connecticut

Lyman Allyn Museum, New London

Illustrations and Text by
SARA EMERSON ROLLESTON

HASTINGS HOUSE   Publishers   NEW YORK

Dedicated to
Harland J. Bascom
Beloved Uncle

Whose forebears contributed to the early founding of Connecticut.

Ensign William Goodrich, the Settler, from Waterbury, Massachusetts, who moved to Wethersfield in 1634 or 1635. He was one of the men who put down the Pequot camp in Mystic in 1637, after the warring tribe massacred and scalped English settlers.

Thomas Bascom, a French Huguenot, who came to this country in 1634, settled in Dorchester, then ventured to Windsor in 1639 as part of the second company to move there. He later went to Northampton.

Michael Griswold, who settled in Wethersfield before 1640.

Thomas Wright, who settled in Wethersfield in 1639.

Elizabeth Alden Seabury, originally from Duxbury, a granddaughter of John Alden, settled in Stonington in 1697 at the time of her marriage. Her daughter, Patience Seabury Latham of Groton, was the mother of Abigail Latham, who married Isaac Griswold of Norwich, Connecticut.

Library of Congress Cataloging in Publication Data

Rolleston, Sara Emerson.
    Historic houses and interiors in southern Connecticut.
    Includes index.
    1. Historic buildings — Connecticut — Pictorial works. 2. Interior decoration — Connecticut — Pictorial works. 3. Connecticut — History — Pictorial works.
I. Title.
F95.R65   974.6   76-7446
ISBN 0-8038-3035-1

Published simultaneously in Canada by
Saunders of Toronto, Ltd., Don Mills, Ontario
Printed in the United States of America

Contents

Hempsted House, New London.

Introduction

A book such as this, which takes us visiting from house to house along the Connecticut coast, serves more than one purpose. It provides an opportunity for the armchair traveller to explore the homes of early New Englanders, to play the game of compare and contrast and draw conclusions concerning the colonists' habits and our own. The very uniformity of the floor plans and room use gives food for thought about the impact of environment on early builders. The concept of the house as a "machine for living" was not first thought of in the twentieth century after all. In New England, where would a man build his chimneystack but right in the heart of the house?

The thoughtful viewer may ponder also the strength of tradition which bound men who learned the builder's craft from father to son, from master to apprentice. Tradition which made for a similarity of style and proportion gives dignity to the simplest village. How different from our accustomed street-scape with its mixture of salt-box, condominium, ranch house and Victorian villa.

Another pleasure the book provides is in the introduction it gives to New Englanders of an earlier day. As house-museums are more thoughtfully researched and interpreted to us, they give a truer picture of the actual families who lived and worked in them. It is this insight into the daily habits of housewives, farmers, ministers and sea captains which enriches a visit to their homes, making it possible to travel in time as well as in space — reaching back for roots in our common humanity.

If, as we sometimes hear, we are becoming a fragmented people, restlessly searching for identity, surely these houses, in pictures and in reality, can give us, as we study and enjoy them, more than the interest of a collection of artifacts however quaint or decorative: a warm feeling of relatedness to the men and women of once-upon-a-time.

JANET G. JAINSCHIGG, President of
The Connecticut League of Historical Societies, and of the
Society for the Preservation of New England Antiquities

Thomas Hooker's House, from John W. Barber's *Connecticut Historical Collections,* New Haven, page 43, 1836. Photograph courtesy of *The Connecticut Historical Society,* Hartford, Connecticut.

Theophilus Eaton's house from Edward R. Lambert's, *History of the Colony of New Haven,* Hitchcock and Stafford. 1838, page 52. Photo courtesy of *The Connecticut Historical Society,* Hartford, Connecticut.

Foreword

The purpose of this book is to offer you a photographic record of the domestic arts of coastal Connecticut from 1639 to 1919. Awareness of the need to preserve America's early heritage, grows every day with the ravages of time. Historical societies and archeological groups are emerging in many older towns and cities to rescue and renovate important domestic arts and architecture of our past. With the added discovery of ancient inventories, diaries, letters, such societies can now more accurately reconstruct and furnish these houses with documentary exactness to "the way they used to be." Apart from historic value, these houses and their artifacts are rich source-material for today's designers, architects, craftsmen, homemakers. Before the industrial revolution — when the artistic merit of home furnishings took a nose dive — the home arts in Connecticut represented the good taste of the early settlers. There was a nobility of proportion, and inventiveness of design, a keen awareness of the fitness of things. These first builders expressed *superb quality* in all the work of their hands — their homes, their furnishings, their lives, their country. True, some of the more sophisticated household wares were imported from England. But the early native country art which sprang from necessity, flourished in Connecticut and gave its first houses great charm. Connecticut's domestic art is rooted in its history.

After the first struggle for survival of the Pilgrims of 1620, Puritans came to Massachusetts in droves. Even the towns of Duxbury, Dorchester, Watertown and Boston were becoming crowded. When news of the fertile valley of Connecticut came, of its mammoth forests of sturdy trees, its waterfront teeming with fish and shellfish, its rivers thriving with salmon, its prospect of a rich fur trade from the bountiful wildlife, the adventurous Massachusetts colonists were determined to set out for these "delightful banks."

In 1634 and 1635 Wethersfield was established by members of the Watertown congregation, Windsor in 1635 by Dorchester families. Hartford was founded in 1636 by Thomas Hooker and his Newtown, now Cambridge, church. Leaving Massachusetts on the last day of May, a hundred men, women and children and a hundred sixty head of cattle and farm animals trekked through the blossoming wilderness under Mr. Hooker's dynamic leadership. Covering ninety miles in two weeks, they inched their way over mountain, waterways, swamps and cut their way through thickets and forests. With no guide but a compass and faith in the guiding hand of their God, these "saints" as they called themselves, sang hymns on the way to their new "promised land."

Arriving in early summer, they had time to raise their houses, clear the land, and plant for a late harvest. Here at Hartford, as at Wethersfield and Windsor, the colonizers were gentlemen of quality and intelligence. Many were new to the drudgery and hardships of pioneering new territory, but they were determined to be free men. With great diligence the little community built its fenced city to withstand the winter's cold, Indian attack, and wolves, wild boars and bears.

The Puritan fathers of our country were men of distinction who could have carved a name for themselves in England. Civil and religious leaders were well educated, the majority at Oxford or Cambridge, and most were men of some experience. Every role necessary for the establishment of a community in the legislative, military, clerical and mercantile areas was filled by well qualified men. They came from fine families and were principled, God-fearing and God-loving people who thought for themselves, their high morality contributing to their good balance and judgment, good taste and manners.

One of these men was Thomas Hooker, who helped to shape this country's growth, giving a greater atmosphere of liberty to Connecticut's government and society than had existed in Massachusetts. Through his learning, experience, and self-discipline, he became wise in his decisions, original in his thinking, daring in his innovations of individual rights and diplomatic in healing differences of opinion. He was friendly with the legislature and did much to advise the formidable men who shaped the Constitution of Connecticut, the first in this country, and in developing the petition for Connecticut's great charter.

The early settlers were used to living well and laid out houses that suited their way of life. Their good taste and refinement is shown in this old drawing of Thomas Hooker's house, with many of the characteristics of the Connecticut plan. It has a central chimney and its windows are leaded, small, and placed high to prevent Indian intrusion. The upstairs projects several inches over the first floor, and bulbous drop-pendants embellish the hood over the doorway, which is centrally located, with an extended entryway.

Another important Southern Connecticut house is that of Theophilus Eaton, who was Governor of the New Haven colony, with John Davenport as its minister. This colony based its law on Biblical law. New Haven was designed to be an elegant, planned city, laid out in plots around a city square. Eaton's house, according to the drawings, was a large one with five chimneys, each one serving several fireplaces. The front is E-shaped. A man of wealth and stature, Eaton was an important merchant connected with the East India Company of England. His house was built around the time New Haven was founded, about 1637.

Henry Whitfield, too, was a man of great wealth. His house was built of grand proportions in 1639, and is probably the earliest example of a stone house in New England that still stands. Most houses were built of oak and with wood timbers. Whitfield, like the other founders of Connecticut's early towns was a minister who brought his band of Puritans to the area which was later named Guilford in 1643.

George Denison, swashbuckling hero and former soldier in England's Cromwellian war, wrote of his "mansion house" where he entertained like a king. It burned in the 18th century and was immediately rebuilt by his grandson, though the plan was different.

The high morality of the first founders of our country gave them a discernment for the best in all areas of their lives, which was manifested in their surroundings. Their houses and their furnishings, sturdily constructed, had a simple, unpretentious beauty and well-proportioned grandeur about them. The builders had the earth's abundance for their use, the plentiful oak, pine, white wood, maple, stone, and shells for mortar. These craftsmen were often ship builders who transferred their skills to architecture in the splicing of timbers and in the use of supporting corbels. Even the pitch of a wall sometimes resembles that of a captain's cabin, as do the proportions of the wall paneling. To withstand the ravages of wind and storm at sea, ships were sturdily built, and the houses were too, against Indian raids, weather, and ferocious beasts. Often prefabricated during the winter, the logs and timbers cut and shaped according to plan, settler's houses could be raised on spring or summer days by the community.

Generation after generation of early Americans were called upon to defend their homes and freedoms at the battle line. As the first army, a handful of men, left Hartford, Windsor and Wethersfield, Thomas Hooker gave it a benediction that outlined the purpose of the 1637 Pequot War, and incidentally every following war. He said, ". . . although gold and silver be wanting you, yet you have that to maintaine which is farre more precious, the lives, liberties and new purchased freedom . . ." Connecticut's victories in this and in following Colonial wars, trained the soldiers for the Revolutionary War.

The founders of Connecticut were zealous in protecting their rights, and citizens took the oath of a free man when they arrived. The first colony to have a Constitution, Connecticut inspired the United Colonies of New England, and foresaw the necessity of establishing its liberties by charter. The petition was fashioned with great care and presented to King Charles II by John Winthrop II, the son of the Massachusetts Bay Governor and one of Connecticut's founders. The charter gave a freer breath cherished by the citizens and when King James II's ambassador, Edmund Andros was to take it back, revoking its rights it was secreted at the conference table, spirited away, and reportedly hidden in a great oak tree. When William and Mary came into power the freedoms established in the charter again came into effect. The charter oak was felled by a storm in 1856 and a piano shown in this book was made from the wood.

Connecticut was the first colony to have its delegate vote to accept the Declaration of Independence. The fervor to be free from injustices and dominating influences encouraged each man and woman to express individual creativity in meeting necessity. The early colonist had to do almost everything for himself and was not afraid to express himself in new ways, whether it was a spoon rack, a "cheast", a great door, or "ye bedstead." His works, were, though at times naive, labors of love, and even the crudest farm pieces display individual charm.

Beginning chronologically with Thomas Hooker's house, the pictures close with the castle designed by his direct descendant, William Gillette, the actor who portrayed Sherlock Holmes around the world. Here are some of the most beautiful historic houses built along the Connecticut Coast, from 1639, through the country's exciting events in the late 17th, the 18th, 19th and early 20th centuries.

To do a book if this sort, one becomes indebted to many. My first gratitude goes to my dear husband, William A. Rolleston, A.I.A., who encouraged and supported this project. The endpaper map is by him. My thanks go to the publisher, Walter Frese, for his good taste and creative imagination. Also to Al Lichtenberg, Art Director, Daian Frese, Editor, and Lee Tobin, Production Manager, I express gratitude, as I do to Mrs. George Thompson and Mrs. John Pearson Smith for stenographic help.

Much appreciation goes to the many historical societies, without whose cooperation this book would not be possible. To their directors, curators and attendants who graciously allowed my photographic intrusions, I am most indebted. Special thanks must be expressed to Mr. and Mrs. Donald Fowler of the Stratford Historical Society, and to Mrs. Gemmell Jainschigg, President of the Society for the Preservation of New England Antiquities, and of the Connecticut League of Historical Societies, for her enthusiasm and Introduction.

As you wander through these historic houses, which you can visit in person during the summer, and a few all year, you will find example after example of America's early domestic art, works created in the atmosphere of freedom, where the individual felt unhampered and was able to express himself creatively, in this "sweet land of liberty."

SARA EMERSON ROLLESTON

WHITFIELD HOUSE, 1639, Guilford.

This fortress of a house, built in 1639 for the leader of a group of English Puritans, Reverend Henry Whitfield, is the oldest stone house in New England. Whitfield, a well-to-do vicar of Ockly, Surry, England, became dissatisfied with the religious and economic domination and persecutions that existed under the reign of Charles I, and with twenty-five other dissident Puritans, sailed for the New World.

A friend of John Davenport, New Haven's famed leader, and George Fenwick, colonizer of Saybrook, it is natural that Whitfield set his compass for Connecticut's shore. On a site between New Haven and Saybrook, land was purchased from the Menuncatuck Indians where the settlement established its roots. Later, in 1643 this area was named Guilford.

William Leete, from Cambridge, later to become a Governor of Connecticut, was a member of this group. As he was familiar with England's stone houses, perhaps he influenced Whitfield to build this L-shaped stone stronghold. Other houses in Connecticut were built of oak, but this stone one would not only be a bulwark against Indian raids and the wiles of the wilderness, but it would be less liable to burn.

The builder of this house was probably Edward Jones, a North Hamptonshire carpenter connected with William Leete. Three other stone houses, now demolished, are attributed to him.

The Colonial Dames of America took the initial efforts in saving this historic landmark and the Federal Government and other private contributors assured the preservation of one of America's great early domestic landmarks. Architect J. Frederick Kelly was in charge of restoration which was completed on October 27, 1937. The house is owned by the state.

The Great Hall, harking back to medieval tradition, is 15 x 33 feet with huge fireplaces or "chimneys" as they were then called, at either end. This room served as a place for church services, town meetings, a refuge for all in emergencies, and a dwelling for the Whitfields. *Above:* View of north chimney.

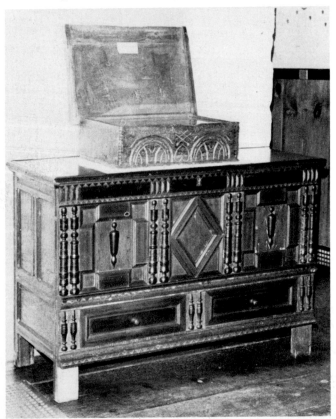

This documented Plymouth chest has a carved Bible Box resting on it.

When the room was in private use, a "room divider," a large barn-like door suspended on hinges, could be dropped from the ceiling, making two rooms. Each room then had its own end-wall chimney. *Above:* South view of the Great Hall.

A study of Governor Leete's famous ox-blood red chair.

The restored kitchen houses a loom and a display of cooking pots and implements used in preparing meals and running a household. The door leads to the cellar. The cupboard holds pewter pieces of different dates. The pottery on the long shelf is Connecticut slipware. Herbs from the kitchen garden outside the kitchen door were dried on a sapling suspended from the rafters.

The sapling lug pole suspended between the inner side walls of the chimney held the early cooking kettles over the flames. Iron cranes, suspended in the hearth's opening, came later.

The Hall Chamber, which would now be called a master bedroom, is over the Great Hall on the northern side. A tiny courting mirror of an irregular shape hangs over the important early painted whitewood chest, a piece which dates from between 1690 and 1710.

Some of the stonework in the bedroom fireplace is the original 1639 masonry. The chest, called a "high daddy," is a country piece. The sturdy chairs are Carver chairs. Pelts were used for rugs. The paddle on the turkey-red linsey-woolsey quilt was for beating the feather bed into shape.

15

The child's room was purposely placed over the warm kitchen. The lid of the hutch table is folded up to make a chair. The cradle is an unusually large one. *Below:* The garret with its 60 degree pitched roof houses a loom, the town clock of The First Congregational Church in Guilford, and includes exhibits of coins and memorabilia of historic Guilford interest.

HYLAND HOUSE, 1660,
Guilford.

Another 17th century house, also in Guilford, the George Hyland House, was built of oak clapboard about twenty years later than the Whitfield's stone one. Here is an example of what developed as the typical Connecticut plan. A central chimney at the back and sandwiched between two rooms downstairs and two upstairs, housed flues for the fireplaces of each of the four rooms. The rear chimney area left space in front of it for a central entrance hall or "porch" as it was called. A ⬐ shaped staircase to the second floor, backed the fireplace wall.

This four-room plan, "two over two" as it is known, with a centered front door, hall, and in back of that the great chimney, was the prototype for many early Connecticut houses.

The great press cupboard between the windows, is American woodwork furniture dating sometime between 1690 and 1700. This piece is on loan to Hyland House by *The Metropolitan Museum of Art*, Gift of Mrs. Russell Sage, 1909.

Originally the kitchen, this room became later the equivalent of our living room of today. The triangular chair in the far corner is a three-legged one and is on loan to Hyland House by *The Metropolitan Museum of Art*, Gift of Mrs. Russell Sage, 1900. It is an English XVI chair of oak. *Below:* The press cupboard is on loan to Hyland House by *The Metropolitan Museum of Art*, Gift of Mrs. Russell Sage, 1909.

The "keeping room," a 19th century term for the best room of the house, was a showplace for the more formal pieces of furniture. The room was used for social occasions, weddings, funerals, and visits from the preacher.

A close up of the cupboard containing a rare collection of Delft plates and flip glasses.

The chimney in the Keeping Room.

Presumably English Delft, this platter with its Chinese pagoda design, seen in the keeping room, would make a beautiful pattern for needlework today.

As families grew, and more space was required, the house plan expanded. The great lean-to kitchen, with possibly a "borning room" and a buttery on either side, with a steep-roofed garret above, was added at the rear of the house. The kitchen fireplace was "flued" into the existing chimney.

This primitive cupboard is painted in ox-blood color. This paint was made by putting iron filings or ox-blood in a buttermilk or sour milk base, and spread very much like our latex paint of today. The plates are Connecticut-made red slipware, and the designs are taken from Indian patterns.

Two views of the 1720 lean-to kitchen. The top picture at right shows clapboard of the original 1660 house. The double spinning wheel, known as a gossip wheel, allows two women to spin yarn and chat at the same time; or a mother might teach her daughter to spin on this dual wheel.

The nine drawer spice box held herbs and spices used for cooking and medicinal purposes. Connecticut had a booming trade with the West Indies, importing molasses, spices, sugar, rum, and indigo, a plant used for dyeing yarn in shades of blue.

Upstairs, the beautiful "bedstead with curtains" is similar to one so described in the inventory of George Hyland's house, taken at the time of his death in 1692. The cradle has unusual lengthwise rockers. The highly sophisticated crewel bedspread is worked in shades of indigo blue wool on ivory linen, in an original pineapple design. *Below:* A loom and weaving equipment are displayed in this second bedroom. The bed is covered with a linsey-woolsey quilt, dyed in indigo blue. A trundle, pull-out bed, fits underneath.

The lean-to of Hyland House was added on by the builder's son in 1720. He also introduced the boldly carved balustrade on the staircase. This house is an example of the Connecticut plan, a "two over two" and added lean-to kitchen with overhead garret. The steep 45 degree roof line gave the house its salt-box profile, and the attic provided sleeping quarters for hired help or children, though children usually slept in a trundle bed. The original clapboard siding of the 1660 house is the inside wall of the garret.

25

THOMAS LEE HOUSE, 1660, East Lyme.

Thomas Lee, Sr. and his family came to this country about 1641 and settled in the vast area then known as Saybrook. His son, the second Thomas Lee, built this house around 1660 and obvious changes were made in it during his lifetime. In 1713 it no doubt was moved to face the changing traffic of a new road. A lean-to kitchen and attic were added then.

Elmer Davenport Keith, authority on old houses, has written of this ancient Lee house: "Today it stands primitive and untouched beyond any monument of the past in Connecticut — nearer to Christopher Columbus than we are today to George Washington by 100 years."

Two views of the front room in the Thomas Lee house. The lintel over the fireplace is one great stone weighing over 1,000 pounds. The stalwart center beam, known as the summer beam, is the main support for the second floor rooms. Thomas Lee III, a justice for the area, held court here in the Judgment Hall.

John Lee, fourth generation of the Lee family in this country, left words of advice in 1716 as his dying charge for future Lee's to follow. They were inscribed on the wall of the parlor.

1735 was the year this wall paneling was probably added to this best parlor. The four-fluted pilasters are the earliest known examples of such half columns.

The 1713 lean-to kitchen is in its original condition. A ship builder obviously constructed the house, for the corbels are similar to those used in shipbuilding of that time.

29 This kitchen view shows a large trencher on the table from which, in the 17th century, everyone ate, each one helping himself.

The parlor chamber upstairs has one of the original windows of the 1660 house, on the left wall by the bed. The 17th century house had small windows of necessity: glass was scarce. Placed high on the walls, they let in less drafts than larger ones would, and were less vulnerable to Indian or wild beast attacks.

The other bedroom, called the "hall chamber" since it was above the "hall" downstairs, has a spinning and needlework area. The turkey-red and white quilt is identified as a wedding quilt by the elaborate heart design applique in the four corners.

The narrow necked basket was for goose feathers, used for making feather beds.

Before even the bicycle was invented, the chief boy's toy was the hobby horse, to emulate his father's means of travel.

The spice box held the imported herbs and spices which were, along with molasses and rum, brought to these shores by schooners from the West Indies.

This bushel basket was woven from hickory splints. The annual growth layers of a felled tree loosen when immersed in water. Each layer is cut into strips for weaving. Recorded in the Lee house is a recipe for making a barrel of soap: 6 bushels of ashes to 24 pounds of grease.

HEMPSTED HOUSE, 1678, New London.

Originally built on land granted to Robert Hempsted in 1645, this house was constructed of unpainted oak by his son Joshua I in 1678, the year that Joshua's only son, namesake and heir, Joshua II was born, the fifth of nine children. Joshua II spent his entire 80 years here, for he inherited his father's estate including the house where he was born. Married, and with a growing family, he started a diary at age 33, diligently recording the events of his life and of the community.

Some of his friends lived in the houses shown in this book — Thomas Lee III who lived in what is now East Lyme, Nathaniel Shaw in New London, George Denison II, Major Eells II of Milford, and Thomas Buckingham of Saybrook. He was a free man, a churchman and a devoted Connecticut citizen. He donated barrels of "cyder" for the local militia on "trayning days" and was always ready to help a fellow being. He was a man of genial kindness, attended Sunday services forenoon and afternoon, and even helped with coffins and burials.

In 1728, a wing was added to Joshua's house by his son Nathaniel for his wife and family. Six additional generations made it the dwelling of ten generations of the same family. The noble house was spared when much of New London was burned by Benedict Arnold and his British forces in 1781. It is furnished with outstanding early 17th and 18th century pieces, including many family heirlooms. This rare heritage home was restored by The Antiquarian and Landmarks Society, Inc. of Connecticut. Through dedicated research it has been preserved as an important example of 17th and 18th century domestic architecture.

Opposite page: Kitchen wash area in Nathaniel Hempsted's part of the house.

The fireplace corner of the great hall has a huge beam lintel over its chimney. The walls are whitewashed plaster. An early settle on the back wall is unique in having a center arm or candle rest. The overhead hood protects against winter drafts.

In the 17th and 18th centuries, it was not unusual for the best bed of the house to be placed in the hall, as is seen here. This great bed, with bottle green woolen draw curtains, might have been used by guests. Many notable pieces of furniture, lighting devices, and an ancient musket are displayed in this room.

This Carver-type chair and the table with its sausage-turned legs were hand-crafted on early hand-mechanized tools.

The early 17th century kitchen displayed many of its cooking implements. Here, several have the decorative heart motif, a symbol used frequently in Connecticut as an emblem of love, unity and brotherhood. The scooped out tree trunk (lower right) was used as a mortar to pound corn into meal.

A spoon rack.

A wall cupboard.

The "new" 1728 kitchen was added to the original 1678 house by Nathaniel Hempsted for his young wife and growing family. A kitchen such as this with its warm constant fires, was the gathering place for family living, like our family rooms of today. Often a bed was a normal part of the kitchen's furnishing. Like others of the period, this one folds up and latches to the wall like a 20th century Murphy bed.

Lime green hangings trimmed in coral on the bed in Joshua Hempsted's room are made from material woven for the Hempsted family in 1700. Silhouetted against whitewashed walls, their textured beauty displays how colorful some of the early interiors were. The pull-out trundle bed has a wainscot headboard.

Another view of the bedroom, a room which glows in the afternoon sun. Joshua Hempsted, a real handyman about the house, remodelled the early window in 1736 to a double sashed one. His diary makes frequent reference to his carpentry work. *Below:* The fireplace wall in the bedroom has closed and open cupboards.

Early Delft as seen in the cupboard in Joshua Hempsted's bedroom.

A small bedroom over the entrance hall has a beautiful coverlet made after the manner of a hooked rug.

LT. WILLIAM PRATT HOUSE, 1645 (old section), 1778 (newer part), Essex, Connecticut.

William Pratt came to this country at a youthful age. When Thomas Hooker made the famous journey from Newtown, Massachusetts, now the town of Cambridge, to the area in Connecticut now known as Hartford, Pratt was among those one hundred who trekked their way through the spring wilderness. Pratt married in June of this same year, 1636. In 1637, he was one of the group of men from Hartford, Wethersfield and Windsor who, after the savage attacks of Pequot Indians, formed a band and though few in number, leveled the Indian camp at Mystic in about an hour. After this major aggressive attack, Connecticut was made safer for colonization.

For his contribution in this battle, William Pratt was given 100 acres of land. This he sold, moved to the vast area then known as Saybrook, and purchased land in the section that has now become Essex.

In about 1645 he built the earliest part of the house. What is now the museum part of the house was added in the mid 18th century.

For many generations, this house remained in the Pratt family, and was finally bequeathed by the 20th century Pratt to a nephew, Samuel Griswold. He acquired an important collection of American antiques, which he bequeathed with the Pratt house to the Society for the Preservation of New England Antiquities. The Society restored Pratt House and furnished it with Mr. Griswold's collection of Connecticut country antiques.

Mustard colored walls made a beautiful foil for the William and Mary gate-leg table, made in the first half of the 18th century, the Spanish footed Queen Anne chairs and the butternut chest with its fifteen drawers.

Although the kitchen fireplace paneling and bolection molding are restorations, they are indicative of what might have covered the walls of this early, large room. The courting mirror, in the upper left hand corner of the print, is one of eleven in the house, an unusually large collection of courting mirrors in this country.

Connecticut red ware pottery, many pieces having Indian designs, is well displayed in this hanging wall cupboard.

The lowboy, made about 1750, is among the many fine mahogany pieces in this parlor furnished with 18th century antiques.

The well proportioned seven-fluted pilasters and overhanging mouldings give architectural elegance to the mantel in the parlor.

The children's room has a fine quilt in turkey-red and white. The hobby horse is a splendid one complete with saddle.

The fishnet canopy on this tester bed is a pleasant summer treatment, as is the white quilt. The corner cupboard is a fine one and displays copper and silver luster ware, popular in this country in the early 19th century.

47   This L-shaped room, one of the most charming in the house, has an English oak chest with an Early-American Bible box resting on it. One of the many courting mirrors in the house is hung above.

EELLS-STOW HOUSE, 1685, Milford.

Built about 1685, the Eells-Stow House in Milford has undergone innumerable additions and alterations. The overhanging gabled roof has an unusual plaster cove, a replacement of its earlier one. Originally built in 1685, by Samuel Eells, the house was purchased later in the 18th century by Captain Stephen Stow. The very great Indian collection of Claude C. Coffin is housed at the Eells-Stow house.

Hanging in the entrance hall is a faithful copy of a portrait of Major Eells, a strong and striking primitive in vivid shades of rose and blue. He was an important military figure in the 17th and early 18th century — his presence added distinction to a military drill, a funeral or a government meeting.

The 18th century mantel no doubt covers a large early fireplace. The cupboard houses an excellent collection of Chinese Export Rose Medallion ware.

The gilt mirror shows how patriotic feelings influenced furniture design; the 13 ball decorations under the cornice represent the original 13 states.

Upstairs, this bedroom houses a costume collection. There are also several pieces of early furniture, the early, heavy Carver type chair being of great importance.

The Carver chair belonged to Nicholas Camp, one of Milford's first settlers in 1639. The chair remained in the Camp family until it was given to the Milford Historical Society by its last 20th century owner.

BUSH-HOLLEY HOUSE, 1685, Cos Cob

The Bush-Holley House at Cos Cob Harbor, is known as "the house that never stopped living." From about 1686 when it is believed to have been first constructed, until 1957 when it was purchased by the Historical Society of the Town of Greenwich, the house has been in constant use.

On land purchased from Indians, this house was undoubtedly built by a Dutch settler, for its architectural details are Dutch rather than English. It is recorded that in 1738 Justus Bush purchased the property and made considerable improvements. In 1740 a Queen Anne staircase was added as well as paneling in most of the rooms. Justus Bush was Dutch; his father, Hendrick Bosch, a swordcutter by trade, came to this country in 1658.

Justus Bush bequeathed the property to his son, David Bush, who added what is known as the 1776 kitchen wing with slave quarters overhead. David Bush became a wealthy miller, with his tide mill close to the harbor. Ships came from New York and other ports for his ground flour, potatoes and other produce. When he died, his fortune amounted to about $25,000, which in those days distinguished him as a man of substantial property.

His two sons inherited this house and property. In 1882, Edward P. Holley bought the house and the surrounding buildings and turned it into an inn. When his daughter married the artist Elmer Livingston MacRae, the house became an artists' gathering place for some of the writers and painters and craftsmen of the period. It was here that Willa Cather, Lincoln Steffens and Wallace Irwin did some of their writing, and here such artistic geniuses as Childe Hassam, John and Alden Twachtman, Louis Comfort Tiffany and Mr. MacRae worked. Paintings, sketches and etchings of some of these now hang on the walls of the Bush-Holley House.

The portrait of this beautiful Dutch lady was painted on wood by A. Rageneau. The Hadley chest is dated 1770. The pewter tankard is a signed Danforth-Boardman piece. Danforth was perhaps Connecticut's most illustrious craftsman of pewter. The hour glass dates from about 1750 and runs only 28½ minutes because the sand has worn so thin after 200 years of ups and downs.

54

The great trestle table 10'4" long by 23¼" wide is made from one plank. Originally it was painted or stained ox-blood red. The base is known as a "shoe trestle." Dating from about 1700, this table is unique in having an underneath shelf.

The 17th century Dutch fireplace in the original kitchen had become enclosed over the years and was not discovered until the house was renovated. The bricks, all original, probably came to this country as ballast on a ship from Holland.

The 1776 kitchen added to the house by David Bush has slave quarters overhead. Cooking was done in the fireplace and baking was done in the oven on the left. The English flintlock musket was the type used in the Revolutionary War. The ox-horn kept the powder for the firearm. This musket belonged to the Holleys and has been in this house almost a century. The exquisite dresser is probably of Hudson River origin. It dates from about 1700 and has a shoe trestle base. Pewter pieces are from the Herbert Ferris collection and were given to Bush-Holley House.

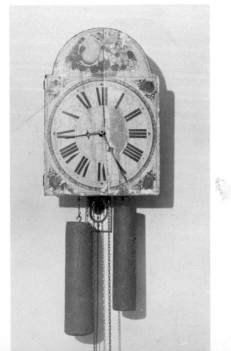

The time piece is known as a Wag-on-the-Wall clock.

The spice chest belonging to the Holleys dates from about 1770. Note a lamb's tongue chamfer on each side. Probably another spice cabinet rested on top of this base.

The wallpaper in the dining room is an exact copy of a paper found in the house when it was under restoration. It was steamed off the walls and on its back was a tax stamp of George II dating the paper before 1760. The paper is in its documentary colors: aqua blue, gray and charcoal.

Portraits of Mrs. David Bush's grandson, a prominent lawyer in Norwalk, and his wife. Judge Benjamin Isaacs and Frances Bryant Isaacs had their portraits done in 1810 by Abraham Tuttle, a local artist who later painted in Vermont. Both husband and wife were born in 1778 and died in 1846.

In 1740 Justus Bush installed this magnificent paneling of pine. Originally painted slate blue, it was repainted in 1800 with a graining to resemble golden oak. Through the years, it has mellowed to a soft, glowing color. In 1920 the Metropolitan Museum of Art tried unsuccesfully to purchase the paneling for its American Wing. The 1685 brick sides of the chimney are in their original herring-bone pattern.

Of great value, this carved Chippendale breakfront piece is a recent acquisition.

Over the pale yellow damask Chippendale sofa hangs an important painting of Mrs. Bush, second wife of David Bush. He too was *her* second husband. The portrait was painted by William Dunlap, who founded the American Academy of Art in 1815. Family miniatures hang on either side.

This kindly lady is Mrs. David Bush, who, in the days of the Revolutionary War when the Church of England was not popular, held services for that church in her home.

The front bedroom has exquisite wood paneling. The Simon Willard clock dates from 1800. The andirons with steeple tops were mentioned by Wallace Nutting in his book. The crewel worked bed and window hangings were done by local women for this room in the manner of 18th century needlework.

The spread is a quilt made in applique and embroidery. It is dated 1810 and signed by its maker, Anne Ingersol, with her date of birth noted in gold thread. It reads, "1789 Little Anne was born." She married Edward Brush in 1811 and went by covered wagon to Indiana. When her husband died, she returned to Greenwich. Over 40 years ago her daughter, in her 80's, gave the Historical Society this spread.

The eagle, this one expertly carved, was one of the popular symbols used in American design to represent freedom, strength, independence, longevity, endurance and depth of vision. The eagle was used in almost all types of design: bottles, quilts, furniture and fabrics.

The Bush-Holley House represents a reconciliation of periods, and stands as a superb example of an historical house that has been in constant use since the 17th century.

MORRIS HOUSE, 1685 and 1780, New Haven.

New Haven's famed John Davenport and Theophilus Eaton established their group of Puritans in England, before coming to the New World in June, 1637. Thomas Morris and his wife Elizabeth were among this group, which, after a year's stay in Boston, journeyed on to the bay of New Haven, where they settled their little colony. New Haven, first known as Quillipiuk, was perhaps the first town in this country to incorporate "city planning", for before building, the town was carefully designed. Eight equal plots were arranged around a large village green. Smaller plots were laid out behind them. The leaders of this cultured group planned an elegant city.

Thomas Morris was given one of the smaller land plots, which he held until he began to accumulate land at Solitary Cove, now Morris Cove. The sizeable acreage of coastal property he had acquired by 1671 fostered his ship building trade. When he died in 1673, his sons, John and Eleazar inherited the property and built on it. John moved to New Jersey, selling all his share including "ye mansion house standing thereon," to his brother Eleazar.

The house was probably built soon after 1680. It and the property remained in the Morris family from generation to generation, the house expanding in size with the growth of the families. The Morris heirs were rooted in New Haven, for it was stipulated in every will until the middle of the 19th century, that the house could not be sold out of the family.

In 1779 the British troops under General Tyron invaded New Haven on July 5th, turning every house in their path into blazes. Morris House was the first, but was rebuilt on its old foundations by Amos Morris the following year. He even added a ballroom! The house was built of white oak frame and hand hewn stone sides from his property, and the plaster was made of burned oyster shell and sand from the beach.

Ownership was transferred to the Pardee family in 1915 when the house was sold to neighbors. They had held property adjacent to the Morris' since the 17th century. William Scranton Pardee died in 1918, leaving the house to the New Haven Colony Historical Society with an endowment for its upkeep.

This front room has been furnished with 17th century antiques. The Carver chair, the English wainscot chair, the pottery and pewter are of rare value. A Puritan family such as the Morris' treasured their great Bible. John Davenport, the minister with whom this family came to New Haven, established laws for his colony based on the Mosaic laws. Oriental rugs, known then as Turkey carpets, were often used as table covers.

This little room adjoining the dining room has fine wainscoted half-paneling and full paneling on the disjointed fireplace wall.

The room, now a dining room, originally boasted a fireplace opening large enough to burn eight-foot logs. American Primitive portraits add to the charm.

The new kitchen is furnished with early American hand-crafted furniture. Of particular interest is the settle which has a shelf beneath its hood. The fireplace has a large beam lintel.

The old kitchen is huge.

A ballroom is on the floor above!

Two of the many bedrooms in Morris House: a front bedroom and an adjoining child's room.

KNAPP TAVERN–PUTNAM COTTAGE, 1690, Greenwich.

Timothy Knapp built his house about 1690. In 1729 he deeded half of it to his son, who used his portion as a tavern to care for the weary traveler between New York and Boston. The trials of traveling in the late 17th and early 18th century tax the imagination, for there were no roads or throughways. Before 1790 when the turnpike era began, traveling was done on horseback or on foot, sometimes through thickets which had to be cut away. Waterways had to be crossed by canoes or rafts, carrying horses and luggage too, for there were no bridges to speak of. The traveling hardships of 1700 have been described first hand in Madame Knight's famous journal.

As towns developed, they were required to have inns, or "ordinaries," and how welcome they were to the weather-beaten, weary traveler. Far from the comforts of today's hostelries, those of the inn of two centuries ago were of a different standard. Mattresses were frequently stuffed with corn husks, and often each bed accommodated five or six guests each. Some had signs requiring guests to remove their boots before going to bed, and some advertised that they changed their linen every fortnight.

In 1779, when the Tories, 1,500 strong, began their invasion of Horseneck (now Greenwich) with its only 150 soldiers, General Putnam was staying at Knapp Tavern. Knowing there would be total disaster if he did not search for help, he heroically plunged through the troops and on to Stamford to gather reinforcements. He returned by nightfall with a little army that followed the retreating Tories, attacking them and retrieving some of the stolen loot and captured prisoners.

Knapp Tavern, now called Putnam Cottage, still retains its original scalloped shingles. The house now belongs to the Putnam Hill Chapter of the DAR. It is being constantly restored to its original appearance, with Colonial gardens and outbuildings.

Restoration by the DAR has uncovered two fieldstone fireplaces on the first floor with a pass-through oven that could be used by either fireplace.

Left and opposite page: Other views of the Putnam Cottage Tavern Room.

This fireplace has two ovens. The pass-through oven which can be used by the adjacent room is hidden by the camera's perspective. *Below:* One of the bedrooms in Putnam Cottage.

Simple country pieces furnish this bedroom. Both bedrooms on the second floor have well proportioned wall paneling on their chimney wall.

A mahogany desk and chairs are to be seen in the large tavern room.

HOYT-BARNUM HOUSE, 1700, Stamford.

This little three room cottage with an attic and cellar, and three fireplaces with a center chimney, stands in the heart of "downtown" Stamford. Originally a farmhouse, its first owner also did iron work. Although small in size, the Hoyt-Barnum House has great collections of local historical items. Its group of early Connecticut pottery is outstanding. Many lighting fixtures of early vintage are here. A collection of 19th century dolls and early toys pleases children visiting this house.

The Hoyt-Barnum House is listed on the National Trust Register of Historic Places.

The big kitchen still retains its original hand-hewn floor boards and wall paneling of vertical boards.

A chest-on-chest of exceptional quality, and a six-boarded chest from early Wethersfield are two distinguished pieces in the Hoyt-Barnum collections.

The fireplace wall in the bedroom.

An early Wethersfield chest.

The ox-blood red corner cupboard houses early Connecticut pottery.

78

An adjustable ratchet candle stand.

The earthenware jug with spout probably held cider, a popular 18th century drink.

A hand-made wooden milk "can" from early Wethersfield.

The wrought iron candle stand fits into a wooden base. In its pinch device it holds dried rush stalks as well, an economy measure, since candles were treasured and harder to come by.

When that zealot of liberty, Lafayette, visited this area in 1824, he was feted with the honor due a conquering hero. As he rode into view, his path was strewn with flowers gathered by children. This platter with his name commemorated the visit. His image was even printed on fabrics and carved on furniture.

This historic brazier was used by Revolutionary soldiers, who warmed a stew, coffee or their frost-bitten fingers over its hot coals.

An early 19th century doll.

A toy pony-drawn cart and a collection of 19th century dolls.

OGDEN HOUSE, about 1700, Fairfield.

This Connecticut farmhouse was probably built in three stages. First came two rooms, a kitchen with a sleeping chamber above. Secondly, two more rooms were added opposite these with a hall and chimney between the two sets of rooms, making the typical "two over two" identified with the Connecticut house plan. Lastly, the lean-to with its steep roofed garret completed this salt-box. The exterior shingles were three feet in length.

The house fell into bad repair over the years, and in the 1930's it was restored by J. Frederick Kelly, the authority on Connecticut architecture at that time. He dated the house as having been built about 1700.

The house was known to have been lived in by David Ogden, a prosperous farmer who, after marrying Jane Sturges in 1750, lived here. The house was filled with children, for of his ten, seven lived to maturity. He died in 1776, and following the custom of the day, an inventory was made of all his belongings. Those inventories are still in existence, and they show Mr. Ogden to have been a man of considerable property.

The lean-to kitchen was reconstructed under the direction of J. Frederick Kelly. In the 18th century kitchen, a folding bed was not uncommon, as is here shown. In winter, this room was the warmest one in the house. The gate-leg table of maple and curly maple dates about 1700-1735, and came from a Fairfield family.

Originally there might have been a curved edge to the table, instead of the straight edge. It has large butterfly hinges. The commodious ladder-back chairs with their five back slats also date from between 1700 and 1735. They are among the first made which have a supplementary turned stretcher under the notched arm rest. This was added, of course, for increased strength, and is considered to be a Connecticut feature. The chairs are of ash and maple and have boldly turned uprights and stretchers.

An important collection of redware pottery is shown on the open shelves of the wall cupboard.

The original kitchen of the 1700 house was here — now the room is a parlor. *Below:* This is a long view of the kitchen.

The dining room has many outstanding pieces of furniture. The desk is a Fairfield one and came from the Wakeman family. It dates from between 1740 and 1760. The chairs are similar to some described in the inventory of Mr. Ogden's furnishings — "6 crook back chairs." The dining table is a Fairfield drop-leaf. The tall pine cased clock is signed and dated, "J. Buckley, Fairfield, 1777." Joseph Buckley, who was born in 1755 and died in 1815, fought in the Revolutionary War from July through December 1775. The painting over the desk is of Luther Allen of Enfield and was painted about 1790.

This portrait of two sisters, all done up in their Sunday best, is an amusing one, with the baby poking its finger in the doll's eye. The sisters are Margaret and Elizabeth Daggett of New Haven.

This beautiful early American portrait of Mr. Burr and his son is a copy of the original, which now hangs in the National Gallery in Washington, D.C.

Opposite page: The upstairs hall has a table and two chairs, locally made in the 18th century.

The "blue chamber" has an indigo quilt, and blue and white check hand-woven valance and hangings made from a length of antique material from Cheshire, Connecticut. The rocker, made from a barrel, is covered in blue quilted cloth.

Incidentally, the tester bed is painted red and can fold up against the wall. It belonged to Thomas Danforth III, the great Connecticut pewter craftsman. The bed wrench, used to tighten the rope springs, is marked "TD". Thomas Danforth worked in pewter, tin, copper, and brass. Born in Middletown, he had many years in his shop in Rocky Hill. In 1807 he went to Philadelphia for a few years, returning to Rocky Hill in 1818. His dates are 1756-1840. Pieces of his work are seen in this book.

The heart and crown rocker in this view of the blue chamber, came from Milford while the desk chair is a country Chippendale one, painted red.

90

The north chamber with its warm reds and soft wood colors, houses an exceptional collection of chests, a pencil post bed, and the portrait of a rather severe matron. The high chest is all in its original condition; even its brasses are in their original state. It came from a Fairfield family.

This primitive water color portrait of a serious child holding an orange and wearing a fancy green dress, is attributed to R. W. Shute and was painted about 1830.

The woman wearing a cap is the portrait of an unknown matron.

DENISON HOUSE, 1717, Mystic.

The colorful 17th century George Denison I, Cromwellian Captain, friend of the Indians, courageous soldier and an independent leader and free thinker, built his house on this site. He called it his "Mansion place," where he and his wife, Ann Borodell Denison, held "grate feasts." The house was demolished by fire in 1717 on the eve of his grandson's marriage. This same grandson, the inheritor of the 200 acres and property of his grandfather, immediately erected the house pictured above using some of the charred timbers from the old house. He and his bride lived there as did eleven successive generations of Denisons. In 1943 Mrs. Ann Borodell Denison Gates bequeathed the house to the Denison Family Association. It was architecturally restored by Frederick Kelly, and the interiors were furnished from the vast collections of Denison heirlooms stored in the attic and outbuildings on the property. Differing eras of the house's history are represented room by room, with an early kitchen, a late 18th century bedroom, an early 1820 sitting room, a Civil War period bedroom, and Mrs. Gates' early 20th century parlor.

The dining area of the great kitchen was the gathering place for big families. Corn and herbs were hung from the ceiling to dry for future winter use. In this unique house can be seen one family's collection of heirlooms through the centuries.

95 The kitchen, representing the Colonial period, displays pewter, cooking utensils, spinning wheel and a notable set of Windsors. The curved trimmer arch supports a hearthstone in the room overhead, a feature found only in New England architecture.

A wooden jointed 16 inch doll was carved by a friendly Indian for a Denison child. It wears English boots, not moccasins!

When crows ravaged cornfields, these crow-decoys were placed to attract other crows — to come within range of the farmer's musket. They are 17 and 18 inches tall.

Close up view of the kitchen fireplace. *Below:* An open shelf for family pewter. The steel blades of knives were polished on the box at the right.

The sitting room is furnished with furniture and bric-a-brac of about 1820. *Below:* The mirror is topped with a phoenix.

Opposite page:
This bedroom is furnished with late 18th century pieces.

This bedroom has been furnished with mahogany and walnut pieces of the Civil War era. *Below:* The living room of the last Denison resident as it was in the early 20th century, furnished with "new" and old pieces.

Buttoned sofa in the 20th century living room.

Fireplace view of Mrs. Ann Borodell Denison Gates' 20th century living room.

The big Winthrop desk, the leather cushioned Windsor, and the cupboard with many rare pieces of china
and glass are family pieces that have always been in this old homestead.

102

JUDSON HOUSE, 1723, Stratford.

Nine generations of Judsons lived in this imposing house in Stratford, from the time it was built, presumably in 1723 by Captain David Judson, until it was sold to Mr. John Wheeler in 1888. In 1891 it was again sold, to two maiden ladies, Celia and Cornelia Curtis, who lived there until the last surviving one willed it to the Stratford Historical Society in 1925 with certain provisos.

This house, built on land, even perhaps the actual site, of original settler William Judson, David Judson's great grandfather, has great quality. The curved pediment over the central entrance door was perhaps the first of its kind in Connecticut; the overhanging roof is also unique. Comparison of the architectural details of Judson House with those of the Second Episcopal Church completed in 1743, show the likelihood that Architect Thomas Salmon,

who came here in 1717, designed both buildings.

Like so many 18th century houses, this one went through changes. Walls were superimposed over older ones, new mantels were added, and new "hardwood" floors put over the original wide planks of 1723. When the Stratford Historical Society became owner, the house was restored to its original 18th century condition, through the supervision of Elmer Keith, authority of architecture of that period. With him was the guiding hand of Abbott Lowell Cummings, then, in 1957, Assistant Director for the Society for the Preservation of New England Antiquities, in Boston. The actual work was done, for the most part, by volunteers who gave of their skills, time and labor. The same spirit of cooperation exists today in the effort to preserve the house and its treasures.

Restoration revealed the beautifully proportioned paneling under layers of superimposed wall coverings. The side pilasters and bolection molding around the fireplace were added where evidence of their existence determined their placement. An Astor piano, dating from about 1800, which had been on loan to Washington's Mount Vernon for 50 years, was returned to the Judson House collection. Furniture of historical interest completes this room.

The craftsman's mark on this pewter teapot is L. T. Curtis.

Opposite page: Judson House doorway

The exquisitely detailed corner cupboard has a duplicate copy in the opposite corner of the room. Both display the superb collection of Canton ware. Additional pieces set the table. *Below:* The Crown and Heart chair in the fireplace corner is a rare and beautiful one.

The cut-corner bowl, Canton pattern, dates from about 1840; its diameter is 9½″. The covered cups with strawberry finials were used for syllabub or baked custard. The sugar bowl is another Canton piece.

The magnificent Canton platter — 19¾″ by 16¼″ — was a gift to the Stratford Historical Society by Mrs. A. M. de Groot. Formerly the platter, and many other pieces of Canton ware in Stratford's superb collection, once belonged to Eliza Hamilton Hawley, the daughter of Alexander Hamilton.

The 8¾″ tall cider flagon dates from about 1800. The foo-dog finial is rare on this Canton pattern ware.

The reticulated fruit basket and underliner is decorated in the Fitzhugh pattern, sometimes done in green, here in blue on white ground.

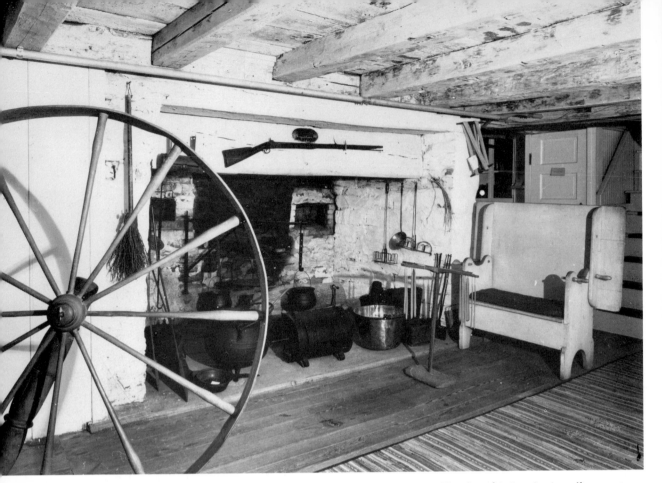

The slave kitchen in the cellar.

The kitchen fireplace is furnished with 18th century cooking equipment. The low bench is where the housewife sat when she tended the fire or stirred the stew.

The kitchen cupboard displays pewter, redware, cheese rounds, and on the top shelf, the slender pitcher poured out cider, a popular colonists' drink.

Upstairs, the 18th century bedroom displays a poster bed with curtains of toile, a 1650 chest, an 18th century wardrobe. The wall paneling is in its original state.

The early 1650 chest has hot water bottles on its top. A courting mirror hangs above it.

Below: This ceramic ink stand, made in a factory in Bow, England, about 1750, belonged to Izrahiah Wetmore, Pastor of the First Church of Christ (Congregational), Stratford, from 1753 to 1780. He was the minister of the Revolution and ardently defended the rights and liberties of the colonies.

Here are two silhouettes of Stratford gentlemen of the 18th century in their high beaver hats: Gideon Tomlinson and Roswell Judson.

The leather writing box belonged to Samuel Johnson, D.D., who was born in Guilford in 1696 and died in Stratford in 1772. He was the first rector of the first parish, in the first diocese outside of the British Isles, at Christ Episcopal Church, Stratford, where he served for nearly forty years, interrupted only by his term as First President of King's College, later to become Columbia University.

THOMAS GRISWOLD HOUSE, 1735, Guilford.

For over 200 years, one family lived in this house, generation after generation. In 1958 the Guilford Keeping Society purchased this 1735 house.

Recent restoration done by the Society is putting the house back in its original state. Nineteenth century dormer windows have been removed. Added walls have been peeled off and paneled walls and a great kitchen fireplace discovered. Layers of linoleum and narrow oak flooring were lifted from the floors, revealing the first wide pine planks of the original house. The house will be completely restored in 1976, displaying its collection of Americana. This house was depicted on a commemorative stamp. The front fence was from the old First Congregational Church belfry.

Rear view of the Thomas Griswold House in Guilford, showing the "Saltbox" profile. The house is now a registered landmark by the National Trust Register of Historic Places.

The front doorway is stunning in its classic simplicity.

The batten door at the rear was made of two thicknesses of 7/8 inch wood, held together by hand-wrought nail studding in a diamond pattern. This double thickness strengthened the door against attack and inclement weather and was added insulation for inside warmth. This door is cited as a rare example of a batten door in J. Frederick Kelly's "Early Domestic Architecture of Connecticut."

The unearthed kitchen fireplace revealed a rare find — three bake ovens!

The front hall staircase has flat balusters, unusual for Connecticut craftsmen who usually turned the spindles and posts.

A corner built-in closed and open cupboard holds kitchen utensils.

A basket made of hickory splints.

An extremely fine example of an early ladder-back chair, this one has trumpet finials, and mushroom hand rests.

Yankee ingenuity devised this labor saving butter churn. Instead of the up and down heaving of the usual churn, here the good wife who made her family's butter, simply had to turn the handle, and the churning was done mechanically.

The dining room has a pine corner cupboard on loan by Dr. Robert Gordon, of Yale University. The Chelsea sprig ware tea set, and the Sheffield candlesticks are 18th century.

This lowboy and gilt mirror are the only Griswold heirlooms in the house.

The "Star of Bethlehem," an album quilt, has the signature of each patchmaker in each star center. It is a quilt of distinction on this pencil-point bedstead.

A Jacquard loomed coverlet of rare quality in bright vermilion and white is shown at the left.

BATES-SCOFIELD HOMESTEAD, 1736, Darien.

Jonathan Bates built his saltbox house in the "Middlesex parish of Stamford town" in 1736. Darien was not so designated until 1820, its first recorded date. The house plan he used was the typical Connecticut two over two with a central chimney and entranceway, or porch, as it was then called. A lean-to kitchen with its steep-roofed garret overhead was all a part of the original building.

About 100 years after it was built, Ezra Scofield purchased the house in 1825. It remained in that family until 1924. The Darien Historical Society obtained it in 1963, moved it, and had it restored to its original design. The furnishings of the house are typical of the period from the 1730's until the 1820's. Landscaping is in keeping with what might have been in earlier days, and a formal geometrically planned herb garden with its board-edged walks is a typical 18th century one. The wing, added at the back of the house, includes a library, club and office. A basement gallery provides for exhibits and lectures.

This beautiful parlor glows with color — mustard yellow walls, shades of gold in the draperies, and the muted golds and rose in the Aubusson carpet. The word parlor comes, of course, from the French verb *parler*, to talk. The magnificent chest-on-chest is a 17th century veneered piece.

The parlor has its original wall paneling, and has been painted a mustard gold color.

This important chair with its sausage turnings, was originally painted. The paint has now been removed, and the carpenter's guide markings are clearly visible. The crewel curtains are of white linen worked in marigold colors and shades of moss and olive green.

The very complete collection of Chinese Export in this corner cupboard was the wedding china of Betsy 124
Davis when she married Markus Miles. The pitcher, however, was a special gift to Markus Miles by a friend
who had borrowed his favorite hunting dog, and shot it accidentally. The pitcher with its hunting scene was
the friend's token of regret.

125 A country pine grandfather clock is a recent acquisition. The homespun linen curtains, worked in shades of rose, pink and lavender, are typical of the crewel work done by the 18th century woman before the Revolutionary war. Needlework of this sort was part of a young girl's education. Local women designed and worked these draperies from adaptations of early American needlework designs.

The kitchen in the Bates-Scofield Homestead. This child's pen kept the baby off the cold floor and out of harm's way.

A foot warmer.

A wall box.

Another view of the kitchen. *Lower Right:* This rare country-made lift-lid and drawer chest, ox-blood red with white fleur-de-lis painted decoration, is identified with similar ones supposedly from the Milford or Woodbury area of Connecticut. The M-shaped design, making legs from the two end boards, is characteristic of these rare chests.

The washstand, with its bucket of water, dish with homemade lye and pork fat soap, and the earthen wash bowl, was where the family washed up before meals.

Dining table in the kitchen.

The buttery.

A redware plate.

This chamber contains equipment for spinning yarn and weaving cloth.

This pencil post bed has a trundle bed underneath it which pulled out at night. Children usually slept in the trundle. Bedsprings were made by stringing the bed frame with rope in a warp and weft open weave. *Below:* This view shows the wall paneling.

A close-up view of the crewel work done by local women for the bed hangings.

SLOAN-RAYMOND-FITCH HOUSE, 1731-1757, Wilton.

Several families have lived in this lovely house from the time the poor weaver, Alexander Sloan, first purchased his four acres of land for $24.00 in 1731 and thereon built his house. Since he had to take out a mortgage of 70 pounds to do this and was unable to repay his debt, he lost the house in 1734. For the next 23 years a blacksmith lived there. In 1757 Clapp Raymond, a colorful captain, the town clerk and a deputy to the Assembly, built the two story front of the house, adding on to the little cottage Sloan had built.

Suddenly elegance and distinction enhanced the humble little saltbox. In 1799 it was sold to Bena-

jan Strong Comstock. In 1823 it was sold with 63 acres to Elias Sturgis, who turned it into a tavern for 17 years. In 1840 the house was sold to Joseph Platt Fitch, with one acre of land. Fitch added four acres to his plot and the property remained in the hands of that family for about 100 years. In 1936 Philip Van Wyck purchased the house and put it in excellent repair. It was again sold in 1968 to Mr. Ralph Piersall who in turn donated it to the Wilton Historical Society on land belonging to Homequity. The Historical Society has furnished the house with outstanding collections of decorative arts which it has been accumulating for many years.

The parlor is furnished with 18th century furniture.

The parlor has many fine examples of early 18th century chairs and a grandfather clock.

Displayed in the dining room is a distinguished collection of Staffordshire pasteware. The windows in the 1757 part of the house have 24 panes.
Most have their original glass.

Fireplace wall in the dining room.

The original kitchen in the Sloan-Raymond-Fitch House in Wilton.

Much redware pottery was made in Norwalk as well as in other sections of Connecticut. Sometimes Indian designs were used to decorate the slipware. At other times names, mottos, and letters of the alphabet were used. "Who Emma," and the phrase "Cheap Money" show the potter even used his ware as a memo pad.

A view of the fireplace. *Below:* "Who Emma!" and "Cheap Money" mottos on the redware plates. Perhaps "Who Emma" was meant to read "Whoa — Emma"!

Connecticut hand-made baskets.

A bedroom upstairs has a beautifully paneled fireplace wall. The American desk is a commodious one. *Below:* Two views of the bedroom showing more of the 18th century antiques, including an imported press cupboard.

HANFORD-SILLIMAN HOUSE, 1764, New Canaan.

The Hanford-Silliman House in New Canaan is a beehive of activity, keeping alive the history, crafts and interests of the past, and offering them to their community in exciting and contemporary ways.

Because the original builder and owner, Stephen Hanford, was a weaver by trade and a licensed tavern keeper as well, these interests have been emphasized in the house displays.

There is a spinning and weaving room. Another room is furnished as an 18th century tavern just off the early kitchen with its expansive hearth.

In 1764, when this house was built, every town by law had to have an ordinary, the 18th century word for a coffee house or tavern where there were fixed prices for a meal and a night's lodging.

Twenty years after Stephen Hanford had built his house, he died in 1784. Four years later his widow sold it to Elisha Leeds, for his newly married daughter, Martha, and her husband, Joseph Silliman. The Silliman family and their descendants lived in the house for the next 130 years. In 1959 The New Canaan Historical Society became owners of this beautiful Connecticut house, making it a landmark of activity.

In addition to the Hanford-Silliman House, the Historical Society has an added complex of buildings: a Tool Museum which also houses a usable early printing press; an Apothecary Shop, New Canaan's first drug store which opened in 1845; an historical library of over 2,500 volumes; a Costume Museum with over 1,000 garments from which to select for special exhibits; and John Rogers' summer studio, with many examples of his work. John Rogers was a summer resident of New Canaan and had his studio near the Hanford-Silliman House. It was moved here to display his story sculpture groups.

He was known as the "people's sculptor," and like Norman Rockwell, he caught the homey attitudes of simple human interest subjects such as "Coming to the Parson," "The School Examination," or "Going for the Cows." He sold 8,000 reproductions of "Coming to the Parson."

Around the chimney are implements for baking and cooking. The high backed settle protected the sitter from draughts. The rocker, an American invention, came into being in the later 17th and early 18th century. The distaff at the left is for making yarn.

The Colonial kitchen was the family room of the 18th century.

Meals were eaten in the kitchen. A dry sink with shelves above, is where the dishes were washed in water that was heated over the fire.

The corner cupboard holds a rare collection of early pewter.

Several views of the tavern room with its superb collection of pewter. Accounts were kept at the tall desk. Eighteenth century chessmen are placed on a folding inlaid chessboard table.

Another view of the tavern room.

Pewter, American and English, from the collection of
Mrs. T. Ferdinand Wilcox and others, is probably the
most outstanding collection on Connecticut's coast.

The 1790 English piano is in excellent condition. Chinese export china is behind the corner cupboard door, and Hepplewhite chairs stand in front of the windows. A floral hooked rug in pastel colors, is of fine workmanship.

This chair was one of the original tavern chairs in Mr. Hanford's inn.

The beautifully hand painted insignia above the piano keys.

The weaving and spinning room includes an old loom as well as a modern one. *Below:* This bedroom up-stairs has a rope strung bed, quilt and hooked rugs, a wash stand with folding mirror and a drop top.

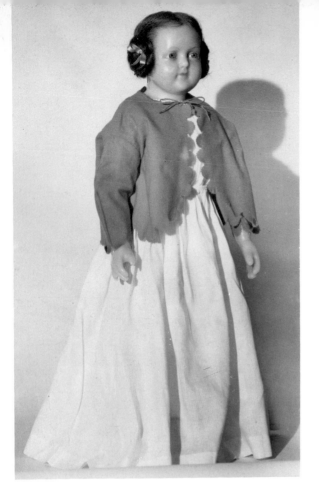

Early doll.

This early hobby horse has remnants of its original barn-red paint still visible in spots.

A Victorian doll.

Above and opposite page: An 18th century doll.

THE SHAW MANSION, 1756, New London.

Hailing from Fairfield, in 1722 Nathaniel Shaw, a 19-year-old youth, went to New London and immediately engaged in sea trade. He became a successful sea merchant doing trade with many parts of the globe. He married in 1730 and in 1735 purchased land on the west bank of the Thames River from George Denison of Westerly. He lived in the wooden building on the property until 1756, when he built the "Mansion."

Shaw engaged 35 Acadians who had been deported to New London when they refused to take the oath of allegiance to Great Britain, and put them to work quarrying stone on his property for his new granite house.

Through the years, many American heroes have visited this imposing house. George Washington was here on April 9, 1776. The room where he slept is much as it was at that time. General Nathaniel Greene, Nathan Hale and Governor Trumbull have been entertained here. Lafayette stopped by in 1824 to pay his respects, but both Mr. Shaw and his son were by then deceased.

Nathaniel Shaw, Jr., son of the builder of the house, was appointed Naval Agent, and the Shaw home was Connecticut's Naval Office. The first naval activity directed by Congress in 1776 emerged from New London.

In 1781 Benedict Arnold and his Tories burned New London, and several small fires were started in the Shaw Mansion. Neighbors rallied to put out the flames, and the house was saved except for a wooden office ell. Later generations of the family built on to the house at this juncture.

After Nathaniel Sr. and his wife had died, Nathaniel Jr. left the property to his brother Thomas, who was unmarried. Thomas' niece, Lucretia Shaw Woodbridge, inherited the house with her husband Elias Perkins. Their descendants lived in the Shaw Mansion until 1907, when it was purchased by the New London Historical Society. Important restorations have been done by the Society, uncovering closed off fireplaces, and discovering a cement wall made to look like paneling. Many pieces of Shaw furniture, portraits, silver, china, books and letters are in this wonderful historic house.

The living room includes a distinguished collection of furniture and accessories, some of which were owned by the original builder of the house, Nathaniel Shaw.

The valuable scroll-top desk is believed to have been designed and crafted by a New London cabinetmaker.

The dining room in the Shaw Mansion.

Portraits of the Shaw family hang on the walls of this front parlor.

Mr. William Johnston painted these portraits of Mary Shaw and her sister-in-law. They hang in the upstairs hall.

By Ralph Earl, these important portraits represent Thomas Shaw, and his niece, Lucretia Shaw Woodbridge Perkins, with her son Nathaniel. They hang in the upstairs hall.

The room which George Washington occupied when he visited Mr. Shaw on April 9, 1776. The fireplace wall is cement, molded to imitate wood paneling.

This is the bed where George Washington slept when he visited Mr. Shaw in 1776. The mahogany stand at the foot of the bed contains a basin used for a footbath.

Here is where George Washington shaved.

This hooped canopy bed is notable for its deep top curve.

BUCKINGHAM HOUSE (1690 Kitchen), 1725-1758, Mystic.

Originally in old Saybrook, this house is now restored at Mystic Seaport. The kitchen dates from about 1690. The Buckingham family were among Connecticut's early settlers. Thomas Buckingham, son of the first Thomas of New Haven and Milford, was educated for the ministry. He supplied the pulpit at Wethersfield in 1663 and 1664, and received 20 shillings a week for his services. In 1670 his ministry took him to what has become Old Saybrook, where he remained until his death.

Buckingham is revered as one of the founders and trustees of Yale, which had its infant days in Old Saybrook. He was custodian of the library which was removed from Branford to the rector's house. Scholars were instructed nearby, and sometimes at the rector's house. The great Uncas, Indian and trusted friend of the English, bequeathed the greater part of his large land acreage in Hebron to Thomas Buckingham, Esq., William Shipman and others. The property became the town of Hebron and its church was the fifteenth in Connecticut. A town could not be recognized until it formed its church.

The kitchen end of the house was, no doubt, built by Thomas Buckingham. Perhaps some of those first Yale students sat before the great hearth fires of this room on cold, snowy days. The room housed the first nucleus of the Yale library. The new house was built by Thomas' grandson, probably between 1725 and 1758. This grandson, Daniel II, bequeathed the house to his son who lived there all his days until he died in 1815. A later generation of the Buckingham family played an important part in the politics of the country: William Alfred Buckingham was Mayor of Norwich, Governor of Connecticut during the War Between the States, and was elected to the United States Senate during the Presidency of Andrew Johnson.

This house, an outstanding example of 18th century Connecticut architecture, is a two over two with the attached lean-to older kitchen. It was slated for destruction to make way for a bridge to cross the Connecticut River, but state authorities realized the historic worth of the ancient house and presented it to Mystic Seaport. It was delivered in two sections, taken by barge to its present site, and restored.

Wallpaper in the front parlor is a reproduction of paper actually found on the walls. *Below:* The panels on the fireplace wall are of identical width.

The kitchen, of earlier vintage than the house, dates from the 1690's. Its wide hearth, able to take 8-foot logs, and its oven at the rear of the chimney indicate its early date, as do the leaded windows and the batten door. Today, an attendant cooks and bakes in this chimney, the name used for a fireplace in the 17th century, and she bakes her stews and baked beans, bread and corn cakes from old recipes.

The early dresser is perhaps a Dutch piece.

Opposite page: The leaded window with diamond shaped glass panes, is typical of 17th century windows.

The dining room in Buckingham House at Mystic Seaport.

An American primitive painting of a baby wearing a bright scarlet dress.

The bedrooms upstairs are furnished with 18th century farm furniture.

KEELER TAVERN, 1733-1769, Ridgefield.

In 1733 Benjamin Hoyt left Deerfield for Ridgefield, taking with him a few home necessities, including a batten door with which he secured the new house he built for himself and his family. After 36 years in his house, he sold it in 1769 to Timothy Keeler. Mr. Keeler married, and opened his house as a tavern. Business thrived and he was forced to build a new, large kitchen to meet the demands of the trade.

Stagecoach travelling was on the increase and roads were being cut and improved all the time. In fact, the turnpike era was just ahead. It lasted from about 1790 through 1810 when it waned, to be picked up again in 1820 through 1840. The stages that carried passengers also carried mail, and since a tavern was a natural stopping place, it is not surprising to find Mr. Keeler the first postmaster in Ridgefield.

Keeler Tavern operated as an inn for 130 years. During the Revolutionary War days, bullets and ammunition were made in the cellar, making it a target for the British. Sometimes the Inn is called the "Cannonball House," for on April 27, 1777, the house was fired upon and the cannon ball still lodges in the northeast corner of the house.

When Timothy died in 1815, his son and daughter carried on the business. But William, the son, died when he was 42, and his sister married her neighbor, Abijah Ressiguie, the head of the carriage works in Ridgefield, a man who lived to be almost 100.

Their daughter carried on when he was too old to manage, and Keeler Tavern became a country inn, a vacation spot for summer guests.

In 1907, Cass Gilbert, architect of the Woolworth Towers, and of the Supreme Court Building in Washington, D.C., bought the commodious tavern for his home. He added the back wing with its spacious dining room, new kitchen and upper chambers. He put in a formal sunken garden with a little pool as well as a summer garden house. In 1955 it was purchased by Mr. and Mrs. Welsh for their home, but it was again sold almost ten years later, in 1966, to the Keeler Tavern Preservation Society.

One of the trellis walkways in the Cass Gilbert garden.

This room, first a kitchen, then turned into a tap room by Thomas Keeler, has the clock and the corner chair that originally were in the house. The high backed settle chair protects from draughts. The checker-board and the chestnut roaster suggest 18th century pastimes.

The hooked rug, "United We Stand," is of 1776 vintage.

One side of the original Keeler Tavern sign.

The Ladies' Parlor was the gathering place for women guests, not permitted in the Tap Room.

The new kitchen was added by Mr. Keeler to accommodate both his growing trade and his growing family of eight children. The pen by the table was to keep the baby protected from cold floors and hot fires. When a pen had wheels, it was called a "Go-cart." The rocker bench on the right had removable fences. A child could safely sleep there with its mother close by.

The mantel in the Ladies' Parlor.

Another view of the Ladies' Parlor.

Napoleon's brother, Jerome Bonaparte ate here! He and his bride stopped here on their wedding trip from Baltimore to Niagara Falls. The linen press with chamfered corners, is painted vermilion; the chairs, black.

The dining room includes portraits of Keeler's daughter and her husband. *Below:* Cass Gilbert salvaged the Adam mantel from Bristol Mansion in New Haven when it was being torn down.

The Dutch influence of New Amsterdam, close by, is seen in the bulbous "turnip" feet of the bed and dresser. *Below:* The dark left wall raises, like a barn door, and can be attached to the ceiling, turning two bedrooms into a ballroom!

WHITEHALL, 1771-1775, Stonington.

Originally built as a retirement home for Dr. Dudley Woodbridge, a well-to-do doctor in Mystic, this 200 year old house was constructed between 1771 and 1775. A spacious, gracious mansion, it retains the early Connecticut plan of two over two with a rear kitchen, yet now the proportions are imposing and much enlarged, embellished with architectural details of the Greek Revival.

Dr. Woodbridge's mansion shows how Connecticut architecture had advanced over a hundred years. The exterior included a gambrel roof. Windows have become much larger with 12 panes over 12 panes. The exquisite design of the doorway with its hand-carved door is impressive in its simplicity and grandeur. Inside, ceilings become high, upstairs as well as downstairs.

The house was lived in by descendants of the Woodbridge family until 1852 when it was purchased by Joseph Wheeler. Succeeding generations of the Wheeler family lived in this country estate

for over a century. In 1962 Dr. DeWitt T. Keach, Professor at Yale, and Mrs. Florence Bentley Keach, the fifth generation owner of Whitehall, were notified that the path of Highway I-95 was to travel right through the historic house, and it would be demolished. It was then that Whitehall was given to The Stonington Historical Society with a new land site of 5 acres, and an initial fund by Mrs. Keach for its removal. The house was then moved to its present location and was painstakingly restored and furnished. Gifts of furniture and accessories as well as purchases have contributed to the furnishing of Whitehall as it may have been in the 18th century.

Dr. and Mrs. Keach's generous gift of Whitehall to The Stonington Historical Society has made it possible to preserve permanently an important house of great quality that exemplifies Connecticut's architectural heritage.

The dining room includes many 18th century pieces of exceptionally fine quality.

The open shelves flanking the fireplace, house 18th century English china.

The living room has many fine antiques, including an early 17th century sunflower chest seen below the portrait.

A corner in the living room includes an early embossed recliner leather chair, above which is a portrait of a seaworthy gentleman of the 18th century, and an early globe.

Two views of the big kitchen. Important is the curved brick trimmer arch at the fireplace's ceiling, which supports the fireplace in the bedroom above.

The borning room, off the kitchen, has a stenciled floor. This room, like those in earlier houses, was off the kitchen, in easy reach of hot water and warmth. Sometimes it was called the "coming and going room" as the elderly and the sick also used this room.

This bedroom is furnished with 18th century furniture. The field bed has an indigo blue and white quilt. The picture below illustrates the fireplace wall, carved from one extremely wide board.

Another beautiful bedroom exhibits an exquisite quilt in shades of tobacco brown and pink. The hooked rug is chalk pink and charcoal. A Victorian child's playpen is at the foot of the bed.

An album quilt made for the minister of the Congregational Church in Stonington has the signatures of the parishioners, who made the individual squares. It is a large quilt in red and white.

The Florence Griswold House in Old Lyme was built in 1817.

FLORENCE GRISWOLD HOUSE, 1817, Old Lyme.

In 1817 William Noyes had Samuel Belcher, who was also the architect of the beautiful Congregational Church in Lyme, build this grandly proportioned house. Some years later, in 1840, this late Georgian house was purchased by an Ely. But it was again sold in 1841, the following year, to Captain Robert Griswold, who brought his young bride to its spacious rooms. Robert Griswold was the Captain of a packet boat that travelled regularly from New York to England.

After Mr. Griswold's death, his wife and daughter used the house as a finishing school where they turned out young ladies properly "cultured" for society.

Florence Griswold, the daughter of Robert Griswold, a musician, after 1901 used the house as a means of support, taking in illustrious boarders, who

were leaders of the academic arts, and were members of the National Academy. Childe Hassam lived there from 1903 to 1915. Other boarders were William Metcalf, Gifford Beal, Walter Griffen and Frank du Mond. Works by these artists are exhibited in the house. At one time, Woodrow Wilson brought his wife here.

The present furnishings have been given to the Historical Society by friends in the community. New England and local Lyme furnishings predominate. Of outstanding merit is the comprehensive china collection originally gathered by the McCurdy family. The house has been furnished to represent the home of an affluent Lyme family of the early 19th century. The harp in the music room was owned by Florence Griswold.

The Victorian bedroom is decorated in shades of peach and charcoal. The trapunto quilt is of exquisite work-manship.

This magnificent corner cupboard holds a few of the pieces of china and pottery from the McCurdy collection.

The fireplace is flanked by 12 over 12 glass windows. Chinese export Rose Medallion china decorates the mantel shelf. A hooked rug of the 19th century, in marigold colors combined with olive and sage greens is of great charm.

DESHAM-ALLYN HOUSE, 1829, New London.

Captain Daniel Desham, a noted and wealthy whaling merchant used New London's harbor as his home port, and it was here that he built his granite mansion in 1829. Its central Palladian window, the stone quoins, and the carved overhanging cornice make this Federal dwelling a house of much distinction. Interior details were taken from the architectural handbook of Asher Benjamin.

In 1851 another successful whaler, Captain Lyman Allyn, bought this house and his descendants lived in it until it became a part of the Lyman Allyn Museum. The house has been furnished with valuable antiques appropriate to the first half of the 19th century.

The hallway between the living and dining rooms also opens onto a terrace and beds of flowers.

The living room with its stunning chandelier, is furnished with Neo-Classic and early 19th century furniture and accessories.

The folding desk includes glassed bookshelves.

The music room with its early piano and harp is where guests often gathered after dinner, to be entertained by "live" performers. Most Victorian ladies were accomplished players of either instrument. *Below:* Another view of the opposite side of the music room.

The dining room in the Desham-Allyn house has a tole plate warmer to the left of the fireplace. A white Chelsea tea set sprigged in ageratum blue is on the sideboard. *Below:* The New London harbor appears in this ship painting in the hall entitled, "Ship Alert — New London."

In close proximity to the Desham-Allyn house is the Lyman Allyn Museum where many important examples of Americana are exhibited. This large American primitive over the bulbous ball-footed desk, is a sensitive study of a New England mother and her child.

A sampler worked by a New London girl in 1821 is well preserved.

The pitcher has a mottled green and brown glaze.

This original Hancock chair, painted black with gold trim and stencil work, has the added feature of having a landscape painted on its back.

STONE HOUSE, 1840, Deep River.

Like Essex, Deep River was a part of the original great expanse known in the early days of Connecticut as Saybrook. This house was built in 1840 from stone quarried from the area. Deacon Ezra Southworth built the house for his bride. The house remained in the hands of the Southworth descendants until 1947 when it was left to the Historical Society by Ada Southworth Munson. Through the years a Victorian porch was added, and the flat roof was altered by introducing a double pitched one.

There are several rooms furnished in the Victorian style. The marine collection is notable. Cut glass was made in Deep River at one time, and a collection of it may be seen here.

The parlor in the Stone House includes 18th and 19th century pieces.

The piano made from the Charter Oak is in the far corner of the room.

The Victorian bedroom has a sleigh bed among its other pieces.

The arched divider separated the sleeping area from the dressing room area in this Victorian bedroom.

LOCKWOOD-MATHEWS MANSION, 1868, Norwalk.

Based on Bramante's plan for St. Peter's Cathedral in Rome, on a smaller scale, this Victorian house of great elegance was the work of the architect, Detlef Lienau, the famed Frenchman who also designed several Newport houses, the "Grosvenor" on Fifth Avenue, the first apartment-hotel to be designed in New York City, in 1871, and other apartments, multiple dwellings and industrial buildings.

The owner of the mansion, LeGrand Lockwood, was a Wall Street "tycoon" of the 19th century. The Gold Panic of '69 affected his affairs and he mortgaged his property. He had lived in his man-

sion only four years when he died in 1872. Although a considerable amount of his loan was repaid, his wife was not able to meet the final payment, and those holding the mortgage sold it in 1876 to Charles Mathews, a New York importer, for $90,-000. In 1941 the City of Norwalk purchased the property after the last descendant of the Mathews family died in 1938.

The Mansion is undergoing intensive restoration. Since there are photographs of each room taken in Lockwood's day, there is an accurate record of how to furnish each room.

The hand-carved mantel, done by imported Italian artisans who were paid 50 cents a day, and many of whom returned to Italy after the mansion was completed, is of English and American walnut. The parquetry floor is inlaid with five different kinds of wood. The embossed wallpaper simulates Moroccan leather. The library was to contain over 3,000 books, maps and manuscripts. The room is at present unfurnished.

The drawing room is one of palatial elegance. A few pieces of the original furniture are gradually coming back to Lockwood Mansion.

GILLETTE CASTLE, 1914-1919, Hadlyme.

Just as we started with the great preacher, Thomas Hooker, who led his pioneer hundred from Newtown, Massachusetts, to the wilds of Connecticut, so we close, many generations later, with a direct descendant of this Puritan leader, William Gillette. He, however, took not to the pulpit but to the stage, captivating the theater world with his portrayal of Conan Doyle's Sherlock Holmes. Fame brought fortune and his assets mounted to three million dollars at that time when there was no income tax.

When 61, he decided to build, not his dream house, but his dream castle. Although he originally chose Long Island for his site, a trip up the Connecticut River on his houseboat altered his plans. The dramatic scenery of the rocky ridges known as the Seven Sisters, the winding river and the magnificent forests fired his artistic imagination. After buying 122 acres, he set about designing the 24-room castle where he spent his last twenty years.

He was architect, designer, decorator for everything in the castle, *his* castle in the air. Thirty masons took five years to build the house.

The plan, like the actor, is dramatic and spectacular. His daring use of open planning, of textured surfaces, of developing the indoor-outdoor look so popular now in California, were in advance of his time, and suggest his knowledge of Frank Lloyd Wright's approach to architecture.

The exterior, however, with its bulky turrets and ramparts, is awkward almost to the point of being grotesque. Most unorthodox, it suggests stage scenery rather than reality. Gillette's house, like that of his forebears, is a barricade, and what a barricade! Granite walls 4 to 5 feet thick at the base taper to about 2 feet thick at the tower. Great iron beams support the weight. All the wood in the building is white oak from the South. The stone is all native Connecticut fieldstone.

Above is a view of the living room looking towards the staircase. Bedrooms open off the balcony. Some of the furniture is built in.

The dining room opens onto the conservatory. The table is on a track that slides forward in front of the built-in seat. The carved relief details on the massive doors, ceilings, light switches and cupboards were designed by Gillette and carved by local craftsmen.

The hand-carved bar is part of the room which connects Gillette's study and the dining room.

This rock garden built in the conservatory includes a little fountain and pool at the far end. The outside terrace is a continuation of the conservatory's pavement.

INDEX

(Page numbers in **bold face** *denote photographs)*

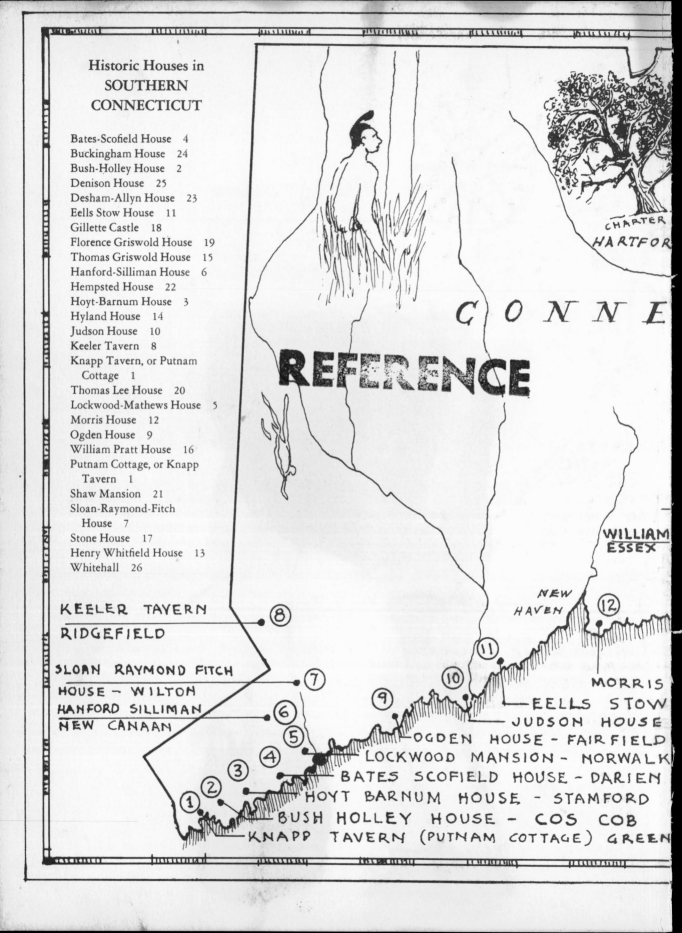

Historic Houses in SOUTHERN CONNECTICUT

REFERENCE

CHARTER
HARTFOR

CONNE

WILLIAM
ESSEX

NEW
HAVEN

KEELER TAVERN
RIDGEFIELD ⑧

SLOAN RAYMOND FITCH
HOUSE — WILTON ⑦
HANFORD SILLIMAN
NEW CANAAN ⑥

⑤

④

③

② ①

⑫

⑪

⑩

⑨

MORRIS
EELLS STOW
JUDSON HOUSE
OGDEN HOUSE - FAIRFIELD
LOCKWOOD MANSION - NORWALK
BATES SCOFIELD HOUSE - DARIEN
HOYT BARNUM HOUSE - STAMFORD
BUSH HOLLEY HOUSE - COS COB
KNAPP TAVERN (PUTNAM COTTAGE) GREEN

INTRODUCTION TO
Solid Modeling
Using SolidWorks® 2007

INTRODUCTION TO
Solid Modeling
Using SolidWorks® 2007

William E. Howard
East Carolina University

Joseph C. Musto
Milwaukee School of Engineering

Burr Ridge, IL   Dubuque, IA   New York   San Francisco   St. Louis
Bangkok   Bogotá   Caracas   Kuala Lumpur   Lisbon   London   Madrid   Mexico City
Milan   Montreal   New Delhi   Santiago   Seoul   Singapore   Sydney   Taipei   Toronto

INTRODUCTION TO SOLID MODELING USING SOLIDWORKS®, 2007

 This book is printed on recycled, acid-free paper containing 10% postconsumer waste.

1 2 3 4 5 6 7 8 9 0 QPD/QPD 0 9 8 7

ISBN 978-0-07-337532-8
MHID 0-07-337532-2

Global Publisher: *Raghothaman Srinivasan*
Executive Editor: *Michael Hackett*
Senior Sponsoring Editor: *Bill Stenquist*
Director of Development: *Kristine Tibbetts*
Developmental Editor: *Lora Kalb*
Executive Marketing Manager: *Michael Weitz*
Senior Project Manager: *Kay J. Brimeyer*
Senior Production Supervisor: *Sherry L. Kane*
Associate Media Producer: *Christina Nelson*
Associate Design Coordinator: *Brenda A. Rolwes*
Cover Designer: *Studio Montage, St. Louis, Missouri*
Compositor: *Visual Q*
Typeface: *10/12 Giovanni; Gill Sans Condensed*
Printer: *Quebecor World Dubuque, IA*
(USE) Cover Image: *Copyright © Commuter Cars Corporation, David Clugston Photography, and Bryan Woodbury; SolidWorks rendering of Tango front suspension by Dave Mounce and Mike Thompson of Commuter Cars Corp.*

Library of Congress Cataloging-in-Publication Data

Howard, William E.
  Introduction to solid modeling using SolidWorks / William E. Howard, Joseph C. Musto.—3rd ed.
    p. cm.—(BEST (Best engineering series and tools))
  Includes index.
  ISBN 978-0-07-337532-8—ISBN 0-07-337532-2 (hard copy : alk. paper)
  1. Computer graphics. 2. SolidWorks. 3. Engineering models. 4. Computer-aided design. I. Musto, Joseph C. II. Title.
T385.H75 2007
620'.00420285536—dc22

                                                            2007013014

www.mhhe.com

About the Authors

Ed Howard is an Assistant Professor in the Technology Systems Department of East Carolina University. Prior to joining ECU, Ed taught for nine years at Milwaukee School of Engineering, where he taught classes in mechanics, finite element analysis, solid modeling, and composite materials. He was also Director of the Mechanical Engineering Technology program. His holds a BS in Civil Engineering and an MS in Engineering Mechanics from Virginia Tech, and a Ph.D. in Mechanical Engineer-ing from Marquette University.

Ed worked in design, analysis, and project engineering for 14 years before beginning his academic career. He worked for Thiokol Corporation in Brigham City, UT, Spaulding Composites Company in Smyrna, TN, and Sta-Rite Industries in Delavan, WI. He is a registered Professional Engineer in Wisconsin.

Joe Musto is an Associate Professor and Director of the Mechanical Engineering Program at Milwaukee School of Engineer-ing, where he teaches in the areas of machine design, solid modeling, and numerical methods. He holds a BS degree from Clarkson University, and both an M.Eng. and Ph.D. from Rensselaer Polytechnic Institute, all in mechanical engineering. He is a registered Professional Engineer in Wisconsin.

Prior to joining the faculty at Milwaukee School of Engineering, he held industrial positions with Brady Corporation (Milwaukee, WI) and Eastman Kodak Company (Rochester, NY). He has been using and teaching solid modeling using SolidWorks since 1998.

BRIEF CONTENTS

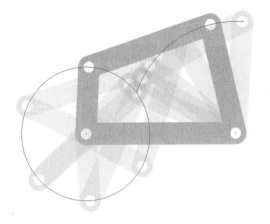

CONTENTS

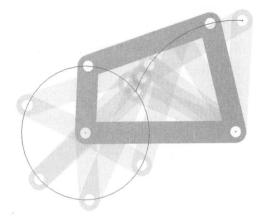

SPECIAL FEATURES

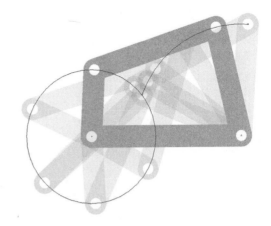

PREFACE

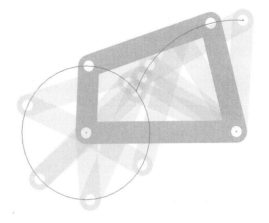

As design engineers and engineering professors, the authors have witnessed incredible changes in the way that products are designed and manufactured. One of the biggest changes over the past 20 years has been the development and widespread usage of solid modeling software. When we first saw solid modeling, it was used only by large companies. The cost of the software and the powerful computer workstations required to run it, along with the complexity of using the software, limited its use. As the cost of computing hardware dropped, solid modeling software was developed for personal computers. In 1995, the SolidWorks Corporation released SolidWorks®95, the first solid modeling program written for the Microsoft Windows operating system. Since then, the use of solid modeling has become an indispensable tool for almost any company, large or small, that designs a product.

A good example of a small company utilizing the power of solid modeling is Commuter Cars Inc. of Spokane, Washington. Commuter Cars has created the Tango, which is featured on the cover of this book. Envisioned as a solution to commuter traffic problems and a way to maximize limited parking, the goal was to design a car that had all of the functionality and features, as well as the weight of a full-sized car, but pack it into the space of a rectangle that would just enclose a motorcycle.

Designing for the level of safety Commuter Cars demanded (the Tango is weighted to maintain a safe rollover threshold and includes race car roll cage protection and 4-point harnesses) had its own challenges, but they also wanted a car that was environmentally friendly and fun. Therefore, they designed it to be powered by electric motors, go from 0 to 60 miles per hour in 4 seconds, and feel and look like a car that anyone would want to drive. SolidWorks software allowed Commuter Cars engineers to fit components, run the suspension and other moving parts through their range of travel, and find interferences, streamlining the design process substantially.

SolidWorks is a registered trademark of SolidWorks Corporation.

Motivation for this Text

When we saw a demonstration of the SolidWorks software in 1998, we were both instantly hooked. Not only was the utility of the software obvious, but the program was easy to learn and fun to use. Since then, we have shared our enthusiasm with the program with hundreds of students in classes and informal training sessions at the Milwaukee School of Engineering, and at East Carolina University and in summer programs with high school students. Most of the material in this book began as tutorials that we developed for these purposes. We continue to be amazed at how quickly students at all levels can learn the basics of the program, and by the sophisticated projects that many students develop after only a short time using the software.

While anyone desiring to learn the SolidWorks program can use this book, we have added specific elements for beginning engineering students. With these elements, we have attempted to introduce students to the design process and to relate solid modeling to subjects that most engineering students will study later. We hope that the combination of the tutorial style approach to teaching the functionality of the software together with the integration of the material into the overall study of engineering will motivate student interest not only in the SolidWorks software but in the profession of engineering.

Philosophy of This Text

The development of powerful and integrated solid modeling software has continued the evolution of computer-aided design packages from drafting/graphical communication tools to full-fledged engineering design and analysis tools. A solid model is more than simply a drawing of an engineering component; it is a true virtual representation of the part, which can be manipulated, combined with other parts into complex assemblies, used directly for analysis, and used to drive the manufacturing equipment that will be used to produce the part.

This text was developed to exploit this emerging role of solid modeling as an integral part of the engineering design process; while proficiency in the software will be achieved through the exercises provided in the text, the traditional "training" exercises will be augmented with information on the integration of solid modeling into the engineering design process. These topics include:

- The exploitation of the parametric features of a solid model, to not only provide an accurate graphical representation of a part but also to effectively capture an engineer's design intent,
- The use of solid models as an analysis tool, useful for determining properties of components as well as for virtual prototyping of mechanisms and systems,

- The integration of solid modeling with component manufacturing, including the generation of molds, sheet metal patterns, and rapid prototyping files from component models.

Through the introduction of these topics, students will be shown not only the powerful modeling features of the SolidWorks program, but also the role of the software as a full-fledged integrated engineering design tool.

The Use of This Text

The text layout and typography have been redesigned to improve readability and make the tutorials more accessible to students. The chapter-long tutorials introduce both basic concepts in solid modeling (such as part modeling, drawing creation, and assembly modeling) and more advanced applications of solid modeling in engineering analysis and design (such as mechanism modeling, mold creation, sheet metal bending, and rapid prototyping). Each tutorial is organized as "keystroke-level" instructions, designed to teach the use of the software. For easy reference, a guide to these tutorials is shown on the inside front cover.

While these tutorials offer a level of detail appropriate for new professional users, this text was developed to be used as part of an introductory engineering course, taught around the use of solid modeling as an integrated engineering design and analysis tool. Since the intended audience is undergraduate students new to the field of engineering, the text contains features that help to integrate the concepts learned in solid modeling into the overall study of engineering. These features include:

- *Design Intent Boxes:* These are intended to augment the "keystroke-level" tutorials to include the rationale behind the sequence of operations chosen to create a model.
- *Future Study Boxes:* These link the material contained in the chapters to topics that will be seen later in the academic and professional careers of new engineering students. They are intended to motivate interest in advanced study in engineering, and to place the material seen in the tutorials within the context of the profession.

While these features are intended to provide additional motivation and context for beginning engineering students, they are self-contained, and may be omitted by professionals who wish to use this text purely for the software tutorials.

The Organization of This Text

The organization of the chapters of the book reflects the authors' preferences in teaching the material, but allows for several different options. We have found that covering drawings early in the course is helpful in that we can have students turn in drawings rather than parts as homework assignments. The eDrawings feature, which is covered in Chapter 2, is especially useful in that eDrawings files are small (easy to e-mail), self-contained (not linked to the part file), and can be easily marked up with the editing tools contained in the eDrawings program.

The flowchart illustrates the relations between chapters, and can be used to map alternative plans for coverage of the material. For example, if it is desired to cover assemblies as soon as possible (as might be desired in a course that includes a project) then the chapters can be covered in the order 1-3-6-7-2-8, with the remaining chapters covered in any order desired. An instructor who prefers to cover parts, assemblies, and drawings in that order may cover the chapters in the order 1-3-4-5-6-7-2-8 (skipping section 4.4 until after Chapter 2 is covered) again with the remaining chapters covered in any order.

Chapters 9 and 10 may be omitted in a standard solid modeling course; however, they can be valuable in an introductory engineering course. Engineering students will almost certainly find use at some point for the 2-D layout and vector mechanics applications introduced in these chapters. Chapter 13 is intended to wrap up a course with a discussion of how solid modeling is used as a tool in the product development cycle.

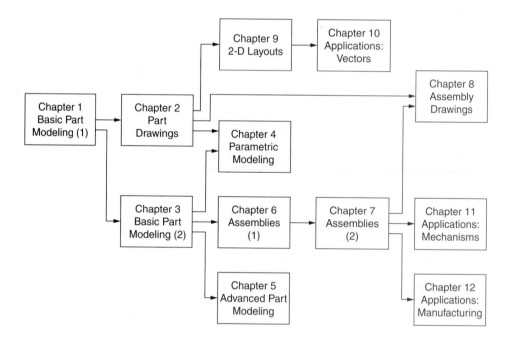

SolidWorks® Student Design Kit Included

The SolidWorks® Student Design Kit 2007–2008 is packaged with this book. The student design kit includes a 150-day license of the following:

- *SolidWorks® 2007:* the standard in 3-D mechanical design software
- *eDrawings® 2007:* a great tool for sharing design information
- *SolidWorks® Animator:* easy-to-use video creation software
- *DWGEditor®:* a handy tool for viewing and editing 2-D drawings
- *MoldflowXpress™ and COSMOSXpress™:* powerful design validation tools

Additional Resources for Instructors

Additional recourses are available on the web at www.mhhe.com/howard. Included on the website are tutorials for three popular SolidWorks Add-Ins, COSMOSWorks®, COSMOSMotion™ and Photo-Works™, and the book figures in PowerPoint format. Instructors can also access model files for all tutorials and problems (password-protected; contact your McGraw-Hill representative for access).

Acknowledgments

We are grateful to our friends at McGraw-Hill for their support and encouragement during this project. In particular, we have enjoyed working with Lora Kalb, our editor, and Bill Stenquist, the sponsoring editor. Laura Hunter of Visual Q created the page design and did the page layouts, assisted by the proofreading and copyediting of Matt Hunter. Brenda Rolwes created the cover design. Also, thanks to Tim Maruna, who encouraged us to initiate this project.

At SolidWorks Corporation, Marie Planchard has continually provided support. The SolidWorks Partner Program team, particularly Magdalen Fryatt, have always always been helpful.

We also want to thank the reviewers whose comments have undoubtedly made the book better. These reviewers included:

Bruce H. Adee, *University of Washington*

Holly K. Ault, *Worchester Polytechnic Institute*

Radha Balamuralikrishna, *Northern Illinois University*

---

eDrawing and DWGEditor are registered trademarks of SolidWorks Corporation. MoldflowXpress, COSMOSXpress, and PhotoWorks are trademarks of SolidWorks Corporation. COSMOSWorks is a registered trademark of Structural Research and Analysis Company. COSMOSMotion is a trademark of Structural Research and Analysis Company.

Beth Carle, *Rochester Institute of Technology*

Lawrence E. Carlson, *University of Colorado*

Karen L. Coen-Brown, *University of Nebraska, Lincoln*

Charles Coleman, *Arkansas State University*

Robert Crockett, *California Polytechnic State University, San Luis Obispo*

Ismail Fidan, *Tennessee Tech University*

Rajit Gadh, *University of California, Los Angeles*

Meung J. Kim, *Northern Illinois University*

Roger L. Ludin, *California Polytechnic State University, San Luis Obispo*

Sara McMains, *University of California, Berkeley*

Charles Ritz, *California Polytechnic State University, Pomona*

Stephen A. Tennyson, *Boise State University*

Mary Tolle, *South Dakota State University*

At the Milwaukee School of Engineering, many of our students and colleagues used early versions of the manuscript and materials that eventually became this text. We thank them for their patience and helpful feedback along the way.

Ed Howard
Joe Musto

PART ONE

ONE

Learning SolidWorks®

CHAPTER 1

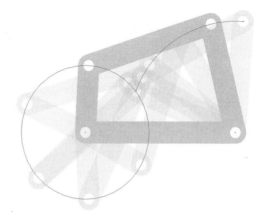

Basic Part Modeling Techniques

Introduction

Solid modeling has become an essential tool for most companies that design mechanical structures and machines. Just 15 years ago, this would have been hard to imagine. While 3-D modeling software existed, it was very expensive and required high-end computer workstations to run. An investment of $50,000 or more was required for every workstation with software, not including training of the operator. As a result, only a few industries used solid modeling, and the trained operators tended to work exclusively with the software.

The dramatic performance improvements and price drops of computer hardware, along with increased competition among software vendors, have significantly lowered the cost barrier for companies to enter the solid modeling age. The software has also become much easier to use, so that engineers who have many other job functions can use solid modeling when required without needing to become software specialists. The SolidWorks®[1] program was among the first solid modeling programs to be written exclusively for the Microsoft Windows environment. Since its initial release in 1995, it has been adopted by thousands of companies worldwide.

This text is laid out as a series of tutorials that cover most of the basic features of the SolidWorks® program. Although these tutorials will be of use to anyone desiring to learn the software, they are written primarily for freshman engineering students. Accordingly, topics in engineering design are introduced along the way. "Future Study" boxes give a preview of coursework that engineering students will encounter later, and relate that coursework to the solid modeling tutorials.

In this first chapter, we will learn how to make a simple part in SolidWorks. We will actually create the same part twice, using different techniques the second time.

---

[1] SolidWorks is a registered trademark of the SolidWorks Corporation, 300 Baker Avenue, Concord, MA 01742.

Chapter Objectives

In this chapter, you will:

- be introduced to the process of engineering design and the concept of concurrent engineering,

- learn how to create and dimension simple 2-D sketches and perform operations to create 3-D shapes from these sketches,

- be introduced to design intent as we create a part, and

- learn how to modify parts.

1.1   Engineering Design and Solid Modeling

The term *design* is used to describe many endeavors. A clothing designer creates new styles of apparel. An industrial designer creates the overall look and function of consumer products. Many design functions concentrate mainly on aesthetic considerations—how the product looks, and how it will be accepted in the marketplace. The term *engineering design* is applied to a process in which fundamentals of math and science are applied to the creation or modification of a product to meet a set of objectives.

Engineering design is only one part of the creation of a new product. Consider a company making consumer products, for example bicycles. A marketing department determines the likely customer acceptance of a new bike model and outlines the requirements for the new design. Industrial designers work on the preliminary design of the bike to produce a design that combines functionality and styling that customers will like. Manufacturing engineers must consider how the components of the product are made and assembled. A purchasing department will determine if some components will be more economical to buy than to make. Stress analysts will predict whether the bike will survive the forces and environment that it will experience in service. A model shop may need to build a physical prototype for marketing use or to test functionality.

During the years immediately following World War II, most American companies performed the tasks described above more or less sequentially. That is, the design engineer did not get involved in the process until the specifications were completed, the manufacturing engineers started once the design was finalized, and so on. From the 1970s through the 1990s, the concept of *concurrent engineering* became widespread. Concurrent engineering refers to the process in which engineering tasks are performed simultaneously rather than sequentially. The primary benefits of concurrent engineering are shorter product develop times and lower development costs. The challenges of implementing concurrent engineering are mostly in communications—engineering groups must be continuously informed of the actions of the other groups.

Solid modeling is an important tool in concurrent engineering in that the various engineering groups work from a common database: the solid model. In a 2-D CAD (Computer-Aided Design) environment, the design engineer produced sketches of the component, and a draftsman produced 2-D design drawings. These drawings were forwarded to the other engineering organizations, where much of the information was then duplicated. For example, a toolmaker created a tool design from scratch, using the drawings as the basis. A stress analyst created a finite element model, again starting from scratch. A model builder created a physical prototype by hand from the drawing parameters. With a solid model, the tool, finite element model, and rapid prototype model are all created directly from the solid model file. In addition to the time savings of avoiding the steps of recreating the design for the various functions, many errors are avoided by having everyone working from a common database. Although 2-D drawings are usually still required, since they are the best way to document dimensions and tolerances, they are linked directly to the solid model and are easy to update as the solid model is changed.

A mechanical engineering system (assembly) may be composed of thousands of components (parts). The detailed design of each component is important to the operation of the system. In this chapter, we will step through the creation of a simple component. In future chapters, we will learn how to make 2-D drawings from a part file, and how to put components together in an assembly file.

1.2 Part Modeling Tutorial: Flange

This tutorial will lead you through the creation of a simple solid part. The part, a flange, is shown in **Figure 1.1** and is described by the 2-D drawing in **Figure 1.2**.

FIGURE 1.1

FIGURE 1.2

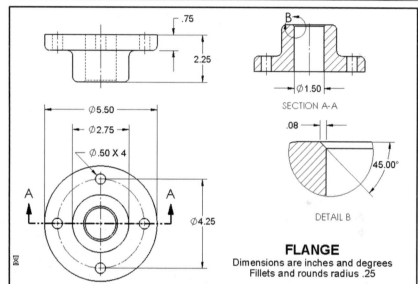

SECTION A-A

DETAIL B

FLANGE
Dimensions are inches and degrees
Fillets and rounds radius .25

FIGURE 1.3

FIGURE 1.4

FIGURE 1.5

Begin by clicking the SolidWorks icon. The SolidWorks Resources Task Pane shown in Figure 1.3 may be displayed. If so, select View: Task Pane from the main menu, as shown in Figure 1.4.

The Task Pane is an interface for accessing files and online resources. It can be toggled on and off by selecting it from the View menu. A check mark by a menu item indicates that the menu item is active; clicking clears the check mark and makes the menu item inactive.

From the main menu, select File: New, as shown in Figure 1.5.

A dialog box will appear, from which you are to specify whether we are creating a part, an assembly, or a drawing (see **Figure 1.6**).

FIGURE 1.6

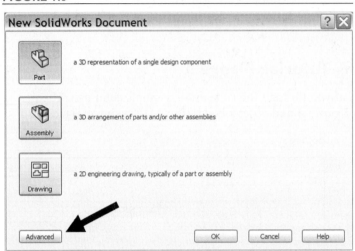

The "Advanced" button at the lower left of the box allows you to toggle between menus with explanatory text ("novice" mode) and menus with simple icons ("advanced" mode, as shown in **Figure 1.7**). We will use the advanced mode in this book.

FIGURE 1.7

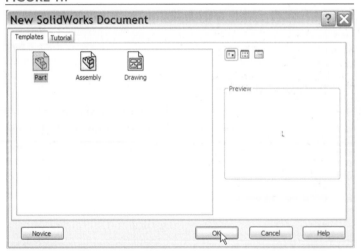

FIGURE 1.8

FIGURE 1.9

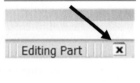

Click on the "Advanced" button. Click on the Part icon to highlight it and then click the OK button. If the Quick Tips box shown in Figure 1.8 is displayed, click the X on the status bar, shown in Figure 1.9, to turn off its display.

Before we begin modeling the flange, we will establish a consistent setup of the SolidWorks environment. The screen layout shown in **Figure 1.10** is similar to the default configuration. The *graphics area* occupies most of the screen. The part, drawing, or assembly will be displayed in this area.

FIGURE 1.10

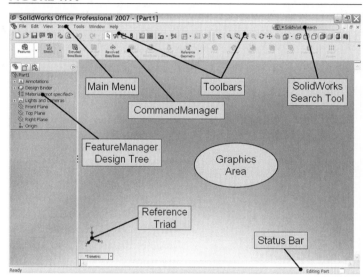

There is a *main menu* at the top of the screen, and a *status bar* on the bottom of the screen. When you move the cursor over any toolbar icon or menu command, a message on the left side of the status bar describes the command. Other information appears at the right side of the status bar, such as whether or not a sketch is completely defined.

FIGURE 1.11

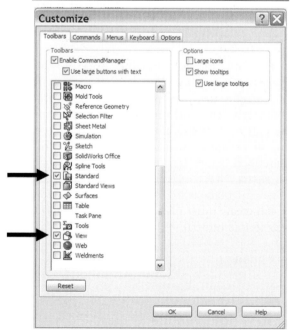

There are a number of *toolbars* that can be displayed. Toolbars allow for the selection of frequently-used commands with a single mouse click. If you right-click on any of the toolbars, a list of available toolbars is displayed, with active toolbars indicated by the depression of the icon beside the toolbar name. Toolbars can also be turned on or off from the Customize command.

From the main menu, select Tools: Customize. Under the Toolbars tab, click to select or deselect toolbars so that only the Standard and View toolbars are selected, as shown in Figure 1.11. Click OK.

The toolbars may be repositioned anywhere on the screen by clicking and dragging with the left mouse button. Typically, they are placed just below the main menu, as shown in **Figure 1.10**.

The *CommandManager* contains most of the tools that you will use to create parts. By default, when working in the part mode, there are two categories of tools in the CommandManager: sketch tools used in creating 2-D sketches, and features tools used to create and modify 3-D features.

Clicking on the Sketch and Features icons at the left of the CommandManager toggles the commands between the 2-D and 3-D tools, as shown in **Figures 1.12** and **1.13**.

FIGURE 1.12

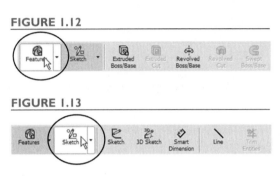

FIGURE 1.13

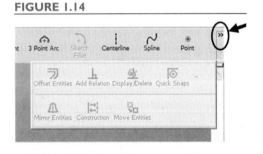

If your screen size/resolution do not allow the display of all of the tools of the Command-Manager, there will be a double arrow at the right end of the CommandManager. Clicking on this double arrow allows the rest of the tools to be shown, as shown in **Figure 1.14**.

FIGURE 1.14

Note that many of the tools on the CommandManager are shown in gray; these are tools that are not available at the current state of the part or sketch. The contents of any toolbar can be added to the CommandManager. In Chapter 3, we will see how to customize toolbars and the CommandManager.

FIGURE 1.15

Just to the left of the drawing area is the *FeatureManager Design Tree*. The steps that you will execute to create the part will be listed in the FeatureManager. This information is important when the part is to be modified. When you open a new part, the FeatureManager lists an origin and three predefined planes (Front, Top, and Right), as shown in **Figure 1.15**. As you select each plane with your mouse, the plane is highlighted in the drawing area. We can create other planes as needed, and will do so later in this tutorial.

We will now set some of the program options.

From the menu, select Tools: Options, as shown in Figure 1.16.

The dialog box contains settings for both the system and for the specific document that is open.

FIGURE 1.16

Under the System Options tab, for the General options, make sure that the box labeled "Input dimension value" is checked, as shown in Figure 1.17. **If it is not, click on the box so that a check mark appears.**

FIGURE 1.17

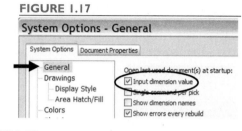

Also under the System Options tab, click on Sketch: Relations/Snaps. Make sure that the box labeled "Grid" is not checked. If it is, click on the box to clear the check mark (see Figure 1.18**).**

Grid-snapping means that when you are sketching, you can place items only at specific points defined by a rectangular grid. While this can be useful for drawing items of a specific size, it is usually not required.

FIGURE 1.18

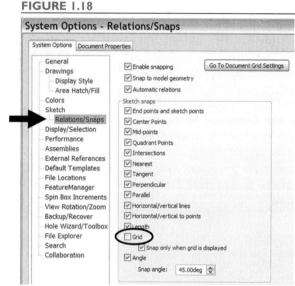

The background color of the modeling area may be gray, with a color gradient to white. If you would prefer a plain white background, follow the next step.

Under the System Options tab, click on Colors. Click on Viewport Background and Edit, as shown in Figure 1.19. **Pick white as the background color, and click OK.**

FIGURE 1.19

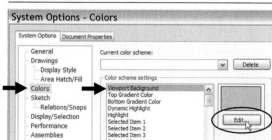

Choose the Plain option for the background appearance, as shown in Figure 1.20.

Under the Document Properties tab, select Detailing. Under Dimensioning standard, select ANSI from the pull-down menu, as shown in Figure 1.21.

FIGURE 1.20

FIGURE 1.21

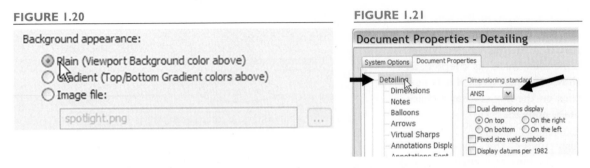

ANSI is the American National Standards Institute, an organization that formulates and publishes the standard drawing practices used by most companies in the United States. European companies are more likely to use the standards of ISO, the International Organization for Standardization.

Under the Document Properties tab, select Grid/Snap and make sure that the "Display grid" box is checked, as shown in Figure 1.22.

Also under the Document Properties tab, select Units. Select IPS (inch, pound, second) as the unit system. Set the number of decimal places for length units to 3, as shown in Figure 1.23. **Click OK to close the dialog box.**

FIGURE 1.22

FIGURE 1.23

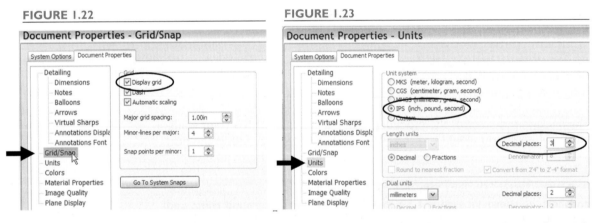

FIGURE 1.24

Any of the options just set can be changed at any time during the modeling process. In Chapter 3, we will learn how to create a *template* that allows us to begin a new part with our preferred settings in place.

We start the construction of the flange by sketching a circle and extruding it into a 3-D disk.

Select the Front Plane by clicking on it in the FeatureManager Design Tree, as shown in Figure 1.24.

The Front Plane will be highlighted in green. The color green indicates that an item is the currently selected item.

Sketch

Begin a sketch by selecting the Sketch group of the CommandManager, and then the Sketch Tool.

A grid pattern appears, signifying that you are in the sketching mode, as shown in **Figure 1.25**.

FIGURE 1.25

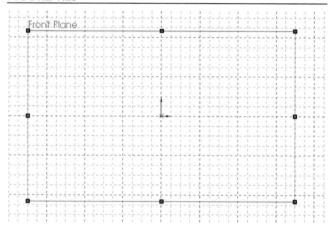

FIGURE 1.26

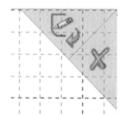

Also, a Sketch icon appears in a triangle at the upper-right corner of the screen, as shown in **Figure 1.26**. (Note: For clarity, most of the images in this text were produced with the grid display turned off. For new users, however, the grid display is a useful reminder that the sketching mode is active.)

Select the Circle Tool.

Circle

FIGURE 1.27   FIGURE 1.28

Notice as you move the cursor into the drawing area that it changes appearance into a pencil with a circle next to it, as shown in **Figure 1.27**. This lets you know that the Circle Tool is active. Move the cursor toward the origin until a red dot appears at the origin, as shown in **Figure 1.28**; this indicates that you will snap to an existing point (in this case the origin) when you click with the mouse. Also, note the small icon next to the origin that signifies a *coincident relation*—the origin and the center point of the circle will share the same location.

A snap adds a relation of the positions of two entities. In this example, when you "snap" to the origin, the circle will be centered at the exact coordinates of x = 0 and y = 0. The relation added when one entity is created by snapping to another can be edited later, if desired. The addition of a snap automatically is a nice feature of the SolidWorks program: snaps are intuitive. It is not necessary to enter the numerical coordinates of the center of the circle.

With the center point highlighted as in Figure 1.28, click and hold the left mouse button and drag the mouse outward to create a circle, as shown in Figure 1.29. Release the mouse button to create the circle.

FIGURE 1.29

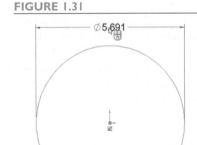

The circle will appear in green. The green color indicates that it is the currently selected item.

Click the esc key to close the Circle Tool and deselect the circle just drawn.

The circle should now appear in blue. At the bottom of the screen, notice that "Under Defined" appears. This is because we have not set the dimension of the circle yet.

When a sketch does not contain enough dimensions and/or relations to define its size and position in space, it is said to be underdefined, and is denoted by blue entities.

Other possible conditions of the sketch are "Fully Defined," when the sketch contains exactly enough dimensions and/or relations to define its size and position in space (denoted by black entities), and "Over Defined," where the sketch has at least one dimension or relation that contradicts or is redundant to the other dimensions and relations (denoted by red entities). Overdefined sketches should be avoided.

Smart
Dimension

Select the Smart Dimension Tool. An icon representing dimension lines and arrows will appear, as shown in Figure 1.30.

FIGURE 1.30

Now click with the left mouse button anywhere on the circle. A dimension will be added to the diameter of the circle. You can drag the dimension to a convenient location. When the dimension is where you want to put it, left click the mouse (see Figure 1.31).

FIGURE 1.31

⌀5.691

A dialog box prompting for the value of this dimension will be displayed, as shown in Figure 1.32. **Enter "5.5" in the box.** (You don't need to enter "in" since that is the default unit, set earlier). **Press the Enter key or click on the check mark to update the dimension.**

FIGURE 1.32

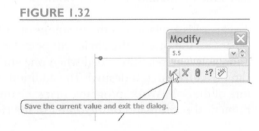

Notice that the circle is redrawn to the correct dimension. The dimension in inches will be displayed, and the circle will become black. Notice at the bottom of the screen in the status bar that the sketch is now Fully Defined. (Note: If we had not snapped to the origin for the circle's center, the sketch would still be underdefined because the circle would not be located in space.)

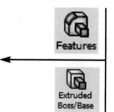

Use the esc key to turn off the Dimension Tool. Now if you double-click on the dimension value, the dialog box reappears and you can change the dimension. Try this, and then use the Undo Tool to return the dimension to 5.5 inches.

Note that you can change the way the dimension is displayed.

Select the dimension by clicking once on the dimension value, and then click on one of the green dots on the arrow heads to change the arrow display. Click and drag on the center green dot to rotate the dimension to a new position.

FIGURE 1.33

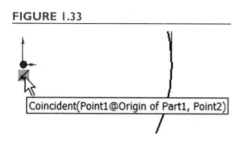

Coincident(Point1@Origin of Part1, Point2)

Next to the center of the circle, an icon shows that a constraint is applied. By moving the cursor over the constraint icon, details about the constraint can be viewed, as shown in **Figure 1.33**. Constraints can be deleted by clicking on the constraint icon to select it, and then pressing the delete key.

FIGURE 1.34

The display of sketch relations can be toggled on and off by selecting View from the main menu and clicking on Sketch Relations, as shown in **Figure 1.34**. Some experienced users prefer to not show the relations because they can cause a sketch to appear cluttered, but new users are advised to keep the relation display turned on.

Now we are ready to turn this 2-D sketch into a 3-D part with the Extruded Boss/Base command.

Select the Features group of the CommandManager, and the Extruded Boss/Base Tool.

The *base feature* is the first solid feature created. Any subsequent solid features are called *bosses*.

Note that the view of the part changes to display a 3-D preview of the extruded solid.

FIGURE 1.35

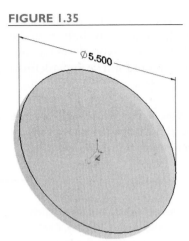

Click and drag the arrow at the center of the circle outward to set the direction of the extrusion. When you release the mouse button, a preview of the extruded solid is shown, as in Figure 1.35.

On the left side of the screen, where the FeatureManager is normally displayed, the PropertyManager is now active. The PropertyManager allows the properties of the selected entity to be viewed and edited. There are several options available for the extrusion, including adding draft (taper) to the part, but for now we only need to adjust the depth of the extrusion.

Set the depth of the extrusion to 0.75 inches, as shown in Figure 1.36. When you click on the check mark, the circle is extruded into a solid disk, as shown in Figure 1.37.

FIGURE 1.36

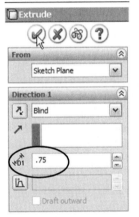

FIGURE 1.37

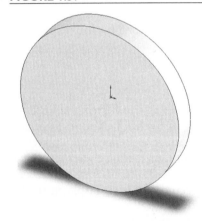

Now that we have a solid part, we can examine the functions of the viewing tools.

On the View toolbar, shown in Figures 1.38 and 1.39, the first icon allows the previous view to be displayed. Next are the zoom tools, indicated by the magnifying glass icons. The Zoom to Fit Tool adjusts the zoom so that the entire model can be viewed. The Zoom to Area Tool allows a viewing window to be selected by dragging out an area on the screen. Zoom In/Out is a dynamic tool that adjusts the zoom in and out as the left mouse button is held and the mouse is moved up and down. Zoom to Selection is active only when an entity (edge, face, sketch, etc.) is selected. The Rotate View Tool is especially useful for visualizing all sides of a model. With this tool active, holding down the left mouse button and moving the mouse causes the model to rotate.

FIGURE 1.38

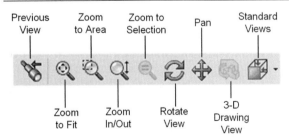

FIGURE 1.39

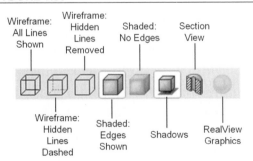

The Pan Tool allows the model to be repositioned on the screen without changing the zoom size. (Note: When using the Zoom In/Out, Rotate View, and Pan Tools, it is necessary to turn them off before proceeding. You can do this either by clicking the tool icon or pressing the esc key.) The 3-D Drawing View Tool is active only when working on drawings. The Standard Views Tool activates a pull-down menu of standard views. These standard views are discussed below.

The appearance of the part can be changed with the display tools. The wireframe tools are sometimes very useful when sketching. Solid views can be displayed either with or without solid lines indicating model edges. The Shadow Tool can be used with either shaded mode to add shadowing to the shaded solid view. A section view can be used to display a cross-section of the part. This is often useful to visualize complex parts. The final tool, the RealView Graphics Tool, allows for a realistic view of the part based on the selected material of the part. This option works only with certain graphics cards, and is not used in this book.

The pull-down menu beside the Standard Views Tool, shown in **Figure 1.40**, allows six views perpendicular to the predefined planes of the part: Top, Bottom, Left, Right, Top, and Bottom views. The Normal To Tool works with a selected plane or sketch, and is useful when working with sketches that are not parallel to one of the predefined planes.

FIGURE 1.40

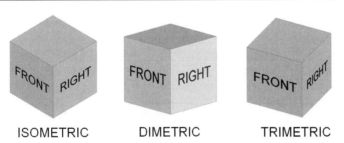

There are three standard pictorial (3-D) views: Isometric, Trimetric, and Dimetric. In an isometric view, the view orientation is such that the angles between the displayed edges of a cube are equal, as shown in **Figure 1.41**.

FIGURE 1.41

ISOMETRIC   DIMETRIC   TRIMETRIC

In a dimetric view, two of the angles are equal, and in a trimetric view all angles are different. The Trimetric View in SolidWorks emphasizes the display of the front of the part, and is the default pictorial view. (As we will discuss later, the front view should be the view that is most descriptive of the part.)

FIGURE 1.42

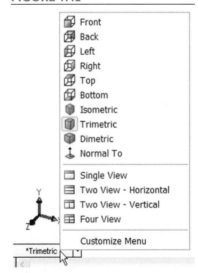

An alternative method for selecting one of the standard views is to use the menu adjacent to the reference triad in the lower left corner of the graphics area, as shown in **Figure 1.42**. This menu also allows selection of a multiview, as will be discussed later in this chapter.

Experiment with the zoom and viewing options. When finished, select a shaded solid display (either with or without edges displayed) and the Trimetric View.

Now we are ready to add to our part. The next feature we will add is the 2.75-inch diameter boss. We could sketch the circle to be extruded on the front or back face of the existing part, but instead we will create a new plane that is 2.25 inches away from the front plane. There are several reasons why we might want to define the part in this manner. One is that we may want to add draft, a slope to the sides of a feature that allows it to be extracted from a mold. If so, then we want our 2.75-inch dimension to apply at the top of the boss, allowing the diameter to get larger closer to its base.

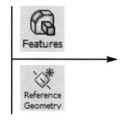

Select the Reference Geometry Tool from the Features group of the CommandManager. From the menu that appears, select Plane (see Figure 1.43).

FIGURE 1.43

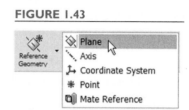

Note that the FeatureManager has been replaced in its usual position by the PropertyManager, where the parameters of the new plane will be defined. However, the FeatureManager is still visible as a "fly out" list to the right of the PropertyManager. By default, the FeatureManager is shown collapsed; that is, only the name of the part is shown. The full FeatureManager can be shown by clicking on the plus sign next to the part name.

Click the plus sign next to the part name (Part1) to expand the FeatureManager. Click on the Front Plane to select it, as shown in Figure 1.44. In the box defining the offset distance, enter 2.25. Click the check mark and the new plane, labeled Plane1, is created.

FIGURE 1.44

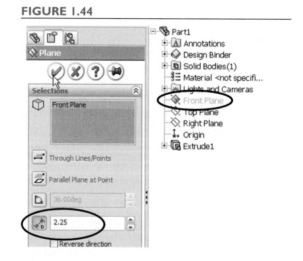

Of course, the Reverse direction box could have been checked if we wanted the new plane to be behind the Front Plane.

Now with Plane1 selected (highlighted in green), open a new sketch by selecting the Sketch Tool from the Sketch group of the CommandManager.

Switch to the Normal To View (Figure 1.45). Notice that in this case, the Normal To View is the same as the Front View.

FIGURE 1.45

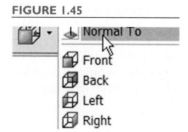

Select the Circle Tool. Sketch a circle centered at the origin, as shown in Figure 1.46. Select the Smart Dimension Tool and add a 2.75-inch dimension to the diameter, as shown in Figure 1.47.

FIGURE 1.46

FIGURE 1.47

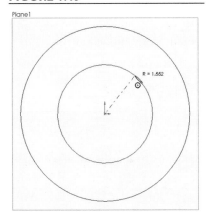

Select the Extruded Boss/Base Tool from the Features group of the Command-Manager, and switch to the Trimetric View (Figure 1.48).

As shown by the preview, the extrusion is going away from the base feature rather than toward it.

Click and drag on the direction arrow so that the extrusion is in the correct direction, as shown in Figure 1.49.

Since we want the extrusion to extend back to the base feature, we can specify that intent in the definition of the extrusion.

In the PropertyManager, select Up To Next from the pull-down menu, as shown in Figure 1.50. Click the check mark to complete the extrusion.

We can turn off the display of Plane1 and of the origin.

From the main menu, select View: Planes, and then select View: Origins.

FIGURE 1.48

FIGURE 1.49

FIGURE 1.50

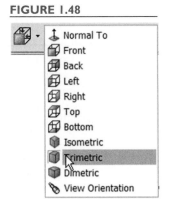

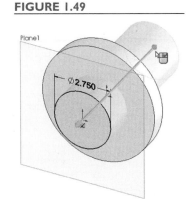

DESIGN INTENT | Planning the Model

As we build the 2.75-inch diameter boss of our flange, we can choose from two existing planes/surfaces or construct a new plane. The choice of constructing a new plane in order to allow us to add draft to our part is an example of design intent. There are many definitions of design intent. Ours is:

Design intent is the consideration of the end use of a part, and possible changes to the part, when creating a solid model.

Throughout this book, we will identify examples of considering design intent when modeling.

Both Plane1 and the origin still exist in the model, but turning off the display of planes and origins results in a less cluttered model view, as shown in **Figure 1.51**.

FIGURE 1.51

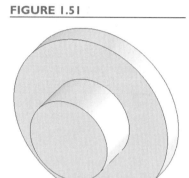

We can change the color of the part at any time.

Click on the part name (Part1) in the Feature-Manager to select it, as shown in Figure 1.52, and click on the Edit Color Tool from the standard toolbar.

In the PropertyManager, choose a new color for the part (see Figure 1.53). Light colors are recommended, as dark colors can make some features difficult to see. **Click the check mark in the Property-Manager to apply the new color.**

You may notice that the circular edges appear to be a series of line segments rather than a smooth curve. You can smooth the appearance of the part by selecting a higher image quality.

FIGURE 1.52

FIGURE 1.53

From the main menu, select Tools: Options: Document Properties: Image Quality. Move the slider bar to the right, as shown in Figure 1.54. Click OK.

FIGURE 1.54

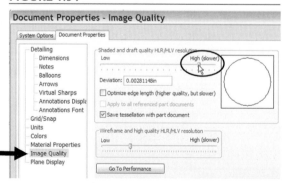

The trade-off for higher image quality is a slight reduction in the speed that the screen is redrawn. However, for simple parts this speed reduction will not be noticeable.

Now let's add the center hole. This time we will select a face to define our sketch plane. As you move the cursor over the front surface, notice that a square icon appears. This indicates that a surface will be selected when you click with the left mouse button. Similarly, a line icon indicates that an edge will be selected.

FIGURE 1.55

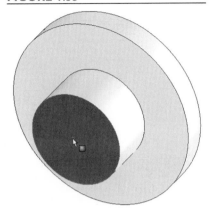

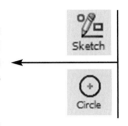
Sketch

With the square icon showing, select the **front face, as shown in** Figure 1.55. It will be highlighted in green. **Select the Circle Tool from the Sketch group of the CommandManager.**

Circle

Note that selecting a sketch tool (in this case the Circle Tool) with a plane or surface selected causes a sketch to automatically be opened. Although for previous sketches we have changed the view orientation so that we are looking normal to the sketch, that is not necessary for simple sketches. We will create this sketch while remaining in the Trimetric View orientation.

FIGURE 1.56

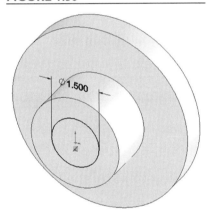

Smart Dimension

Drag out a circle centered at the origin. Select the Smart Dimension Tool and dimension the circle diameter as 1.5 inches, as shown in Figure 1.56.

Features

Now select the Extruded Cut Tool from the Features group of the CommandManager. Select the type as Through All in the PropertyManager, as shown in Figure 1.57. **Click the check mark to complete the cut. The result of this operation is shown in** Figure 1.58.

Extruded Cut

We will now add the four bolt holes.

FIGURE 1.57

FIGURE 1.58

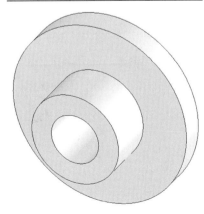

Select the surface shown in Figure 1.59. Switch to the Normal To View. Select the Circle Tool from the Sketch group of the CommandManager, and drag out a circle centered at the origin, as shown in Figure 1.60. In the PropertyManager, check the "For construction" box shown in Figure 1.61.

FIGURE 1.59   FIGURE 1.60   FIGURE 1.61

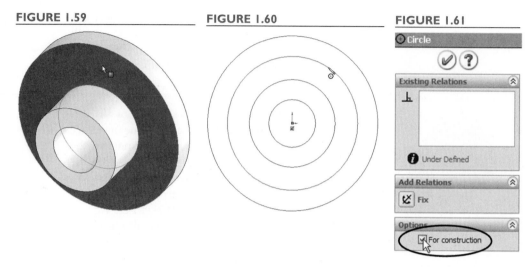

Construction entities help you locate and size sketch parameters, and are indicated by dashed-dotted lines. The circle just drawn represents the bolt circle.

Select the Smart Dimension Tool. Add a 4.25-inch diameter dimension to the circle, as shown in Figure 1.62.

FIGURE 1.62

Select the Circle Tool. Move the cursor to the top quadrant point on the construction circle, as shown in Figure 1.63. Note the red diamond that appears, along with the coincident and vertical relation icons. Drag out a circle. Select the Smart Dimension Tool and add a diameter dimension of 0.50 inches, as shown in Figure 1.64.

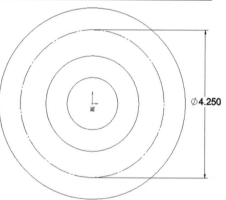

FIGURE 1.63   FIGURE 1.64

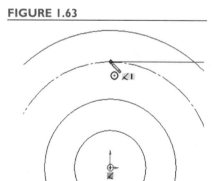

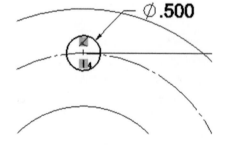

The sketch is now fully defined.

FIGURE 1.65

Select the Extruded Cut Tool from the Features group of the CommandManager, and extrude a hole with a type of Through All. Click the check mark.

The first bolt hole is now in place, as shown in the trimetric view in **Figure 1.65**. Notice that in the FeatureManager, all of our procedures are being recorded. To more easily identify features for later modifications, we can rename features.

FIGURE 1.66

- ⊕ Extrude1
- ◇ Plane1
- ⊕ Extrude2
- ⊕ Cut-Extrude1
- ⊕ Cut-Extrude2

FIGURE 1.67

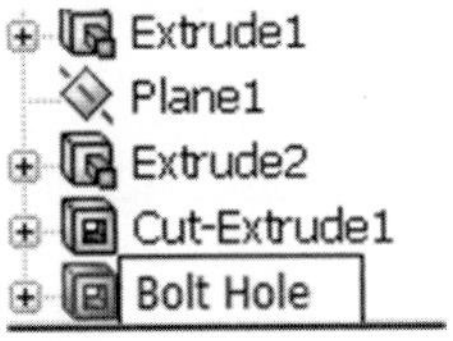

- ⊕ Extrude1
- ◇ Plane1
- ⊕ Extrude2
- ⊕ Cut-Extrude1
- ⊕ Bolt Hole

Click once on Cut-Extrude2 to select and highlight the name, as shown in Figure 1.66. Type "Bolt Hole" to rename the feature, as shown in Figure 1.67. Press the Enter key to accept the new name.

We could create the other three holes in the same manner, but it is easier to copy the single hole into a circular pattern. Also, since our design intent is for the holes to exist in a circular pattern, it makes sense to construct them that way. If we later change the diameter of the holes, the diameter of the bolt circle, or the number of holes, it will be easy to do if we have created them in a pattern.

Make sure that the first bolt hole is selected. From the Features group of the CommandManager, select the Circular Pattern Tool.

FIGURE 1.68

In the PropertyManager, **Figure 1.68**, the first box is shaded in pink, indicating that this box is selected for input. This box is where the axis of the circular pattern is to be specified. Although we could create an axis, that is not necessary. Any cylindrical feature of the part has an axis associated with it; we can use one of these axes as the axis for our pattern.

From the main menu, select View: Temporary Axes. Select the axis at the center of the part, as shown in Figure 1.69. In the PropertyManager, set the number of features to 4, as shown in Figure 1.70.

FIGURE 1.69

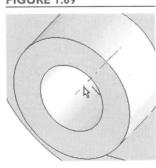

FIGURE 1.70

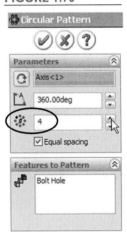

DESIGN INTENT — Selecting a Modeling Technique

The three fillets are added in this tutorial in a single step by selecting the three edges to be filleted within a single fillet command. With this method, only the first fillet is dimensioned. Another way to add the fillets is to close the Fillet Tool after each fillet is created, so that the fillets are created in three separate steps. The preferred method depends on how you wish to edit the fillet radii. If you want all of the fillets to always have the same radius, then the first method allows one value to be changed for all three fillets. If you prefer to edit the fillets separately, then the second method provides an editable dimension for each fillet.

The "Equal spacing" box should be checked, and the angle set to 360 degrees. The preview of the pattern should now show four equally spaced bolt holes, as shown in Figure 1.71. Click the check mark to complete the pattern. From the main menu, select View: Temporary Axes to turn off the display of the axes, and the part should now appear as in Figure 1.72.

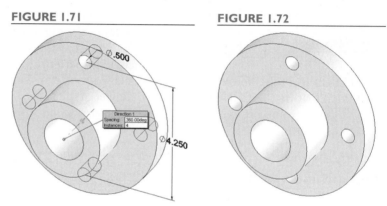

FIGURE 1.71　　　　　FIGURE 1.72

Now let's finish the flange by adding fillets to three of the sharp edges. A fillet is a feature that rounds off a sharp edge. Actually, a fillet is a rounded edge created by adding material, while a round is created by removing material. Fillets and rounds are created with the SolidWorks software by the same command.

Fillet

From the Features group of the CommandManager, select the Fillet Tool. Select the three edges indicated in Figure 1.73 to be filleted. (Be sure to see the line next to the cursor, as shown in Figure 1.74, to indicate that an edge and not a face is being selected.)

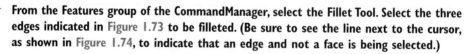

FIGURE 1.73　　　　　FIGURE 1.74

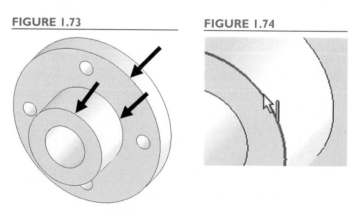

FIGURE 1.75

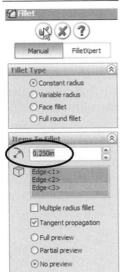

In the **PropertyManager, enter the radius as 0.25 inches, as shown in** Figure 1.75. **Click the check mark to add the fillets, shown in** Figure 1.76.

FIGURE 1.76

Display of tangent edges is often undesirable. The display of tangent edges can be controlled from the Options menu.

From the menu, select Tools: Options. Under the System Options tab, under Display/Selection, choose Removed as the Part/Assembly tangent edge display option, as shown in Figure 1.77. **Click OK. The part should appear as in** Figure 1.78.

FIGURE 1.77

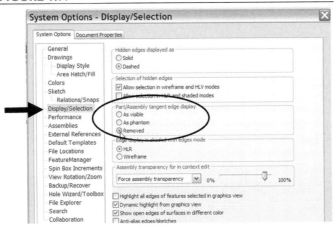

FIGURE 1.78

Now we can add the chamfer to the center hole. A chamfer is a conical feature formed by removing material from an edge.

From the Features group of the CommandManager, select the Chamfer Tool. Select the inner edge of the center hole, as shown in Figure 1.79.

FIGURE 1.79

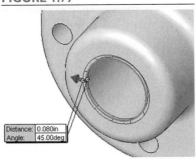

FIGURE 1.80

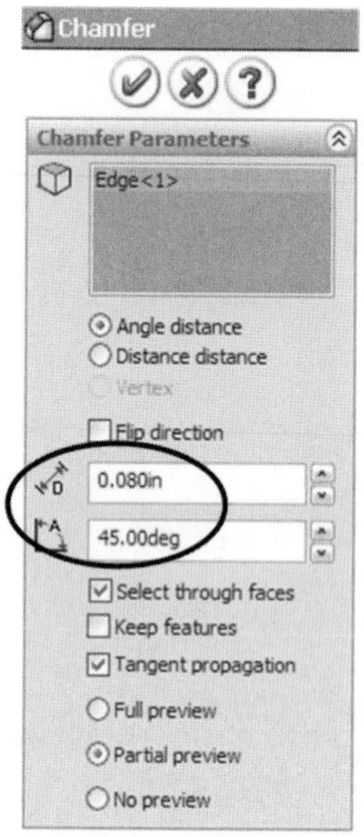

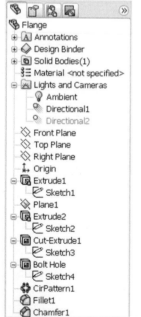

Set the parameters to 0.080 inches and 45 degrees, as shown in Figure 1.80, and click the check mark to finish.

The chamfered part is shown in Figure 1.81.

From the main menu, select File: Save. Browse to the directory where you want to save the part, and save the part with the file name "Flange." Make sure that the file type is "part file", as shown in Figure 1.82. (The file extension will be .SLDPRT.)

FIGURE 1.81

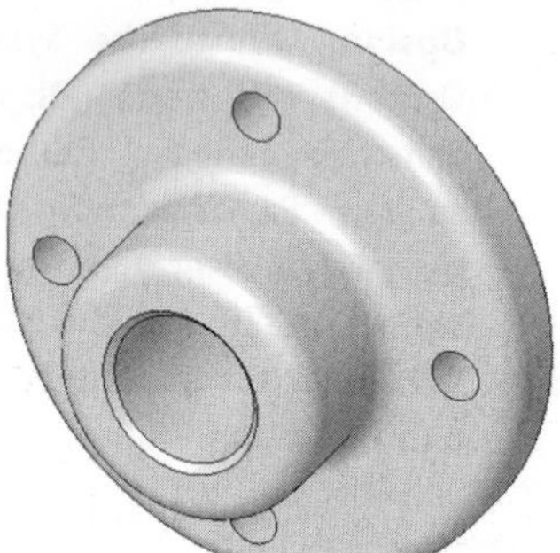

FIGURE 1.82

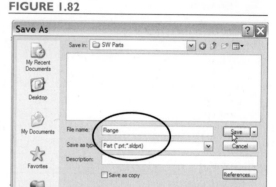

Leave the part file open for the next section, in which we will learn how to make modifications to the part.

1.3 Modifying the Flange

FIGURE 1.83

One of the main advantages of solid modeling is the ability to make changes easily. As we have observed, the FeatureManager has recorded all of the operations required to make the flange, as shown in Figure 1.83. If you click on the plus sign next to each feature, we see that the sketch associated with each feature is stored, as well.

Let's change the first item that we created by increasing the diameter of the base from 5.5 to 7 inches.

FIGURE 1.84

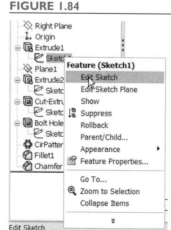

Right-click Sketch1 in the FeatureManager, and select Edit Sketch from the pop-up menu, as shown in Figure 1.84. Double-click the 5.5-inch dimension, and change it to 7.0 inches, as shown in Figure 1.85.

FIGURE 1.85

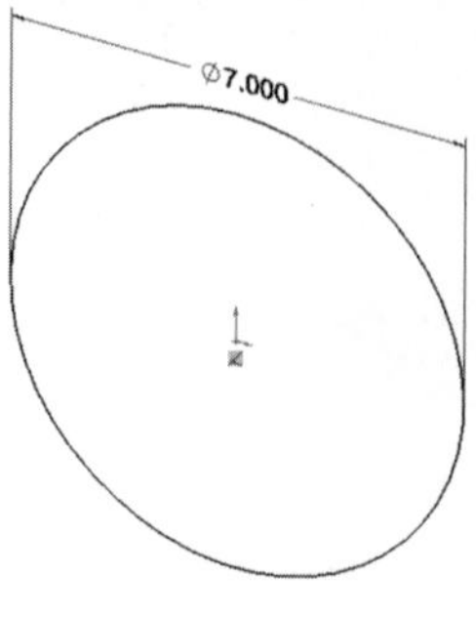

⌀7.000

When you close the sketch by clicking on the icon in the upper-right corner of the screen (see **Figure 1.86**), the part will be updated to the new dimension, as shown in **Figure 1.87**.

An even easier way to edit the sketch dimensions or the extrude depth is illustrated next.

Double-click the icon next to Extrude1 in the FeatureManager.

All of the dimensions used to create the feature are displayed, as shown in **Figure 1.88**. The sketch dimensions are shown in black, while the feature dimensions (in this case the extrude depth) are shown in blue.

FIGURE 1.86

FIGURE 1.87

FIGURE 1.88

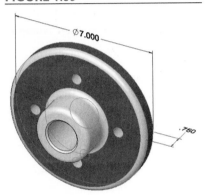

Double-click the diameter dimension and change it back to 5.5 inches. Click the Rebuild Tool.

To add draft to the boss, select Extrude2 from the FeatureManager, right-click and select Edit Feature, as shown in Figure 1.89. In the PropertyManager, turn the draft on (see Figure 1.90) and set the angle to 3 degrees. Check the "Draft Outward" box so that the boss increases in size as it is extruded. Click the check mark to finish.

FIGURE 1.89

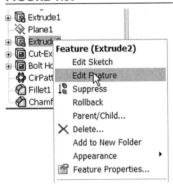

FIGURE 1.90

The draft will be easier to see from a top or side view. You can show the front, top, and right views along with the current (trimetric) view with the Four-View option. Before displaying the Four-View window, we will set an option that controls how the views are displayed.

FIGURE 1.91

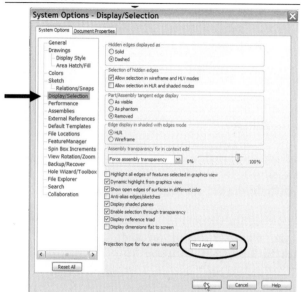

From the main menu, select Tool: Options: System Options: Display/Selection. From the pull-down menu near the bottom of the dialog box, select "Third Angle", as shown in Figure 1.91.

The third-angle option displays the front, top, and right views, with the front view in the lower left position (standard for most US drawings), while the first-angle option displays the front, top, and left views, with the front view in the upper left position (standard for most European drawings). We will discuss first-angle and third-angle projections further in Chapter 2.

Select the pull-down menu below the Reference Triad, and select the Four-View window, as shown in Figure 1.92.

The drafted feature can be seen clearly in the top and right views, as shown in Figure 1.93.

FIGURE 1.92

FIGURE 1.93

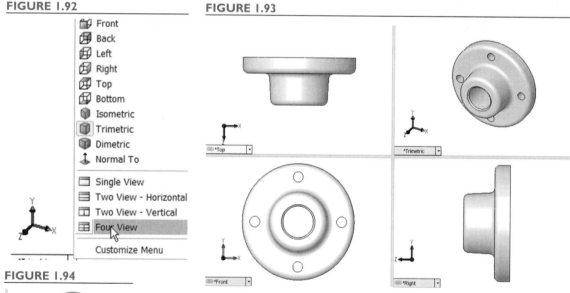

To revert to a single view, select Single View from the pull-down menu under the Reference Triad in any of the windows, as shown Figure 1.94.

FIGURE 1.94

Finally, right-click on CirPattern1 in the FeatureManager and select Edit Feature. Change the number of holes from four to six, as shown in Figure 1.95.

FIGURE 1.95

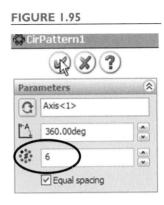

The modified part is shown in Figure 1.96.

These last two changes illustrate the importance of considering design intent when modeling. If the first boss had been extruded from the base feature, then adding draft would have required us to change the diameter of the boss, calculating the diameter that will result in a 2.75-inch diameter at the top of the boss when draft is included. By sketching in a plane at the top of the boss, the critical 2.75-inch dimension can be maintained easily. Also, by constructing the holes as a circular pattern instead of individually, the number of holes could be modified easily.

Close the part window by clicking on the X in the upper-right corner of the part window, as shown in Figure 1.97. **Do not save the changes to the file.**

FIGURE 1.96

FIGURE 1.97

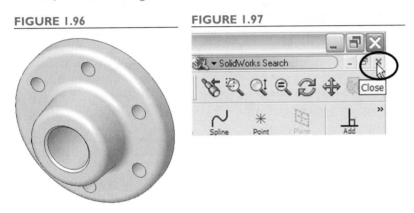

1.4   An Alternate Method of Modeling the Flange

Here is a different approach to creating the body of the flange. Several sketching features are introduced here.

FIGURE 1.98

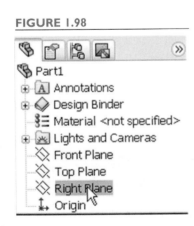

From the main menu, select File: New, or click on the New File icon. Click on the Part icon and click OK. As in Section 1.2, select Tools: Options from the main menu and under Document Properties, set the units to IPS, the number of decimal places to 2, and the dimensioning standard to ANSI. Click on the Right Plane in the FeatureManager, as shown in Figure 1.98. **Switch to the Right View. From the Sketch group of the CommandManager, select the Line Tool.**

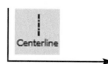

As noted earlier, if a plane or flat surface is selected, then selecting a sketching tool automatically opens a new sketch on that plane or surface.

Sketch the profile of horizontal and vertical lines shown in Figure 1.99, with all lines above and to the left of the origin. Select the Centerline Tool, and sketch a horizontal centerline from the origin, as shown in Figure 1.100.

FIGURE 1.99

FIGURE 1.100

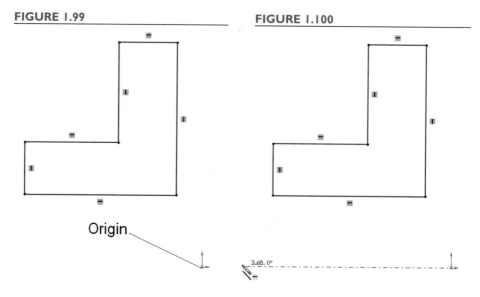

Now we will add dimensions to the sketch. Our first dimension will define the diameter of the center hole.

Select the Smart Dimension Tool. Click on the centerline, and then on the horizontal line defining the center hole.

Notice that if you place the dimension above the centerline, a radius dimension is added, as in **Figure 1.101**. If you drag the dimension below the centerline, a diameter dimension is added, as in **Figure 1.102**. Since our part is dimensioned by diameters, we will build the part that way.

FIGURE 1.101

FIGURE 1.102

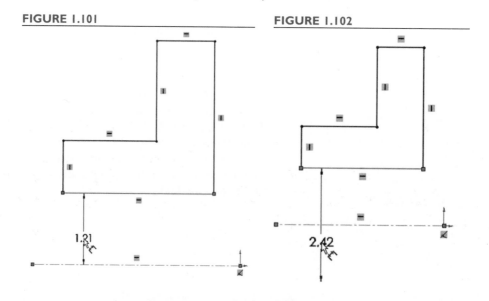

Add the 1.5-inch diameter dimension as shown in Figure 1.103. Add dimension to the other diameters as shown in Figure 1.104. With the Smart Dimension Tool still active, click once on the horizontal line defining the 0.75-inch thickness of the flange. Place a linear dimension. Repeat for the horizontal line defining the 2.25-inch overall height of the flange, as shown in Figure 1.105.

FIGURE 1.103   **FIGURE 1.104**

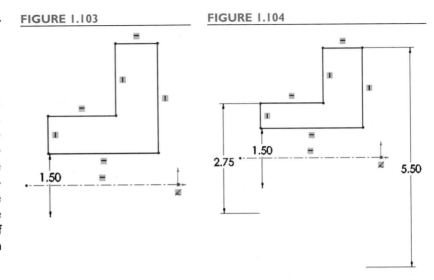

FIGURE 1.105

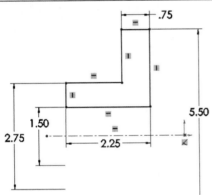

The sketch is still underdefined, as the horizontal position of the sketch relative to the origin is not defined. We will set the location of the back of the flange to be in the same plane as the origin by adding a relation.

Click the esc key to turn off the Dimension Tool. Click on the vertical line of the sketch defining the bottom of the flange, and then, while holding the ctrl key, the origin, as shown in Figure 1.106.

FIGURE 1.106

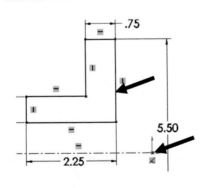

The ctrl key allows you to make multiple selections. In the PropertyManager, shown in Figure 1.107, any existing relations between the selected items are displayed. Below the Existing Relations box, there are Add Relation tools. In this case, there are three possible relations between the two points: Midpoint, Coincident, and Fix. Selecting Midpoint would set the midpoint of the line at the origin. This would result in an error, since that relation would contradict the diameter dimensions set earlier. Selecting Fix simply locks the selected entities in their existing locations. We want to select the Coincident relation, which moves the sketch entities so that the origin lies on the projection of the line.

FIGURE 1.107

In the PropertyManager, select a Coincident relation, and click the check mark.

The sketch is now fully defined.

DESIGN INTENT   Sketch Relations

Relations are used extensively in sketching. In many cases, relations are used instead of dimesions to help to fully define a sketch. Consider the two lines shown here. If these two lines are to be perpendicular, then we could add

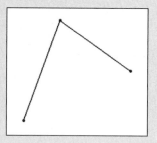

a 90-degree dimension between them. We can achieve the same result, however, by adding a perpendicular relation between the two lines. To do so, we select one line by clicking on it, and while holding down the ctrl key, selecting the second line. The PropertyManager shows any relations between the selected entities, and provides tools for adding new relations. In this case, the Perpendicular icon is selected, and the lines become perpendicular. Note that if the display of sketch rela-

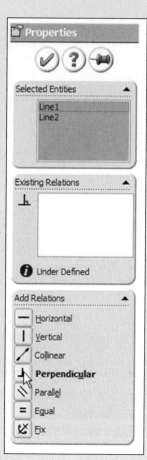

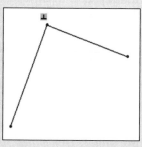

tions is turned on (from the View menu), then an icon indicating perpendicularity is shown.

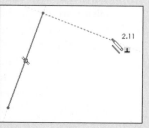

Relations can be added automatically, as well. When drawing the second line, dashed guidelines appear along and perpendicular to the first line are displayed on the screen. If the endpoint of the second line is placed along one of the perpendicular guidelines, then a perpendicular relation is added.

Relations can also be added to individual entities. In these cases, the relations are relative to the predefined coordinate system and origin. For example, if we select the line shown here, any relations involving that line are displayed in the PropertyManager. Clicking the Vertical icon in the Add Relations area of the PropertyManager causes the line to be vertical.

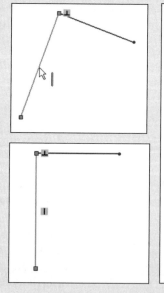

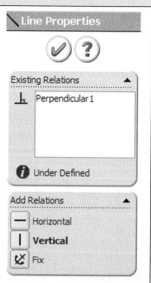

Relations can be deleted if necessary by selecting one of the entities associated with the relation, selecting the relation in the PropertyManager, and pressing the delete key. If the sketch relation icons are displayed on the screen, then relations can be deleted by selecting the appropriate icon and pressing the delete key.

Equal relations are particularly useful for minimizing the number of dimensions required to fully define a sketch. For example, the sketch here will be used to form a link with two holes.

The advantage of this approach is seen if the hole size is to be modified. Changing the .5-inch dimension will cause the diameters of both circles to change.

A list of the relation icons is shown here. All are common in 2-D sketches except for the last two: the Pierce relation is used in multiple-sketch applications such as sweeps and lofts, and the Along X relation is used in 3-D sketches (there are similar Along Y and Along Z relations).

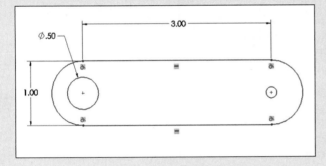

Rather than adding a .50-inch dimension to the second circle, an Equal relation can be added by selecting both circles and clicking the Equal icon in the PropertyManager. The diameter of the second circle will then be equal to that of the first circle.

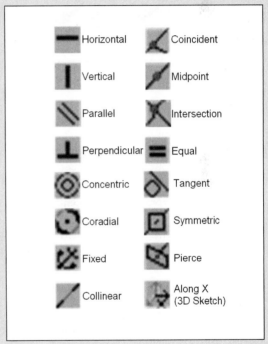

Horizontal		Coincident	
Vertical		Midpoint	
Parallel		Intersection	
Perpendicular		Equal	
Concentric		Tangent	
Coradial		Symmetric	
Fixed		Pierce	
Collinear		Along X (3D Sketch)	

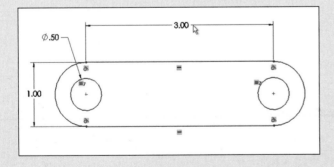

Sketch Fillet

The fillets can also be added to the sketch. **Select the Sketch Fillet Tool. In the PropertyManager, set the radius to 0.25 inches, as shown in Figure 1.108, and then select the point at the corner of two lines to be filleted. With the Sketch Fillet Tool still active, select the other two points corresponding to filleted edges, as indicated in Figure 1.109. Click on the check mark or press the esc key to end the fillet operation.**

FIGURE 1.108

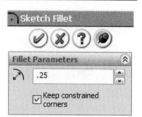

The sketch should now appear as in **Figure 1.110**.

FIGURE 1.109

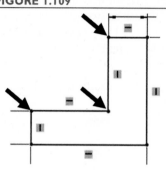

FIGURE 1.110

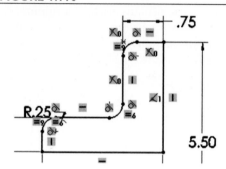

Notice that several relations have been added automatically to the sketch. Each fillet is tangent to its two adjacent edges, and the fillets themselves are equal in radius. A complex sketch can sometimes become cluttered by the numerous relation icons displayed. If desired, you can turn off the display of the relations.

From the main menu, select View: Sketch Relations.

The sketch should now appear as in **Figure 1.111**. Note that the sketch relations can be toggled off and on as desired.

We will now add the chamfer to the sketch. Although there is no Sketch Chamfer Tool on the Sketch Tools toolbar, there is a chamfer command that can be accessed from the main menu under Tools: Sketch Tools: Chamfer. However, we will create the chamfer manually in order to introduce more sketching tools and techniques.

FIGURE 1.111

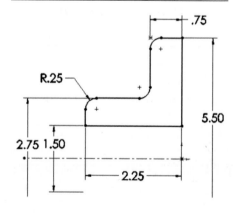

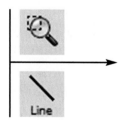

Line

Select the Zoom to Area Tool and drag a box around the area where the chamfer is to be added. Select the Line Tool.

Begin the line with the coincident icon next to the cursor, as shown in Figure 1.112, indicating that the end of the new line will snap to the vertical line. Note: Do not snap to the midpoint of the line.

Drag the line diagonally, ending on the horizontal line, as shown in Figure 1.113. Select the Trim Entities Tool.

FIGURE 1.112

FIGURE 1.113

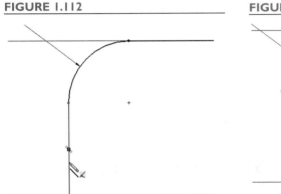
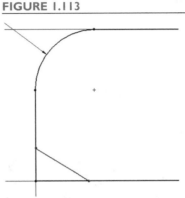

There are several options for trimming entities. The simplest for trimming away portions of one or two entities is the "Trim to closest" option. With this option selected, clicking on a sketch entity will cause it to be trimmed up to the closest intersection with another entity.

FIGURE 1.114

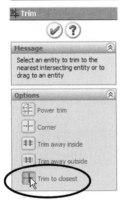

FIGURE 1.115

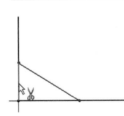

In the PropertyManager, choose Trim to Closest, as shown in Figure 1.114. Click on the portion of the vertical line that extends beyond the diagonal line, as shown in Figure 1.115. Repeat for the portion of the horizontal line that extends beyond the diagonal line. Click Yes in the dialog box that appears.

The results of the trimming operations are shown in Figure 1.116.

FIGURE 1.116

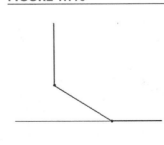

We will now add two dimensions. The Smart Dimension Tool creates a type of dimension that corresponds to our selections. For example, we earlier dimensioned a circle by clicking once on the circle. The result was a diameter dimension. When we clicked on a line, a linear dimension along the length of the line was created. When we clicked on two parallel lines, the result was a dimension defining the distance between the lines. Here we will create a linear dimension between a point and a line, and an angular dimension between two nonparallel lines.

DESIGN INTENT | Choosing the Initial Sketch Plane

The choice of the initial sketch plane for a part should be considered before beginning a new part. Standard drawing practice is to orient the part so that the Front View is the model view that best describes the part. When we constructed the flange earlier, we selected the Front Plane as the sketch plane for the first feature. The result was the proper orientation of the part, with the Front View being the most descriptive of the standard views.

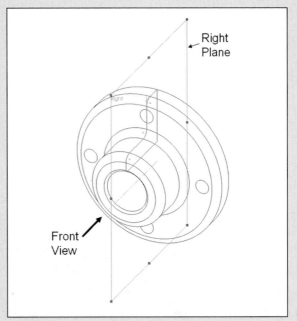

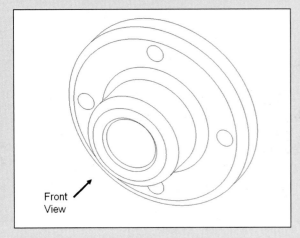

Now that we are creating the same part by revolving the part's cross-section about the centerline, we must sketch the section in either the Right or Top Plane to maintain the same part orientation.

We have selected the Right Plane. Although the plane associated with a sketch can be changed by right-clicking the sketch in the FeatureManager and by selecting Edit Sketch Plane subsequent operations may be affected and errors could result. It is good practice to carefully consider the desired orientation of the part before modeling, and selecting the appropriate sketch plane accordingly.

DESIGN INTENT | Keeping It Simple

The main flange body has been modeled in two different ways: with a series of extrusion, fillet, and chamfer operations, and with a single revolution. Which is the better method? Although the final models are identical, editing and troubleshooting are more difficult with the second method. Many errors encountered when modeling parts are associated with sketches: duplicate entities, open contours, endpoints that do not meet, and overdefined sketches are all common mistakes that can be difficult to detect and correct in complex sketches. The best approach is simplicity: use many simple steps rather than a few complex steps. Following this approach will result in models that are easier to edit and debug.

Select the Smart Dimension Tool. Click once on the point indicated in Figure 1.117, and then the line indicated. Enter the value of the dimension as 0.08 inches. Click on the diagonal line and then the horizontal line, and place an angular dimension setting the chamfer angle at 45 degrees, as shown in Figure 1.118.

Smart Dimension

FIGURE 1.117   **FIGURE 1.118**

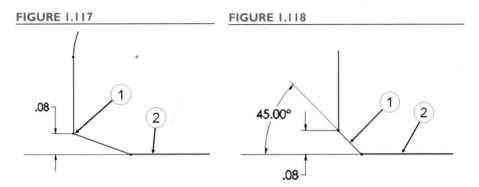

Note that the sketch is underdefined. When we trimmed away the end of the horizontal line, the 2.25-inch diameter was deleted, since it dimensioned that line. We need to add that dimension back to the sketch.

Select the Zoom to Fit Tool. With the Smart Dimension Tool still active, click on each of the lines defining the top and bottom of the flange, as shown in Figure 1.119. Add the 2.25-inch height dimension.

The completed sketch is shown in Figure 1.120.

FIGURE 1.119   **FIGURE 1.120**

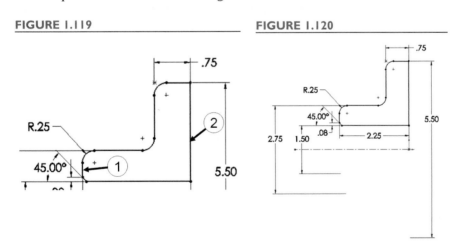

Features

Select the Revolved Boss/Base Tool from the Features group of the Command-Manager.

Revolved Boss/Base

By default, the revolution is a full 360 degrees about the sketch's centerline, as shown by the preview of the revolution in **Figure 1.121**.

Click the check mark in the PropertyManager to complete the revolution.

The resulting solid body is shown in **Figure 1.122**.

FIGURE 1.121

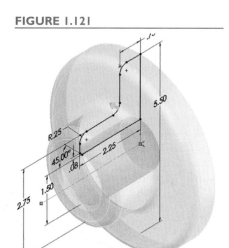

FIGURE 1.122

Select the surface shown in Figure 1.123. Switch to the Normal To View. Select the Circle Tool from the Sketch group of the CommandManager, and drag out a circle on the selected surface, in the approximate location shown in Figure 1.124. Select the Smart Dimension Tool, and dimension the diameter of the hole as 0.50 inches, as shown in Figure 1.125.

FIGURE 1.123

FIGURE 1.124

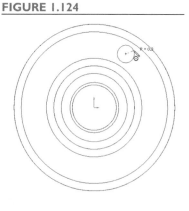

FIGURE 1.125

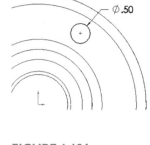

FIGURE 1.126

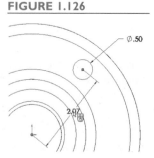

We will now add a second dimension that defines the radius of the bolt circle.

With the Smart Dimension Tool active, click once on the center of the new circle and then click on the origin to create a linear dimension, as shown in Figure 1.126.

Note that depending on where you drag out the dimension, you can create a radial dimension, as shown in **Figure 1.126**, a vertical dimension as shown in **Figure 1.127**, or a horizontal dimension, as in **Figure 1.128**. Note the "lock" icon beside the cursor, as shown in **Figure 1.129**. Pressing the right mouse button locks the dimension style regardless of where the dimension is placed.

FIGURE 1.127

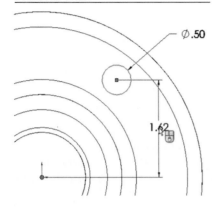

FIGURE 1.128

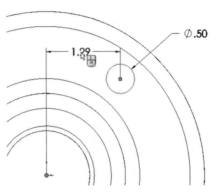

FIGURE 1.129

FIGURE 1.130

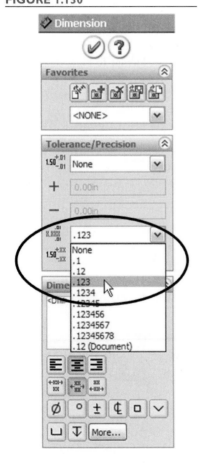

Place the dimension as a radial dimension. Enter "4.25/2". The software performs the math. To display the dimension to three decimal places, select .123 from the pull-down menu in the PropertyManager, as shown in Figure 1.130. The sketch should now appear as in Figure 1.131.

FIGURE 1.131

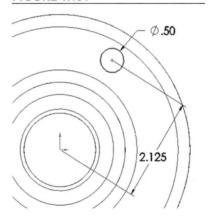

Note that the sketch is still underdefined. This is because the circle that we drew is not tied to any angular location.

DESIGN INTENT Planning for Other Uses of the Model

Why did the circle defining the first bolt hole need to be aligned directly above the origin with the vertical centerline? This step was not absolutely necessary. Imagine that you were given the job of drilling the four bolt holes into a "blank" flange. Where would you drill the first hole? It doesn't matter, as long as the other three holes are equally spaced relative to the first hole.

In this case, leaving the sketch underdefined would have been OK. However, later we will make a 2-D drawing of the flange, and placing the first hole directly above the center of the flange (the origin) in the drawing is the preferred orientation. Since the drawing will be made directly from the part, orienting the bolt holes in the part will make creation of the drawing easier.

FIGURE 1.132

Click the esc key to turn off the Smart Dimension Tool. Click on the center point of the new circle, and, while holding down the ctrl key, select the origin. As noted earlier, the ctrl key allows multiple items to be selected. **In the PropertyManager, click Vertical to align the two points, as shown in Figure 1.132, and click the check mark to close the PropertyManager.**

The bolt-hole circle is now located directly above the origin, as shown in **Figure 1.133.** Note that the sketch is now fully defined.

FIGURE 1.133

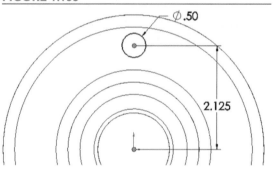

FIGURE 1.134

From the main menu, select **Tools: Sketch Tools: Circular Pattern. Click on the circle to identify it as the item to be repeated. In the Property-Manager, make sure that the center of the pattern is x = 0 and y = 0 (the origin), the number of steps is 4, the angle is 360 degrees, and the Equal spacing box is checked, as shown in Figure 1.134. A preview of the pattern is shown in Figure 1.135. Click the check mark to complete the pattern.**

FIGURE 1.135

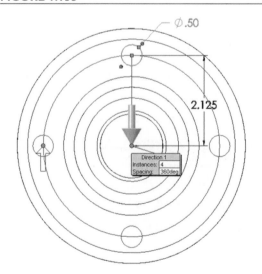

FIGURE 1.136

Select the Extruded Cut Tool from the Features group of the CommandManager. Set the type as Through All, and click the check mark to create the holes, which are shown in Figure 1.136.

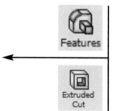

The volume and mass of the flange can be calculated. The first step in this process is to identify the material of the part. The program has a materials library containing the properties of many common materials.

In the FeatureManager, right-click on Material, and select Edit Material, as shown in Figure 1.137. In the Materials Editor that appears, select 6061 Aluminum Alloy, as shown in Figure 1.138.

FIGURE 1.137

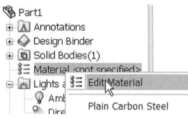

FIGURE 1.138

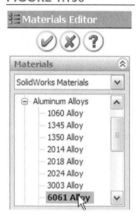

If you scroll to the bottom of the PropertyManager, the properties of the selected material are shown. (See Figure 1.139.) We see that the aluminum 6061 has a density of 0.0975 pounds-mass per cubic inch.

FIGURE 1.139

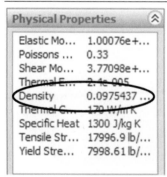

Click the check mark to apply the material.

From the main menu, select Tools: Mass Properties.

FIGURE 1.140

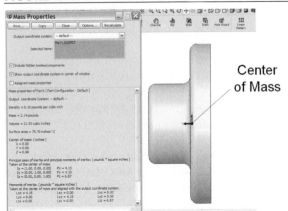

Center of Mass

The dialog box shown in **Figure 1.140** shows the mass properties of the part. The volume of the part is 21.93 cubic inches and its mass of 2.14 pounds (to be absolutely correct, we should express the mass of the flange as 2.14 pounds-mass or the weight of the flange as 2.14 pounds.) Also, the program locates the center of mass (0.68 inches from the back face of the flange), and calculates surface area and moments of inertia. (See the Future Study box.)

Finally, we can give our flange a realistic look by applying a texture to the surfaces.

Select the entire part by clicking on the part name in the FeatureManager. Select the Textures Tool from the Standard toolbar. In the PropertyManager, select Metal: Cast: Cast Rough, as shown in Figure 1.141. Use the slider bar to adjust the grain size as desired, as shown in Figure 1.142. Click the check mark.

FIGURE 1.141

FIGURE 1.142

Textures can also be applied to individual surfaces. For example, a part might be cast with certain critical surfaces machined.

The completed model is shown in **Figure 1.143**.

FIGURE 1.143

FUTURE STUDY

Dynamics (Kinetics)

In physics, you learned Newton's Second Law:

$$F = ma$$

or the forces (F) acting on a body equal the mass of the body (m) times its acceleration (a). For mechanical engineers designing machines with moving components, application of this law results in the forces required to move a body in a particular manner. In the field of engineering materials, the development of lightweight, strong materials allows moving components to be moved at extremely high accelerations, resulting in higher performance.

The form of Newton's Second Law written above applies to bodies moving in linear or translational motions. Most machine components also move in rotational motions. Newton's First Law for rotational motions is:

$$T = I\alpha$$

or the torques (T) acting on a body equal the mass moment of inertia (I) times the angular acceleration (α) of the body. This mass moment of inertia is a function of the body's mass and the way in which the mass is distributed relative to the axis of rotation. For example, consider the two wheels shown here. The two wheels are the same diameter and have the same weight, but the wheel on the left has a mass moment of inertia almost twice that of the wheel on the right. If the wheels were mounted onto shafts, it would take twice as much torque to bring the wheel on the left up to speed as it would the wheel on the right (over the same period of time). While a low mass moment of inertia is usually desirable, a notable exception is a flywheel.

The inertia of a flywheel in an engine rotating at a high speed makes it difficult to slow down. As a result, the rotational speed of the engine remains smooth despite small fluctuations in power.

The calculation of mass and mass moments of inertia for complex shapes can be tedious. Therefore, the use of solid modeling software to perform these calculations saves time for engineers performing these types of analysis.

PROBLEMS

P1.1 Create a solid model of the stepped shaft, using Extruded Boss/Base and Fillet features.

FIGURE P1.1A

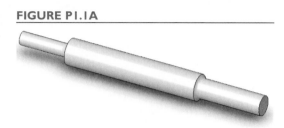

FIGURE P1.1B

Dimensions are in inches

P1.2 Use an Extruded Boss to create a solid model of a 2-foot long segment of a W8X31 steel wide-flange beam (The designation W8X31 denotes wide-flange beam family, 8 inches nominal depth, weight of 31 pounds per foot.) Set the material type to plain carbon steel and find the weight of the part in pounds. Dimensions shown are inches.

Use Equal relations so that the part cross-section is modeled using only the dimensions shown. Use a fully defined sketch of the cross-section.

FIGURE P1.2A

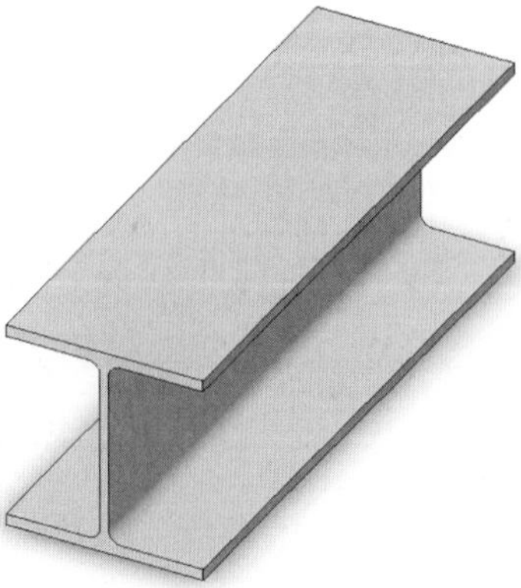

FIGURE P1.2B

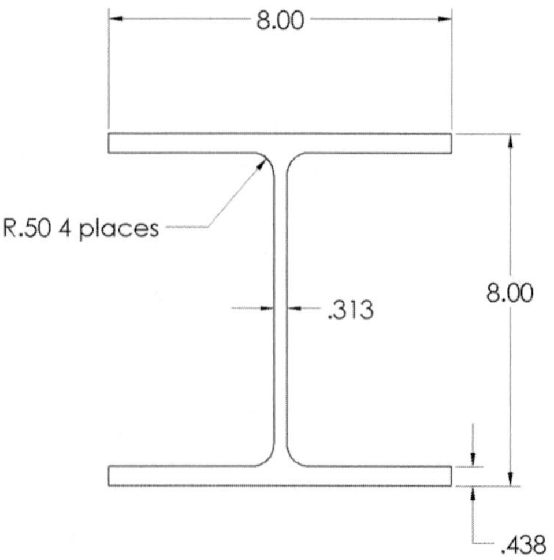

P1.3   Create a solid model of the pulley. Create the cross-section, revolve it into a solid, and then add the keyway. Set the material to cast carbon steel and find the weight of the pulley. Dimensions shown are inches.

Use Equal relations so that the part cross-section is modeled using only the dimensions shown. Use a fully defined sketch of the cross-section.
(Answer: Weight = 8.26 lb)

FIGURE PI.3A

FIGURE PI.3B

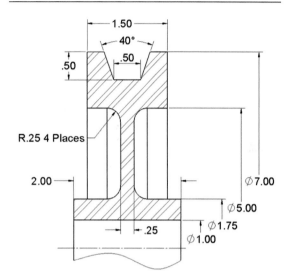

FIGURE PI.3C

Detail of Keyway:

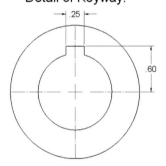

P1.4 Create a solid model of a 5-inch-diameter sphere. Find the formulas for volume and surface area of a sphere, and compare the values calculated from these formulas with those obtained from the mass properties option.

To create the sphere, sketch and dimension a circle, and draw a line connecting the top and bottom quadrant points of the circle. Trim away the left half of the circle. Add a vertical centerline from the center of the semi-circle, and revolve the sketch 360 degrees about the centerline. Note: Be sure that you have only one centerline in the sketch. Multiple centerlines cause the Revolve command to fail. Also, the complete circle cannot be revolved, as the sketch to be revolved cannot cross the centerline.

FIGURE P1.4A   **FIGURE P1.4B**

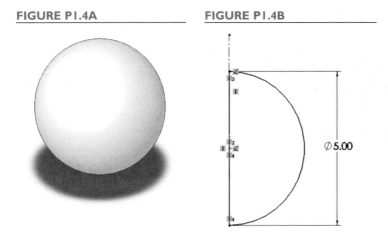

P1.5 Create a solid model of this plastic pipe tee. A tee is used to connect pipes together. The type of tee shown here is used to join pipes with solvent welding. A chemical is applied to the inside of the socket, and the pipe is then forced into the socket. The solvent softens the plastic, and when the solvent dries, a strong, permanent joint is created. The sockets are tapered slightly to allow for a tight fit with the pipe.

Set the material to PVC Rigid and find the weight of the tee. Dimensions shown are inches.

(Answer: Weight = 0.1044 pounds. Click the Options tab in the Mass Properties box and increase the number of decimal places, if necessary.)

FIGURE P1.5A   **FIGURE P1.5B**

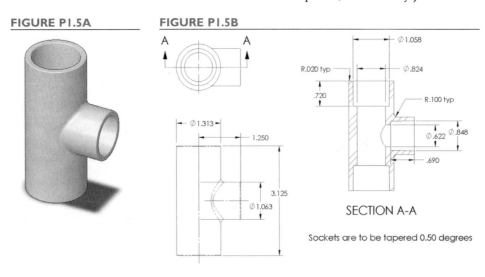

SECTION A-A

Sockets are to be tapered 0.50 degrees

P1.6   Create a solid model of this 2-mm-thick steel bicycle disk brake rotor. Calculate the mass of the part, using AISI 304 stainless steel as the material. Dimensions shown are mm.

Note: Although this part can be modeled with a single extrusion from a complex sketch, you will find it easier to extrude a solid disk and then use a series of simple extruded cuts and circular patterns.

FIGURE P1.6A

FIGURE P1.6B

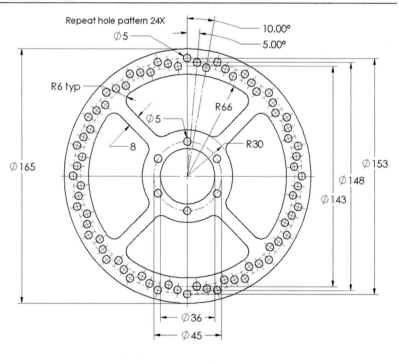

P1.7   Create a solid model of the pleated filter element. Dimensions shown are inches, and the diameter dimensions shown are nominal dimensions. There are 36 pleats in the part, and the part is 8 inches long.

To create this part, start a sketch with two construction circles representing the nominal inner and outer diameters. Add and dimension two lines representing one pleat, and use a circular pattern to copy these two lines into the other 35 positions. Select the Extruded Boss Tool. Since the sketch is an open contour, a thin-feature extrusion will be created. Set the thickness to 0.02 inches, and set the type as Mid-Plane.

FIGURE P1.7A

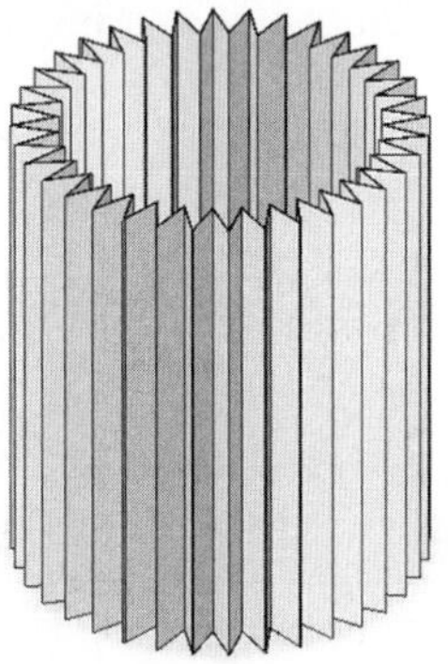

FIGURE P1.7B

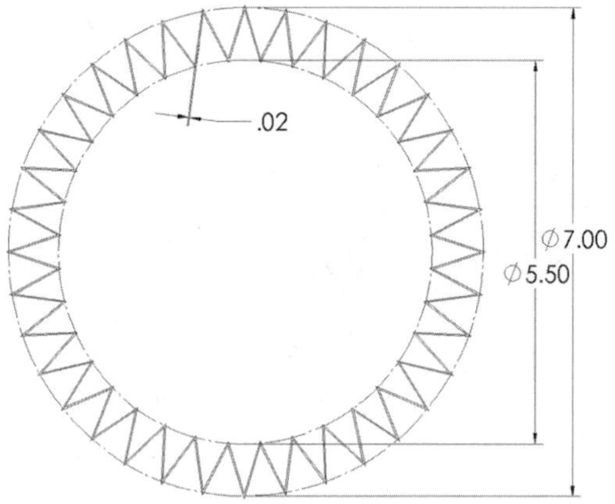

CHAPTER 2

Engineering Drawings

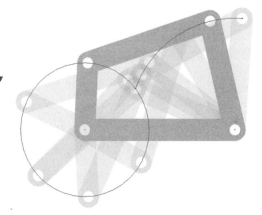

Introduction

Even companies that design parts exclusively with solid modeling software still need to produce 2-D drawings. A multiple-view 2-D drawing is the best way to document the design, showing all of the dimensions necessary to produce the part. Since no manufacturing process can produce "perfect" parts, the tolerances (variations from the stated dimension of a part) allowed for important dimensions are also shown on 2-D drawings.

The SolidWorks program allows for 2-D drawings to be quickly and easily produced from 3-D models. The drawing will be fully associative with the part file, so that changes to the part will be automatically reflected in the drawing, and vice versa.

2.1 Drawing Tutorial

In this tutorial, a 2-D drawing of the flange from Chapter 1 will be made.

Open the SolidWorks program. Click on the New Document Tool. Select the Drawing icon, as shown in Figure 2.1, and click OK.

FIGURE 2.1

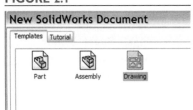

---

[1] eDrawings is a registered trademark of the SolidWorks Corporation, 300 Baker Avenue, Concord, MA 01742.

As if you were making a drawing by hand, your first step is to select the size and type of paper to be used. Later we will look at using sheet formats with a title block, but for now let's use a blank 8-1/2 X 11-inch sheet (A-Landscape).

Choose a paper size of A-Landscape, and click on the box labeled "Display sheet format" to clear the check mark, as shown in Figure 2.2. Click OK to close the dialog box.

If the Model View box appears in the PropertyManager, as shown in Figure 2.3, click on the X to close the box.

FIGURE 2.2

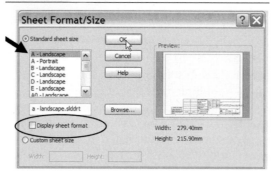

FIGURE 2.3

Before bringing in the flange model data, we will set a few options.

Select Tools: Options from the menu. Under the System Options tab, select Drawings: Display Style, and set the hidden line and tangent displays as shown in Figure 2.4.

FIGURE 2.4

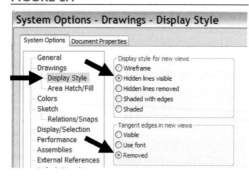

Hidden lines are usually displayed in standard drawing orthographic views, but not in section or detail views. Tangent edges are usually not shown on drawing views. Whether or not to show hidden and tangent edges is sometimes dependent on the complexity of the part. As we will see later, we can change these display options for each model view.

FIGURE 2.5

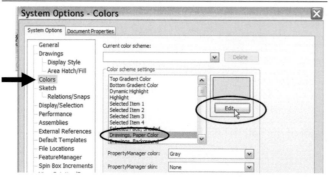

Select Colors: Drawings, Paper Color. Select Edit, as shown in Figure 2.5. Select white for the paper color and click OK.

Under the Document Properties tab, select Detailing and set the dimensioning standard to ANSI, and turn on the automatic display of center marks and center lines for circular features, as shown in Figure 2.6. Select Units, and set the Unit system to IPS (inch, pound, second), and the decimal places to 2, as shown in Figure 2.7. Set the decimal places for angles to zero. Click OK.

FIGURE 2.6

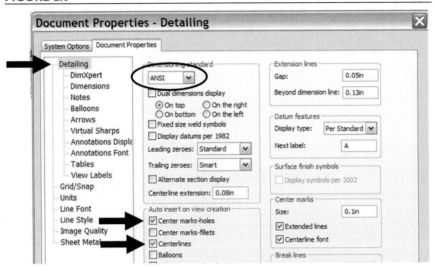

FIGURE 2.7

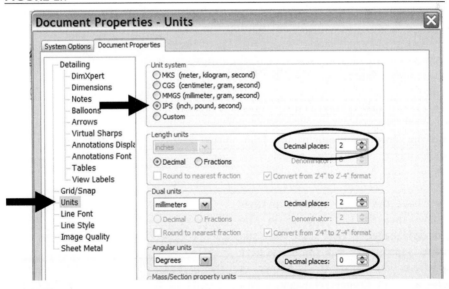

Although the part was modeled with the decimal places set to 3, the number of decimals does not affect the accuracy of the model, only the way dimensions are displayed. For a drawing, the number of decimal places should be related to the tolerance level of most of the dimensions.

FIGURE 2.8

Before adding our drawing views, we will set the type of projection to third angle. The third-angle option displays the front, top, and right views, with the front view in the lower left position (standard for most US drawings), while the first-angle option displays the front, top, and left views, with the front view in the upper left position (standard for most European drawings). For example, consider the part shown in **Figure 2.8**. The first- and third-angle projections of this part are shown in **Figure 2.9**.

FIGURE 2.9

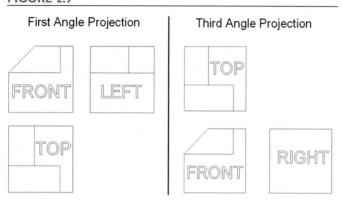

First Angle Projection | Third Angle Projection

In the drawing space, right-click and select **Properties** from the menu that appears. Set the **Type of projection** to **Third Angle**, as shown in **Figure 2.10**, and click **OK** to close the Sheet Properties box.

FIGURE 2.10

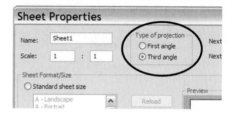

When we modeled a part in Chapter 1, we found most of the commands we needed in the CommandManager. In the drawing mode, the CommandManager has three groups of commands by default: Drawings, Sketch, and Annotations. The group is changed by clicking on the appropriate icon at the left of the CommandManager.

We are now ready to import the geometry from the part file.

From the **Drawings** group of the CommandManager, select the **Model View** Tool.

If you have the flange open in another window, then it will appear in the PropertyManager. If not, then click the **Browse...** button and find the flange part file where you stored it, as shown in **Figure 2.11**. In PropertyManager, select **Multiple Views** and click on the front and top views to select them, as shown in **Figure 2.12**. Click the check mark to place the views.

FIGURE 2.11

FIGURE 2.12

FIGURE 2.13

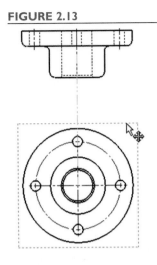

As you pass the cursor over each drawing view, notice that a rectangular box that defines the boundary of that view appears. Moving the cursor over the drawing view boundary displays the move arrows, as shown in Figure 2.13. When the move arrows are displayed, you can click and drag the drawing view to a new location. Note that the views remain in alignment as they are moved.

Note that we need only the front and top views for this part, since the right view shows no information that cannot be seen in the top view. Also, note that the drawing scale was automatically selected. You can override the scale by right-clicking in the drawing area, selecting properties, and defining a new scale.

Now we will import the dimensions that were used to create the model.

Select the Model Items Tool from the Annotations group of the CommandManager. In the PropertyManager, select Entire model as the source, as shown in Figure 2.14. Also check the boxes labeled "Import items into all views" and "Elimate duplicates." Click the check mark to import the model items (dimensions) into the view.

Dimensions are imported as shown in Figure 2.15. While the PropertyManager for Model Items contains options for controlling the import of dimension, notes, tolerances, etc., accepting the default options is usually sufficient.

FIGURE 2.14   **FIGURE 2.15**

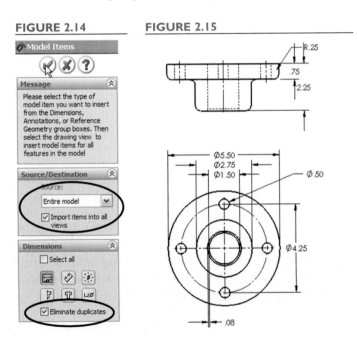

You can click and drag on the value of any dimension to reposition it within its associated drawing view.

Click and drag the dimensions on the drawing sheet so that they can all be clearly seen.

DESIGN INTENT Inserting Dimensions

In Chapter 1, we learned how to orient the model so that the front view was the view that best describes the part. Similarly, more dimensions will be applied to the front view than to the other views. For this simple part, we brought dimensions into both views at the same time. For more complex parts, importing dimensions into the views one at a time allows for more control over where dimensions are placed. It is good practice to always insert dimensions to the front view first. Dimensions can be moved from one view to another, as will be demonstrated later in the tutorial.

DESIGN INTENT Exploiting Associativity

In Chapter 1, we defined the position of the bolt holes in two ways: first by adding a construction circle and adding a diameter dimension to that circle, and second by adding a radial dimension from the center. At the time, there seemed to be no real advantage to either method. When dimensioning the drawing, however, we see that drawing a bolt circle and dimensioning its diameter is the preferred way to show the radial position of the bolt holes. If the distance were defined by a radial dimension, then we could simply delete the radial dimension in the drawing, add a construction circle, and add a new dimension. However, the new dimension would not be associative with the part. That is, changing the added 4.25-inch dimension would not change the bolt hole positions, and changing the radial dimension in the part would not cause the drawing dimension to be updated. Therefore, maintaining full associativity between the part and the drawing would require editing of the part file.

FIGURE 2.16

You can also change how the arrows are displayed on linear dimensions, such as for the 2.25-inch dimension shown in **Figure 2.16**. When you click once on the dimension value to select it, the dimension will appear in green and dots will appear on the arrowheads. When you click on one these dots, the arrowheads will switch from outside to inside or vice versa, as shown in **Figure 2.17**.

The options for changing the appearance of dimensions, dimension lines, and leaders are numerous, and we will cover only a few in this text. By right-clicking on any dimension and selecting Display Options or Properties, you will find that it is easy to change the appearance of the dimension.

FIGURE 2.17

The font for any dimension can be changed individually, but if you want to change the font type or size for all dimensions, you can do that from the Document Properties menu.

Select Tools: Options from the menu. Under Document Properties, select Annotations Font: Dimension, and select a font and font size. The font size may be input in inches or points. Click OK to apply the selected font.

A section view will help show the center hole and the chamfer more clearly.

Select the Section View Tool from the Drawings group of the CommandManager.

The line tool becomes active when the Section View Tool is selected, as shown by the line icon next to the cursor. Since we want to draw our line exactly through the center of the part, we need to "wake up" a center mark and quadrant points for placement of the line's endpoints.

FIGURE 2.18

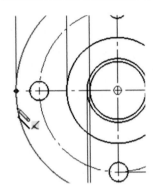

Without clicking any mouse button, move the cursor over the edge of one of the circular features, as shown in Figure 2.18, and hold it there momentarily. Move the cursor outside of the edge of the flange. When the dotted line appears that indicates alignment with

FIGURE 2.19

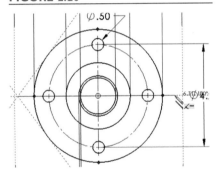

a quandrant point, as in Figure 2.19, click and drag a horizontal line completely through the part, as shown in Figure 2.20 (make sure that the horizontal icon appears by the line before clicking).

FIGURE 2.20

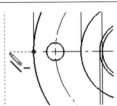

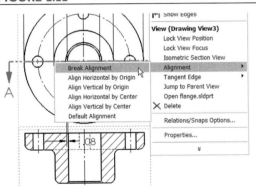

When you finish the line, a section view is created. Move the cursor to place the section view. By default, the view will be kept in alignment with the front view. Drag the section view well away from the other views, and click once to place the view, as shown in Figure 2.21.

FIGURE 2.21

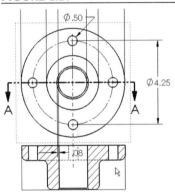

Right-click within the section view boundary box, and from the menu that appears, select Alignment: Break Alignment, as shown in Figure 2.22. Move the cursor over the edge of the section view boundary box so that the move arrows appear. Click and drag the view to a new location on the sheet, as shown in Figure 2.23.

FIGURE 2.22

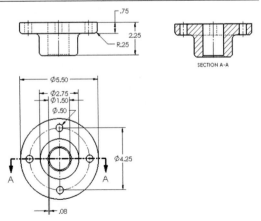

FIGURE 2.23

When we created the section view, the direction of the view relative to the section line was down, toward the bottom of the sheet. This resulted in a section view that is upside-down from our preferred orientation of the part. This is easily modified.

Double-click on the section line in the front view. The arrows defining the direction of the section will be reversed, as shown in Figure 2.24.

FIGURE 2.24

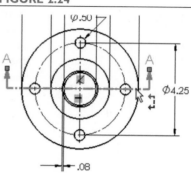

The section view will not be immediately reversed. Instead, it appears crosshatched, indicating that it needs to be rebuilt.

Click the Rebuild Tool in the Standard toolbar.

The section view appearance is now consistent with the direction of the section arrows, as shown in Figure 2.25.

FIGURE 2.25

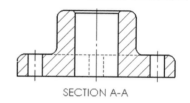

SECTION A-A

Section views are usually shown without the hidden lines displayed.

Select the section view, and click on the Wireframe with Hidden Lines Removed Tool from the View Menu.

FIGURE 2.26

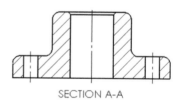

SECTION A-A

The section view should now appear as in Figure 2.26.

The chamfer is difficult to see at the default scale (1:2). A detail view that enlarges the chamfer region will be helpful.

Select the Detail View Tool from the Drawings group of the CommandManager.

The Circle Tool will be activated automatically. Drag out a circle around the area to be included in the detail view, as shown in Figure 2.27. Move the cursor to the position where you want the detail view to appear, and click to place the view, as shown in Figure 2.28.

FIGURE 2.27

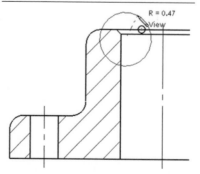

R = 0.47

FIGURE 2.28

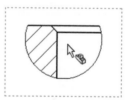

DETAIL B
SCALE 1 : 1

FIGURE 2.29

Note that the detail view has a scale of 1:1. The scale of any drawing view can be changed, and we will change the scale of the detail view to enlarge the chamfer area further.

With the detail view selected, check the "Use custom scale" box in the PropertyManager, and change the scale to 2:1, as shown in Figure 2.29. Click the check mark to apply the scale.

Dimensions can be imported into section and detail views. In this case, the 45-degree angle of the chamfer can be seen best in the detail view.

Click in the white space of the detail view boundary box to select this view, and select the Model Items Tool from the Annotations group of the CommandManager. Click the check mark to import dimensions into the view. The 45-degree dimension will be added, as shown in Figure 2.30. Press esc to deselect the detail view.

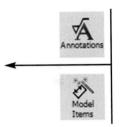

FIGURE 2.30

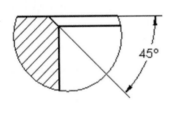

DETAIL B
SCALE 2:1

We would also like to show the 0.080-inch width of the chamfer on the detail view, but that dimension has already been imported into the front view. A dimension will be imported only once, so that the drawing is not over-dimensioned. We could simply add a new dimension to the detail view and delete it from the front view, but doing so would cause the associativity with the part to be lost for that dimension. Instead, we will move the dimension from the front view to the detail view.

Press and hold the shift key. Click and drag the 0.080-inch chamfer dimension from the front view into the detail view boundary box. It is not necessary to place the dimension exactly where it belongs. When you release the mouse button, the dimension will be moved into the detail view. Release the shift key, and drag the dimension to its final position, as shown in Figure 2.31.

FIGURE 2.31

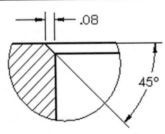

DETAIL B
SCALE 2:1

Using the same procedure, move the 1.50-inch diameter dimension to the section view. Hole diameters are usually dimensioned in the view in which the holes appear as circles, but in this case the front view will be less cluttered if we show the dimension in the section view.

FIGURE 2.32

Change the font of the labels on the section and detail views by clicking on each text group, clearing the check from the "Use document's font" box in the PropertyManager, and clicking on the Font button, as shown in Figure 2.32. Increase the size of the font.

Your drawing should now appear as in Figure 2.33.

FIGURE 2.33

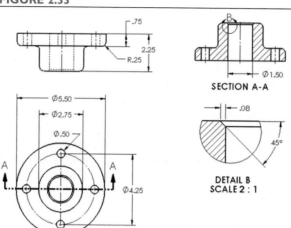

As we noted earlier, the number of decimal places displayed in the drawing will relate to the tolerances applied to that dimension. Often, certain dimensions are more critical than others and will need to have tolerance values specified. For example, suppose that the center 1.5-inch diameter hole needs to have a tight tolerance to allow for a good fit with the part that will be inserted into the hole. When that dimension is selected, a number of options appear in the PropertyManager.

FIGURE 2.34

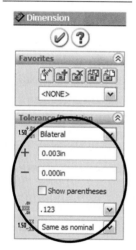

Click on the number portion of the 1.50-inch dimension. In the PropertyManager, shown in Figure 2.34, select a tolerance type of Bilateral from the drop-down menu. Enter a plus value of 0.003 and a minus value of 0.000. In the Precision Box for the dimension (the box that has .12 displayed), use the pull-down menus to select .123 (3 decimal places). Click the check mark to apply the format to the dimension.

The dimension should now appear as in Figure 2.35, indicating that the diameter can be no smaller than the 1.500-inch nominal dimension, but can be up to 0.003 inches larger. It may be necessary to click and drag the Section A-A label to allow room for the dimension with tolerances.

FIGURE 2.35

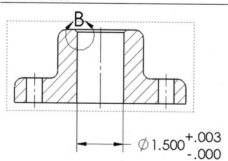

In addition to dimensions with tolerances, *geometric tolerances* are often added to drawings in order to fully define the acceptable limits of a part's geometry. For example, suppose that the back surface of the flange is to mate to another part with a gasket between the two parts to create a seal. If the back of the flange is warped, it may not allow for a proper seal, even if all dimensional tolerances are met. To ensure a good surface for sealing, we might need to add a flatness specification.

FUTURE STUDY

Manufacturing Processes, Geometric Dimensioning and Tolerancing, and Metrology

In this example, we placed a relatively tight tolerance on the diameter of the center hole so that a tight fit could be realized between the flange and the part that fits into the hole. How do you know what the tolerance should be? Perhaps a better question is: what tolerance is required for the part to function as designed in an assembly? The answer to this question will in many cases dictate the manufacturing process that can be used. Many engineering students study manufacturing processes, but it is impossible to learn the specific details of all of the manufacturing processes in use today. On the job, engineers should learn as much as possible about the manufacturing processes used by their company and its suppliers, in order to understand what tolerances are practical and economical.

Applying dimensions and tolerances to engineering drawings is a more complex topic than it first appears. For example, consider a simple part such as a pin that is required to fit into a hole. If we simply define the diameter of the pin and place tolerances on the diameter, are we sure that the pin will fit into the hole? What if the pin is bent slightly? Its diameter might be within the limits defined by the tolerance, but it may not work in its intended purpose. The process of Geometric Dimensioning and Tolerancing (GD&T) allows a designer to specify the acceptable condition of a part, considering its function. In the example we just discussed, a straightness tolerance might be required. In the drawing tutorial in this chapter, we added a flatness specification to a surface that was important for sealing. Proper application of GD&T standards can actually reduce the cost of making many parts, since they allow control of the important features of a part more efficiently than simply tightening the tolerance values of all dimensions. At many companies, the detailing of drawings is performed by a drafting department, and engineers document designs with less-formal drawings and sketches. At many smaller companies, however, engineers detail their own drawings. For these engineers, study of GD&T standards and practices is necessary.

A related area of study is metrology, the science of measurements. Many features are difficult to measure accurately with traditional methods, and computer-controlled Coordinate Measuring Machines (CMMs) are now widely used in industry. Using statistical methods with measured data, quality assurance engineers track variations and work to control the processes that are used to produce the components. This method of Statistical Process Control (SPC) allows problems to be detected and corrected before reject parts are produced.

FIGURE 2.36

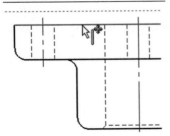

Geometric Tolerance

In the top view, click on the line corresponding to the back surface of the flange, as shown in Figure 2.36. Select the Geometric Tolerance Tool from the Annotations group of the CommandManager.

In the dialog box, select the flatness symbol from the pull-down symbol menu, as shown in Figure 2.37. Enter 0.010 as the value for Tolerance 1, and a preview of the tolerance call-out will appear, as shown in Figure 2.38. Click to place the annotation in the desired location. Click OK to apply the tolerance, and drag the call-out box to the desired location, as shown in Figure 2.39.

Since we are not using a title block with default tolerances shown, we will specify them in a note.

FIGURE 2.37

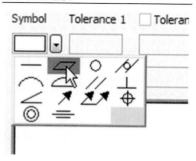

FIGURE 2.38

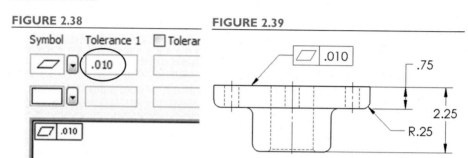

FIGURE 2.39

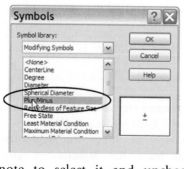

Select the Note Tool from the Annotation group of the CommandManager. Drag the cursor to the approximate location where the note will be placed (near the bottom of the drawing), and click. Choose a font type and size from the toolbar that appears. In the text box that appears at the location where you clicked, begin typing the text of the notes shown in Figure 2.40.

FIGURE 2.40

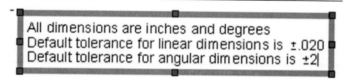

All dimensions are inches and degrees
Default tolerance for linear dimensions is ±.020
Default tolerance for angular dimensions is ±2

Use the Enter key to start a new line. The ± symbol is inserted by clicking on the Add Symbol Tool in the PropertyManager (Figure 2.41) and selecting Plus/Minus from the list of available symbols, as shown in Figure 2.42. Click outside of the text box to place the note. Press the esc key to turn off the Note Tool; otherwise, subsequent mouse clicks will place duplicate notes on the drawing.

FIGURE 2.41

FIGURE 2.42

If desired, you can change the font type and size by clicking on the note to select it and unchecking Use document font in the PropertyManager and then select the Font button. A new font or font size can then be chosen.

Since we defined all of the fillets with a single fillet command in the part, only one of the fillets is dimensioned in the drawing. We might prefer to call out the fillet radius in a note, yet maintain associativity with the part.

Double-click on the notes. Move the cursor to the end of the last line and press the Enter key to move to a new line. Type in "All fillets and rounds are to be." Click on the .25-inch dimension, as shown in Figure 2.43. The dimension's value will appear in the text box. Click outside of the text box to end editing of the note. The completed note is shown in Figure 2.44.

FIGURE 2.43

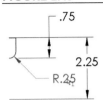

FIGURE 2.44

> All dimensions are inches and degrees
> Default tolerance for linear dimensions is ±.020
> Default tolerance for angular dimensions is ±2
> All fillets and rounds are to be R.25

FIGURE 2.45

If you change the value of the radius, then the value in the note will change accordingly. Now that the fillet radius is shown in a note, displaying it on the drawing is unnecessary. However, deleting the dimension will produce an error, since the note links to the value of the dimension. Therefore, we will hide the dimension.

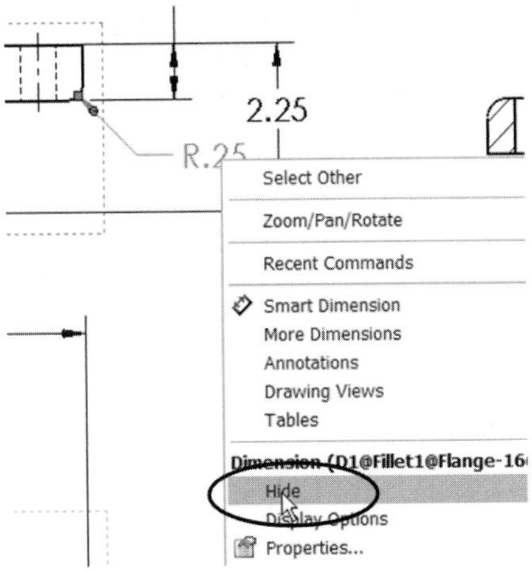

Right-click on the R.25 dimension and select Hide from the menu, as shown in Figure 2.45.

If you want to show the dimension later, you can do so by selecting Hide/Show Annotations from the main menu. Any hidden dimensions will show up light, as shown in **Figure 2.46**, and clicking on them will change them back to visible dimensions. Similarly, clicking on visible dimensions will hide them. This is good method for hiding several dimensions at once. When finished, select Hide/Show Annotations again or press the esc key to return to the normal editing mode.

FIGURE 2.46

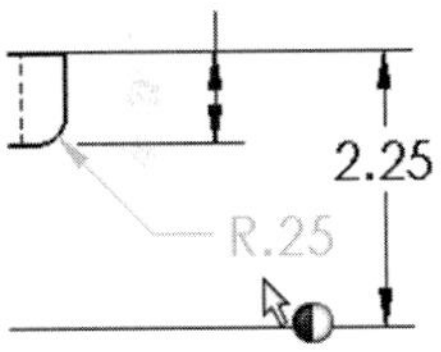

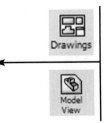

A pictorial view such as a trimetric view can often be helpful in interpreting a 2-D drawing.

Select the Model View Tool from the Drawing group of the CommandManager. The part can be selected by double-clicking the part name in the PropertyManager. In the PropertyManager, select the Trimetric View as the orientation of the new model view, and the shaded with edges mode as the display style, as shown in Figure 2.47. Move the cursor to the desired location of the new view, and click to place the view.

FIGURE 2.47

Right-click on the trimetric view, and select Tangent Edge: Tangent Edges with Font, as shown in Figure 2.48.

Move the drawing views and notes around the sheet so that they can all be seen clearly. Add a note identifying the scale as 1:2. To see how the drawing will look when printed, select the Print Preview Tool.

FIGURE 2.48

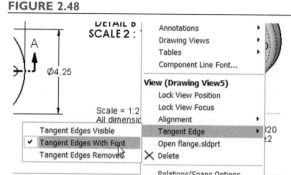

Your drawing should appear similar to **Figure 2.49**.

FIGURE 2.49

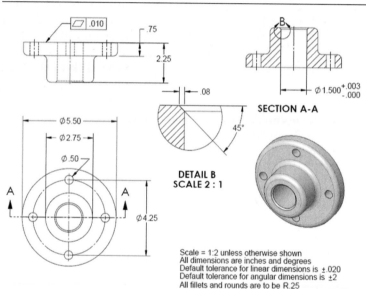

Select File: Save and save the drawing as "Flange," with a file type of .slddrw (SolidWorks Drawing).

Open the Flange part file, and experiment with changing dimensions and noticing the updating of the drawing. Similarly, change some drawing dimensions and observe the changes in the part.

A tool which can be helpful in visualizing a drawing view is the 3-D Drawing View Tool, which is found on the View Toolbar. With any of the standard drawing views or the section view selected, selecting the 3-D Drawing View tool allows you to rotate that view within its boundaries, as shown in **Figure 2.50**.

FIGURE 2.50

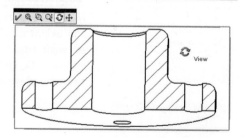

Clicking the check mark in the pop-up toolbar next to the drawing view turns the 3-D Drawing View Tool off and resets the view to its 2-D orientation. (If the 3-D Drawing View Tool is not present on your View Toolbar, you may access the the command from the main menu by selecting View: Modify: 3D Drawing Tool.)

2.2 Creating a Drawing Sheet Format

Most engineering drawings include a title block and a border. The title block can include a large amount of information. In addition to basic data, such as the name of the part, the part number, the scale, the date created, etc., many companies require the names or initials of reviewers who must approve the drawing before it is released to users. Some require a revision history that tracks changes made to the drawing. Others require the listing of information about where the part described on the drawing is used in assemblies.

The SolidWorks program includes several default title blocks and borders, called *sheet formats*. These sheet formats can be edited to fit the particular needs of a company. The sheet formats are different for every standard paper size. In this section, we will create a simple sheet format for an A-size drawing. Our format will include some basic information without taking up much room on the sheet. Rather than modifying an existing title block, we will build ours from scratch.

Open a new drawing. Choose A-Landscape as the paper size; leave the "Display sheet format" box unchecked, as shown in Figure 2.51. **If the Model View command starts automatically, check the X in the PropertyManager to close it, as shown in** Figure 2.52.

FIGURE 2.51

FIGURE 2.52

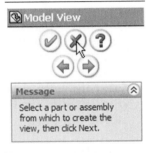

Note that you can prevent the Model View command from starting automatically by clearing the check mark from the box labeled "Start command when creating new drawing" in the PropertyManager. However, since we will usually be creating a drawing from an existing part, we will allow the command to continue to start automatically.

FIGURE 2.53

Select Other	
Zoom/Pan/Rotate	▶
Recent Commands	▶
✧ Smart Dimension	
More Dimensions	▶
Annotations	▶
Drawing Views	▶
Tables	▶
Sheet (Sheet1)	
Edit Sheet Format	
Add Sheet...	
✕ Delete	
🗗 Properties...	
Relations/Snaps Options...	
⯆	

Right-click in the drawing space. Select Edit Sheet Format, as shown in Figure 2.53.

In a drawing, you can toggle between editing the drawing itself and editing the sheet format, which contains the title block and border.

Sketch

Rectangle

Select the Rectangle Tool from the Sketch Group of the CommandManager. Drag out a rectangle that fills most of the page, as shown in Figure 2.54.

Right-click on any toolbar, and select Line Format from the list of available toolbars, as shown in Figure 2.55. With the rectangle still selected, choose a heavier line weight from the Line Format Toolbar, as shown in Figure 2.56.

FIGURE 2.54

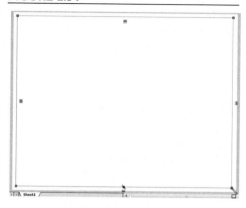

FIGURE 2.55

FIGURE 2.56

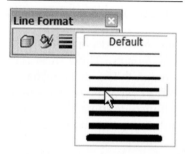

FIGURE 2.57

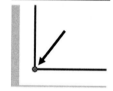

FIGURE 2.58

FIGURE 2.59

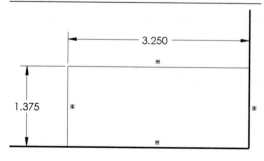

Click on the lower left corner of the rectangle to select it, as shown in Figure 2.57. In the PropertyManager, input its x and y coordinates as 0.375 inches each, as shown in Figure 2.58. Click on the Fix icon.

Note that if your default units are mm, you need to change to the ips system by selecting Tools: Options: Document Properties: Units from the main menu.

Select the upper right corner of the rectangle. Set its coordinates to x = 10.625 inches and y = 8.125 inches. Fix this point.

In the lower right corner of the sheet, drag out a rectangle from the corner of the border. Select the Smart Dimension tool, and dimension the rectangle as 3.25 inches by 1.375 inches, as shown in Figure 2.59.

FIGURE 2.60

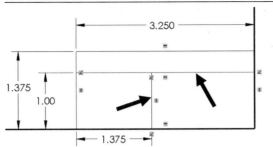

Select the Line Tool, and add the horizontal and vertical lines shown in Figure 2.60. Be sure that the endpoints snap to lines and not specific points (such as midpoints).

Select the Smart Dimension Tool, and add the 1-inch and 1.375-inch dimensions shown.

FIGURE 2.61

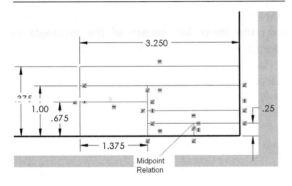

Midpoint

Select the Line Tool, and drag out a horizontal line from the midpoint of the vertical line shown in Figure 2.61 to the vertical line on the right side of the title block.

Add the other three lines shown in Figure 2.62, and add dimensions and relations as shown so that the drawing is fully defined.

FIGURE 2.62

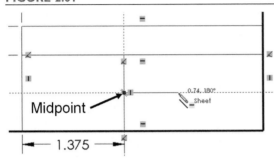

Midpoint Relation

We will now hide the dimensions just added.

From the main menu, select View: Hide/Show Annotations. Click on each dimension, and it will turn gray, as shown in Figure 2.63. When all dimensions are selected, press the esc key to hide them.

FIGURE 2.63

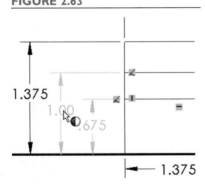

You do not need to turn off the display of the sketch relations; they will not appear when we toggle back from editing the sheet format to editing the drawing.

Before adding the text to the block, we can set the font that we want to use. The font for each text entity can be specified individually, but changing the default font will minimize the number of individual edits that are required.

Line

Smart Dimension

Line

From the main menu, select Tools: Options. Under Document Properties, select Annotations Font: Note. In the dialog box, select Arial as the font. Choose the "Points" option for the size, and enter 10 as the size, as shown in Figure 2.64. Click OK to choose the font, and OK again to close the Options box.

FIGURE 2.64

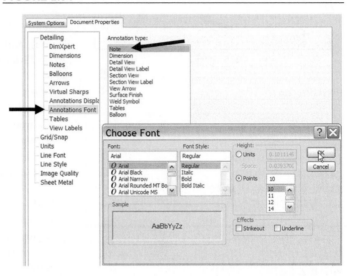

Annotations

Note

Select the Note Tool from the Annotations group of the CommandManager. Click in any blank area to place the note, and type in the text as shown in Figure 2.65, using the Enter key to move to a new line. Choose the Center tool to center the text within the box. Click outside of the text box, and press the esc key to end the Note command (if you do not press the esc key, then you can click in different areas of the drawing to place the same note in multiple locations). Click and drag the note to the position shown in Figure 2.66.

FIGURE 2.65

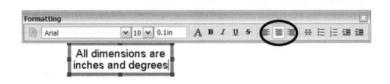

FIGURE 2.66

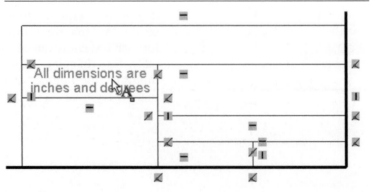

FIGURE 2.67

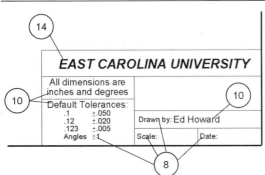

Add the rest of the text shown in Figure 2.67, adding your school/ company name and your name to the title block. Use the font sizes shown in Figure 2.67. When opening a new note, select the font size before typing in the text. Font sizes can be easily changed by double-clicking each note and selecting a new font size.

FIGURE 2.68

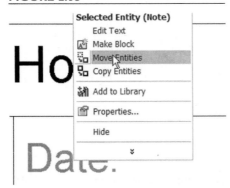

Note that it is sometimes difficult to move a text entity to the position desired because of auto-aligning features. To have more precise control when locating a note, you can right-click on the text and select Move Entities, as shown in Figure 2.68. Drag the text to the position desired and click to place it.

We will now add the scale value to the drawing, linking it to the drawing sheet's scale.

Open a new note. In the PropertyManager, select the Link to Property Icon, as shown in Figure 2.69. From the pull-down menu in the dialog box, select "SW—Sheet Scale," as shown in Figure 2.70, and click OK.

FIGURE 2.69   **FIGURE 2.70**

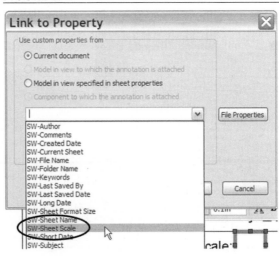

The sheet's scale will now be added to the title block, as shown in **Figure 2.71**. If the scale of the drawing is changed, the title block will update automatically.

Click outside the text box, and press the esc key to end the Note command. Right-click in the drawing area and select Edit Sheet, as shown in Figure 2.72.

FIGURE 2.71

FIGURE 2.72

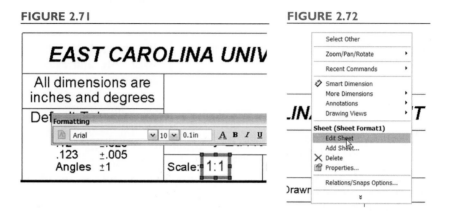

The title block and border are now in the background, and cannot be edited without toggling back to Edit Sheet Format.

From the main menu, select File: Save Sheet Format. Give the sheet a unique name and save it to the default directory, as shown in Figure 2.73. Close the drawing. Select No when asked if you want to save the drawing file.

The drawing sheet format just created can be selected when beginning a new drawing, and can be applied to existing drawings. We will now apply the format to the flange drawing.

Open the flange drawing created earlier. Right-click in the drawing space (away from any drawing view) and select Properties. In the Sheet Properties box, select the sheet format just created from the pull-down list, as shown in Figure 2.74. Check the box labeled "Display sheet format" and click OK.

FIGURE 2.73

FIGURE 2.74

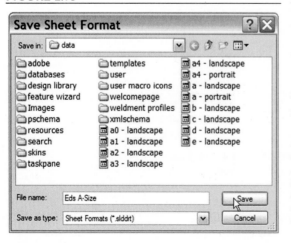

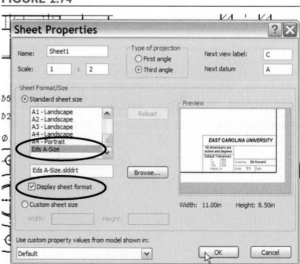

Move the drawing views as necessary. Delete the notes concerning units and tolerances, which are now covered in the title block. Add notes showing the drawing title and the date. The finished drawing is shown in Figure 2.75. Save the drawing for use in the eDrawings tutorial that follows.

FIGURE 2.75

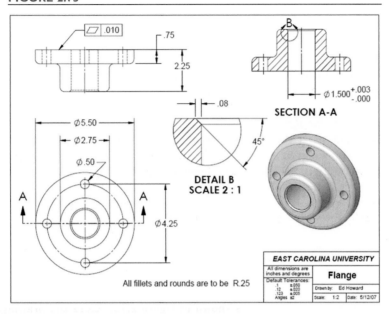

2.3 Creating an eDrawing

One disadvantage of using drawings that are fully associative with part files is that in order to share the file with other users, they must have access to both the drawing file and the associated part file. One option for sharing drawings without transferring the part file is to create a *detached drawing*. When you open a detached drawing, it is not necessary to have the model file loaded. In addition to viewing and printing the drawing, annotations can be added to the drawing. When the model is required, for example if you attempt to edit a dimension imported from the model, then you are prompted to load the model from which the drawing was created. To save a drawing as a detached drawing, choose File: Save As from the main menu and select a file type as "Detached Drawing".

Another option for sharing drawings with others, including those who do not have access to SolidWorks software, is to create an eDrawing. The eDrawings Viewer can be downloaded for free, and the eDrawings Publisher also allows the creation of executable files that can be read on any computer. Even within organizations using SolidWorks software, eDrawings are extensively used to share information. Markup tools allow users to make comments and corrections, and the small file sizes of eDrawings make exchange of data via e-mail more practical.

To save a SolidWorks drawing as an eDrawing, simply select File: Save As from the main menu and select eDrawing (.edrw) as the file type. The eDrawing file format is very efficient, and file sizes produced are small. For example, the file sizes of the part and drawing files of the flange in Chapters 1 and 2 are:

- Part file: 215 kB
- SolidWorks drawing file: 311 kB
- eDrawings file: 70 kB

The eDrawings file is smaller than most image files (.bmp, .pdf, etc.) that could be used to electronically communicate a drawing, but as we will see, an eDrawing is more than a 2-D image. The viewer can rotate any of the drawing views in 3-D space.

To create an executable file or to mark up an eDrawing, it is necessary to have the eDrawings program installed on your computer.

Open the flange drawing file that you saved in the previous section. From the main menu, select Tools: Add-Ins. If the box next to eDrawings is not checked, click on the box to activate eDrawings, as shown in Figure 2.76. By checking the "Start Up" box, you can have the eDrawings Add-In loaded whenever you start a new SolidWorks session. Click OK.

FIGURE 2.76

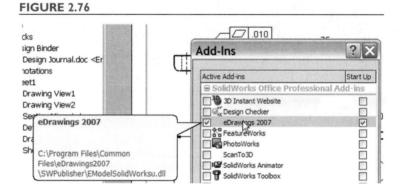

Select File: Publish eDrawing from the main menu. An eDrawing is created and the eDrawings Publisher is opened, as shown in Figure 2.77.

FIGURE 2.77

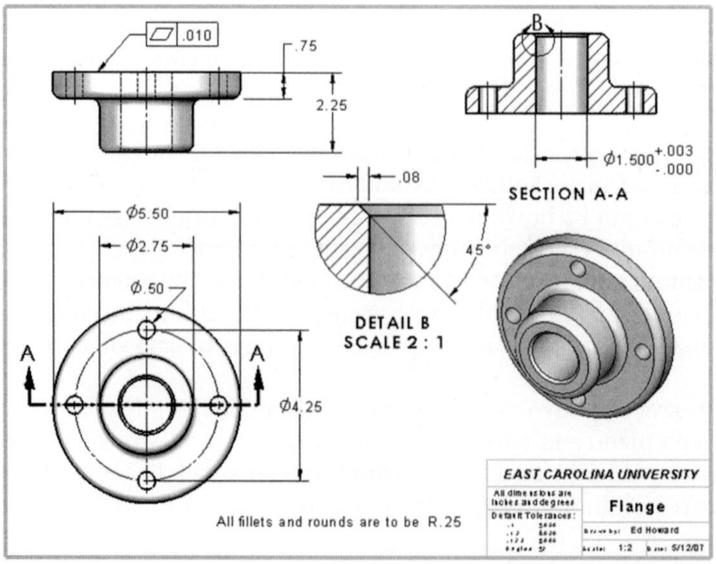

Note: Once you have installed the eDrawings Publisher to your computer, you can open the program from the Start menu on your computer or an icon on your desktop. Installing eDrawings as a SolidWorks add-in simply provides easy access to the program from the SolidWorks environment.

By default, the eDrawing views are displayed in the shaded mode. The display mode can easily be changed to show line drawings.

Click on the Shaded icon.

The eDrawings Viewer allows drawings to be animated. The Play Tool automatically switches from one view to another. The Next Tool allows you to control the animation steps.

Click the Next Tool repeatedly to switch from one view to another, including section and detail views.

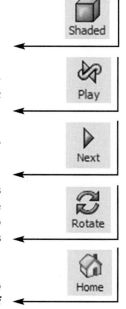

FIGURE 2.78

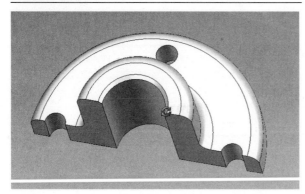

When the Section View is active, select the Rotate Tool. Click and drag to rotate the model view, as shown in Figure 2.78.

Select the Home Tool to return to an overview of the drawing.

An important feature of eDrawings is that comments can be added by reviewers. To illustrate, we will add a comment for draft (taper to allow the part to be easily removed from a mold) to be added to the outer surface of the 2.75-inch diameter boss.

Select the Markup Tool from the left side of the screen.

Select the Options button, as shown in Figure 2.79.

FIGURE 2.79

In the box that appears, you can set preferences for your comments. Several reviewers can add comments to the same drawing, and each reviewer can have a unique color.

Enter a name for the reviewer, and select a color and font type/size, as shown in Figure 2.80. Click OK.

From the markup tools, select the Cloud with Leader Tool. Click on the edge to be drafted, as shown in Figure 2.81. In the pop-up box that appears, type in the text of the comment, as shown in Figure 2.82. Click the check mark to close the box, and then click at the location where the comment is to be placed. The comment as it appears on the drawing is shown in Figure 2.83.

FIGURE 2.80

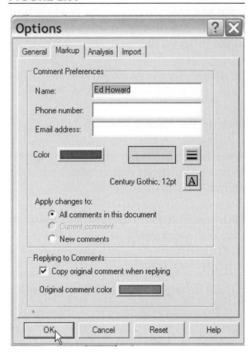

FIGURE 2.81

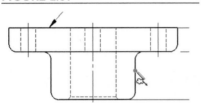

FIGURE 2.82

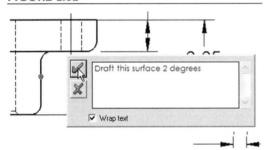

FIGURE 2.83

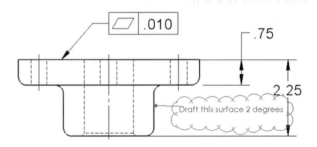

Comments are listed on the left side of the screen, as shown in Figure 2.84, allowing the person making the corrections to the drawing to see who made each comment. In this way, eDrawings allow efficient collaboration among different groups working on a project.

We can also "Stamp" a drawing, much as paper drawings can be stamped to limit its distribution, identify it as proprietary, etc.

FIGURE 2.84

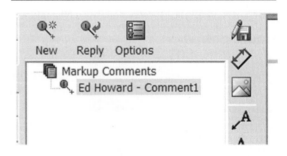

Select the Stamp Tool. Select a stamp from the menu, and click to place it on the drawing, as shown in Figure 2.85. You can drag the corners of the stamp to resize it.

Stamp

FIGURE 2.85

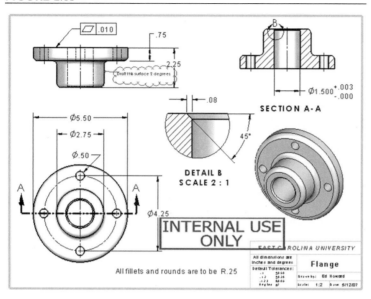

Note that a stamp becomes permanent when the eDrawing is saved, so the recipients cannot delete it.

There are several options for saving and sending eDrawings files. Files can be e-mailed directly from the eDrawings Publisher.

Send

Select the Send Tool.

Several options are available, as shown in Figure 2.86. To send the drawing to someone without the eDrawings Viewer, it is necessary to save an executable file, which includes the Viewer. Since the executable file contains the eDrawing Viewer, the file is much larger than the file saved with the .edrw format. In this example, the .exe file is 2100 kB, as compared with the 59 kB file size of the .edrw file. Since many companies have firewalls that prevent .exe files from being received (because of the possibility of viruses), it may be necessary to send the file as a zipped file or as an html. Both of these options result in the eDrawings Viewer being sent along with the eDrawing.

FIGURE 2.86

Send As

- eDrawings file (.edrw, .eprt, .easm,)
  Requires recipient to have eDrawings Viewer installed.
- Zip (.zip)
  Firewall friendly. Sends an exe file embedded in a zip file. Recipients may require an application to unzip the file.
- HTML page (.htm)
  Firewall safe. Displays the eDrawings file within an HTML page that can be viewed using Internet Explorer. Automatically installs the eDrawings Viewer.
- Executable (.exe)
  Least firewall friendly. Very likely to get stripped from the email by virus protection software.

  OK   Cancel   Help

Select cancel to close the Send box. Select File: Save from the main menu, save the eDrawing as an .edrw file, and close the eDrawings Publisher.

PROBLEMS

P2.1   Create a SolidWorks drawing of the beam section described in Problem P1.2. Include front and side views in your drawing.

FIGURE P2.1

P2.2   Create a SolidWorks drawing of the pulley described in Problem P1.3. Include front and side views in your drawing, as well as a section view. Show a detail view of the keyway region.

FIGURE P2.2

P2.3   Create an eDrawing of the pulley from Problem P2.2.

P2.4 Create a SolidWorks drawing of the plastic pipe tee described in Problem P1.5. Include front and side views in your drawing, as well as a section view.

FIGURE P2.4

P2.5 Create an executable eDrawing of the pipe tee from Problem P2.4. (This problem requires the eDrawing add-in.)

P2.6 Create a SolidWorks drawing of the brake rotor described in Problem P1.6. Include front and side views in your drawing.

FIGURE P2.6

P2.7 Create an eDrawing of the brake rotor from Problem P2.6.

CHAPTER 3

Additional Part Modeling Techniques

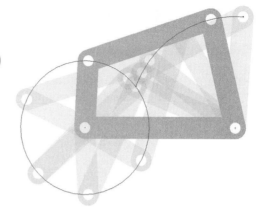

Introduction

The flange part modeled in Chapter 1 required the use of a number of basic solid modeling construction techniques. In this chapter, some additional construction and dimensioning techniques will be explored. The part that will be modeled in this chapter is a wall-mounted bracket, as shown in **Figure 3.1**.

FIGURE 3.1

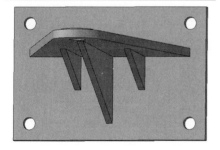

This bracket has some features that will allow us to explore some new modeling techniques:

- It has one plane of symmetry, allowing us to exploit the mirroring capabilities of the program.

- It has a linear hole pattern, which can be readily constructed using the SolidWorks program.

- It has three reinforcing ribs, which can be created with the extruded boss command used earlier or with a rib tool.

In this chapter, a tutorial for modeling this bracket will be presented. Before beginning this tutorial, we will learn how to customize the SolidWorks environment.

Chapter Objectives

In this chapter, you will:

- learn how to customize the SolidWorks environment by modifying the toolbars and the CommandManager,

- learn how to save preferences for options in template files,

- construct centerlines, and use them to locate sketch features through the addition of relations,

- use the Dynamic Mirror Tool to create symmetric sketches about a centerline,

- perform a new type of extrusion called a Mid-Plane Extrusion,

- add ribs with the Rib Tool,

- use the Mirror Tool to create symmetric features about a symmetry plane, and

- create a linear hole pattern.

3.1   Customizing the SolidWorks Environment

Open a new part file. Click on the Front Plane in the FeatureManager to select it.

We will begin by drawing a circle. However, rather than selecting the Circle Tool from the Sketch group of the CommandManager, as we did in Chapter 1, we will select the Circle Tool from the main menu.

From the main menu, select Tools: Sketch Entities: Circle, as shown in Figure 3.2. Drag out a circle, as shown in Figure 3.3 (the size of the circle is not important).

FIGURE 3.2

FIGURE 3.3

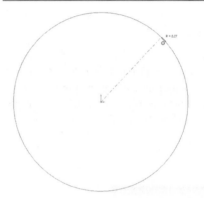

Press the esc key to turn off the Circle Tool. From the main menu, select Insert: Boss/Base: Extrude, as shown in Figure 3.4. Click the check mark in the Property Manager to create a solid disk, as shown in Figure 3.5.

FIGURE 3.4

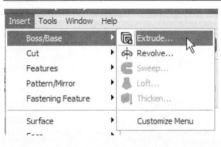

FIGURE 3.5

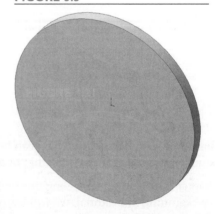

The edges of the disk might look rough on the screen. For a smoother appearance, you may wish to adjust the image quality by selecting Tools: Options from the main menu, and using the slider bar in the Image Quality dialog box found under the Document Properties tab, as described in Chapter 1.

Now we will add a cylindrical boss, using the toolbars to specify sketch and feature commands.

Right-click on any of the open toolbars (but not the CommandManager). A list of available toolbars is displayed, with open toolbars indicated by the icon being "pressed" down. Click on Features, as shown in Figure 3.6. Right-click on a toolbar again, and click on Sketch. Finally, right-click on a toolbar and click on Standard Views.

The Features, Sketch, and Standard Views toolbars are now displayed. Toolbars for 2-D operations (Sketch) are generally placed along the right edge of the screen, toolbars for 3-D operations (Features) are generally placed along the left edge, and general tools (Standard Views) are generally placed near the top of the screen. If they are not, you may wish to click on them, and drag them to the appropriate positions.

Select the front face of the part, as shown in Figure 3.7. Click on the Circle Tool in the Sketch toolbar, as shown in Figure 3.8.

FIGURE 3.6

FIGURE 3.7

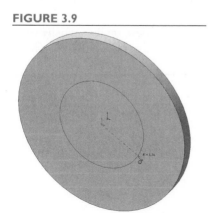

FIGURE 3.8

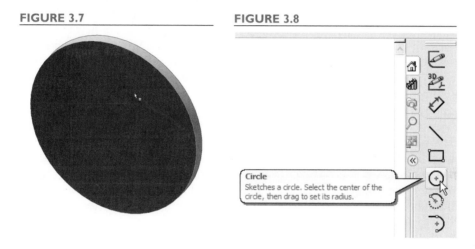

Circle
Sketches a circle. Select the center of the circle, then drag to set its radius.

Drag out a circle, as shown in Figure 3.9.

Select the Extruded Boss/Base Tool from the Features toolbar, as shown in Figure 3.10. Enter a distance for the circle to be extruded, and click the check mark to complete the extrusion, which is shown in Figure 3.11.

FIGURE 3.9

FIGURE 3.10

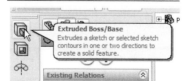

Extruded Boss/Base
Extrudes a sketch or selected sketch contours in one or two directions to create a solid feature.

Existing Relations

FIGURE 3.11

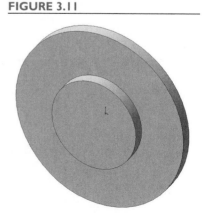

FIGURE 3.12

We have now activated sketch and feature tools in three different ways:

- from the CommandManager
- from the Main Menu
- from Toolbars

The CommandManager is a newer addition to SolidWorks. Many experienced users prefer to use the toolbars instead, since they are accustomed to doing so. There is another advantage to using the toolbars: tools can be accessed with a single mouse click. With the CommandManager, it is necessary to select either the Sketch group or the Features group before selecting the desired tool, if the appropriate group is not already displayed. The CommandManager can be turned off and on in the same manner as any toolbar, by right-clicking on a toolbar and clicking on Command-Manager on the menu that appears.

In this book, we have chosen to use the CommandManager for sketch and feature tools because the tool names are displayed along with the icons. For new users, this is a helpful feature. We use the Standard, View, and Standard Views toolbars because many of the commands on these toolbars can be used at the same time sketch or feature commands are being used. For example, we might begin an extrusion command from the CommandManager, and realize that a different view mode or orientation might be helpful in setting the extrusion parameters. We can click on any of the view tools from the toolbar without interrupting the extrusion process. We use the main menu to call up commands that are not commonly used. For example, we may want to add an ellipse to a sketch. Rather than adding the Ellipse Tool to the Sketch toolbar, we select Tools: Sketch Entities: Ellipse from the main menu. However, if the types of parts that you model use ellipses regularly, then the Ellipse Tool can be added to the toolbar. We will now learn how to modify toolbars.

Right-click on any of the toolbars (but not the CommandManager). Near the bottom of the menu that appears, click on Customize, as shown in Figure 3.12. Check the boxes labeled "Show tooltips" and "Use large tooltips" if you would like to have a pop-up box describe each tool as you pass your cursor over it (such as those shown in Figures 3.8 and 3.10). You may also want to select the "Large icons" option, depending on your screen size and resolution.

First, we will delete an unused tool from the toolbar.

Move the cursor over the RealView Graphics Tool on the View toolbar, as shown in Figure 3.13. Click and drag the icon into the modeling area, as shown in Figure 3.14.

FIGURE 3.13

FIGURE 3.14

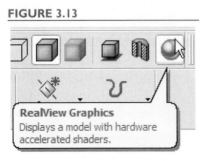

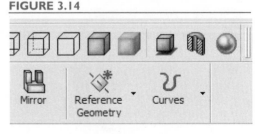

This will remove the RealView Graphics Tool from the menu. If you have a graphics card that supports RealView, then you might want to add it back later. (Note: if your toolbars do not fit onto the screen, so that it is necessary to click on an arrow on the right edge of the screen to display all of the icons on the toolbar, then it may be necessary to drag the toolbar to a different location before adding and/or removing tools. Click and drag the toolbar to a location where its entire contents can be seen, make any desired changes, and then drag the toolbar back to its desired location.)

We will now add a tool to a toolbar. The following step will add the Four View Tool to the Standard Views toolbar. If this tool already appears on your computer, you may duplicate the steps shown with any other tool.

In the dialog box, click on the Commands tab and select Standard Views from the list of categories.

FIGURE 3.15

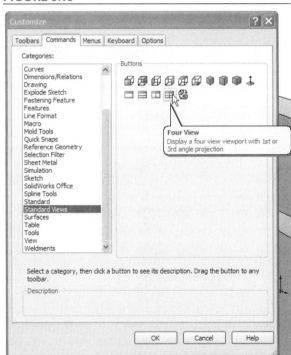

A group of icons representing the available tools for this category is displayed. If you have the Tooltips active, then moving the cursor over each icon displays the tool name and gives a brief description of that tool, as shown in **Figure 3.15**.

Click on the Four View Tool and drag it onto the Standard Views toolbar, next to the Dimetric View Tool, as shown in Figure 3.16. Click OK to close the dialog box. The Four View Tool now is included on the Standard Views toolbar, as shown in Figure 3.17.

FIGURE 3.16

We will see how to customize the CommandManager. Any toolbar can be shown on the CommandManager.

FIGURE 3.17

Right-click on the CommandManager, and select Customize CommandManager from the menu that appears, as shown in Figure 3.18.

FIGURE 3.18

A list of toolbars is displayed, with the toolbars currently on the CommandManager indicated with check marks, as shown in Figure 3.19. Click the box for the Standard Views toolbar, and then click anywhere in the modeling area to close the menu.

FIGURE 3.19

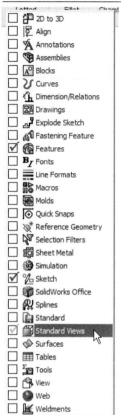

The Standard Views Tools are now available from the CommandManager, as shown in Figure 3.20. Note that the tools are the same as those on the toolbar. When tools are added or removed from the toolbar, then those changes are reflected in the CommandManager.

FIGURE 3.20

Right-click on the Command-Manager, and select Customize CommandManager. Click on the Standard Views to remove the check mark, and click in the modeling area to close the menu.

Since the standard views can be selected from the pull-down menu on the Views toolbar or from the menu in the lower left corner of the drawing area, it is not necessary to have them on the CommandManager. If you would like to have one-click access to the standard views, then leave the Standard Views toolbar displayed. In a later chapter, when making a sheet metal part, we will add the Sheet Metal Tools to the CommandManager.

Note that when you make changes to a toolbar, you do not need to save the changes. The modifications will be automatically saved.

Document options are not automatically saved. For example, if the default system of units is millimeters/grams/seconds and you usually work in inches/pounds/seconds, then you must change the options for every new part. However, you can change the default options by modifying the template in which they are saved. The following steps demonstrate the modification of the default part template. If you use a shared computer, then you may prefer to change the options every time and leave the defaults as set.

Optional steps for modifying the part template:

Open a new part file. From the main menu, select Tools: Options, as shown in Figure 3.21. Under the Document Properties tab, set the following options as desired (recommended values in parentheses):

- **Grid/Snap (Display grid)**
- **Units (inch/pound/second, number of decimal places = 2 or 3)**
- **Colors (a light color for the Shading color)**
- **Image Quality (move slider bar to High)**

Click OK to close the Options box.

Note that only options under the Document Properties tab are saved in a template. Changes to System Options will apply to all subsequent documents, whether a template is saved or not.

From the main menu, select File: Save As. In the dialog box, use the pull-down menu to select Part Templates as the file type, as shown in Figure 3.22. Click on the file named "Part" to select it, and click Save. When asked if you want to replace the default template, click Yes. Close the part file.

FIGURE 3.21

FIGURE 3.22

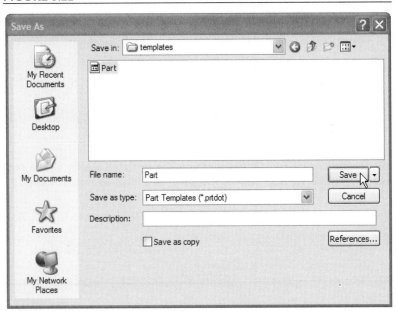

When you open a new part file, the settings just saved will be applied. You may also save templates with other names. For example, you can have a "Part mm" template for use when modeling a part in millimeters and a "Part in" template for modeling a part in inches. Templates are especially useful with drawings. You can save templates for different unit systems, drawing sizes, and title blocks.

3.2   Part Modeling Tutorial: Bracket

Open a new part file. Be sure that dimensions are set to inches (with two decimal places displayed) and the Display Grid option is on.

FIGURE 3.23

Click on the Front Plane in the FeatureManager to select it, as shown in Figure 3.23.

Click on the Sketch icon so that the Sketch group of tools is displayed in the CommandManager. Click the Rectangle Tool.

Now left-click anywhere in the drawing area and while holding down the left mouse key, drag out a rectangle, as shown in Figure 3.24.

FIGURE 3.24

x = 4.52, y = 2.31

Don't worry about the locations of the corner points; we will add dimensions that will size and locate the rectangle.

Click on the Smart Dimension Tool, and dimension the horizontal side of the rectangle to 6 inches and the vertical side to 4 inches, as shown in Figure 3.25.

FIGURE 3.25

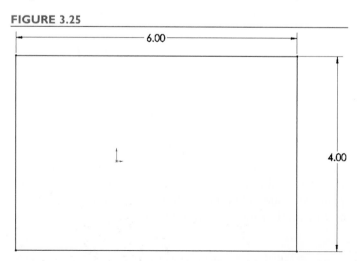

6.00

4.00

Note that the sides of the rectangle are shown blue, and the status bar at the lower-right corner of the screen shows that the sketch is "Under Defined." Although we have fully defined the size of the rectangle, we have not specified its position. We can do this by adding dimensions from the origin to two of the sides, or by using a centerline for construction. We will use the centerline approach.

Click on the Centerline Tool. Drag a diagonal line, snapping from corner to corner of the rectangle.

The dimensioned sketch with the centerline added should appear as shown in **Figure 3.26**.

FIGURE 3.26

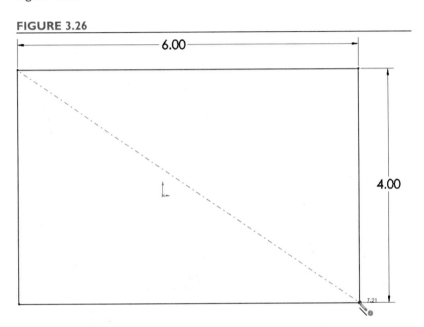

A relation will now be added to locate the rectangle so that it is centered at the origin.

Click the esc key to turn off the Centerline Tool. Hold down the ctrl key, and use the left mouse button to select both the centerline and the origin.

Recall that the ctrl key is used to make multiple selections.

In the PropertyManager, select Midpoint to add a relation between the centerline and the origin, as shown in Figure 3.27. Click the check mark to apply the relation.

The rectangle is now both dimensioned and located, so the sketch is fully defined.

FIGURE 3.27

Features

Extruded
Boss/Base

Click on the Features icon and then the Extruded Boss/Base Tool. In the PropertyManager, enter 0.25 inches as the thickness, and click on the check mark, as shown in Figure 3.28.

A solid object has been created, as shown in **Figure 3.29**.

The horizontal boss of the bracket will now be constructed. The feature will be sketched in a plane 1.25 inches below the top surface of the base part. To accomplish this, we will first need to create the reference plane to be used for sketching.

Select the top surface of the base part (see Figure 3.30).

FIGURE 3.28

FIGURE 3.29

FIGURE 3.30

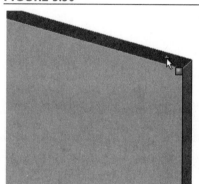

Be sure that the face is selected (a square symbol will appear next to the cursor).

FIGURE 3.31

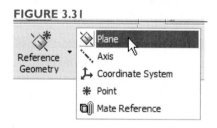

From the Features group of the CommandManager, select Reference Geometry: Plane, as shown in Figure 3.31. In the PropertyManager, click the check box to reverse the direction, and set the distance to 1.25 inches (see Figure 3.32). Click the check mark to create the plane, which will be named Plane1.

The boss feature will now be sketched in this new plane. The symmetry of the boss about the Right Plane will be exploited in the creation of the sketch.

FIGURE 3.32

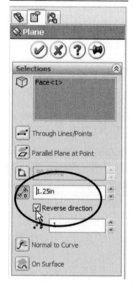

Select the Top View. Use the Pan Tool to place the part toward the top of the screen, as shown in Figure 3.33. Press the esc key to turn off the Pan Tool.

FIGURE 3.33

We will use mirroring to assist in construction of the symmetric sketch. This will require that we draw a centerline first.

If Plane1 is not selected (highlighted in green), then click on Plane1 in the Feature-Manager. Select the Centerline Tool from the Sketch group of the Command-Manager, and drag a line from the origin downward. As you drag the line downward, a vertical relation symbol by the cursor shows that the line will be vertical (see Figure 3.34).

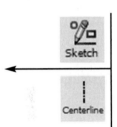

FIGURE 3.34

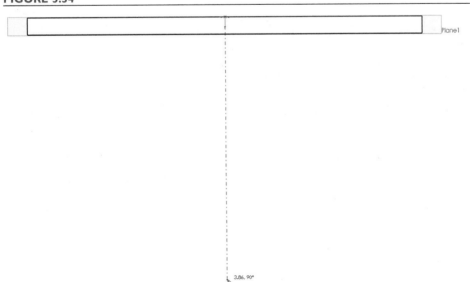

With the centerline selected, go to the main menu and select Tools: Sketch Tools: Dynamic Mirror, as shown in Figure 3.35.

Drawing features added now will be mirrored about the centerline.

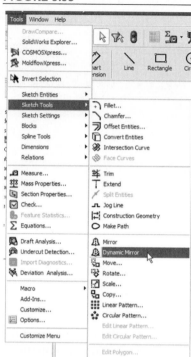

Select the Line Tool (solid line, not the centerline), and move the cursor near the edge of the previously created solid.

A coincident relation symbol will appear next to the cursor to show that you are snapping to the edge, as shown in Figure 3.36.

While holding down the left mouse key, drag a line downward at an angle (Figure 3.37).

When you release the mouse key, you will see that the line you were drawing and another line that is a mirror image are created. Note that a symmetric relation has been created between the lines.

FIGURE 3.35

FIGURE 3.36

FIGURE 3.37

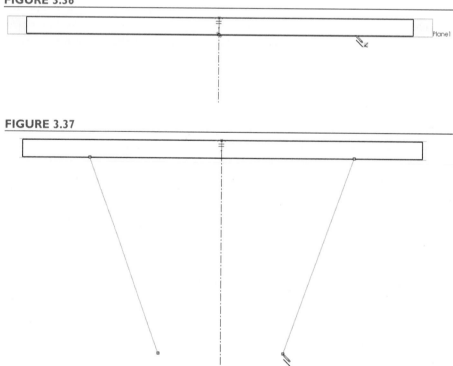

FIGURE 3.38

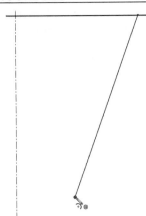

Select the Tangent Arc Tool. Move the cursor to the endpoint of the line, so that the concentric relation symbol appears next to the cursor, indicating that the arc will begin at the endpoint of the line (see Figure 3.38). Hold down the left mouse button and drag out an arc, with the endpoint on the centerline, as shown in Figure 3.39. Deselect the Dynamic Mirror tools from the main menu to end mirroring. The arc that you drew will remain tangent to the first line, no matter how the dimensions of the sketch are changed. Your sketch should now appear as shown in Figure 3.40. Of course, this is not exactly what we want: the two arcs should be tangent to each other. Therefore, we will add a relation to the two arcs.

FIGURE 3.39

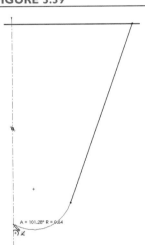

FIGURE 3.40

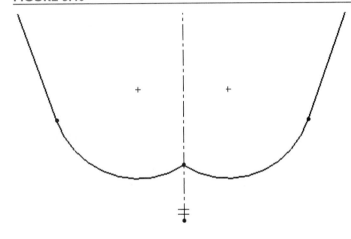

FIGURE 3.41

Select the two arcs, and click Concentric in the Property-Manager, as shown in Figure 3.41. Click the check mark to add the relation.

The two arcs are now tangent to each other, as shown in Figure 3.42. Note that we could have specified a tangent relation instead of the concentric relation, but there are two possible solutions to the tangent relation. To ensure that the geometry is the way we want it, the concentric relation provides only one solution.

FIGURE 3.42

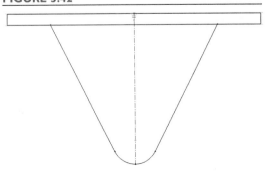

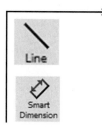

Line

Smart Dimension

Select the Line Tool, and finish the sketch with a horizontal line connecting the two free ends of the sketch, as shown in Figure 3.43. Select the Smart Dimension Tool, and dimension the sketch as shown in Figure 3.44. Add the 0.75 inch radius first.

Note that the 7-inch dimension is to the back of the bracket.

FIGURE 3.43

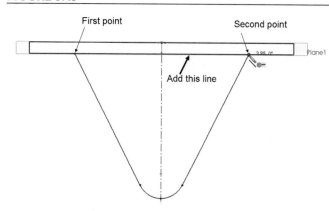

First point

Second point

Add this line

FIGURE 3.44

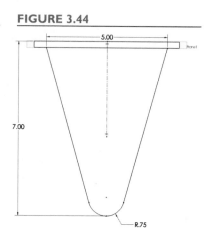

Features

Extruded Boss/Base

Select the Extruded Boss/Base Tool from the Features Group of the Command-Manager. Click the Reverse Direction icon in the PropertyManager, as shown in Figure 3.45, and extrude the part downward 0.25 inches. Change to the Trimetric View to preview the extrusion, and click the check mark to complete the operation.

The bracket should appear as shown in Figure 3.46.

FIGURE 3.45

FIGURE 3.46

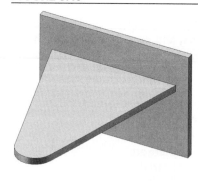

Now we will add a raised cylindrical feature for reinforcement near what will become a mounting hole.

Select the top surface of the horizontal extruded boss, as shown in Figure 3.47. Select the Top View.

FIGURE 3.47

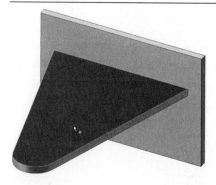

We want to locate the raised area concentric with the rounded tip of the boss. In order to establish this relation, we will first need to "wake up" the arc that makes up this rounded tip, allowing the center point to be used as a snap point in our sketch.

FIGURE 3.48

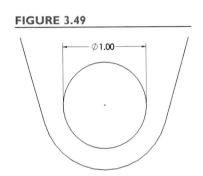

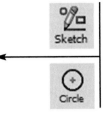

Sketch

Circle

Select the Circle Tool from the Sketch group of the CommandManager. Move the cursor into the sketching window, and hold the pointer (without clicking) over the arc (see Figure 3.48, which is shown in wireframe mode for clarity).

The center point of the arc now appears, and it can be used as a snap point for the center of the circle.

FIGURE 3.49

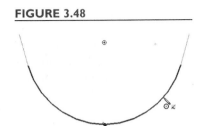

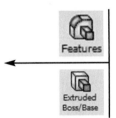

Smart Dimension

Drag out a circle, starting at the center mark. Select the Smart Dimension Tool, and dimension the circle to be 1 inch in diameter (see Figure 3.49).

Features

Extruded Boss/Base

Select the Extruded Boss/Base Tool from the Features group of the CommandManager. Extrude the sketch upward for a distance of 0.050 inches, as shown in Figure 3.50.

A reinforcing rib will now be added to the part. This will be created using a new type of extrusion, called a Mid-Plane Extrusion.

FIGURE 3.50

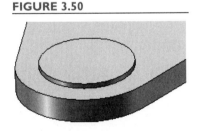

Sketch

Line

Select the Right Plane from the Feature-Manager, and select the Right View. Select the Line Tool from the Sketch group of the CommandManager, and sketch in the line shown in Figure 3.51. The endpoints of your line should snap to the edges of the solids, but not to any specific point on the edges. Recall that a coincident relation symbol next to the cursor indicates that you are snapping to the edge.

FIGURE 3.51

FIGURE 3.52

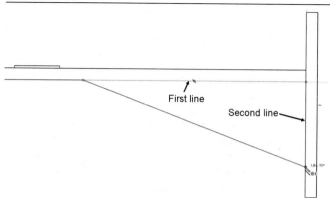

Add one horizontal and one vertical line coincident with the edges of the solid (snap to the end-points of the first line and the inter-section point of the edges), completing the profile of the rib, as shown in Figure 3.52.

Smart Dimension

Select the Smart Dimension Tool, and dimension the sketch as shown in Figure 3.53.

FIGURE 3.53

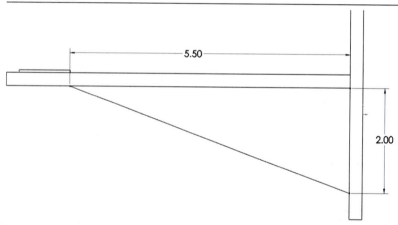

5.50

2.00

Features

Extruded Boss/Base

Select the Extruded Boss/Base Tool from the Features group of the CommandManager. In the PropertyManager, select Mid Plane as the type from the pull-down menu (see Figure 3.54), and enter a thickness of 0.1875 inches (see Figure 3.55). Click the check mark to complete the extrusion.

FIGURE 3.54

FIGURE 3.55

Unlike the one-sided blind and "up to next" extrusions used previously, the mid-plane type extrudes material in *both* directions, from the sketch plane outward. For a Mid-Plane Extrusion, the thickness entered is the *total* thickness of material after the extrusion. A front view of the part shows that the rib is symmetric about the Right Plane (see **Figure 3.56**).

FIGURE 3.56

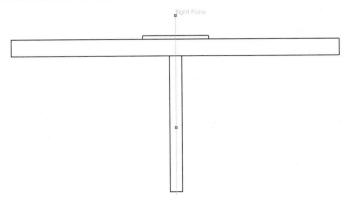

The next rib will be added in a slightly different manner, using the Rib Tool. But first, we must create a new plane for the rib. So far, we have used the CommandManager to create a plane. Here, we will use a drag-and-drop technique that is similar to that used in other Windows applications.

FIGURE 3.57

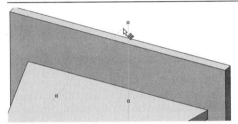

FIGURE 3.58

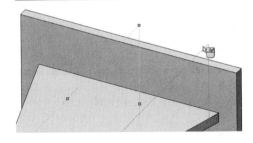

Select the Trimetric View. Click on the Right Plane in the FeatureManager to select it. Hold down the ctrl key, and move the cursor over one of the lines defining the plane until the move arrows appear, as shown in Figure 3.57. Click and drag the mouse to the right. When the mouse button is released, a new plane is created, as shown in Figure 3.58. In the PropertyManager, set the offset distance to 1 inch, as shown in Figure 3.59. Click the check mark to complete the definition of the new plane, which will be labeled Plane2.

FIGURE 3.59

FIGURE 3.60

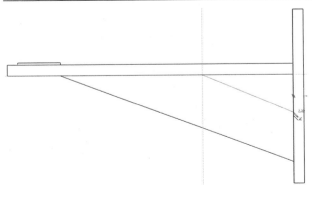

Select the Line Tool from the Sketch group of the CommandManager. Draw a diagonal line as shown in Figure 3.60, snapping the endpoints to the edges of the solids (but not to any specific points).

Smart
Dimension

Select the Smart Dimension Tool and add the dimensions shown in Figure 3.61.

For the first rib, we added two lines to close the sketch and used an Extruded Boss command to complete the rib. A rib can be created from an open sketch using the Rib Tool.

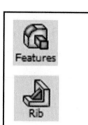

Features

Rib

Select the Rib Tool from the Features group of the CommandManager. In the FeatureManager, set the thickness to 0.1875 inches, as shown in Figure 3.62.

FIGURE 3.61

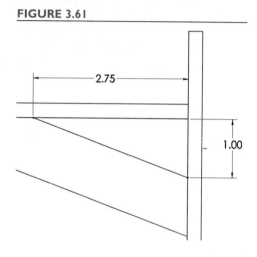

FIGURE 3.62

The thickness can be set to be offset from the plane in either direction, or so that the rib is symmetric about the plane (similar to the Mid-Plane Extrusion used for the first rib). By default, the middle of the three buttons, designating a rib symmetric about the plane, is selected. For the extrusion direction, the rib can be defined as parallel to the plane of the sketch (default) or normal to the plane. Neither of these settings needs to be changed for our rib.

Check the "Flip material side" box, as shown in Figure 3.62, **so that the arrow defining the rib direction points toward the part, as shown in** Figure 3.63. **Click the check mark to complete the rib, which is shown in** Figure 3.64.

FIGURE 3.63

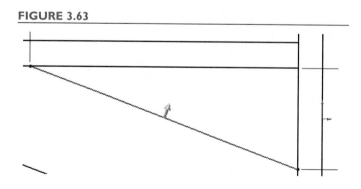

FIGURE 3.64

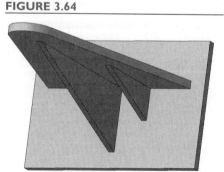

FIGURE 3.65

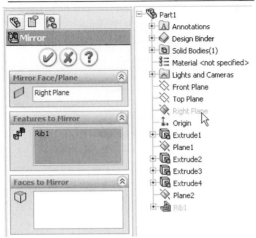

Earlier, we used the Dynamic Mirror Tool to create symmetric elements within a sketch. A similar tool, the Mirror Tool, is used to create symmetric features in a part. We will use this tool to create the final rib.

Select the Mirror Tool from the Features group of the Command-Manager. In the PropertyManager, the Mirror Face/Plane box is active (highlighted in pink), as shown in Figure 3.65. Click on the Right Plane in the FeatureManager, which has "flown out" to the right of the PropertyManager. It may be necessary to click on the plus sign next to the part name to expand the FeatureManager before selection. The rib just created should be listed as the feature to mirror. If it is not, click that box to make it active and select the rib from the FeatureManager.

A preview of the final rib is displayed, as shown in **Figure 3.66**.

Click the check mark to complete the rib.

The three ribs are shown in **Figure 3.67**.

FIGURE 3.66

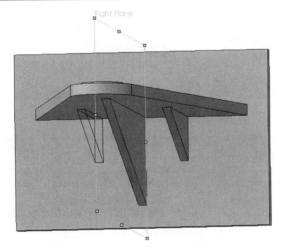

The holes will now be added to the part.

FIGURE 3.67

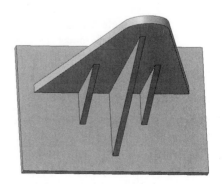

Select the top surface of the raised circle, as shown in Figure 3.68. Select the Circle Tool from the Sketch group of the CommandManager. Select the top view.

As before, it is necessary to "wake up" a center mark at which the hole will be centered.

Move the cursor to the edge of the rounded end of the part, or the circular edge of the reinforced area, without clicking a mouse button. This will cause the center mark to be displayed, as shown in Figure 3.69.

FIGURE 3.68

Click and drag out a circle from the center mark. Select the Smart Dimension Tool, and dimension the diameter of the circle as 0.50 inches, as shown in Figure 3.70.

FIGURE 3.69

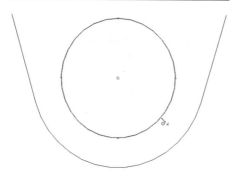

FIGURE 3.70

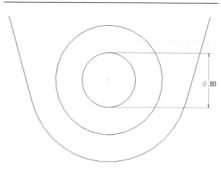

Ø.50

Select the Extruded Cut Tool from the Features group of the CommandManager, and select Through All as the type. Click the check mark to complete the hole, which is shown in Figure 3.71.

The four-hole bolt hole pattern used to mount the bracket to the wall will now be added. This will be done by creating a single hole, and then defining a *pattern* based on this hole. In Chapter 1, a *circular pattern* was used to create a bolt hole pattern in the flange. In this exercise, a new type of pattern known as a *linear pattern* will be introduced.

The first step will be the creation of a single bolt hole.

FIGURE 3.71

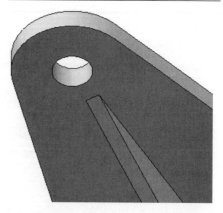

Select the large vertical face of the base part as shown in Figure 3.72. Select the
Circle Tool from the Sketch group of the CommandManager, and sketch a circle
near the upper-left corner of the face. Select the Smart Dimension Tool and dimension the hole diameter as 0.375 inches, as shown in Figure 3.73.

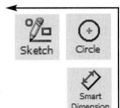

FIGURE 3.72

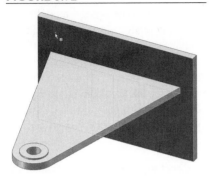

FIGURE 3.73

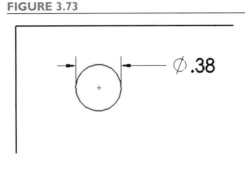

Note that the diameter dimension is displayed to two decimal places, since that is
the option that we set for this part. However, the dimension is stored to the same
accuracy we entered.

FIGURE 3.74

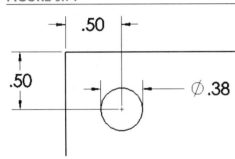

Add linear dimensions between the
circle and the edges, as shown in
Figure 3.74.

Select the Extruded Cut Tool from the
Features group of the Command-
Manager, and select Through All as the
type. Click the check mark to com-
plete the hole, which is shown in
Figure 3.75.

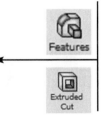

With this single hole defined, a linear
hole pattern can now be created.

FIGURE 3.75

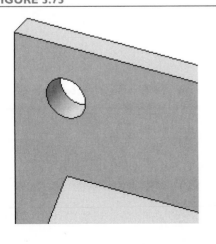

With the new hole selected, select the
Linear Pattern tool from the Features
group of the CommandManager.

The feature Cut-Extrude2 will be
shown in the "Features to Pattern"
box, indicating that this is the base
feature for the linear pattern. The
"Direction 1" box in the Property-
Manager will be highlighted in pink;
this allows the first linear direction of
the pattern to be established.

DESIGN INTENT   Symmetry in Modeling

In this chapter, we used mirroring techniques for sketch entities and features to define symmetric elements in a part. The four mounting holes in the bracket, which were created with a linear pattern, could have been defined with mirror commands. The advantage of doing so would be that if we change the dimensions of the vertical portion of the bracket (6 inches by 4 inches), the hole positions would be updated to the correct positions. The same associativity between the hole locations and the size of the bracket can be added if a linear pattern is used, but will require the addition of equations, which will be explained in Chapter 4.

Using symmetric elements in a part is good modeling practice. If a part contains planes of symmetry, plan your model to take advantage of those planes. In the bracket model, we centered the initial sketch about the origin. This placed the part so that the Right Plane coincided with the symmetry plane of the entire part, and the Top Plane coincided with an additional symmetry plane of the vertical portion of the part.

FIGURE 3.76

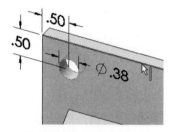

Click on the top horizontal edge of the rectangular base to establish the first direction, as shown in Figure 3.76. In the PropertyManager, set the Direction I distance to 5 inches and the number of instances to 2, as shown in Figure 3.77. The Direction 2 box in the PropertyManager will be highlighted pink.

A preview of a second patterned hole will appear, as shown in Figure 3.78.

FIGURE 3.77

FIGURE 3.78

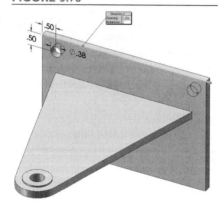

FIGURE 3.79

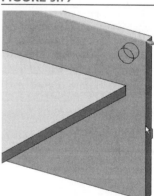

Click on the right vertical edge of the rectangular base to establish the second direction of the pattern, as shown in Figure 3.79.

FIGURE 3.80

FIGURE 3.81

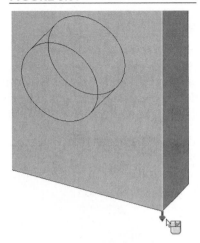

In the **PropertyManager,**
set the **Direction 2** distance to be **3 inches** and
the number of instances
to be **2,** as shown in
Figure 3.80.

**If the preview of the pat-
terned holes shows that
the pattern is created in
the wrong direction,
click on the arrow at the
end of the edge defining
the pattern direction, as
shown in Figure 3.81.**

**When the preview of the pattern appears correct, as shown in
Figure 3.82, click the check mark to complete the pattern.**

The completed part is shown in Figure 3.83.

Save the part file.

FIGURE 3.82

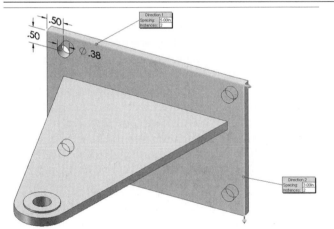

FIGURE 3.83

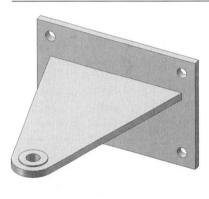

PROBLEMS

P3.1   Create a solid model of a structural tee section by creating the sketch shown in **Figure P3.1A** on the Front Plane and mirroring it about the centerline. Use relations as appropriate to fully define the sketch. Extrude it using a Mid-Plane Extrusion to a total thickness of 36 inches to create the model shown in **Figure P3.1B**.

FIGURE P3.1A   **FIGURE P3.1B**

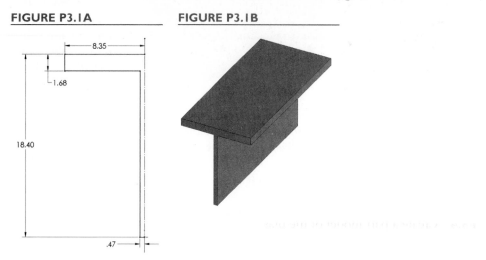

P3.2   The cross-section of a W14 x 370 Wide-Flange Beam is shown in **Figure P3.2A**. Create a model of a 36-inch long segment of a W14 x 370 beam by creating the sketch shown in **Figure P3.2B** and mirroring it about the two centerlines. (Note: This must be done in two steps. Select the items to be mirrored and one of the centerlines, and then select the Mirror Entities Tool. Then select all entities to be mirrored and the other centerline and select the Mirror Entity Tool. Only one centerline can be selected for each mirror operation.) Extrude the sketch to yield the beam section shown in **Figure P3.2C**. Set the material type to Plain Carbon Steel and find the weight of the beam segment.

(Answer: 1101 lb)

FIGURE P3.2A   **FIGURE P3.2B**   **FIGURE P3.2C**

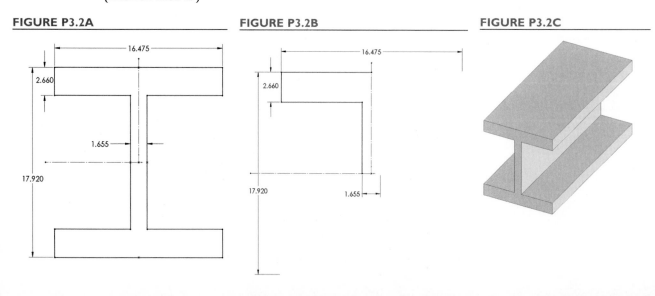

P3.3 Modify the wide-flange beam segment of P3.2 by adding six 1 inch-diameter holes to each end of the beam, as shown in **Figure P3.3A**. The locations of the holes are shown in **Figure P3.3B**. Create a single hole, and use a linear pattern to place the other five holes in one end. Then use a mirror command to place the holes in the other end.

FIGURE P3.3A

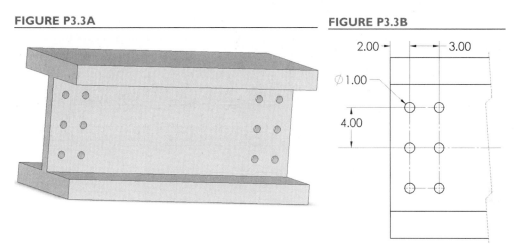

FIGURE P3.3B

P3.4 Create a part model of the plastic bracket shown in **Figure P3.4A** and detailed in **Figure P3.4B**. Use symmetry in your model so that if you change the width of the part from 2 to 3 inches, the rib and hole placements remain symmetric, as shown in **Figure P3.4C**.

FIGURE P3.4A

FIGURE P3.4B

FIGURE P3.4C

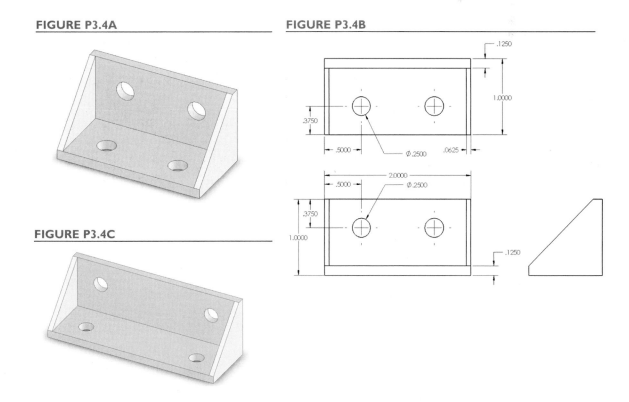

P3.5   Create a model of the perforated board shown in **Figure P3.5A** by the following procedure:

a.   Begin with a 4-inch by 2-inch sketch, centered at the origin using a centerline and a relation (**Figure P3.5B**, on the next page).

b.   Extrude the sketch 0.1 inch.

c.   Create and locate a square thru-hole, as shown in **Figure P3.5C**. (Note: Add a point to the intersection of the diagonal centerlines so that you can dimension to the center of the rectangle.)

d.   Use a linear pattern to create an evenly spaced 40 x 20 grid of holes.

FIGURE P3.5A   **FIGURE P3.5B**

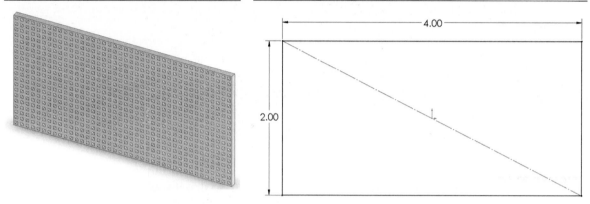

FIGURE P3.5C

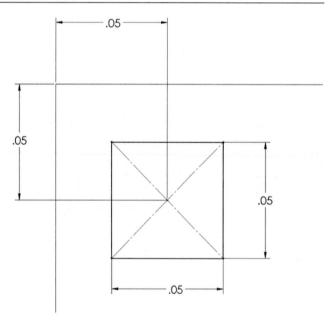

P3.6 Create a solid model of a hacksaw blade (as shown in **Figure P3.6A**, with a close-up view of the teeth shown in **Figure P3.6B**), using a linear patterned cut to create the saw teeth. Follow the procedure outlined below.

a. Begin by creating a sawblade "blank," using the dimensions shown in **Figure P3.6C** and extruding the shape to a 0.02-inch depth.

b. Sketch a single tooth profile, and extrude a cut through the blank (see **Figure P3.6D**).

c. Create a linear pattern to copy the tooth profile the length of the sawblade.

FIGURE P3.6A

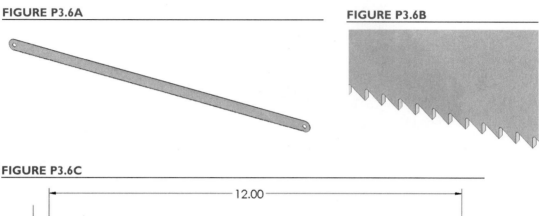

FIGURE P3.6B

FIGURE P3.6C

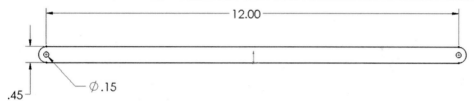

FIGURE P3.6D

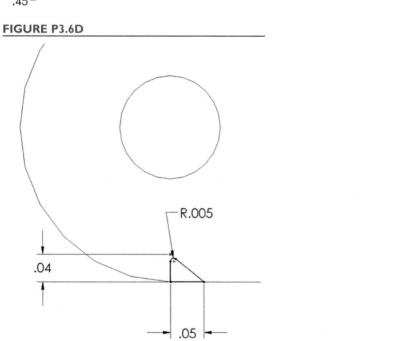

P3.7 Create a solid model of the muffin pan shown in **Figure P3.7A** and detailed in **Figure P3.7B**. The entire pan is 0.050 inches thick. Each of the 12 muffin wells is 3 inches in diameter at the top, is 1.5 inches deep, and has tapered sides, as shown in **Figure P3.7C**. The entire top surface and the insides of the muffin wells are to be coated with a nonstick material. Find the surface area that will be coated. (Hint: The Mass Properties Tool gives you the surface area of the entire part, but to get the surface area for a single surface or a specific group of surfaces, select the surface(s), using the ctrl key to select multiple items, and select Tools: Measure from the main menu.)

FIGURE P3.7A

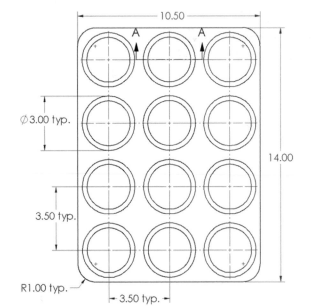

FIGURE P3.7B

FIGURE P3.7C

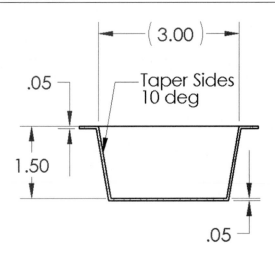

CHAPTER 4

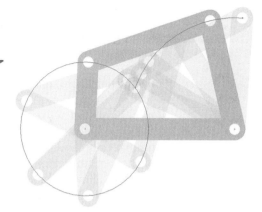

Use of Parametric Modeling Techniques

Introduction

One of the tremendous advantages of solid modeling software is the ability to represent geometric relationships in a parametric form. In a parametric model, the description of the model contains both a geometric description (shape, interconnectivity, etc.) and specific numerical parameters (dimensions, number of instances, etc.). Consider, for example, a simple parameterized solid model of a cylinder; the definition of the model contains both a geometric description defining the primitive shape (cylinder), and two numeric parameters (radius and length) to fully define the model. A whole "family" of cylindrical parts of different radii and lengths could be modeled with a single parameterized model, with only a numeric table of values used to differentiate the various parts in the family.

The Linear Pattern Tool used to define the hole pattern in Chapter 3 is another good example of a parameterized model; the geometric information used to describe a hole pattern includes:
- the shape of the hole (circular)
- the type of extruded cut ("through all")

The numeric parameters that must also be defined include:
- the vectors (axes) that define the two directions of the pattern
- the two "repeat" dimensions along the two directions
- the number of instances of the holes in each direction

Changes can be readily made to the parameters to update the model, without requiring any changes to the geometric information.

This concept of using numeric parameters to drive a solid model can be exploited in design. One powerful tool that can be employed is the development of mathematical relationships (equations) that relate the values of two or more parameters in a model.

Chapter Objectives

In this chapter, you will:

- learn how to display a section view of a model,

- use the Covert Entities Tool to convert the silhouette of a solid part into a sketch line,

- use the Draft Tool to add draft to an existing solid part,

- select the contour to be used for a feature from a multiple-contour sketch,

- perform a revolved cut operation,

- develop equations to embed parameterized relationships into a solid model,

- use a design table to create a family of similar parts, and

- create a multiple-configuration part drawing.

103

In our hole pattern, for example, we might want to restrict our model so that the number of instances of holes in one direction is always the same as the number of instances of holes in the other direction. This is accomplished by relating the two parameters together with an equation, for example:

(# of instances along Direction 2) = (# of instances along Direction 1)

Once this parameterized relationship is established, any change made to the *independent parameter* (the number of instances of holes along Direction 1) would automatically update the value of the *dependent parameter* (the number of instances of holes along Direction 2), and the model would be updated accordingly. This allows the engineer to embed design intelligence and "rules-of-thumb" directly into solid models.

In this chapter, an example of a mechanical part that contains embedded equations to drive specific parameters will be presented. In addition, the tutorial will introduce some new modeling operations that have not yet been utilized in the preceding chapters.

4.1   Modeling Tutorial: Molded Flange

Sketch

Circle

Smart
Dimension

In this exercise, we'll create the flange shown here in **Figure 4.1**. Since this is to be a molded part, we'll add draft to the appropriate surfaces.

Begin by starting a new part, and selecting the Front Plane from the FeatureManager. Select the Circle Tool from the Sketch group of the CommandManager. Drag out a circle centered at the origin. Select the Smart Dimension Tool and add a 6-inch diameter dimension, as shown in Figure 4.2.

Select the Extruded Boss/Base Tool from the Features group of the CommandManager. Extrude the sketch outward to a thickness of 0.25 inches.

FIGURE 4.1

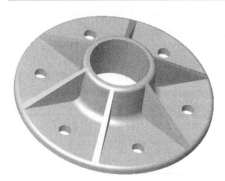

FIGURE 4.2

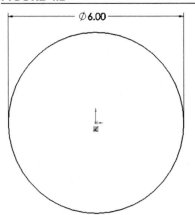

Features

Extruded
Boss/Base

FIGURE 4.3

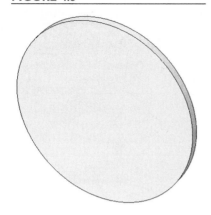

The extruded solid is shown in **Figure** 4.3.

Since the next feature will be drafted, we will define its dimensions in a new plane and extrude its sketch back toward the rest of the part. Therefore, we need to create a new construction plane offset from the Front Plane.

Begin by selecting the Front Plane from the FeatureManager.

The selected plane will be highlighted in green.

While holding down the ctrl key, click and drag the plane outward. Make sure that the move arrows, as shown in Figure 4.4, appear before clicking. Release the mouse button, and the new plane is previewed, as shown in Figure 4.5.

FIGURE 4.4

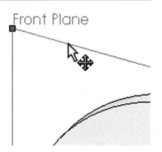

FIGURE 4.5

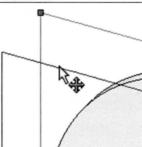

In the PropertyManager, set the offset distance to 1.5 inches, as shown in **Figure** 4.6, and click the check mark to complete the operation.

FIGURE 4.6

The new plane will be labeled Plane1 in the FeatureManager. A cylindrical boss will now be extruded with a draft from this new plane back toward the base feature.

FIGURE 4.7

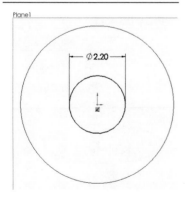

With the new plane (Plane1) selected, select the Circle Tool from the Sketch group of the CommandManager. Drag out a circle from the origin. Select the Smart Dimension Tool and dimension the circle's diameter as 2.2 inches, as shown in **Figure** 4.7.

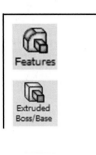

Features

Extruded
Boss/Base

Select the Extruded Boss/Base Tool from the Features group of the CommandManager, and set the direction such that the boss is extruded toward the base. Change the type of extrusion to Up to Next. (Note: If Up to Next is not available, then the extrusion direction is incorrect.) Turn the draft on. Set the draft angle to 3 degrees and check the "Draft outward" box, as shown in Figure 4.8. Click on the check mark to complete the extrusion.

FIGURE 4.8

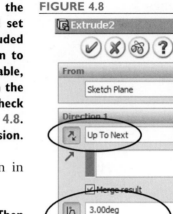

The result of the drafted extrusion is shown in Figure 4.9.

Select View: Planes from the main menu. Then select View: Origins from the main menu.

Sketch

These steps will toggle the display of planes and origins from on (menu icon depressed) to off (icon not depressed).

Circle

Select the face shown in Figure 4.10. Select the Circle Tool from the Sketch group of the CommandManager. Drag out a circle centered at the origin. Select the Smart Dimension Tool. Dimension the circle's diameter at 1.8 inches, as shown in Figure 4.11.

Smart
Dimension

FIGURE 4.9

FIGURE 4.10

FIGURE 4.11

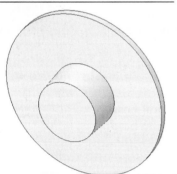

Features

Extruded
Cut

Select the Extruded Cut Tool from the Features group of the CommandManager. Select Through All as the type, turn the draft on, and set the draft angle to 2 degrees. Make sure that the "Draft outward" box is checked, as shown in Figure 4.12.

FIGURE 4.12

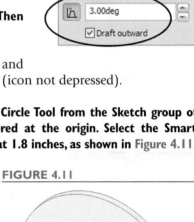

FIGURE 4.13

Click the check mark to apply the cut, which is shown in Figure 4.13.

To see the effect of the draft on the hole, viewing the model with a section view is helpful.

Select the Section View Tool from the View toolbar. In the PropertyManager, select the middle button, representing the Top Plane, as shown in Figure 4.14.

The section view of the model is previewed, as shown in Figure 4.15.

FIGURE 4.14

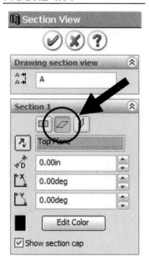

FIGURE 4.15

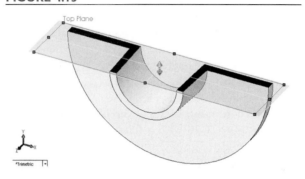

Reverse the direction of the section by clicking on the icon next to the plane selection box, as shown in Figure 4.16.

The new preview of the section view is shown in Figure 4.17.

FIGURE 4.16

FIGURE 4.17

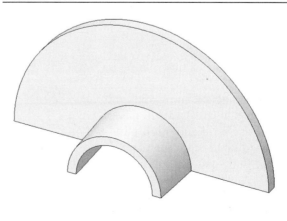

Click the check mark to apply the settings for the section view. Switch to the Bottom View.

The cross-section of the part, as shown in **Figure 4.18**, clearly shows the drafted center hole. The section view will be displayed until turned off with the Section View Tool.

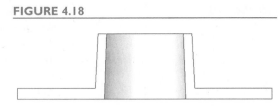

FIGURE 4.18

Click the Section View Tool to return to the display of the entire model.

Fillet

Before adding the ribs and holes, we will fillet several of the sharp edges of the part.

Start by selecting the Fillet Tool.

Since two of the edges are to have the same radius, we can add these radii at the same time.

Set the radius to 0.125 inches, and select the two edges shown in Figure 4.19.

Be sure to select the edge and not the face. If a face is selected, then all of the edges of that face will be filleted.

Click the check mark to apply the fillets. Using a similar procedure, fillet the edge shown in Figure 4.20 with a fillet radius of 0.25 inches.

FIGURE 4.19

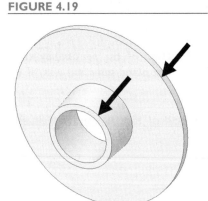

FIGURE 4.20

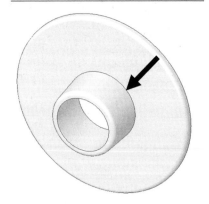

The filleted part is shown in **Figure 4.21**.

FIGURE 4.21

A number of stiffening ribs will now be added to the part. This will be done by creating a single rib and duplicating it a number of times using a circular pattern. The first rib in the pattern will now be created.

Sketch

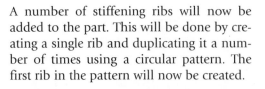
Sketch

Select the Top Plane from the Feature-Manager. Select the Sketch Tool from the Sketch group of the CommandManager to open a sketch. Choose the Bottom View.

FIGURE 4.22

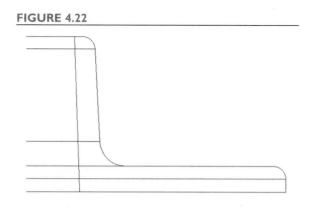

Choose the Wireframe Tool. Zoom in on the right side of the part, as shown in Figure 4.22.

Since the rib will blend into the fillet radii, we need to select the intersections of the radii with the plane. While the edge of the solid part appears to be a line when viewed from this perspective, there is no physical sketch line associated with it; however, we can construct a line coincident with this projected solid edge by using the Convert Entities Tool.

Move the cursor to the intersection of the top fillet and the plane. When you have positioned the cursor at the appropriate location, the silhouette symbol will appear (Figure 4.23). Click to select this silhouette.

FIGURE 4.23

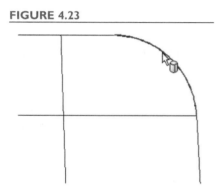

With the silhouette selected, click the Convert Entities Tool.

This will add to your sketch an arc that is coincident with the silhouette of the fillet.

Do the same for the other fillet, so that there are now two arcs in the active sketch, as shown in Figure 4.24.

Select the Line Tool. Move the cursor over the top arc so that the coincident relation icon appears, as shown in Figure 4.25, indicating that the endpoint of the line will snap to the arc. Do not snap to the midpoint of the arc.

FIGURE 4.24

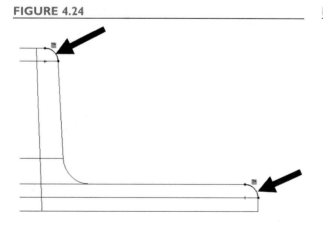

FIGURE 4.25

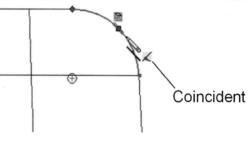

Coincident

Click and drag a line to the other arc. Place the endpoint so that the coincident and tangent relation icons appear, as shown in Figure 4.26. Press esc to turn off the Line Tool.

Zoom in on the fillet at the top of the part, as shown in Figure 4.27. A tangent relation should have been added automatically to the arc and the line. If the relation did not add automatically, then add it manually by selecting both entities (use the ctrl key to select more than one entity) and adding a tangent relation in the PropertyManager.

We will now trim away the portions of the arcs that are not needed in the sketch.

To see the sketch entities more clearly, choose the Shaded Display Tool (without the edges shown). As shown in Figure 4.28, the sketch entities are easy to see if the part edges are not shown.

Zoom in on the intersection of one of the arcs and the line. Select the Trim Entities Tool. Choose "Trim to closest" as the trim option, as shown in Figure 4.29. Click to trim the portion of the arc to be removed, as shown in Figure 4.30.

FIGURE 4.26

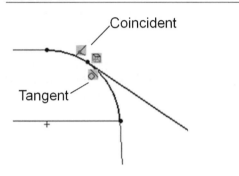

FIGURE 4.27

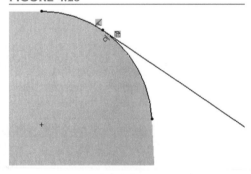

FIGURE 4.28

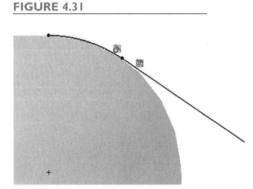

FIGURE 4.29

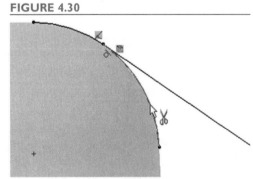

The result of the trimming operation is shown in Figure 4.31.

FIGURE 4.30

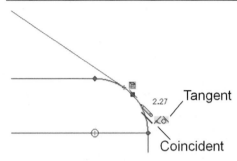

FIGURE 4.31

FIGURE 4.32

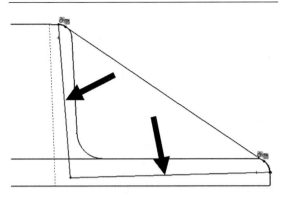

Repeat this process on the other arc/line intersection.

Choose the Wireframe with hidden edges displayed mode. Add the two lines indicated in Figure 4.32 to close the sketch contour. (The two lines do not have to be vertical and horizontal, but should both lie within the edges of the part, so that there will be no gaps when the sketch is extruded into a solid rib.)

Features

Select the Extruded Boss/Base Tool from the Features group of the Command-Manager. Extrude the rib with a Mid-Plane Extrusion with a thickness of 0.125 inches.

Extruded Boss/Base

FIGURE 4.33

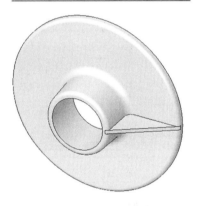

The result is shown in Figure 4.33.

Since this is a molded part, we will need to add a draft to the rib. However, unlike the base feature and the first extruded boss, the necessary draft on the rib is not in the same direction as the extrusion; therefore, the draft on the rib will be added as a secondary operation.

Select the Draft Tool.

Draft

The Draft PropertyManager will appear. First we must specify a neutral plane, from where the draft originates. The Neutral Plane box will be highlighted pink.

Select the top of the flange as the neutral plane. Be sure that you select the face, as indicated by the square symbol.

FIGURE 4.34

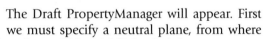

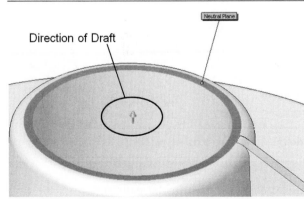

Direction of Draft

The arrow points in the direction for which the thickness decreases (see Figure 4.34). Therefore, this draft is in the correct direction.

In the Draft PropertyManager, click on the box for the Faces to Draft.

The Faces to Draft box will be highlighted in pink.

Select one side face of the rib. Use the Rotate View Tool to rotate the view and select the face on the other side of the rib also. The selected faces will be highlighted, as shown in Figure 4.35.

FIGURE 4.35

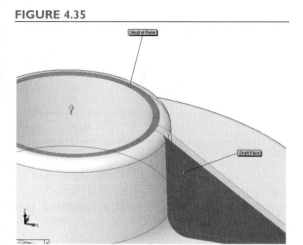

Set the draft angle at 2 degrees, as shown in Figure 4.36, and click the check mark.

The effect of the draft can be seen clearly from the front view, as shown in Figure 4.37.

FIGURE 4.36

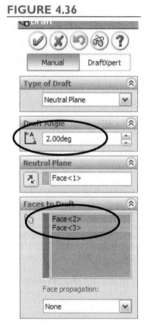

FIGURE 4.37

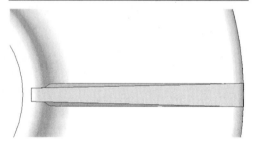

FIGURE 4.38

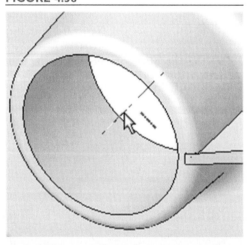

Select the Circular Pattern Tool. Select View: Temporary Axes from the main menu.

Click on the center axis to define it as the axis of rotation, as shown in Figure 4.38.

Both the rib *and* the draft must be copied in the circular pattern.

Click in the "Features to Pattern" box to activate it, and select both the rib (Extrude3) and the draft from the FeatureManager, as shown in Figure 4.39.

(It may be necessary to click on the plus sign next to the part name to expand the fly-out FeatureManager.)

Check the "Equal Spacing" box. Set the number of instances to 6, and click on the check mark to complete the pattern.

The resulting part is shown in **Figure 4.40**.

FIGURE 4.39

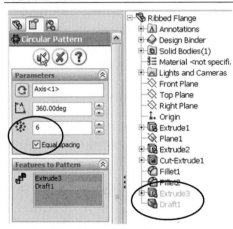

FIGURE 4.40

FIGURE 4.41

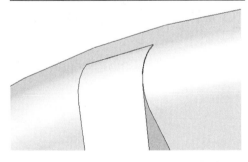

While the geometry of the flange appears to be satisfactory, there is an area where the faces do not blend smoothly. This mismatch occurs at the intersection between the rib and the fillet, as shown in **Figure 4.41**. Note that we have a flat part (the rib) mating with a curved part (the fillet). Although they match perfectly at the mid-plane of the rib, as the rib is extruded outward its surface is slightly higher than the fillet's. Although the mismatch is small, this type of mismatch can result in errors when exporting the geometry to a rapid prototyping system, tool path program, or finite element program.

FIGURE 4.42

One way to remove the mismatch is to cut away the high surfaces of the rib. Think of this operation as sweeping a cutting tool around the part. We will want our tool to match the contour of the rib mid-plane. This is most easily done by copying the sketch that was used to create the rib.

In the FeatureManager, click on the plus sign beside the rib (Extrude3) to display the sketch used to create the rib. Select the sketch by name (Figure 4.42). From the main menu, select Edit: Copy.

DESIGN INTENT Using an Underdefined Sketch

When we copied the sketch used to create the rib, the new sketch was underdefined. This is because entities in the original sketch were linked to the silhouettes of the flange edges, but the copied sketch entities were not. The new sketch could not be recreated in the same way as the original sketch, because the silhouette edges were changed when the rib was extruded. One method of using a fully defined sketch for the second sketch would be to create the sketch in the Right Plane rather than the Top Plane. Since there is no rib at that location, the silhouette edges could be used to define the sketch entities. However, if the number of ribs is changed later to four or eight, then an error would result because the silhouette edges would not be present.

While ideally we would like to be able to change any parameters of a model and have it rebuild correctly, sometimes that result is difficult to achieve. The intent when creating this part is to allow the number of ribs and holes to be changed. Our method of creating the part allows this intent to be realized.

Select the Top Plane, and select Edit: Paste from the main menu.

A new sketch that is identical to the one used to create the rib is placed in the Top Plane, as shown in **Figure 4.43**.

FIGURE 4.43

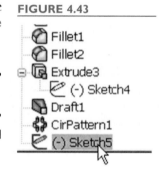

Right-click on the new sketch in the FeatureManager, and select Edit Sketch.

Add the lines shown to complete the "cutting tool" geometry as shown in Figure 4.44, including a vertical centerline from the origin.

Features

Select the Revolved Cut Tool from the Features group of the CommandManager.

FIGURE 4.44

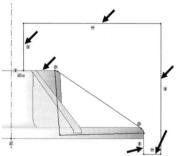

Revolved
Cut

In the PropertyManager, a default angle of 360 degrees is set, as shown in **Figure 4.45**. However, no preview of the cut is shown in the graphics area. This is because there is more than one closed contour within the sketch. We could remove the lines from the original sketch that are not needed in the new sketch, but an easier method is to simply identify the portion of the sketch that is to be used for the new feature. Note that in the PropertyManager, the box labeled "Selected Contours" is highlighted.

FIGURE 4.45

FIGURE 4.46

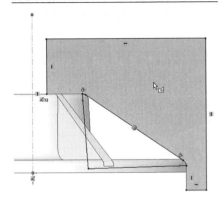

Click in the region of the sketch that makes up the "cutter" to be revolved, as shown in Figure 4.46. Click the mark to complete the cut.

The result is a smooth transition in the problem areas, as shown in Figure 4.47. Note that the top of the rib is no longer flat, but rather has a slight curvature now.

The holes will now be added.

Select the face shown in Figure 4.48.

FIGURE 4.47

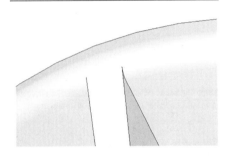

FIGURE 4.48

Select the Circle Tool from the Sketch group of the CommandManager. Draw a circle centered at the origin. Check the "For construction" box in the PropertyManager. Select the Smart Dimension Tool, and dimension the circle diameter as 4.5 inches, as shown in Figure 4.49.

Select the Centerline Tool and draw two centerlines, both originating from the origin. One of the centerlines should be horizontal and the other diagonal, as shown in Figure 4.50. Select the Smart Dimension Tool and add a 30-degree angular dimension between the centerlines.

FIGURE 4.49

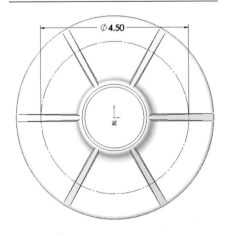

FIGURE 4.50

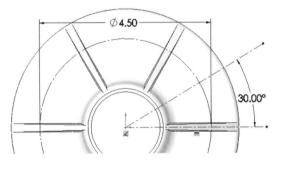

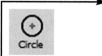

Select the Circle Tool. Move the cursor to the intersection of the construction circle and the diagonal centerline, so that the intersection icon appears, as shown in Figure 4.51.

Drag out a circle. Select the Smart Dimension Tool and add a 0.375-inch diameter dimension to the circle, as shown in Figure 4.52.

FIGURE 4.51   FIGURE 4.52

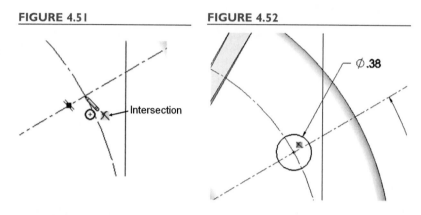

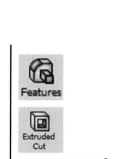

Select the Extruded Cut Tool from the Features group of the CommandManager. Set the type as Through All, and click the check mark to create the first hole.

Select the Circular Pattern Tool. Create a six-hole pattern.

The finished part is shown in **Figure 4.53**.

In the next section, we will add equations to link the rib and hole patterns. This will be easier to do if we rename these features.

In the FeatureManager, rename the extrusion defining the first rib "Rib," the first circular pattern "Rib Pattern," the first bolt hole "Bolt Hole," and the second circular pattern "Hole Pattern," as shown in Figure 4.54. Save the part.

FIGURE 4.53   FIGURE 4.54

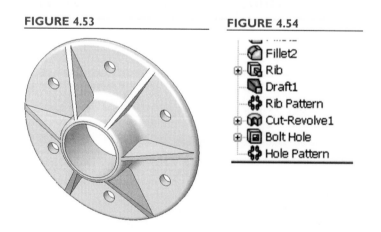

- Fillet2
- Rib
- Draft1
- Rib Pattern
- Cut-Revolve1
- Bolt Hole
- Hole Pattern

4.2   Creation of Parametric Equations

The use of parametric equations embedded in models to control dimensions is a powerful engineering tool. These equations can be used to embed design intelligence directly into solid models. In this section, the flange created in Section 4.1 will be modified to include parametric equations relating the hole pattern to the rib pattern.

With the flange model open, select Tools: Equations from the main menu.

The Equations dialog box will appear.

In the Equations dialog box, click the Add button, as shown in Figure 4.55.

FIGURE 4.55

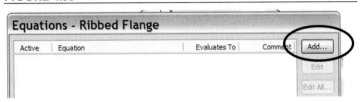

The Add Equation dialog box will appear, as shown in **Figure 4.56**. This dialog box allows for equations relating model parameters to one another to be added to the model.

Double-click on the Hole Pattern in the FeatureManager.

This will display the parameters (6 holes, 360° spacing) in the model window.

Click on the "6" parameter (denoting the number of instances) in the model window, as shown in Figure 4.57.

FIGURE 4.56

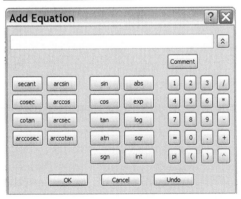

FIGURE 4.57

Note that the symbol denoting this parameter ("D1@Hole Pattern") now appears in the Add Equation dialog box. We can now establish a parametric relationship driving this parameter (the number of holes in the pattern) with another parameter in the model. When considering our design intent, the number of holes in the pattern is not necessarily an independent design choice; most likely, we simply want to ensure that there is one hole centered between each pair of stiffening ribs. Therefore, we will establish a parametric equation tying the number of holes in the pattern directly to the number of ribs in the Rib Pattern.

Click on the equal sign in the equation box, as shown in Figure 4.58.

Since the parameter representing the number of holes in the Hole Pattern is on the left side of this equal sign, the number of holes is a driven parameter; whatever expression is entered on the right side of the equal sign will determine its value. Note that since this value is now a driven parameter, it cannot be directly modified anymore.

FIGURE 4.58

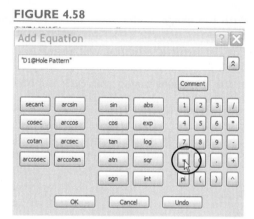

The right side of the equation will now be added.

Double-click on the Rib Pattern to display the parameters associated with it. Click on the "6," as shown in Figure 4.59, to complete the equation.

The equation is shown in Figure 4.60.

Select OK to add the equation. The Equations dialog box now shows the equation and the value that is calculated for the equation (6), as shown in Figure 4.61. Click OK to close the dialog box.

FIGURE 4.59

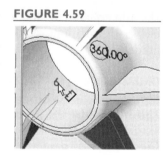

FIGURE 4.60

Add Equation

"D1@Hole Pattern" = "D1@Rib Pattern"

FIGURE 4.61

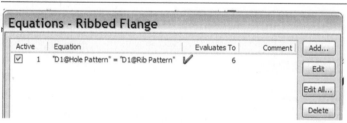

Equations - Ribbed Flange

Active	Equation		Evaluates To	Comment
☑ 1	"D1@Hole Pattern" = "D1@Rib Pattern"	✓	6	

Add...
Edit
Edit All...
Delete

This equation establishes a parametric relation that ties the number of holes in the hole pattern directly to the number of ribs in the rib pattern. We will test the equation at this point.

Double-click the Rib Pattern to display its parameters, and double-click on the value "6" (the number of ribs in the pattern) and change it to "3." Click the check mark, and then click the Rebuild Tool to rebuild the model.

FIGURE 4.62

The model will be rebuilt, with the Rib Pattern modified and the driven Hole Pattern modified as well, as shown in Figure 4.62.

While the number of holes is correctly tied to the number of ribs, our design intent may not be satisfied by this model. Note that the angular location of the holes was set at 30 degrees from the center of a rib; this centered the hole between two ribs when there were six ribs in the pattern, but it no longer provides for centering of the holes when the number of ribs is modified. We will create a new parametric equation to establish the relationship required by our design intent; the equation will drive the angular dimension of the holes so that they are centered between the ribs.

From the main menu, select Tools: Equations. In the Equations dialog box, click Add. Double-click the Bolt Hole in the FeatureManager to display the dimensions associated with the bolt hole.

The angular spacing between ribs is 360 degrees divided by the number of ribs. The first hole is located at one-half of this value away from the first rib. Therefore, the equation required to set the angular dimension to the desired value will be:

Angular Dimension = 1/2 (360/Number of Ribs) or

Angular Dimension = 180/Number of Ribs

FIGURE 4.63

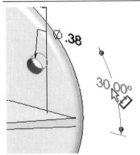

With the hole dimensions still displayed, select the angular dimension locating the hole, as shown in Figure 4.63. In the Add Equation dialog box, click the "=" sign. Type the number 180, and click the "/" sign.

Double-click on the Rib Pattern in the Feature-Manager to display the associated parameters. Select the parameter that represents the number of ribs by clicking on the number 3 in the model window, as shown in Figure 4.64.

FIGURE 4.64

The new equation should be as shown in Figure 4.65.

FIGURE 4.65

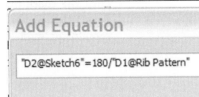

Add Equation

"D2@Sketch6"=180/"D1@Rib Pattern"

Click OK to close the Add Equation dialog box.

The Equations box confirms that the dimension will equal 60 degrees with the current number of ribs (3), as shown in **Figure 4.66**.

FIGURE 4.66

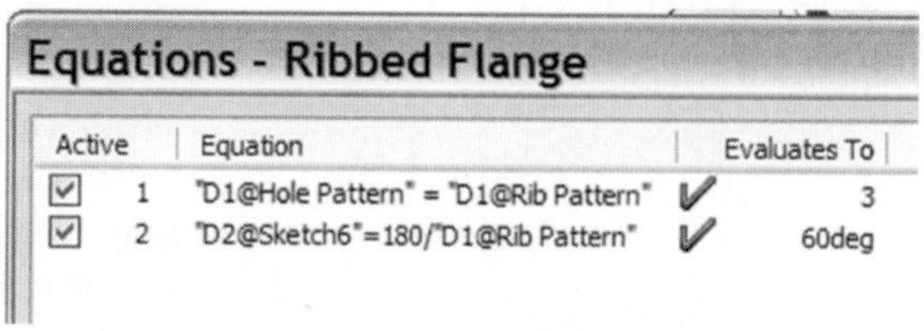

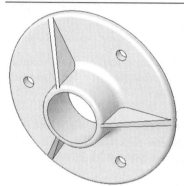

Active	Equation		Evaluates To
☑ 1	"D1@Hole Pattern" = "D1@Rib Pattern"	✓	3
☑ 2	"D2@Sketch6"=180/"D1@Rib Pattern"	✓	60deg

Click OK to close the Equations box and then rebuild the model.

The result is shown in **Figure 4.67**.

FIGURE 4.67

Change the number of ribs to other values and check to see that the number and locations of the holes change in a consistent manner.

Another example is shown in **Figure 4.68**.

Note that there is a difference between *driving* and *driven* parameters. In this example, the number of ribs is a free design choice, and is therefore a driving parameter. As such, it appears only on the right side of the equal sign in parametric equations. Conversely, the number of holes and the angular hole location are driven parameters; they are determined by the choice of number of ribs, and appear on the left side of the equal sign in parametric equations. Since their values are set by the values established by the driving parameters, driven parameters cannot be modified directly in the model.

FIGURE 4.68

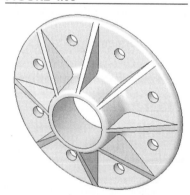

Perform the following demonstration to verify this.

Double-click on the Hole Pattern in the FeatureManager to display the associated parameters in the model window. Double-click on number of holes in the pattern, to try and change the value.

FIGURE 4.69

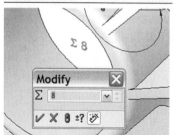

The "Σ" symbol displayed beside the value (see **Figure 4.69**) indicates that the dimension is controlled by an equation and cannot be changed.

Click the check mark to close the message box. Reset the number of ribs and holes to six, rebuild the model, and save the part file.

4.3 Modeling Tutorial: Cap Screw with Design Table

Note: This tutorial requires Microsoft Excel to be installed on your computer.

In this section, we will create a family of similar parts. Many parts are defined this way, especially common parts such as fasteners, washers, seal rings, and so on. Rather than creating separate model files and drawings for every different part, a single part with multiple configurations is made. A single drawing can be made to define the parameters of all of the different configurations. The specifications of the dimensions that define each configuration are contained in a spreadsheet called a *design table*.

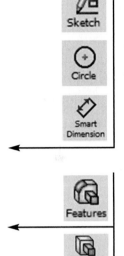

FIGURE 4.70

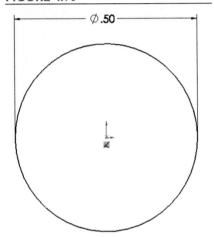

Open a new part. Select the Right Plane from the FeatureManager, and select the Circle Tool from the Sketch group of the CommandManager. Draw a circle centered at the origin. Select the Smart Dimension Tool, and dimension the diameter of the circle as 0.50 inches, as shown in Figure 4.70.

Select the Extruded Boss/Base Tool from the Features Group of the Command-Manager, and extrude the circle 1.50 inches, in the direction shown in Figure 4.71.

Select the face shown in Figure 4.72.

FIGURE 4.71

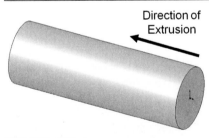

Direction of Extrusion

FIGURE 4.72

FIGURE 4.73

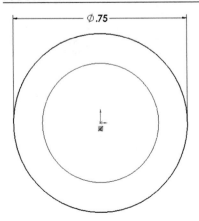

Select the Circle Tool from the Sketch group of the CommandManager. Draw a circle centered at the origin. Select the Smart Dimension Tool and dimension the diameter of the circle as 0.75 inches, as shown in Figure 4.73.

Features

Extruded
Boss/Base

Select the Extruded Boss/Base Tool from the Features Group of the CommandManager, and extrude the circle 0.50 inches to form the head of the screw, as shown in Figure 4.74.

Select the top of the screw head, as shown in Figure 4.75.

FIGURE 4.74

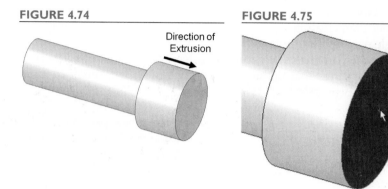

Direction of
Extrusion

FIGURE 4.75

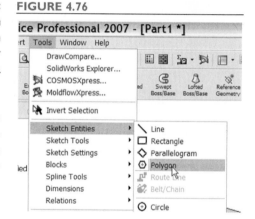

From the main menu, select Tools: Sketch Entities: Polygon, as shown in Figure 4.76. Drag out a polygon from the origin, as shown in Figure 4.77. By default, the number of sides is six (a hexagon).

Press the esc key to turn off the Polygon Tool, and click on one of the sides of the hexagon to select it. In the PropertyManager, add a Horizontal relation to the side.

The hexagon will appear as in Figure 4.78. Note the horizontal relation icon.

FIGURE 4.76

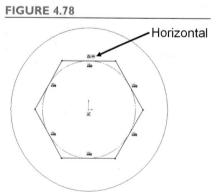

Sketch

Smart
Dimension

Select the Smart Dimension Tool from the Sketch group of the CommandManager, and add a 0.375-inch dimension between two opposite sides of the hexagon, as shown in Figure 4.79.

FIGURE 4.77

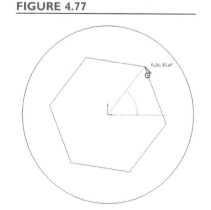

FIGURE 4.78

Horizontal

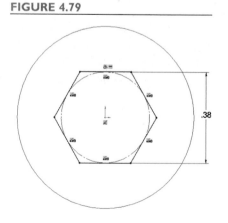

FIGURE 4.79

FIGURE 4.80

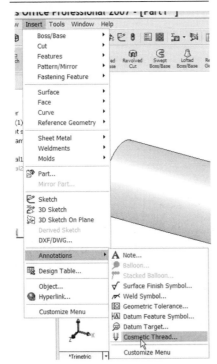

The sketch is now fully defined.

Select the Extruded Cut Tool from the Features group of the CommandManager, and extrude a cut 0.245 inches deep to form the hex socket in the head, as shown in Figure 4.80.

Features

Extruded
Cut

Screw threads are rarely modeled as solid features, since they can be cumbersome to create and can significantly slow down the performance of your computer. Also, since they are standardized, the thread profiles are not required in order to specify them on a drawing. Rather, *cosmetic threads*, graphical features used to show the threaded regions, are much more commonly used. Cosmetic threads can be added to any cylindrical feature.

FIGURE 4.81

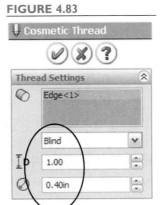

Select the edge where the threads will begin, as shown in Figure 4.81.

Select Insert: Annotations: Cosmetic Thread from the main menu, as shown in Figure 4.82.

Set the thread length as 1.00 inch, and the minor diameter as 0.40 inches, as shown in Figure 4.83. Click the check mark to add the thread. Switch to the front view. The resulting thread display is shown in Figure 4.84.

FIGURE 4.82

FIGURE 4.83

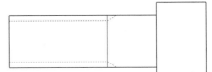

FIGURE 4.84

The minor diameter is the diameter at the "root" of the thread. The actual minor diameter value of a UNF (unified series fine) 1/2-inch thread is 0.408 inches. Since the minor diameter of the cosmetic thread is only for display purposes, using an approximate value is acceptable.

If preferred, the cosmetic thread can be displayed with a shaded thread pattern on the surface rather than with the dashed lines shown in **Figure 4.84**. If you want to change the display mode of the cosmetic thread, choose Tools: Options from the main menu, and under the Document Properties tab, click on Annotations Display. Click on the "Shaded cosmetic threads" box, as shown in **Figure 4.85**. The resulting display is shown in **Figure 4.86**.

FIGURE 4.85

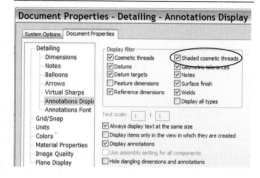

Note that some limited-release versions of the software may not support the display of shaded threads.

The definition of the thread appears in the FeatureManager, attached to the cylindrical feature that is to be threaded, as shown in **Figure 4.87**.

FIGURE 4.86   **FIGURE 4.87**

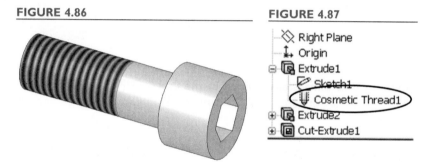

Save the part file.

We have now defined one configuration of the cap screw. To define more configurations, we are going to create a design table.

We will need to access all of the dimensions used to create the part.

To show the dimensions, right-click on Annotations in the FeatureManager, and select Show Feature Dimensions, as shown in Figure 4.88.

FIGURE 4.88

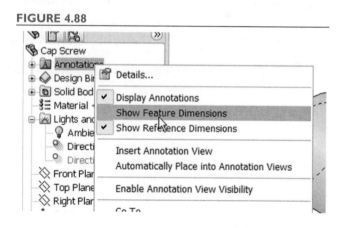

Move the dimensions around the screen so that they are all easily visible, as shown in Figure 4.89.

The isometric view is used here. Since the dimension text is aligned with the plane in which it was created, the isometric view allows for the best display of all dimensions.

If desired, the display of dimensions can be changed so that the text is always oriented relative to the screen by selecting Tools: Options: System Options: Display/ Selection and checking the box labeled "Display dimensions flat to screen."

From the main menu, select Insert: Design Table.

In the PropertyManager, select Blank as the type. Under Edit Control, select the second option, so that dimensions defined in the table cannot be edited outside of the table. Clear all of the options for automatically adding new rows and columns, as shown in Figure 4.90. Click the check mark to begin creation of the design table.

A window containing a Microsoft Excel spreadsheet appears in the modeling area. (Note: Be careful not to click in the white area of the modeling area while editing the design table. Doing so will close the design table. If you accidentally close the design table before you are finished editing, right-click on the design table in the FeatureManager, and select Edit Table from the menu.)

The first row contains the title of the table. In the second row, beginning with cell B2, the parameters to be specified by the table will be identified.

With cell B2 selected, double-click the 0.50-inch dimension defining the diameter of the shank of the screw, as shown in Figure 4.91.

Note that the SolidWorks name for this dimension, "D1@Sketch1," is shown in cell B2, as shown in Figure 4.92. Also, the value for this dimension is shown in cell B3.

FIGURE 4.89

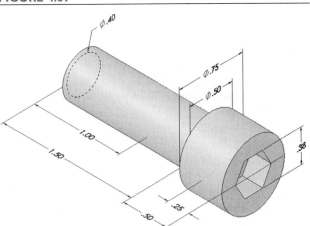

FIGURE 4.90

FIGURE 4.91

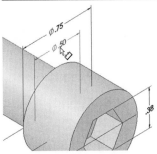

FIGURE 4.92

	A	B	C	D
1	Design Table for: Cap Screw			
2		D1@Sketch1		
3	First Instance	0.5		
4				
5				

With cell C2 highlighted, double-click the 1.5-inch dimension defining the length of the bolt. Repeat for these other dimensions, as shown in Figure 4.93:

FIGURE 4.93

	A	B	C	D	E	F	G	H
1	Design Table for: Cap Screw							
2		D1@Sketch1	D1@Extrude1	D1@Sketch2	D1@Extrude2	D1@Sketch3	D1@Cut-Extrude1	D1@Cosmetic Thread1
3	First Instance	0.5	1.5	0.75	0.5	0.375	0.245	1

D2: Head diameter (0.75 in.)
E2: Head height (0.50 in.)
F2: Hex width (0.375 in.)
G2: Hex depth (0.245 in.)
H2: Thread length (1.00 in.)

The dimension names assigned by the program are not descriptive of the functions of the dimensions. We can add descriptive names in a new row (these descriptive names will be especially helpful if we include the design table in a drawing, as we will do later in this tutorial).

Right-click on the "3" defining the row number of the spreadsheet, and select Insert from the menu, as shown in Figure 4.94.

FIGURE 4.94

	A	B	C	D
1	Design Table for: Cap Screw			
2		D1@Sketch1	D1@Extrude1	D1@Sketch:
				0.7

- Cut
- Copy
- Paste
- Paste Special...
- Insert
- Delete

In the new row, type the descriptive name in each column, as shown in Figure 4.95. **Be sure to leave cell A3 blank.**

FIGURE 4.95

	A	B	C	D	E	F	G	H
1	Design Table for: Cap Screw							
2		D1@Sketch1	D1@Extrude1	D1@Sketch2	D1@Extrude2	D1@Sketch3	D1@Cut-Extrude1	D1@Cosmetic Thread1
3		Diameter	Length	Head Diameter	Head Height	Hex Width	Hex Depth	Thread Length
4	First Instance	0.5	1.5	0.75	0.5	0.375	0.245	1

Below the row containing the SolidWorks dimension names, Column A is reserved for the name of each part configuration.

Click cell A4, and type the name "Part 101," as shown in Figure 4.96. **Enter "Part 102" and "Part 103" in cells A5 and A6, respectively. Enter the values shown in** Figure 4.97 **as the dimensions for the two new configurations.**

FIGURE 4.96

	A	B
1	Design Table for: Cap Screw	
2		D1@Sketch1
3		Diameter
4	Part 101	0.5
5		

FIGURE 4.97

	A	B	C	D	E	F	G	H
1	Design Table for: Cap Screw							
2		D1@Sketch1	D1@Extrude1	D1@Sketch2	D1@Extrude2	D1@Sketch3	D1@Cut-Extrude1	D1@Cosmetic Thread1
3		Diameter	Length	Head Diameter	Head Height	Hex Width	Hex Depth	Thread Length
4	Part 101	0.5	1.5	0.75	0.5	0.375	0.245	1
5	Part 102	0.75	2	1.125	0.75	0.635	0.37	1.5
6	Part 103	1	3	1.5	1	0.75	0.495	2

FIGURE 4.98

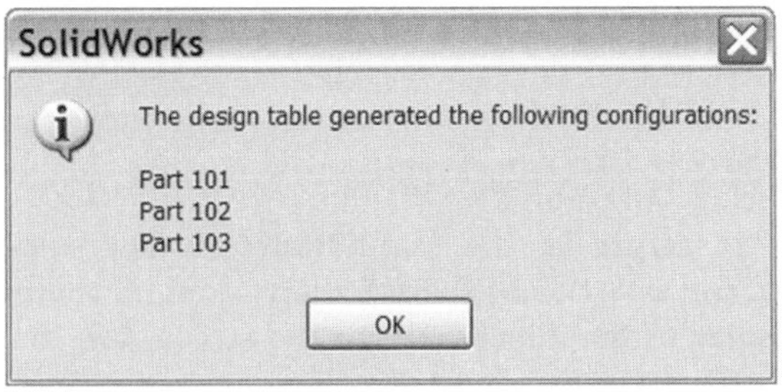
SolidWorks
The design table generated the following configurations:
Part 101
Part 102
Part 103
OK

Click in the white space in the modeling window, outside of the spreadsheet window. This will cause the design table to close, and a message will be displayed that indicates the new configurations have been created, as shown in Figure 4.98. Click OK.

Note that the part has not changed on the screen. That is because the default configuration is the one with the dimensions used to model the part originally. To view the new configurations created from the design table, we need to use the ConfigurationManager.

At the top of the FeatureManager, there are tabs corresponding to the FeatureManager, PropertyManager, and ConfigurationManager. (There could be other tabs as well, if certain add-ins are present.) Click on the icon representing the ConfigurationManager, as shown in Figure 4.99.

In the ConfigurationManager, double-click on Part 103, as shown in Figure 4.100.

The part is rebuilt to the dimensions specified in the design table for Part 103, as shown in Figure 4.101. Dimensions controlled by the design table may appear in a different color on your screen. We will see how to define the color for these dimensions later in this tutorial

FIGURE 4.99

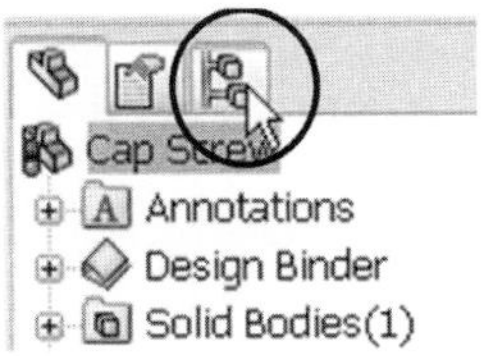
Cap Screw
Annotations
Design Binder
Solid Bodies(1)

FIGURE 4.100

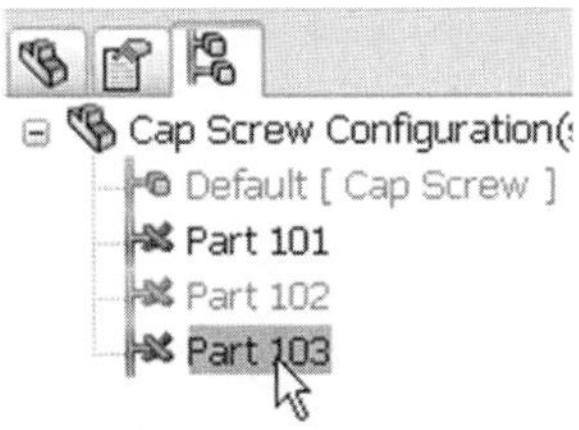
Cap Screw Configuration(
Default [Cap Screw]
Part 101
Part 102
Part 103

FIGURE 4.101

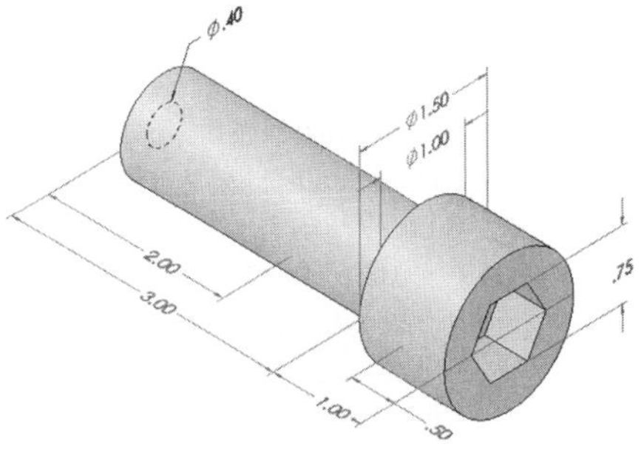
Ø.40
Ø1.50
Ø1.00
2.00
3.00
1.00
.50
.75

One dimension that was left unchanged is the minor thread diameter of the cosmetic thread. Since this is not a dimension used to define the part, we did not include it in the design table. However, we would like to have the display of the cosmetic thread look reasonable on the screen. We can add an equation to control this dimension.

From the main menu, select Tools: Equations.

Click Add to create a new equation. Click on the dimension representing the minor thread diameter (0.400). In the equation box, type "=0.8*" after the name of the minor diameter dimension ("D2@Cosmetic Thread1") and click on the dimension representing the diameter of the bold shank (ϕ1.00). The equation should appear as shown in Figure 4.102.

FIGURE 4.102

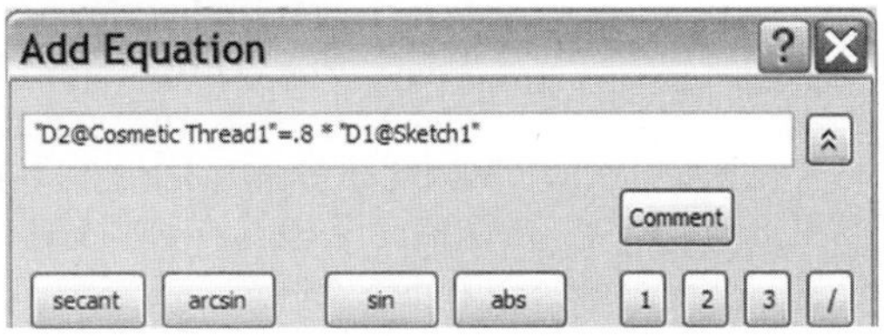
Add Equation
"D2@Cosmetic Thread1"=.8 * "D1@Sketch1"
Comment
secant
arcsin
sin
abs
1
2
3
/

Click OK to add this equation, and OK again to close the Equation box.

Click the Rebuild Tool.

The updated thread diameter is shown in **Figure 4.103**.

Click on the FeatureManager tab to return to the FeatureManager. Right-click Annotations in the FeatureManager, and select Show Feature Dimensions, as shown in Figure 4.104, to turn off the display of the dimensions on the screen. Save the part file.

FIGURE 4.103   FIGURE 4.104

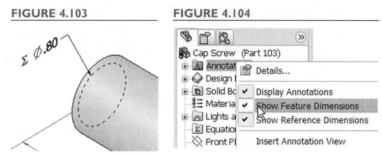

4.4   Incorporating a Design Table in a Drawing

We now will make a single drawing that details all three configurations of the cap screw.

Open a new drawing. Choose an A-size landscape sheet size, and either uncheck the "Display sheet format" box for a plain sheet, or select the sheet format that you created in Chapter 2.

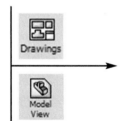

If the Model View command does not start automatically, then select the Model View Tool from the Drawings group of the CommandManager. If desired, check the box labeled "Start command when creating new drawing", as shown in Figure 4.105. Click on the Cap Screw in the Open documents box, or browse to find it. Click the Next arrow in the PropertyManager.

Select "Multiple views," and select the Front and Right views. Choose the wireframe display style with the hidden lines visible, as shown in Figure 4.106.

FIGURE 4.105

Next

FIGURE 4.106

Click the check mark to create the views, which are shown in Figure 4.107.

FIGURE 4.107

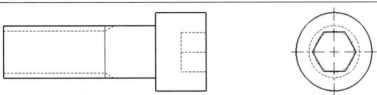

FIGURE 4.107

The model views that are created reflect the configuration that is current when the drawing is created. The configuration used for any model view can be changed by right-clicking on that view and selecting Properties from the menu that appears. For this tutorial, the configuration used is not important.

FIGURE 4.108

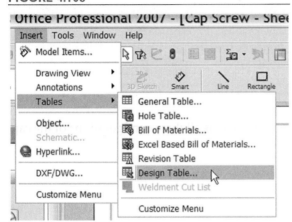

With one of the drawing views selected, select Insert: Tables: Design Table from the main menu, as shown in Figure 4.108.

The design table is inserted into the drawing, as shown in **Figure 4.109**. The design table can be moved on the drawing sheet by clicking and dragging it, but the format of the table is not what we want. There are blank rows and columns visible, dimensions are shown to only the number of decimal places we input, and so on. We will now edit the table to improve its appearance.

FIGURE 4.109

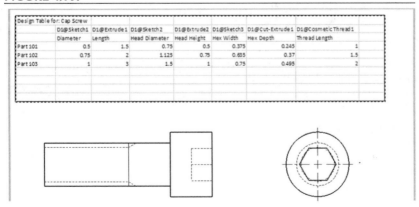

Design Table for: Cap Screw

	D1@Sketch1	D1@Extrude1	D1@Sketch2	D1@Extrude2	D1@Sketch3	D1@Cut-Extrude1	D1@Cosmetic Thread1
	Diameter	Length	Head Diameter	Head Height	Hex Width	Hex Depth	Thread Length
Part 101	0.5	1.5	0.75	0.5	0.375	0.245	1
Part 102	0.75	2	1.125	0.75	0.635	0.37	1.5
Part 103	1	3	1.5	1	0.75	0.495	2

Double-click on the design table, and you will be taken back to the part screen, with the spreadsheet open in a window, as shown in Figure 4.110.

FIGURE 4.110

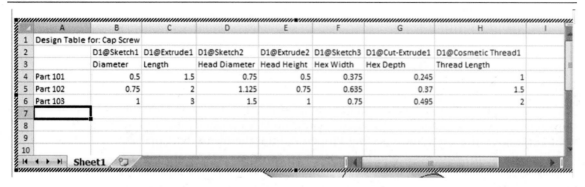

Remember that the design table is a Microsoft Excel spreadsheet, and we will be editing it the same way we would edit any other Excel spreadsheet. To begin, the first two rows do not need to be displayed on the drawing. We cannot delete them, since they contain information necessary to the design table, but we can hide them.

Click and hold the mouse key on the number 1 on the left side of the spreadsheet, and drag the cursor down onto the 2 and release. Rows 1 and 2 will be highlighted. Right-click, and select Hide from the menu, as shown in Figure 4.111.

Select Columns B–H. Click the Center icon on the Excel menu, as shown in Figure 4.112.

FIGURE 4.111

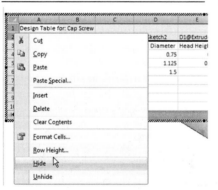

FIGURE 4.112

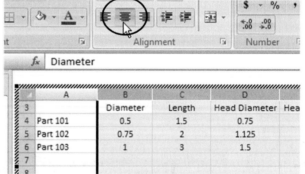

Click on the blank cell in the upper-left corner, which selects the entire spreadsheet. Increase the font size to 14 pt from the pull-down menu, as shown in Figure 4.113. You may also change the font, if desired.

FIGURE 4.113

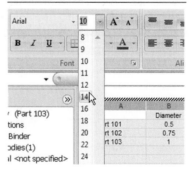

FIGURE 4.114

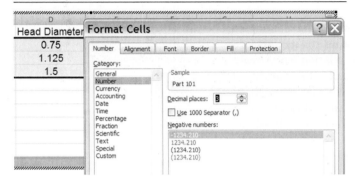

Adjust the column width of each column by clicking and dragging on the line between two column numbers, as shown in Figure 4.114.

Select the cells containing numbers by clicking and dragging across the range of cells. Right-click and choose Format Cells from the menu. Under the Number tab, set the number of decimal places to 3, as shown in Figure 4.115.

FIGURE 4.115

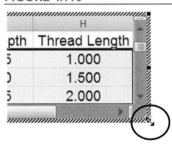

FIGURE 4.116

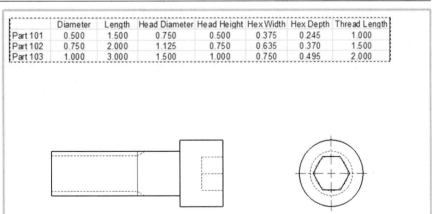

Finally, move the handles on the bottom and right of the spreadsheet so that only cells with values are displayed, as shown in Figure 4.116.

Click outside of the spreadsheet to close it. From the main menu, select Window and click on the drawing name to return to the drawing.

Click on the Rebuild Tool to update the design table in the drawing, which now appears as shown in Figure 4.117.

FIGURE 4.117

	Diameter	Length	Head Diameter	Head Height	Hex Width	Hex Depth	Thread Length
Part 101	0.500	1.500	0.750	0.500	0.375	0.245	1.000
Part 102	0.750	2.000	1.125	0.750	0.635	0.370	1.500
Part 103	1.000	3.000	1.500	1.000	0.750	0.495	2.000

We will now insert the dimensions from the part into the drawing.

Before adding dimensions to the drawing, we need to add a view. Since the depth of the hex cavity needs to be dimensioned, we will add a section view of the head. This will let us avoid dimensioning a hidden feature. It is good practice to refrain from using hidden lines for dimensioning.

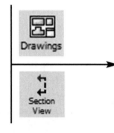

Zoom in on the head of the screw in the front view. Choose the Section View Tool from the Drawings group of the Command-Manager. Hold the cursor momentarily at the midpoint of the top edge of the head to "wake up" this feature, and then move the cursor to the right, as shown in Figure 4.118. The coincident relation icon should appear, indicating that the cursor is aligned horizontally with the midpoint of the top edge of the head. Click and drag a horizontal line through the head, as shown in Figure 4.119. Note the coincident and horizontal relation icons. When you click to complete the line, you will see a message that a partial section view will be created, as shown in Figure 4.120. Click Yes to complete the view.

FIGURE 4.118

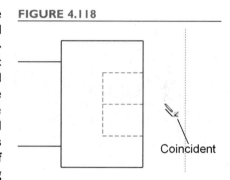

FIGURE 4.119

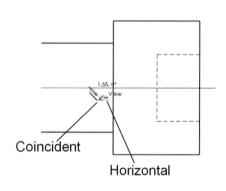

FIGURE 4.120

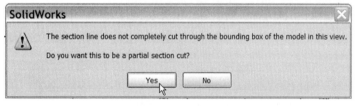

Drag the section view away from the front view and click to place it. Right-click, and choose Alignment: Break Alignment, as shown in Figure 4.121.

FIGURE 4.121

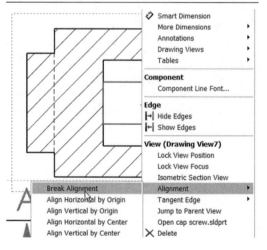

You will now be able to click and drag the section view to any location on the sheet, as shown in Figure 4.122.

FIGURE 4.122

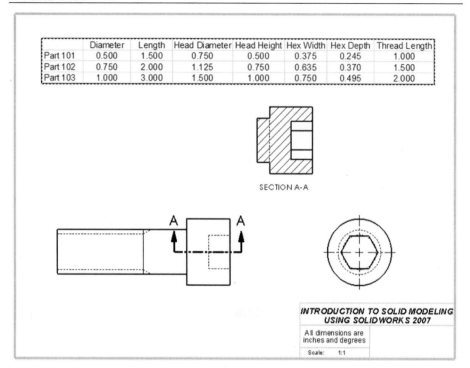

	Diameter	Length	Head Diameter	Head Height	Hex Width	Hex Depth	Thread Length
Part 101	0.500	1.500	0.750	0.500	0.375	0.245	1.000
Part 102	0.750	2.000	1.125	0.750	0.635	0.370	1.500
Part 103	1.000	3.000	1.500	1.000	0.750	0.495	2.000

SECTION A-A

INTRODUCTION TO SOLID MODELING USING SOLIDWORKS 2007

All dimensions are inches and degrees

Scale: 1:1

FIGURE 4.123

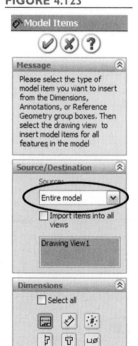

We will now add dimensions to the drawing. Since we want most of the dimensions to appear in the front view, we will import dimensions into that view first.

Select the front view. Select the Model Items Tool from the Annotations group of the CommandManager. In the PropertyManager, select Entire Model as the source, as shown in Figure 4.123. Make sure that the box labeled "Import items into all views" is unchecked. Click the check mark to apply the dimensions.

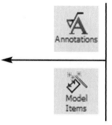

Repeat for the right view and then for the section view, so that all dimensions are imported, as shown in Figure 4.124.

FIGURE 4.124

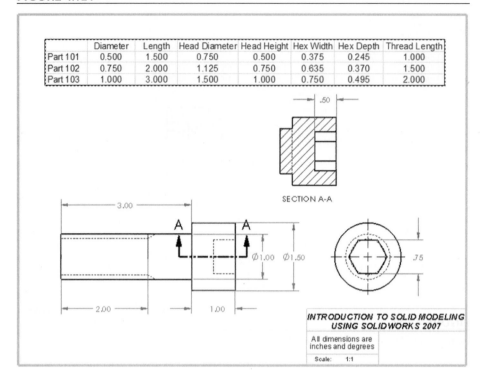

	Diameter	Length	Head Diameter	Head Height	Hex Width	Hex Depth	Thread Length
Part 101	0.500	1.500	0.750	0.500	0.375	0.245	1.000
Part 102	0.750	2.000	1.125	0.750	0.635	0.370	1.500
Part 103	1.000	3.000	1.500	1.000	0.750	0.495	2.000

The dimensions defined by the design table may be shown in a different color than black. (The default color is magenta.) While this may be desirable in the part file, for the drawing we would prefer that all dimensions be displayed in black.

Select Tools: Options from the main menu. Under the System Options tab, select Colors and scroll down the list of entities to find "Dimensions, Controlled by Design Table," as shown in Figure 4.125. Select Edit, and set the color to black.

FIGURE 4.125

Move the dimensions and/or views on the screen so that they are all visible. Move the head diameter dimension to the right view, as shown in Figure 4.126.

(Recall that to move a dimension from one view to another, click and drag it while holding down the shift key.)

The dimensions displayed are those for one configuration. To make this drawing one that defines the dimensions for all configurations, we need to display the dimension names in the drawing views.

FIGURE 4.126

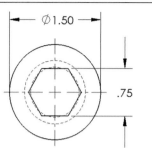

FIGURE 4.127

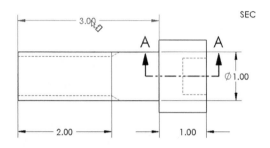

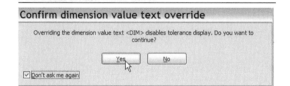

FIGURE 4.129

Confirm dimension value text override

FIGURE 4.130

Click on the dimension defining the length, as shown in Figure 4.127. **In the PropertyManager, replace the "<DIM>" in the Dimension Text box and type in "Length," as shown in** Figure 4.128. **A message will appear, warning you that any tolerances specified for this dimension will not be displayed (see** Figure 4.129). **Check the "Don't ask me again" box, and click Yes.**

Repeat for the other dimensions. Add notes, if desired, to complete the drawing, as shown in Figure 4.130.

FIGURE 4.128

	Diameter	Length	Head Diameter	Head Height	Hex Width	Hex Depth	Thread Length
Part 101	0.500	1.500	0.750	0.500	0.375	0.245	1.000
Part 102	0.750	2.000	1.125	0.750	0.635	0.370	1.500
Part 103	1.000	3.000	1.500	1.000	0.750	0.495	2.000

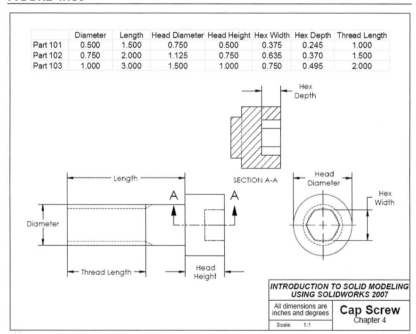

INTRODUCTION TO SOLID MODELING
USING SOLIDWORKS 2007

All dimensions are inches and degrees   **Cap Screw**
Chapter 4

Scale: 1:1

PROBLEMS

P4.1   Consider the flange model developed in Chapter 1. Create a "blank" for this part (without the holes) as shown in **Figure P4.1A**, using the following procedure:

a.   Sketch a 5.5 inch diameter circle on the Top Plane, and extrude it upward 2.25 inches to create a solid cylinder (**Figure P4.1B**).

b.   In the Front Plane, sketch a "cutting tool" to create the flange "blank" from the solid (**Figure P4.1C**).

c.   Use the Cut: Revolve command to create the blank.

FIGURE P4.1A   **FIGURE P4.1B**

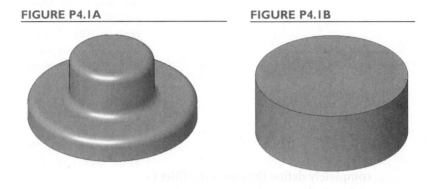

FIGURE P4.1C

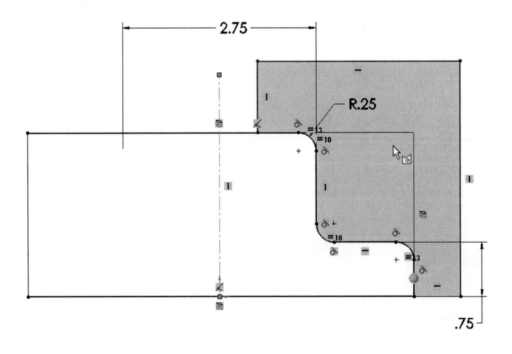

P4.2 Create a solid box as shown in **Figure P4.2A**. Using equations, set the depth $d = 2w$, and the height $h = 3w$, where the width w is the driving dimension. Show the box for a few different values of the driving dimension, as shown in **Figure P4.2B**.

FIGURE P4.2A   **FIGURE P4.2B**

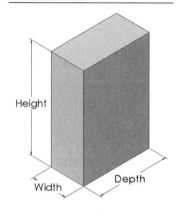

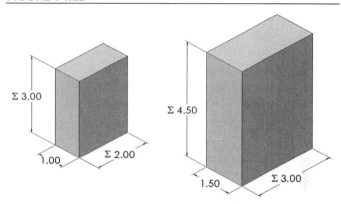

P4.3 Model the bracket shown in **Figure P4.3A**. Use only the dimensions shown in **Figure P4.3B**; use relations and symmetry as required so that these dimensions completely define the part. (The fillet radius, 0.125 inches, is the same for the three fillets.)

FIGURE P4.3A

Add equations to the drawing so that these relationships exist between the dimensions:
1. Height = 0.40 (Width)
2. Leg Width = 1/2 (Height)
3. Hole Spacing = Width minus 2 inches
4. Hole Location = 1/2 (Height minus 0.25 inches)
5. Slot Width = 1/2 (Hole Spacing)
6. Slot Location = 1/2 (Leg Width)

Check to see that the equations work for Width values from 3 to 8 inches.

FIGURE P4.3B

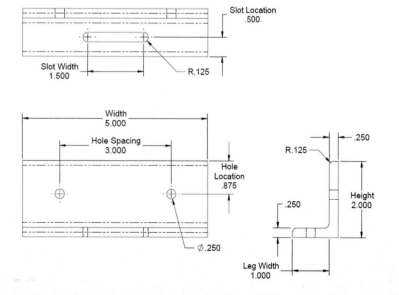

P4.4   In this exercise, you will model a part in which an integer design parameter (number of holes) is controlled by an equation.

    a.   Model the part shown in **Figure P4.4A**. Use a linear pattern to place the second hole. Show all of the dimensions by right-clicking on Annotations in the FeatureManager and clicking on "Show Feature Dimensions."

    b.   Add an equation so that the number of holes is equal to the length of the part (4 inches in the current configuration) divided by two. Therefore, there will be one hole for every 2 inches of length. Show only the dimensions shown in **Figure P4.4B** by right-clicking on each of the other dimensions and selecting "Hide."

    c.   Change the length of the part to 5 inches, as shown in **Figure P4.4C**. Note that the program has rounded the value of the equation (2.5) to the closest integer value (3).

    d.   Add a second equation to change the value of the dimension specifying the location of the first hole so that the holes will be centered on the part, as shown in **Figure P4.4D**.

Experiment with several values of length to show that the equations produce the desired results, as shown in **Figures P4.4E** and **Figure P4.4F**.

FIGURE P4.4A

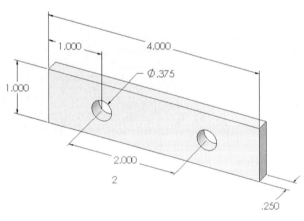

FIGURE P4.4B

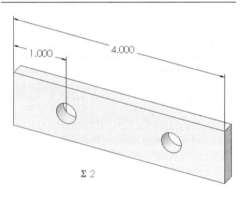

FIGURE P4.4C

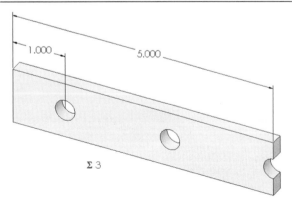

FIGURE P4.4D

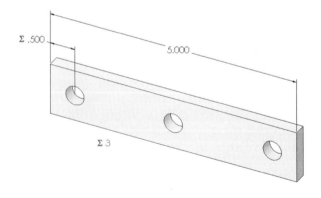

FIGURE P4.4E

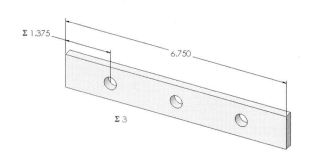

FIGURE P4.4F

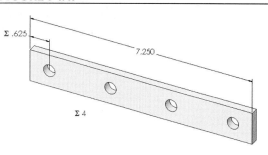

P4.5 Use a design table to create the W18 series of wide-flange shape beams, according to **Figure P4.5** and **Table P4.5**. The model of the beam should be extruded to 36 inches in all configurations.

FIGURE P4.5

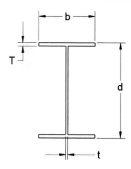

Table P4.5

Designation	Depth d	Flange width b	Flange thickness T	Web thickness t
W18 x 106	18.73	11.200	0.940	0.590
W18 x 76	18.21	11.035	0.680	0.425
W18 x 50	17.99	7.495	0.570	0.355
W18 x 35	17.70	6.000	0.425	0.300

Note: All dimensions in inches.

P4.6 Create a multiconfiguration drawing of the model created in **Figure P4.5**.

P4.7 Make a copy of the flange created in Chapter 1, which is shown in **Figure P4.7A** with some of the dimensions hidden. Create three different configurations of the flange (the flange as created in Chapter 1 will be the first configuration), using both equations and a design table, as detailed below.
  a. Add two equations:
    (1) The boss diameter (2.75 in.) is equal to one-half of the flange diameter (5.50 in.).
    (2) The center hole diameter (1.50 in.) is equal to the boss diameter minus 1.25 inches.
  b. Create a design table to define the dimensions of two additional configurations, as specified in **Table P4.7**.

FIGURE P4.7A

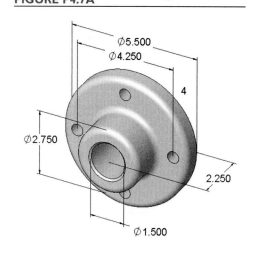

Table P4.7

Flange	Diameter	Height	Bolt circle diameter	Number of bolt holes
Part 1	5.5	2.25	4.25	4
Part 2	7.0	3.00	5.25	6
Part 3	8.0	3.50	6.25	8

Note: All dimensions in inches.

c. Make a 2-D drawing showing the three configurations, with only the dimensions that change shown, as in **Figure P4.7B**. This type of drawing is used often in product literature and catalogs to illustrate the relative sizes of different parts.

Insert three front views and three top views in the drawing. Right-click on each view and select Properties, and select the appropriate named configuration for each view. Hide unwanted dimensions by selecting View: Hide/Show Annotations from the main menu and selecting the dimensions to be hidden. Press the esc key to return to the normal drawing mode.

There are two ways to align the drawing views with each other. To precisely align the views, select a view, right-click, and choose Align: Align Horizontal by Origin, and select another view to align to. Repeat until all views are aligned. If only approximate alignment is needed, turn on the grid display from Tools: Options and use the gridlines to align the views.

FIGURE P4.7B

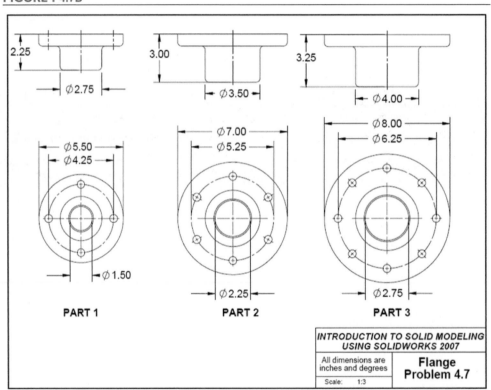

CHAPTER 5

Advanced Concepts in Part Modeling

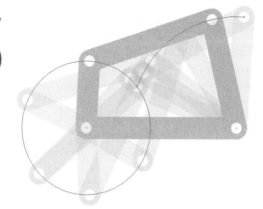

Introduction

The parts that we have made so far have been made primarily with extruded and revolved bases, bosses, and cuts. In this chapter, we will introduce several other tools for creating and modifying parts, including the *Loft*, *Sweep*, and *Shell* Tools.

5.1

A Lofted and Shelled Part

In this exercise, we will construct the business card holder shown in **Figure 5.1**. Note that the top of the part is rounded, while the bottom of the part is rectangular. These dissimilar shapes will be joined into a solid with the Loft Tool. Also, notice that the part is not solid, but rather is hollow underneath, as the view in **Figure 5.2** shows. The Shell Tool allows this type of construction to be easily modeled.

FIGURE 5.1

FIGURE 5.2

Chapter Objectives

In this chapter, you will:

- create a lofted feature from multiple sketches,

- use the Shell Tool to create a thin-wall part,

- learn how to change the order in which features are created and modified,

- create raised letters on a part, and

- create a feature by sweeping a cross-section around a planar or 3-D path.

141

Open a new part. Select the Top Plane, and then select the Rectangle Tool from the Sketch group of the CommandManager. Drag out a rectangle.

Select the Centerline Tool, and add a centerline from one corner of the rectangle to the opposite corner. Press the esc key to turn off the Centerline Tool.

Select the centerline and the origin, and add a Midpoint relation, centering the rectangle about the origin.

Select the Smart Dimension Tool, and dimension the rectangle to be 5.50 inches by 2.00 inches, as shown in Figure 5.3.

FIGURE 5.3

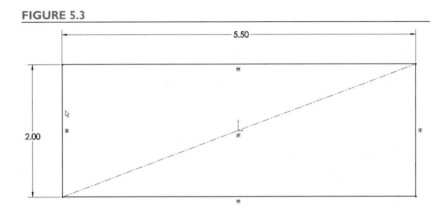

In previous tutorials, upon completing a sketch we have then used a features tool to convert the sketch into a 3-D object. However, a lofted feature requires at least two sketches. Therefore, we will close this sketch and begin the second sketch.

Close the sketch by clicking on the icon indicated in Figure 5.4, in the upper-right corner of the screen.

FIGURE 5.4

The second sketch, which will define the top of the part, will be created in a new plane.

Select the Top Plane from the FeatureManager. Select the Features group of the CommandManager. Click on the Reference Geometry Tool, and choose Plane from the options listed, as shown in Figure 5.5. In the Property-Manager, set the offset distance at 1 inch.

FIGURE 5.5

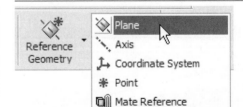

Make sure that the new plane is above the Top Plane, as shown in Figure 5.6 (click on the icon next to the offset distance to change the direction, if necessary), and click the check mark to create the new plane.

FIGURE 5.6

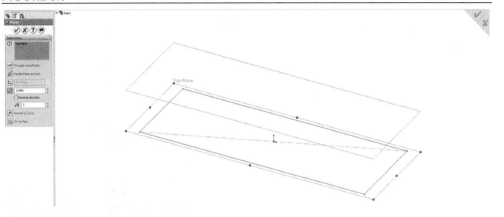

Select the Line Tool from the Sketch Group of the CommandManager.

Draw two horizontal lines, as shown in Figure 5.7, and add an Equal relation to them. Also add a vertical relation between two corresponding endpoints.

Select the Tangent Arc Tool. Drag an arc between corresponding endpoints of the two lines. Be sure to snap to the endpoint of the line for both arc endpoints, as shown in Figure 5.8.

FIGURE 5.7

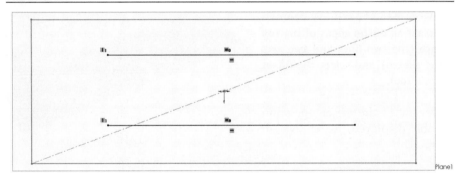

FIGURE 5.8

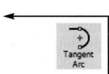

FIGURE 5.9

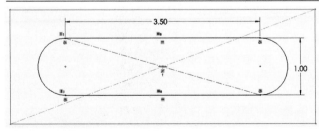

Repeat for the other ends of the lines. Select the Centerline Tool, and add a diagonal centerline. Add a Midpoint relation between the centerline and the origin. Select the Smart Dimension Tool, and add the dimensions shown in Figure 5.9 to fully define the sketch. Close the sketch.

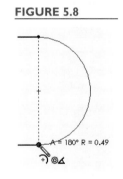

Both of the sketches required for the lofted feature are now in place.

Select the Lofted Boss/Base Tool from the Features group of the CommandManager. Now click on each of the two sketches, near corresponding corners, as shown in Figure 5.10.

The lofted feature will be created based on a "guide curve." The guide curve is created based on the location of the selection of the sketches, as previewed in Figure 5.11. Click the check mark to complete the loft. The resulting part is shown in Figure 5.12.

FIGURE 5.10

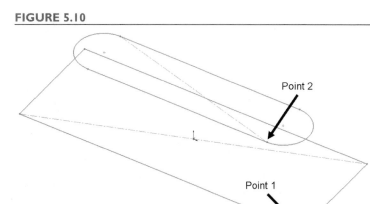

Point 2

Point 1

FIGURE 5.11

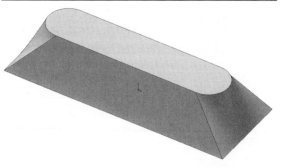

Profile(Sketch2)

Select the top surface of the part. Select the Sketch Tool from the Sketch group of the Command-Manager. With the ctrl key depressed, select all of the edges of the top surface (the two lines and two arcs of the sketch), and select the Offset Entities Tool.

A preview of the offset operation will be displayed, as shown in Figure 5.13.

FIGURE 5.12

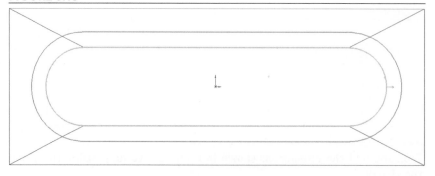

FIGURE 5.13

FIGURE 5.14

In the PropertyManager, set the offset distance as 0.20 inches. Check the Reverse box, as shown in Figure 5.14, so that the offset entities are inside of the edges of the face, as shown in Figure 5.15. Click on the check mark to finish.

FIGURE 5.15

FIGURE 5.16

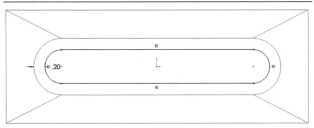

The finished sketch is shown in Figure 5.16. Note that the 0.20-inch offset distance is shown as a dimension that can be edited by double-clicking it.

Before cutting the shape of the sketch into the part, we need to consider the design intent. We want this cut to be blind, so that the cards sit on the bottom of the hole, but we want the cut depth to vary with the overall height of the card holder. Therefore, neither a Blind nor Through All type of cut will work. Rather, we will specify the depth of cut so that the bottom of the cut is a fixed distance above the bottom of the card holder.

FIGURE 5.17

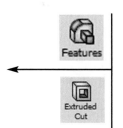

Select the Extruded Cut Tool from the Features group of the CommandManager. Switch to the Trimetric View. In the PropertyManager, set the type of extrusion to Offset From Surface, as shown in Figure 5.17. As the surface, we want to select the bottom face of the part.

To select the bottom surface, we could switch to Bottom view or rotate the model until the bottom view is visible, but in the steps that follow, we will learn a handy technique for selecting a nonvisible surface *without* rotating the model from the trimetric view.

FIGURE 5.18

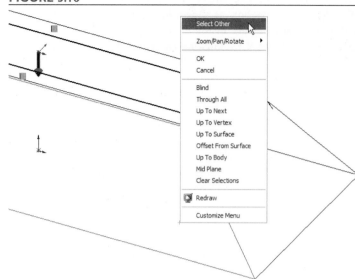

Move the mouse above the bottom face. Do not click the left button; doing so would select the visible outer surface. Right-click, and choose Select Other from the menu, as shown in Figure 5.18.

With the bottom face highlighted, as shown in Figure 5.19, click the left mouse button.

If there were other possible selections available, they could be selected from the pop-up menu that is shown in Figure 5.19.

In the PropertyManager, set the offset distance as 0.125 inches, as shown in Figure 5.20, and click the check mark to complete the cut.

FIGURE 5.19

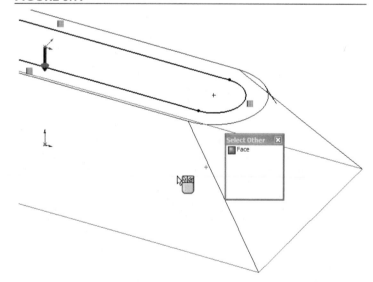

FIGURE 5.20

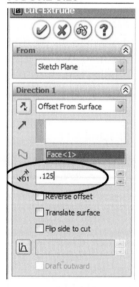

FIGURE 5.21

The resulting geometry is shown in Figure 5.21.

We will now introduce the Shell command. This command is often used with molded plastic parts to create thin-wall geometries. Since the part we are modeling does not need to have any significant strength, making the part solid would be a waste of material. We will make the wall thickness of the part a constant 0.060 inches.

Select the bottom face of the part as the face to be removed, as shown in Figure 5.22. Select the Shell Tool from the Features group of the CommandManager. In the PropertyManager, set the wall thickness to 0.060 inches, as shown in Figure 5.23. Click the check mark to complete the shell operation, the results of which are shown in Figure 5.24.

FIGURE 5.22

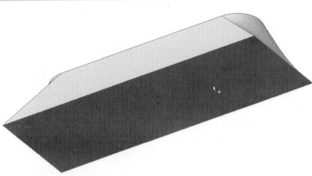

FIGURE 5.23

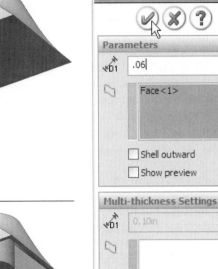

FIGURE 5.24

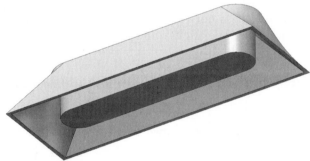

Select the Fillet Tool from the Features group of the CommandManager. In the PropertyManager, set the fillet radius of 0.10 inches. Select the top face, as shown in Figure 5.25, and click the check mark to apply the fillets.

Note that fillets are usually applied to edges, not faces. Selecting a face causes all of the edges of that face to be filleted, as shown in Figure 5.26.

Select the Fillet Tool again. Select one of the edges at the bottom of the cavity as shown in Figure 5.27 (as long as the Tangent propagation box is checked, then the fillet will be extended completely around the bottom edge). Set the radius as 0.050 inches, and click the check mark to apply the fillet.

FIGURE 5.25

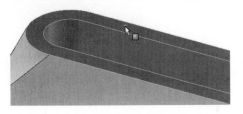

FIGURE 5.26

FIGURE 5.27

Although our part appears to be finished, there is a problem that may not be evident from examining the part from standard views. We will use a section view to get a better look at the problem areas.

Select the Front Plane from the FeatureManager. Select the Section View Tool. Click the check mark, and the cross-section of the part is displayed, as shown in Figure 5.28.

Zooming in on the filleted edges shows the problem. Because the filleting was performed after the shell operation, the wall is thinner than desired at the upper corners, as shown in **Figure 5.29**. (Similarly, the wall is thicker than desired in the lower corners.)

FIGURE 5.28

FIGURE 5.29

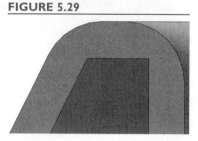

To correct this problem, we could fillet the sharp corners to maintain a constant wall thickness. We could also shell the part *after* creating the fillets. This is the easier way to produce the constant wall thickness. It is not necessary to delete the shell and fillet operations and redo them in the proper order; we can simply reorder them in the FeatureManager.

Click on the Shell in the FeatureManager, as shown in Figure 5.30, and hold down the left mouse button.

Drag the cursor until the arrow points below the two fillets, as shown in Figure 5.31.

Release the mouse button, and the features are reordered, as shown in Figure 5.32.

FIGURE 5.30

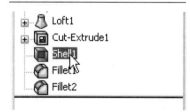

FIGURE 5.31

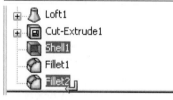

FIGURE 5.32

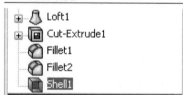

The wall thickness is now constant, as shown in **Figure 5.33**. Note that not all features can be reordered, as some operations will be based on geometries created by prior operations.

FIGURE 5.33

Click on the Section View Tool.

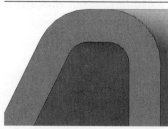

This will toggle off the display of the section view.

Text can be added to a part as a sketch entity and then extruded into raised or embossed letters. We will add a part number in raised letters to the bottom of the part.

FIGURE 5.34

Switch to Bottom View and open a sketch on the flat surface shown in Figure 5.34 **by selecting the Sketch Tool from the Sketch group of the CommandManager.**

FIGURE 5.35

From the main menu, select Tools: Sketch Entities: Text, as shown in Figure 5.35. **In the PropertyManager, type in the text, as shown in** Figure 5.36 **(it is not necessary to select**

FIGURE 5.36

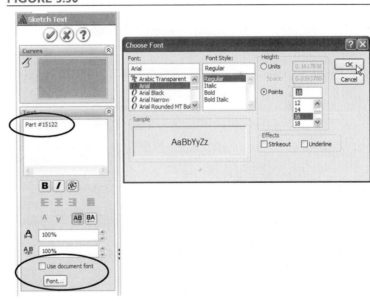

a curve to align the text along).

By default, the font specified in the Options will be used. To use another font, click on the "Use document font" box to uncheck it, which will allow you to select the Font button and edit the type and size of the font.

FIGURE 5.37

Click in the sketch at the approximate location of the text, and then click the check mark in the Property-Manager to close the text box. The text can now be moved by clicking and dragging it around the sketch. Center the text on the face, as shown in Figure 5.37.

Features

If necessary, dimensions can be added to the marker at the lower left of the text to positively locate the text.

Extruded
Boss/Base

Select the Extruded Boss/Base Tool from the Features group of the Command-Manager.

Extrude the sketch 0.020 inches out from the part, as shown in Figure 5.38.

FIGURE 5.38

This card holder may be made from a translucent plastic. The SolidWorks program allows parts to be displayed in the color desired, and also for optical properties such as transparency and shininess to be set.

FIGURE 5.39

Select the part name from the FeatureManager (so that the entire part is selected), and select the Edit Color Tool.

In the PropertyManager, select a gray color, and move the transparency slider bar toward the right, as shown in Figure 5.39. Click the check mark to apply the desired color and properties.

The translucent part is shown in **Figure 5.40**.

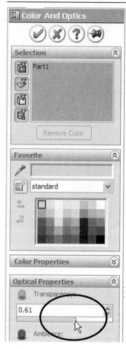

FIGURE 5.40

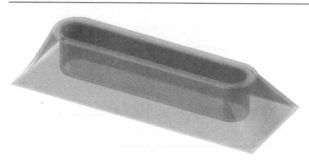

Save this part for use in future exercises.

Note that more than two sketches can be used to create a lofted feature. Consider the three sketches shown in **Figure 5.41**.

FIGURE 5.41

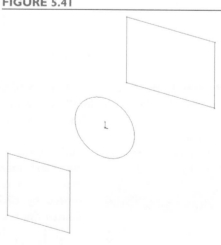

FUTURE STUDY

Industrial Design

In this chapter, we created a part by using the Loft command to smoothly blend two shapes. Engineers in many industries are sometimes reluctant to use this type of construction, since the resulting surfaces are difficult to define mathematically. This makes the geometry difficult to specify on engineering drawings and often impossible to make with traditional manufacturing methods.

Complex geometries have always been an important tool for *industrial designers*. Industrial designers are important members of product development teams, but perform a different task than do design engineers. The Industrial Designers Society of America defines the role of the industrial designer as:

> The industrial designer's unique contribution places emphasis on those aspects of the product or system that relate most directly to human characteristics, needs and interests. This contribution requires specialized understanding of visual, tactile, safety and convenience criteria, with concern for the user. (www.idsa.org)

The image that many associate with industrial designers is that of an artist working on a clay model of an automobile, creating the shapes that would eventually be seen on the showroom floor. The clay model would eventually be digitized by measuring thousands of points on the surface in order to define the shape for the tooling used to stamp the sheet metal body parts. Industrial designers now create many of their models with the "virtual clay" of solid modeling software, computer-controlled machining centers, and rapid prototyping machines.

The roles of design engineer and industrial designer have begun to overlap as they have access to a similar set of product development tools. However, engineers should recognize and utilize the unique capabilities of industrial designers within the product design process.

The lofted solid created from these sketches is shown in **Figure 5.42**.

Also, an additional sketch defining a *guide curve* can be introduced, allowing more control over the loft. **Figure 5.43** shows a guide curve added to the three previous sketches.

FIGURE 5.42

FIGURE 5.43

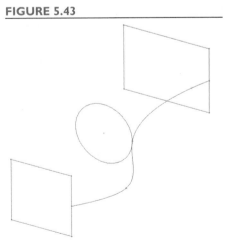

The resulting solid is shown in **Figure 5.44**.

FIGURE 5.44

5.2 Parts Created with Swept Geometry

In this section, we will learn how to create a solid by "sweeping" a cross-section along a path. We will start with a simple part in which the path is planar. Later, we will use a helix curve to form a helical spring. In the next section, we will introduce the 3-D sketch, which will be used to define a sweep path in 3-D space.

The first part that we will create is the bent tubing section shown in **Figure 5.45**. We begin by creating the sweep path. The geometry of the sweep path, which defines the centerline of the tubing, is shown in **Figure 5.46**.

FIGURE 5.45

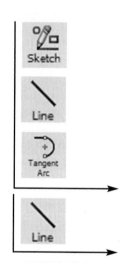

FIGURE 5.46

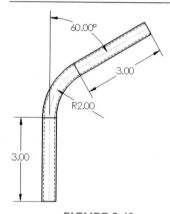

Open a new part. Select the Top Plane from the FeatureManager. Choose the Line Tool from the Sketch group of the CommandManager, and draw a vertical line beginning at the origin. Choose the Tangent Arc Tool, and drag out an arc from the endpoint on the line, as shown in Figure 5.47.

Choose the Line Tool. Drag out a line from the endpoint of the arc along the path that is tangent to the arc, as shown in Figure 5.48.

FIGURE 5.47

FIGURE 5.48

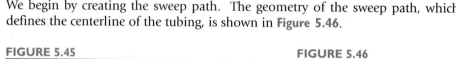

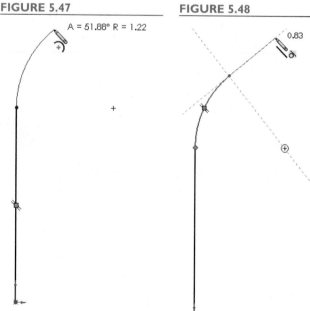

FIGURE 5.49

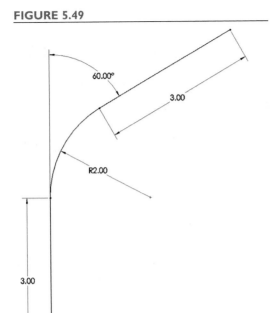

Select the Smart Dimension Tool, and add the dimensions shown in Figure 5.49. The sketch should be fully defined. Close the sketch by clicking on the icon in the upper right corner of the graphics area, as shown in Figure 5.50.

FIGURE 5.50

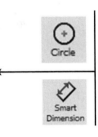

Select the Front Plane from the FeatureManager. Select the Circle Tool, and drag out two circles, both centered at the origin. Select the Smart Dimension Tool, and add diameter dimensions of 0.40 and 0.50 inches, as shown in Figure 5.51. Close the sketch.

FIGURE 5.51

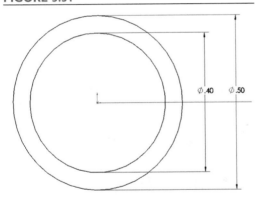

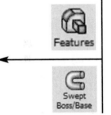

Select the Swept Boss/Base Tool from the Features group of the CommandManager. In the PropertyManager, select the sketch containing the two circles (Sketch2) as the Profile, the cross section to be swept, and select the first sketch defining the geometry of the tubing centerline (Sketch1) as the Path of the sweep, as shown in Figure 5.52. A preview of the swept geometry is shown in Figure 5.53. Click the check mark to complete the operation.

FIGURE 5.52

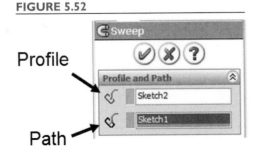

FIGURE 5.53

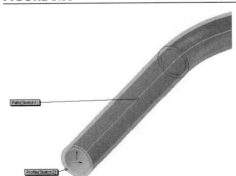

The completed part is shown in **Figure 5.54**.

In the next exercise, we will use a more complex sweep path, a helix, to create a helical spring.

FIGURE 5.54

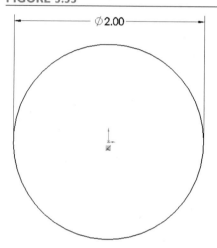

Open a new part. Select the Front Plane from the FeatureManager. Select the Circle Tool from the Sketch group of the CommandManager. Draw a circle centered at the origin. Select the Smart Dimension Tool, and dimension the circle's diameter as 2 inches, as shown in Figure 5.55.

From the main menu, select Insert: Curve: Helix/Spiral, as shown in Figure 5.56.

A helix can be defined by specifying any two of the following three quantities:

1. The height, or overall length of the helix,

2. The pitch, the distance between similar points on successive turns of the helix, and

3. Revolutions, the total number of complete turns of the helix.

We will define the height and the number of revolutions and allow the pitch to be calculated.

Select Height and Revolution in the "Defined by" box. Set the height to 6 inches, the number of revolutions to 8, and the starting angle to 135 degrees, as shown in Figure 5.57.

FIGURE 5.55

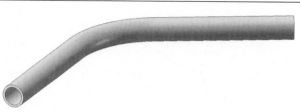

FIGURE 5.56

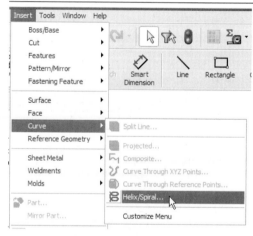

FIGURE 5.57

FIGURE 5.58

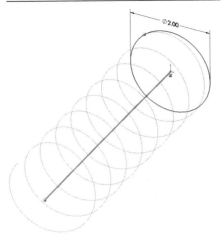

A preview of the helix geometry is shown in **Figure 5.58**. The start angle is not critical here. If the start angle is set to a multiple of 90 degrees, then we could define our profile sketch in either the Right or the Top Plane. We have chosen an arbitrary angle to illustrate the procedure for creating a plane at the end of a path sketch.

Click the check mark to accept the helix definition and close the sketch.

We will now create a new plane at the end of the helix, perpendicular to the helix at that point.

Select the Features group of the CommandManager. Click on the Reference Geometry Tool, and choose Plane, as shown in Figure 5.59. Click once on the helix curve, and then click on the endpoint of the curve. In the PropertyManager, note that "Normal to curve" has been automatically selected as the plane definition, as shown in Figure 5.60. A preview of the new plane is shown in Figure 5.61. Click the check mark to create the plane.

FIGURE 5.59

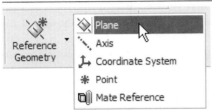

FIGURE 5.60

FIGURE 5.61

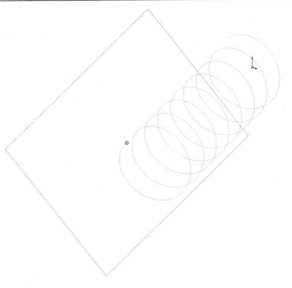

Sketch

Circle

With the new plane selected, choose the Circle Tool from the Sketch group of the Command-Manager. Drag out a circle, as shown in Figure 5.62.

It is not possible to snap the center of the circle to the endpoint of the helix. Rather, we will use a *pierce* relation. The pierce relation is defined between a point and a curve, and sets the point at the location where the curve "pierces" the sketch containing the point.

FIGURE 5.62

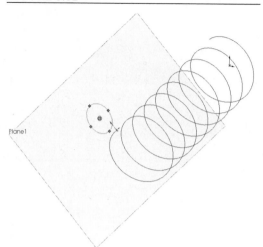

Smart
Dimension

Click on the center point of the circle to select it. While holding down the ctrl key, select the helix. In the PropertyManager, click on Pierce, as shown in Figure 5.63. Click the check mark to add the relation. Choose the Smart Dimension Tool, and add a 0.25-inch diameter dimension to the circle. The sketch should now be fully defined, as shown in Figure 5.64. Close the sketch.

Features

Swept
Boss/Base

Choose the Swept Boss/Base Tool from the Features group of the CommandManager. In the PropertyManager, choose the sketch containing the 0.25-inch-diameter circle as the Profile, and the helix as the Path, as shown in Figure 5.65. Click the check mark to complete the sweep operation.

FIGURE 5.63

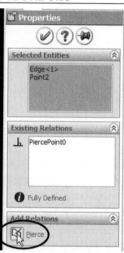

FIGURE 5.64

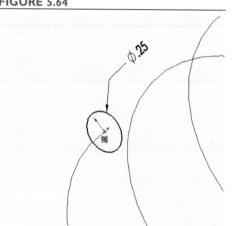

FIGURE 5.65

FIGURE 5.66

The completed spring is shown in **Figure 5.66**. In this exercise, we used a curve in 3-D space as the sweep path. This curve was created from a 2-D sketch (a circle). In the next section, we will use the more general 3-D Sketch Tool to define the sweep path in three-dimensional space.

5.3 A Part Created with a 3-D Sketch as the Sweep Path

The use of a 3-D sketch as a sweep path allows more complex parts to be created. As the name implies, a 3-D sketch contains entities in 3-D space, whereas typical sketches contain entities that exist in a plane. Not all sketch entities are available in a 3-D sketch.

In this exercise, we will model the handlebars shown in **Figure 5.67**. Since the handlebars are defined in metric units, we will need to set the units accordingly.

FIGURE 5.67

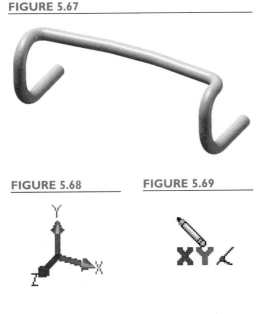

Open a new part. Select Tools: Options from the main menu. Under the Document Properties tab, select Units, and choose MMGS (millimeters, grams, seconds).

Choose the 3-D Sketch Tool from the Sketch group of the CommandManager (or from Insert: 3-D Sketch from the main menu).

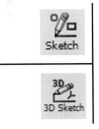

FIGURE 5.68   **FIGURE 5.69**

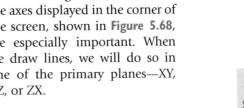

When working with 3-D sketches, the axes displayed in the corner of the screen, shown in **Figure 5.68**, are especially important. When we draw lines, we will do so in one of the primary planes—XY, YZ, or ZX.

Select the Line Tool from the Sketch group of the CommandManager.

Note that beside the cursor, the plane that the line will be drawn in is displayed, as shown in **Figure 5.69**. We want our first two lines to be sketched in the ZX plane, so we will change this orientation before proceeding.

Press the tab key, which causes the sketch plane to cycle between the three principal planes. Stop when the plane selected is ZX, as shown in Figure 5.70.

FIGURE 5.70

Drag out a line from the origin along the X axis, as shown in Figure 5.71. Make sure that the "Along x-axis" relation icon is displayed before releasing the mouse button.

From the endpoint of the first line, drag out a diagonal line, as shown in Figure 5.72.

FIGURE 5.71

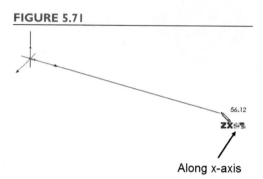

When dimensioning a 3-D sketch, not all of the options available with 2-D sketches can be used. For example, if we try to add a dimension from the origin to the endpoint of the second line, only the straight-line distance between the two points can be displayed. If we want to dimension the x and y distances from the origin to the point, then the use of a centerline is necessary.

FIGURE 5.72

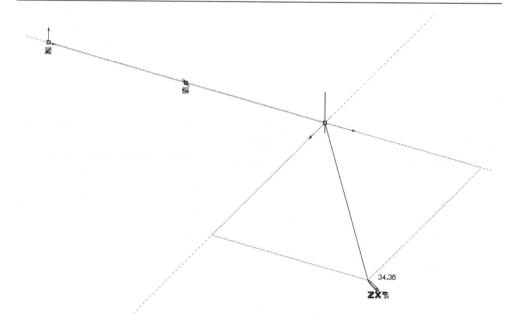

Select the Centerline Tool. Make sure that the ZX designation still shows beside the cursor. Drag out a centerline from the origin along the Z axis, as shown in Figure 5.73.

Centerline

FIGURE 5.73

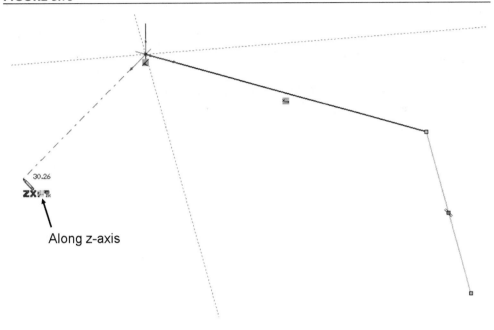

Along z-axis

FIGURE 5.74

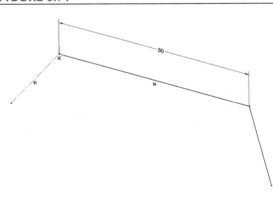

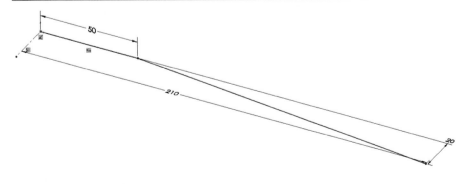

Smart Dimension

Select the Smart Dimension Tool. Click once on the first solid line drawn, and place a 50 mm dimension, as shown in Figure 5.74.

Add other dimensions between the last endpoint of the second solid line and the centerline, and between the last endpoint of the second solid line and the first solid line, as shown in Figure 5.75.

FIGURE 5.75

The other lines of the sketch will be drawn in the YZ plane.

FIGURE 5.76

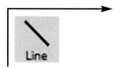

Select the Line Tool. Press the tab key until YZ is shown as the drawing plane, as shown in Figure 5.76. (If the plane does not change when you press the tab key, then click once on the axis display in the corner to "reset" this feature.)

Drag out a line from the last endpoint of the second solid line in the Z-direction, as shown in Figure 5.77.

Drag a line downward (in the –Y direction), as shown in Figure 5.78.

FIGURE 5.77

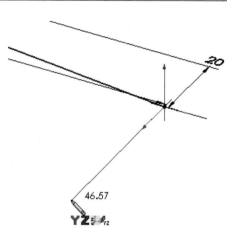

FIGURE 5.78

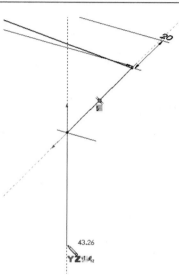

Drag the last line in the –Z direction, as shown in Figure 5.79.

Select the Smart Dimension Tool. Add the dimensions shown in Figure 5.80.

FIGURE 5.79

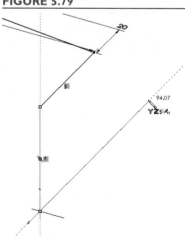

FIGURE 5.80

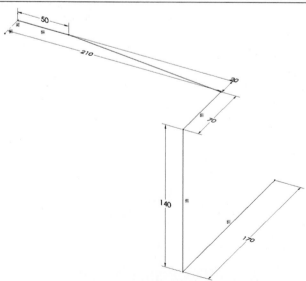

Note that the sketch is not fully defined. 3-D sketches are more difficult to fully define than are 2-D sketches. Although a line may be drawn in a specific plane, it is not *locked* into that plane unless it is aligned with one of the principal axes. We could fix some of the endpoints to fully define the sketch, but that is not necessary.

We will now add fillets to the sharp corners of our sketch. The fillet radii to be added are shown in **Figure 5.81**.

Sketch Fillet

Select the Sketch Fillet Tool. Add the fillets one at a time. The finished sketch is shown in Figure 5.82.

Close the sketch.

FIGURE 5.81   **FIGURE 5.82**

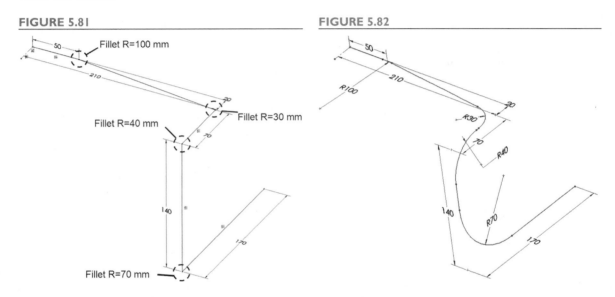

Select the Right Plane from the FeatureManager. Select the Circle Tool. Drag out two circles from the origin, as shown in Figure 5.83.

Add diameter dimensions of 25.4 mm and 23.4 mm, as shown in Figure 5.84.

FIGURE 5.83   **FIGURE 5.84**

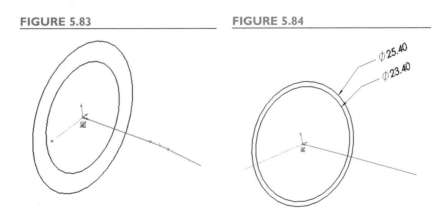

(Although most bicycle components are specified in metric units, a 1-inch outer handlebar diameter, 25.4 mm, is a standard size.)

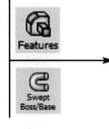

Close the sketch.

Select the Swept Boss/Base Tool from the Features group of the CommandManager. In the Property-Manager, select the 2-D sketch just completed as the profile and the 3-D sketch as the path, as shown in Figure 5.85.

Click the check mark to complete the sweep, as shown in Figure 5.86.

Select the Mirror Tool. In the PropertyManager, select the Right Plane as the mirror plane, as shown in Figure 5.87, and click the check mark.

FIGURE 5.85

FIGURE 5.86

FIGURE 5.87

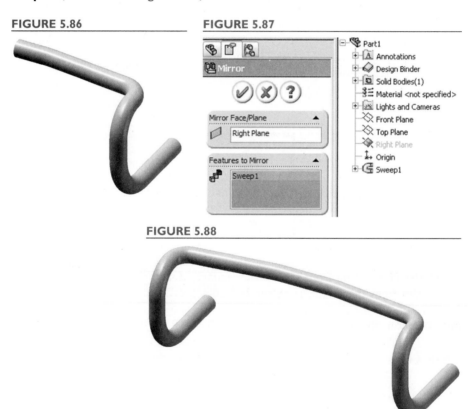

FIGURE 5.88

The completed handlebars are shown in **Figure 5.88**.

We will now determine the mass of the handlebars, which will be made from 6061 aluminum.

Right-click on Material in the FeatureManager. Select Edit Material and select 6061 Alloy from the list of aluminum alloys. Click the check mark to apply the material.

FIGURE 5.89

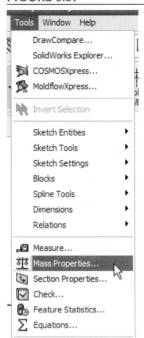

Select Tools: Mass Properties from the Main Menu, as shown in Figure 5.89.

The mass of the handlebars is calculated at about 221 grams, as shown in Figure 5.90.

FIGURE 5.90

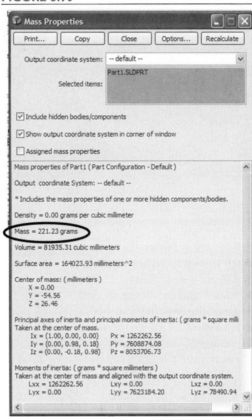

PROBLEMS

P5.1   Create the solid object shown in **Figure P5.1** with a loft between a square base and a circular top (dimensions are in inches).

FIGURE P5.1

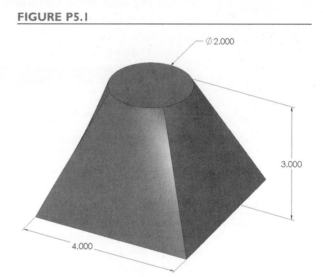

P5.2   Create the part shown in **Figure P5.2A**. Create the sketch shown in **Figure P5.2B** in the Top Plane. Create a new plane 4 inches above the Top Plane, and create the second sketch consisting of the two arcs and two lines indicated in **Figure P5.2C**, snapping to corresponding points of the first sketch. Create a loft between the two sketches to finish the part. All dimensions are in inches.

FIGURE P5.2A

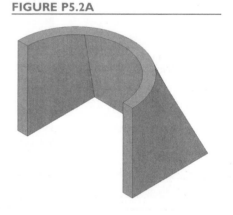

FIGURE P5.2B

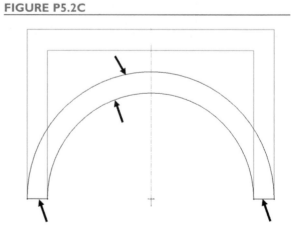

FIGURE P5.2C

P5.3   Create the part shown here, with a circular cross-section of 1-inch diameter. All dimensions are in inches.

FIGURE P5.3A   **FIGURE P5.3B**

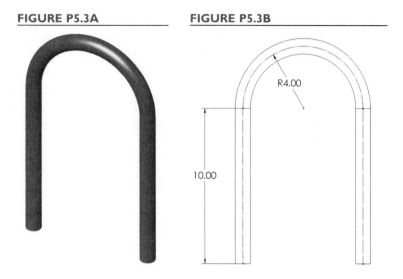

P 5.4   Create the shape shown in **Figure P5.4A** as a loft defined by the two ellipses and one circle shown in **Figure P5.4B**. All dimensions are in inches.

FIGURE P5.4A   **FIGURE P5.4B**

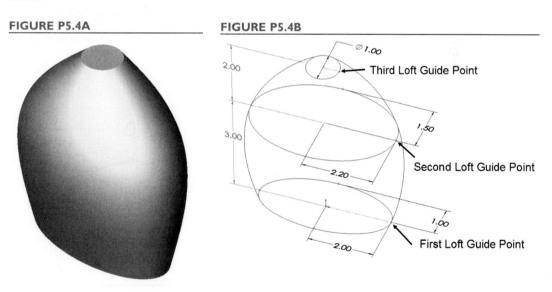

To create an ellipse, choose Tools: Sketch Entity: Ellipse from the main menu. Drag out a circle from the origin, as shown in **Figure P5.4C**, and then click and drag a point on the edge of the circle to "flatten" it into an ellipse, as shown in **Figure P5.4D**. Snap points are created at four locations on the ellipse; use these points to define the semimajor and semiminor axes of the ellipse. Add a centerline from the origin to one of the snap points, as shown in **Figure P5.4E**, and set it to horizontal or vertical to correctly align the ellipse and fully define the sketch.

When defining the 1-inch circle for the top of the loft, add a center line to the horizontal quadrant point, as shown in **Figure P5.4F**. This will provide the final guide point for the loft (see **Figure P5.4B**).

FIGURE P5.4C

FIGURE P5.4D

FIGURE P5.4E

FIGURE P5.4F

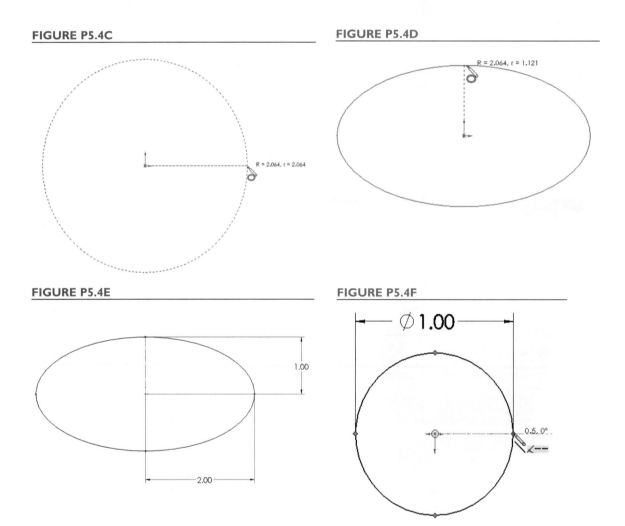

P5.5 Turn the shape created in **Figure P5.4** into the bottle shown in **Figure P5.5A**. Extrude a circular neck, as shown in **Figure P5.5B**, add a 0.25-inch fillet to the neck-to-body junction, and use the Shell Tool to hollow the bottle, leaving a 0.020-inch wall thickness. What is the volume of the space within the bottle? (Hint: To find the volume, move the rollback bar to just before the shell command, as shown in **Figure P5.5C** and find the volume of the solid before shelling. Then move the rollback bar past the shell, and find the volume of the bottle itself. The difference in the two volumes is the volume contained within the bottle.)

*(Answer: 40.8 cubic inches, although the answer may vary if guide points other than those shown in **Figure P5.4B** are used)*

FIGURE P5.5A

FIGURE P5.5B

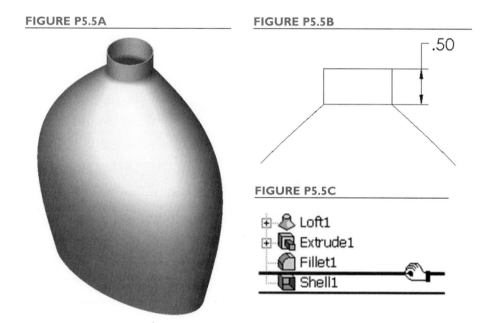

.50

FIGURE P5.5C

⊞ Loft1
⊞ Extrude1
   Fillet1
   Shell1

P5.6 Model a bent tube with 0.5-inch outer diameter and 0.375-inch inner diameter to join the ends of the two tubes shown in **Figure P5.6A**. Follow the route shown by the centerlines in **Figure P5.6A**, and add 1-inch radius fillets to the corners.

The completed model is shown in **Figure P5.6B**.

FIGURE P5.6A

FIGURE P5.6B

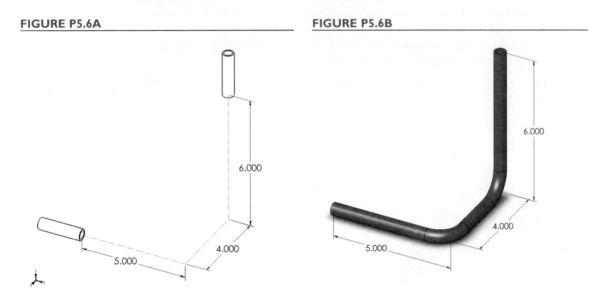

P5.7 Repeat Problem P5.6, using a different path. Use a tube geometry that minimizes the tube length while maintaining a straight section at each end, as shown in **Figure P5.7**.

FIGURE P5.7

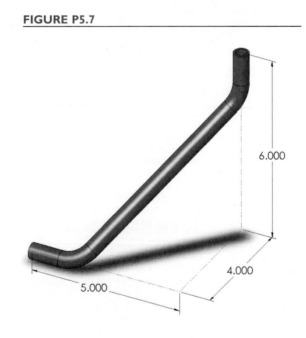

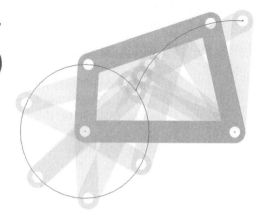

CHAPTER 6

Building Assembly Models from Part Models

Introduction

In the preceding chapters, the development of solid models of parts was covered in detail. In this chapter, methods for combining such part models into complex, interconnected solid models will be described. These types of models, composed of interconnected part models, are called *assembly models*.

The assembly that will be constructed in this chapter is a model of a hinged hatch, as shown in **Figure 6.1**.

The chapter will begin with a tutorial describing the construction of the part models of four components used in this assembly. After the models are constructed, they will be interconnected first into a simple subassembly, and then into a more complex assembly model. The subassembly and assembly models will be used in subsequent chapters to demonstrate some advanced assembly modeling features.

FIGURE 6.1

Chapter Objectives

In this chapter, you will:

- create holes using the Hole Wizard,
- learn to import part models into an assembly,
- define assembly mates between parts, and
- create subassemblies, and use them within larger assemblies.

6.1 Creating the Part Models

Before an assembly can be created, the parts to be assembled must be modeled. In this first step, solid models of the four components will be created.

The first model that we will create is the hinge component.

Start a new part model, and sketch a horizontal line from the origin and a tangent arc in the Front Plane, as shown in Figure 6.2.

Add the dimensions shown in Figure 6.3. Add a centerline from the center of the arc to the endpoint of the arc. In the PropertyManager add a horizontal constraint to the centerline, as shown in Figure 6.3.

FIGURE 6.2

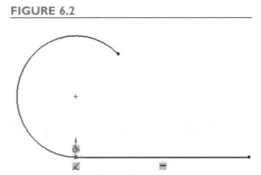

FIGURE 6.3

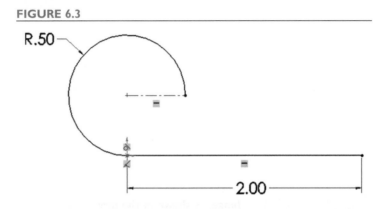

FIGURE 6.4

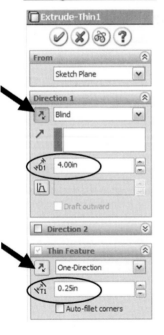

The sketch should now be fully defined. While in previous exercises we have used sketches with closed contours to make extrusions, in this case we will use the open-contour sketch to create a *thin-feature* extrusion.

Create an Extruded Base. Note that the Thin Feature box is checked, since the sketch contour is open. Set the extrusion depth at 4 inches and the thickness at 0.25 inches, as shown in Figure 6.4. Change the directions as necessary so that the extrusion and thickness directions are as shown in the preview in Figure 6.5.

The completed extrusion is shown in Figure 6.6.

FIGURE 6.5   FIGURE 6.6

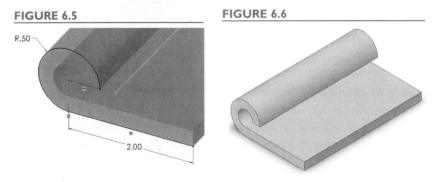

FIGURE 6.7

Select the top horizontal surface of the hinge, as shown in **Figure 6.7**, for the next sketch.

Go to a top view. Sketch the 1-inch square area to be cut away from the basic hinge shape, as shown in **Figure 6.8**. Use snaps and/or relations to align the edges of the square with the edges of the hinge, so that the sketch is fully defined with only the single dimension shown.

FIGURE 6.8

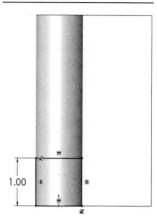

Use the Extruded Cut Tool to cut Through All in both Direction 1 and Direction 2, as shown in **Figure 6.9**.

The result of the cut is shown in **Figure 6.10**.

FIGURE 6.9

Select the extruded cut from the FeatureManager, and define a linear pattern to create another instance of this feature 2 inches along the horizontal edge of the hinge, as shown in the preview in **Figure 6.11**.

The completed pattern is shown in **Figure 6.12**. A pattern of countersunk screw holes will now be added to the hinge. Since fastener holes are generally of standard dimensions, an intelligent design tool known as the Hole Wizard will be used to create the holes.

FIGURE 6.10

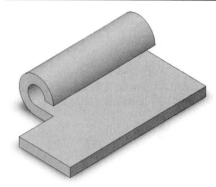

FIGURE 6.11

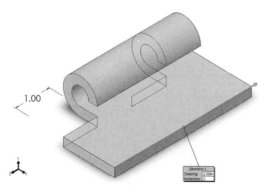

FIGURE 6.12

From the main menu, select Insert: Features: Hole: Wizard, or click on the Hole Wizard Tool from the Features group of the CommandManager.

The Hole Wizard dialog box appears. The Hole Wizard can be used to create holes to accommodate most standard fastener types. We will create countersunk holes for #10 flat head wood screws.

FIGURE 6.13

In the Hole Specification PropertyManager under the Type tab, click to set the hole specification to Countersunk. Set the Standard to Ansi Inch, the Type to Flat Head Screw (82), the size to #10, and the End Condition to Through All, as shown in Figure 6.13. Click the Positions tab in the PropertyManager to initiate the Hole Position PropertyManager.

We are now prompted to enter the hole location, as shown in Figure 6.14. We will create a single hole, and replicate it using a linear pattern.

Change to a top view. Place the center of the hole by clicking in the approximate location shown in Figure 6.15.

FIGURE 6.14

FIGURE 6.15

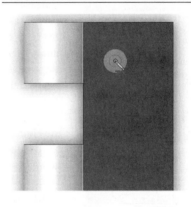

Select the Smart Dimension Tool, and add dimensions to the hole location as shown in Figure 6.16.

Click the check mark to create the hole, which is shown in Figure 6.17.

FIGURE 6.16

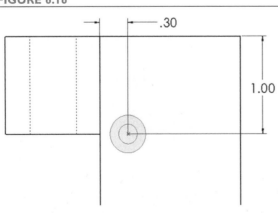

FIGURE 6.17

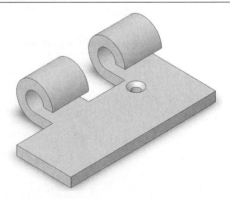

Select the new hole from the FeatureManager, and create a linear pattern with four total instances of the hole, spaced 2 inches along the long side of the hinge and 0.9 inches along the short side, as shown in the preview in Figure 6.18.

The final model of the hinge is shown in **Figure 6.19**. Since it will be used in a later assembly it must be saved.

FIGURE 6.18   **FIGURE 6.19**

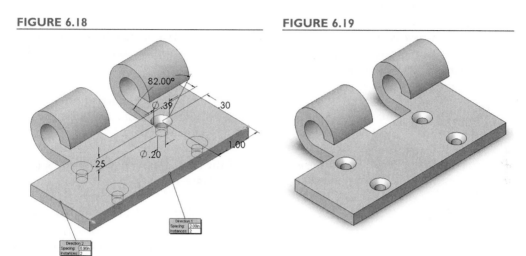

Save this using the file name "hinge," and close the file.

Now, the second major component in the first subassembly will be created.

Open a new part, and sketch a 16-inch by 16-inch square in the Front Plane, centered about the origin. Extrude it 2.5 inches.

This base feature is shown in **Figure 6.20**.

On the front face, sketch a 10-inch square centered about the origin. Extrude it 1 inch from the face.

This completes the second component, as shown in **Figure 6.21**. When we assemble the parts later, it will be helpful if they are different colors.

FIGURE 6.20   **FIGURE 6.21**

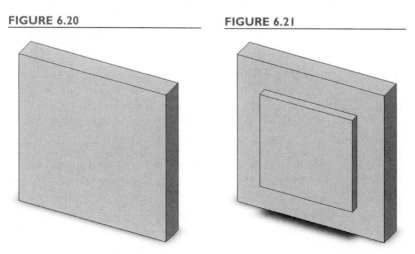

> If desired, select the part name from the FeatureManager, and select the Edit Color Tool. Pick the new color for the hatch, and click the check mark to close the Color PropertyManager.

Save it using the file name "hatch." Close the file.

A model of the hinge pin will now be created.

Open a new part, and sketch a 0.5-inch diameter circle in the Front Plane, centered at the origin. Extrude it 4 inches. Add a 1-inch diameter cap on the pin, extruding it 0.25 inches.

FIGURE 6.22

The pin is shown in **Figure 6.22**. Again, using a new color for this component will aid in visualization of the final assembly.

Change the color of the part, if desired, and save the part in a file named "pin." Close the file.

The final component needed for the assembly is a frame.

Open a new part, and in the Front Plane sketch a 25-inch square centered at the origin. Extrude it to a depth of 4 inches. Extrude a 14-inch square cut (centered on the front face of the component), yielding the part shown in Figure 6.23.

Change the color, if desired. Save this part in a file named "frame," and close it.

FIGURE 6.23

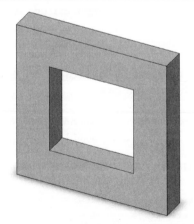

These four parts will now be used to create a model of the hatch assembly.

6.2   Creating a Simple Assembly of Parts

The features of the software that we will employ are the *assembly* capabilities. *Assemblies* are complex solid models that are made up of simpler part models, with specifically defined geometric relationships between the parts. The SolidWorks program provides us with the ability to relate surfaces and other geometric features of one part to those of another part as follows:

- *Define two flat surfaces as **coincident**: This places the two flat surfaces in the same plane.
- *Define two flat surfaces as **parallel**.
- *Define two flat surfaces a preset **distance** apart:* This makes the two surfaces parallel, with a specified distance between them.

- *Define two lines or planes as **perpendicular** to one another.*
- *Define two lines or planes at a preset **angle** to one another.*
- *Define a cylindrical feature as **concentric** with another cylindrical feature:* This aligns the axes of two cylindrical features.
- *Define a cylindrical feature as **tangent** to a line or plane.*

FIGURE 6.24

These geometric relationships are called *mates*. There are many other geometric relationships that can be accommodated as well.

In this section, a tutorial will be presented in which we will create a simple assembly by attaching a set of hinges to the hatch component, as shown in **Figure 6.24**. This assembly will be used in the following section as a small assembly (subassembly) within a larger assembly.

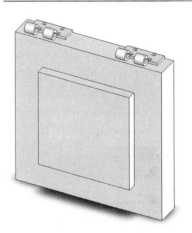

FIGURE 6.25

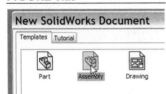

To begin creating an assembly model, select File: New from the main menu. Click on the Assembly icon (Figure 6.25), and click OK.

A new assembly window will be created. For the purposes of this assembly, the main "base" part will be the hatch. We will begin by importing this component into the assembly.

FIGURE 6.26

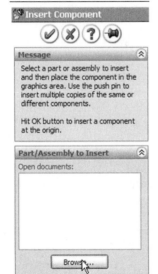

In the PropertyManager, any open parts will be displayed. Since we have closed our part files, click on Browse to find the hatch file, as shown in Figure 6.26. (Note: If the box shown does not appear when you start a new assembly, select Insert: Component: Existing Part/Assembly from the main menu.)

Browse to the location where the hatch file was saved, as shown in Figure 6.27, and open it. If necessary, change the "File of type" option to Part (*.prt, *.sldprt) to find the part files.

FIGURE 6.27

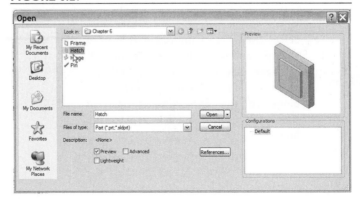

DESIGN INTENT Planning an Assembly Model

When we imported the first part into our assembly, we were careful to locate the part at the origin of the assembly space. More precisely, we made the origin of our part model coincident with the origin of the assembly space, and therefore also made the Front, Top, and Right planes of our part model coincident with the corresponding planes in the assembly space. This is not strictly necessary; we could have located the origin of the part model anywhere in the assembly space. However,

by taking advantage of the default Front, Top, and Right planes (as well as the origin), we can use these as references for the addition of new features (such as holes, bosses, etc.) at the assembly level (as we will do in Chapter 7), as well as in construction of assembly drawings (as we will do in Chapter 8). Judicious choice of the location of the first part we bring into an assembly can simplify subsequent tasks, if we anticipate our future use of the assembly model.

FIGURE 6.28

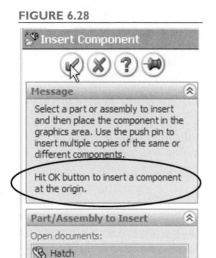

As prompted by the message shown in Figure 6.28, click the check mark (the OK button) to insert the hatch part at the origin.

This will import the hatch model into the assembly, with the origin of the hatch coincident with the origin of the assembly window.

FIGURE 6.29

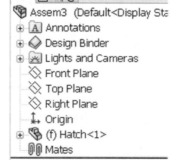

Note that the name of the component (hatch) now appears in the FeatureManager (**Figure 6.29**). The designation (f) means that the component is "fixed"; it is fully constrained in the assembly window, and cannot be moved or rotated. Note the Mates group at the bottom of the FeatureManager. As we define the geometric relations between components, these relations will be stored under this Mates group.

The hinge component will now be brought into the assembly. Note that the CommandManager has an Assemblies group containing many of the tools we will use in assembling the components.

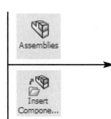

Select the Insert Component Tool from the Assemblies group of the Command-Manager. Select Browse, and find the hinge file. Click Open, and move the hinge to the approximate position shown in Figure 6.30. Click to place the hinge.

FIGURE 6.30

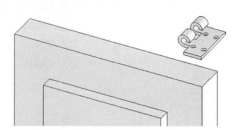

This will import the hinge component, with its origin located at the point selected. The exact position and orientation are not important at this point, since the Mate Tool will be used to establish the position and orientation with respect to the base part.

Note that the name of the hinge component now appears in the FeatureManager, with the (–) designation preceding it. This designation indicates that the component is "floating," and can be moved or rotated (as its degrees of freedom allow).

Although the CommandManager contains Move Component and Rotate Component Tools, parts can also be moved or rotated directly with click-and-drag operations.

Click on the hinge with the left mouse button, and, while holding the button down, drag the hinge to a new position, as shown in Figure 6.31. Hit esc to exit this mode.

Click on the hinge with the right mouse button and, while holding the button down, rotate the hinge to a new orientation, as shown in Figure 6.32. Hit esc to exit this mode.

FIGURE 6.31

FIGURE 6.32

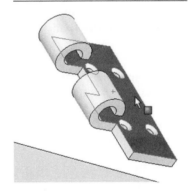

More control over the move and rotate commands is available with the Triad Tool. The Triad Tool can be activated from the right-click menu of a component.

Right-click on the hinge and select Move with Triad from the menu, as shown in Figure 6.33.

FIGURE 6.33

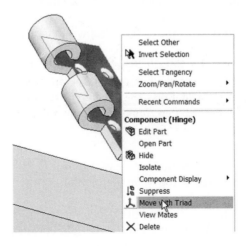

The Triad Tool is shown in **Figure 6.34**. The arrows correspond to the principal axes of the assembly. Click and drag on one of the arrows, as shown in **Figure 6.35**, to translate the part in that direction. Click and drag on one of the circles, as shown in **Figure 6.36**, to rotate the part within the plane defined by that circle.

FIGURE 6.34

FIGURE 6.35

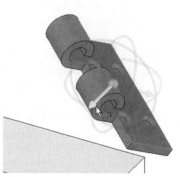

FIGURE 6.36

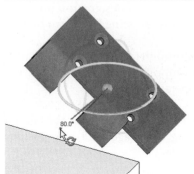

Experiment with moving and rotating the hinge component with the Triad Tool. Place the hinge in the approximate position and orientation shown in Figure 6.37. Click in the white space around the hinge to turn off the Triad Tool.

While it is not strictly necessary to place the component in its approximate position and orientation prior to defining mate instructions, doing so can remove ambiguity and simplify the establishment of the mates.

FIGURE 6.37

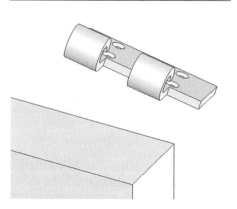

The Mate Tool will now be used to establish the first geometric relationship between the hinge and the hatch.

Click the Mate Tool from the Assemblies group of the CommandManager.

This brings up the Mate PropertyManager.

Using the Rotate View Tool, rotate the view so that the bottom face of the hinge can be seen. Press the esc key to turn off the Rotate View Tool. Select the bottom face (Figure 6.38).

The name of the surface will appear in the pink area of the Mate dialog box.

FIGURE 6.38

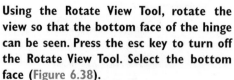

If you select something incorrectly during a mate operation, you can clear the selection box at any time by right-clicking in the assembly window and selecting the Clear Selections option.

FIGURE 6.39

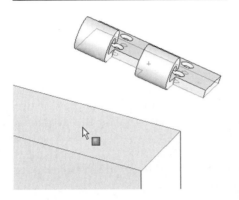

Return to a Trimetric or Isometric View, and select the top face of the hatch component (Figure 6.39).

In the Mate dialog box, the selected faces are shown, and a list of possible mates is shown (Figure 6.40). By default, a coincident mate is selected when two flat surfaces are selected. This means that the two selected faces will be coplanar. The hinge will move to satisfy the selected mate configuration, as shown in Figure 6.41.

FIGURE 6.40

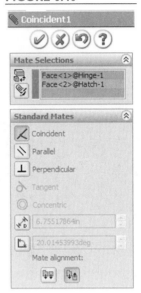

The Mate Alignment Tools in the dialog box are important because there is often more than one configuration that meets the specification of the selected mate. For example, the hinge could be upside-down and the selected mate could still be satisfied. An advantage of placing and orienting a component before applying mates is that the default alignments of the mates are usually correct. However, we will illustrate the use of the Mate Alignment Tools before applying the mate to the hatch and hinge.

FIGURE 6.41

FIGURE 6.42

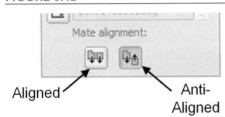

Aligned   Anti-Aligned

Toggle between the Aligned and Anti-Aligned Tools, as shown in Figure 6.42. Note that the hinge is flipped, as shown in Figure 6.43. Choose the tool which results in the proper alignment.

To better view the effect of the mate, switch to the Right View.

As shown in Figure 6.44, the bottom of the hinge and the top of the hatch are coplanar.

FIGURE 6.43

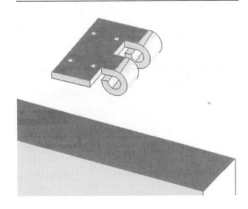

FIGURE 6.44

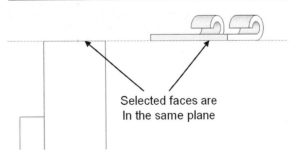

Selected faces are In the same plane

FIGURE 6.45

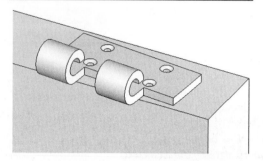

Click the check mark in the Mate dialog box or the pop-up box to apply the mate.

Click and drag the hinge to the approximate position shown in **Figure 6.45**.

Note that the hinge component can be moved with respect to the fixed hatch component, but that the two mated faces remain coplanar. That is the geometric effect of the mate.

A second mate will now be added to provide additional location information for the hinge relative to the fixed hatch component.

Rotate the view orientation so that the back face of the hatch is visible.

With the Mate dialog box still open (select the Mate Tool if you closed it accidentally), select the two faces shown in **Figure 6.46**. Click the check mark to apply this second coincident mate.

The result of the mate is shown in **Figure 6.47**.

FIGURE 6.46

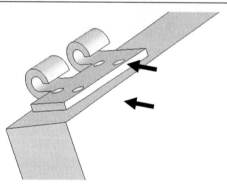

FIGURE 6.47

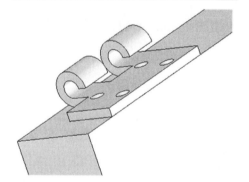

Switch to the Isometric View, and select the two faces shown in **Figure 6.48**.

In this case, we do not want to apply the default coincident mate. Rather, we want these faces to be a specific distance apart.

FIGURE 6.48

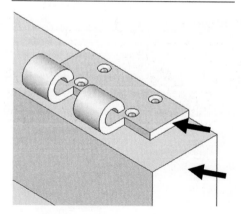

Select a distance mate from the Mate dialog box or the pop-up box, as shown in Figure 6.49. Set the distance to 1 inch, as shown in Figure 6.50.

FIGURE 6.49

FIGURE 6.50

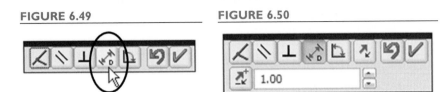

A distance mate has two possible configurations. If you check the Flip Dimension box, then the other configuration is selected, as shown in Figure 6.51.

With the mate defined correctly, as in Figure 6.52, click the check mark to apply the mate.

FIGURE 6.51

FIGURE 6.52

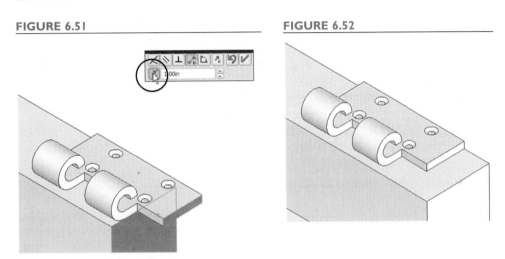

Click esc to close the Mate dialog box. Try to move the hinge by clicking and dragging it.

A message appears, as shown in Figure 6.53, stating that the part cannot be moved. The three mates that we have applied have completely defined its position and orientation relative to the fixed hatch.

A second hinge will now be added to the assembly. Since the second hinge will be identical to the first, no new component must be created. A second instance of the first hinge can simply be added to the assembly.

FIGURE 6.53

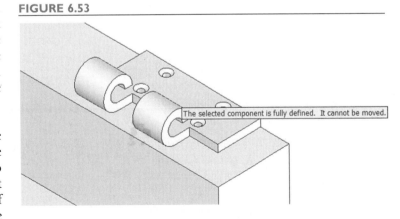

The selected component is fully defined. It cannot be moved.

FIGURE 6.54

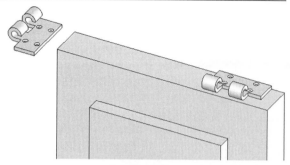

Select the Insert Component Tool, and browse to the hinge file. Place the hinge into the assembly window, as shown in Figure 6.54.

FIGURE 6.55

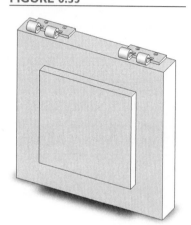

Using a procedure similar to the one outlined previously in this chapter, add two coincident mates and a distance mate to fully constrain the second hinge in the position shown in Figure 6.55.

Once defined, mates can be easily modified. For instance, assume that a redesign specified that the location of the second hinge should be 4 inches from the mated edge rather than 1 inch.

FIGURE 6.56

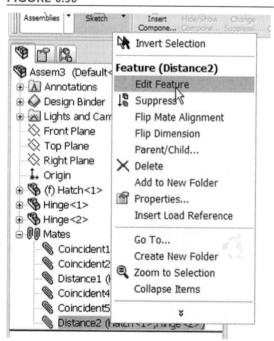

Click the + sign next to the Mates entry in the FeatureManager. Locate the distance mate associated with the second hinge (called Distance2), and right-click on the mate name, as shown in Figure 6.56. Select the Edit Feature option.

The PropertyManager associated with this mate will reopen, allowing for editing of the mate.

FIGURE 6.57

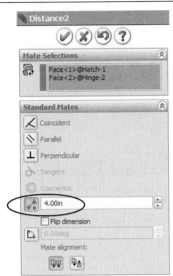

Change the value of the distance to 4.00 inches, as shown in Figure 6.57. Accept the change by clicking the check mark.

The resulting position of the second hinge is shown in Figure 6.58.

FIGURE 6.58

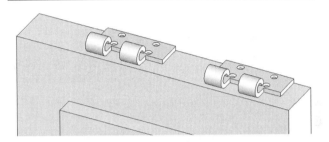

In this way, a parameter of the mate can be readily redefined. Since we will want to continue with the 1-inch value rather than the modified 4-inch value, we will revert to the previous value.

Press the esc key to close the Mate dialog box. Click the Undo Tool to revert to the 1-inch dimension. Save the assembly file using the name "door," and close the file.

Note that the new file has the extension .SLDASM, indicating that it is a SolidWorks assembly file.

6.3 Creating a Complex Assemby of Subassemblies and Parts

FIGURE 6.59

In this section, we will create a new assembly using the door assembly created in the previous section as a subassembly. The assembly will be a model of a hinged hatch, shown in Figure 6.59.

The assembly will also make use of the hinge pin and frame parts created in Section 6.1.

FIGURE 6.60

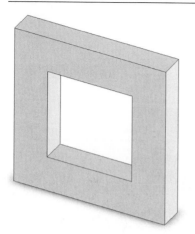

Open a new assembly. If the Insert Component PropertyManager does not open automatically, select the Insert Component Tool from the Assembly group of the CommandManager. Browse to the frame file, and place it at the origin (Figure 6.60).

In the next step, the door assembly created in the previous section will be used as a subassembly within the new assembly. An assembly can be inserted just like a part.

Select the Insert Component Tool, and click the Browse button. In the dialog box, change the "Files of type" option to assembly files, or All Files, and locate the file door.SLDASM. Select it, and click Open (Figure 6.61).

FIGURE 6.61

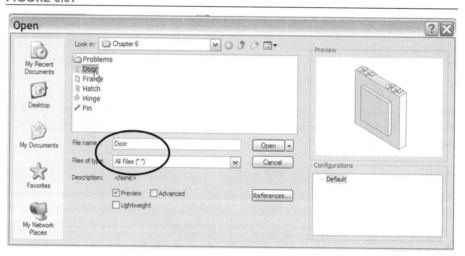

FIGURE 6.62

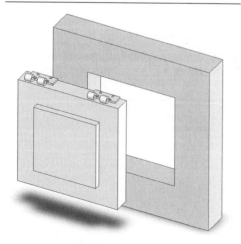

Drop the subassembly into the assembly window in the approximate position shown in Figure 6.62 by clicking.

While the door is an assembly and not a part, it can be handled (mated, rotated, moved, etc.) just like a part component in the assembly window.

Right-click and drag on the door subassembly to rotate it into the approximate orientation shown in Figure 6.63, with the curved portion of the hinges toward the frame.

Select the Mate Tool, and select the side faces of both the hatch part of the door assembly and the frame, as shown in Figure 6.64. Define a 4.5-inch distance mate between the faces. Press the esc key to close the Mate dialog box.

FIGURE 6.63

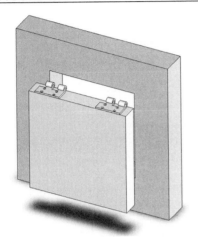

FIGURE 6.64

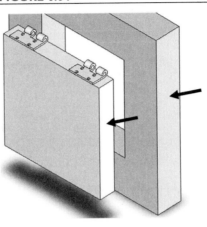

Instances of the hinge parts will now be added to the frame.

Select the Insert Component Tool. Choose Browse, and change the "File of type" back to part files. Select the hinge part. Drop it into the assembly, and rotate and move the hinge to place it into the approximate location and orientation shown in Figure 6.65.

Click on the Mate Tool to begin a mate. Instead of rotating the view orientation to select the bottom face of the hinge, move the cursor over the hinge, right-click, and choose Select Other, as shown in Figure 6.66. With the back face highlighted, as shown in Figure 6.67, click the left mouse button.

FIGURE 6.65

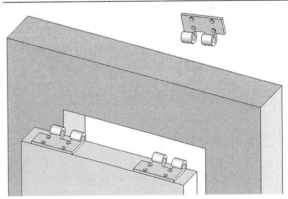

FIGURE 6.66

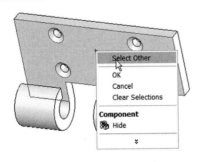

FIGURE 6.67

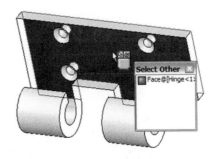

Select the front face of the frame (Figure 6.68). Click the check mark to apply a coincident mate.

The next mate will align the faces of the two hinges to be engaged.

Select the face shown in Figure 6.69 on the hinge that was just mated to the frame.

FIGURE 6.68

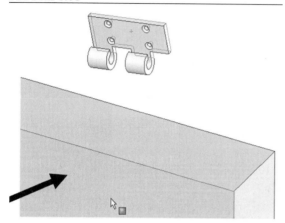

FIGURE 6.69

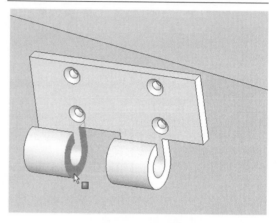

FIGURE 6.70

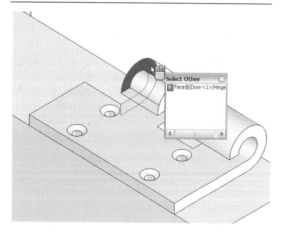

Also select the corresponding face on the hinge mounted to the hatch, as shown in Figure 6.70. Click the check mark to apply a coincident mate.

The effect of the mate can be most easily seen from the Front View, as shown in Figure 6.71.

These two faces now lie in the same plane, but additional mates are required to fully constrain the desired relationship between these components. The hinges will now be brought together to share a common axis of rotation.

FIGURE 6.71

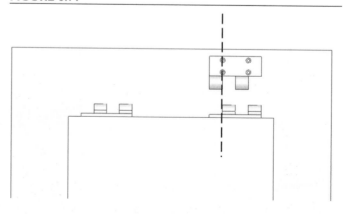

Select the cylindrical inner faces of each of the two hinges to be mated (Figure 6.72).

By default, a concentric mate will be previewed between the two cylindrical faces, as shown in **Figure 6.73**.

Click the check mark to apply the mate.

FIGURE 6.72

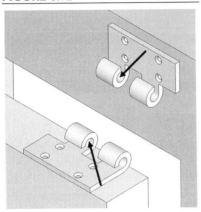

FIGURE 6.73

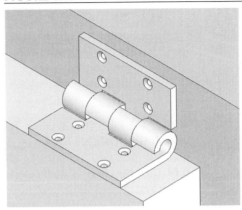

The final mate required will locate the hinge on the frame.

If necessary, click and drag the hatch downward until the top of the hinge is below the top of the frame.

Select the top surfaces of the hinge and frame, and apply a 2-inch distance mate, as shown in Figure 6.74. Close the Mate PropertyManager.

The hinge mate is now fully defined. We can see the effect of the mates by attempting to move the hatch.

FIGURE 6.74

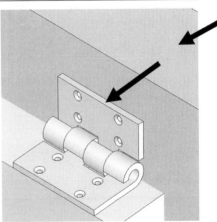

Click and drag on the hatch, as shown in Figure 6.75.

Note that the hatch has a degree of freedom about the hinge, but is constrained against all other types of motion.

FIGURE 6.75

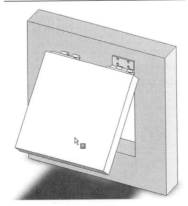

FIGURE 6.76

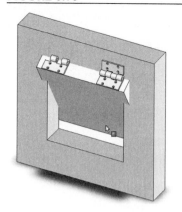

Note also that the hatch can apparently rotate through the frame, as shown in **Figure 6.76**. This is due to the fact that only geometric relations between the entities have been defined, but no true physical characteristics have been imparted to the objects. (We will learn how to use interference detection to limit the motion of the model in Chapter 7.)

Insert a second hinge part, and add mates to place it as shown in Figure 6.77.

We will now add pins to the assembly.

FIGURE 6.77

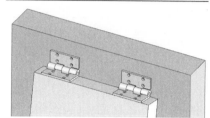

FIGURE 6.78

Choose the Insert Component Tool. Click on the pushpin icon, in Figure 6.78. This will enable the insertion of multiple parts. Browse to find the pin, and click two locations to place in the assembly, as shown in Figure 6.79. Click the check mark to close the Insert Component PropertyManager.

To aid in the selection of small details, a *filter* is sometimes used. When a filter is active, only certain entities can be selected. We are adding mates between faces, so a filter that allows only faces to be selected will be helpful.

FIGURE 6.79

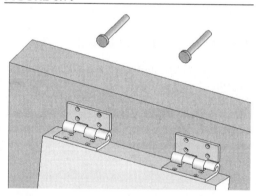

FIGURE 6.80

From the Standard toolbar, select the Toggle Selection Filter Toolbar Tool, as shown in Figure 6.80.

In the Selection Filter toolbar, select the Filter Faces Tool, as shown in Figure 6.81.

Whenever a filter is active, a filter icon appears beside the cursor, as shown in **Figure 6.82**.

FIGURE 6.81

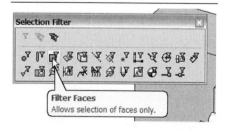

FIGURE 6.82

FIGURE 6.83

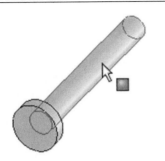

Select the Mate Tool, and select the cylindrical face of the pin, as shown in Figure 6.83. (Note that with the filter set, you cannot select an edge.)

Select one of the cylindrical faces of the hinge, as shown in Figure 6.84. (Either the outer or the inner face may be selected; since they are concentric, the resulting mate will be the same.)

FIGURE 6.84

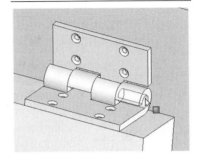

The pin and the hinge will align concentrically in the preview of the mate. If necessary, change the alignment (from anti-aligned to aligned, or vice versa) of the mate to orient the head of the pin appropriately, and drag the pin to the position shown in Figure 6.85. Click the check mark to apply the mate.

FIGURE 6.85

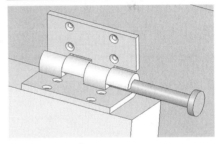

Select the face on the hinge shown in Figure 6.86, and then the underside of the head of the pin, as shown in Figure 6.87.

Click on the check mark to apply the mate, the result of which is shown in Figure 6.88. Close the Mate PropertyManager.

Using this procedure, duplicate the assembly of the second pin.

FIGURE 6.86

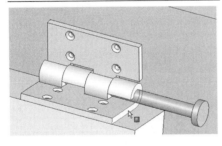

FIGURE 6.87

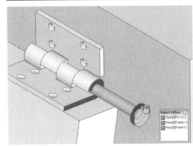

FIGURE 6.88

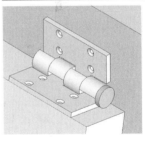

FIGURE 6.89

The assembly is now complete, as shown in Figure 6.89. It will be used in subsequent chapters, so it must be saved. However, it is a good idea to clear any filters when they are no longer needed.

Select the Clear All Filters Tool, as shown in Figure 6.90. Click on the X in the corner of the toolbar to close it.

FIGURE 6.90

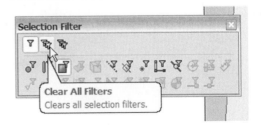

Save the assembly in a file entitled "hatch assembly."

PROBLEMS

P6.1   Create a 6.5 inch x 2.5 inch x 2 inch block. Using the Hole Wizard, add a hole counterbored for a 1/2 inch socket head cap screw with a depth of 2 inches (see **Figure P6.1A**). Use a linear pattern to create a pattern of four evenly spaced holes in the block with a distance of 1.5 inches between hole centers. The resulting block is shown in **Figure P6.1B**, and a section view is shown in **Figure P6.1C**.

FIGURE P6.1A

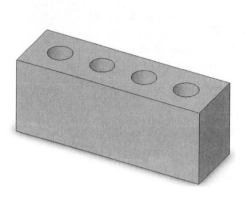

FIGURE P6.1B

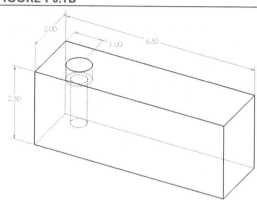

FIGURE P6.1C

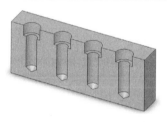

P6.2   Using the parts created in Chapter 6, create a working assembly model of a single hinge (**Figure P6.2**).

FIGURE P6.2

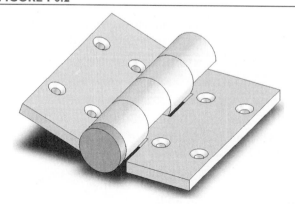

P6.3 Create solid models of a 5 ft. long, 1.5 in. diameter pole (**Figure P6.3A**), and a 4 in. diameter sphere with a 1.5 in. diameter hole in it (**Figure P6.3B** and **Figure P6.3C**). Using these models and the flange model created in Chapter 1 (**Figure P6.3D**), create an assembly model of a flagpole (**Figure P6.3E**).

FIGURE P6.3A

FIGURE P6.3B

FIGURE P6.3C

SECTION A-A

FIGURE P6.3D

FIGURE P6.3E

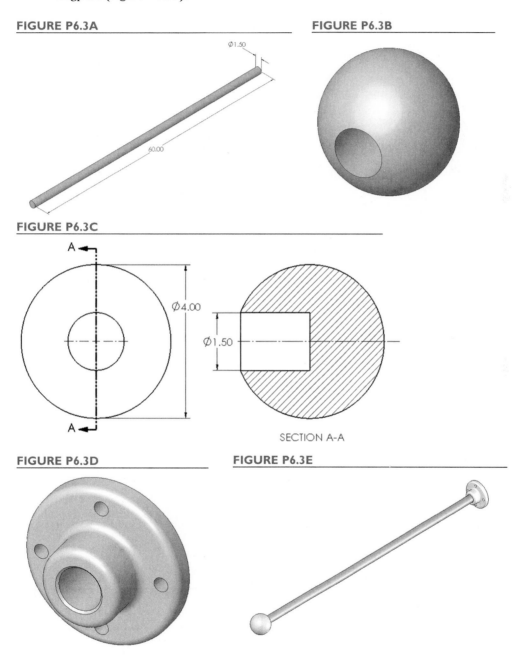

P6.4   Create solid models of the shaft segment shown in **Figure P6.4A** and **Figure P6.4B**,
and the key shown in **Figure P6.4C**. Create an assembly with these two parts and the
pulley model described in Problem P1.3. The finished assembly is shown in
exploded state in **Figure P6.4D** and in normal state in **Figure P6.4E**. (Note: We will
learn how to create an exploded view in Chapter 7.)

FIGURE P6.4A

FIGURE P6.4B

FIGURE P6.4C

FIGURE P6.4D

FIGURE P6.4E

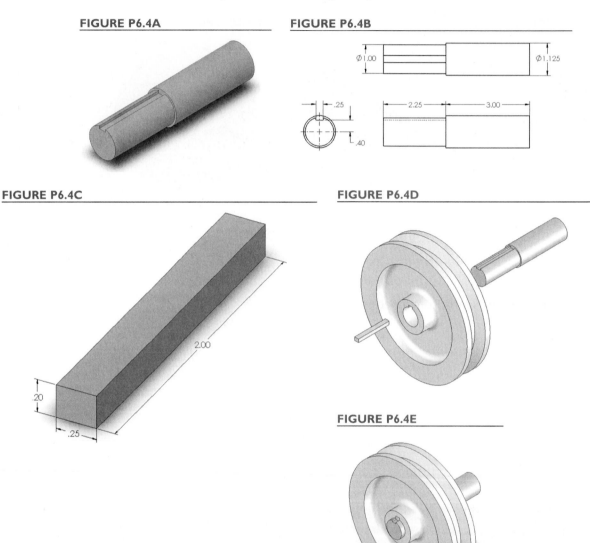

P6.5 Create models of the 2x4 members shown in **Figure P6.5A**. (Note that 2x4s have actual finished dimensions of 1.5 x 3.5 inches.) Create an assembly from these 2x4s as shown in **Figure P6.5B**. Consider creating one or more subassemblies to reduce the total number of mates required.

FIGURE P6.5A   **FIGURE P6.5B**

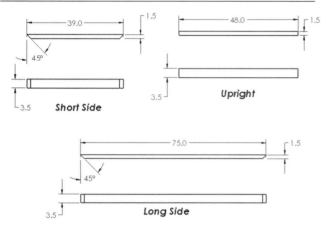

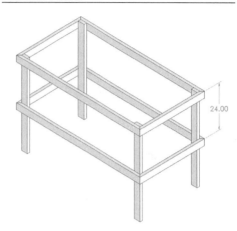

P6.6 Using simple components (flat boards, 2x4s, etc.), design a shelving unit for your room or apartment. Customize your design so that some items that you own (TV, stereo, etc.) will fit on the shelves.

P6.7 The atomic crystal structures of metals are often modeled using spheres to represent atoms. The structure illustrated in **Figure P6.7A** is called a *body-centered cubic* structure. Create a model of this crystal structure as follows:

FIGURE P6.7A

1. Create a 2-inch diameter sphere part model.

2. Open a new assembly.

3. Open a 3-D sketch in the assembly.

4. Add lines to create a box shape, as shown in **Figure P6.7B**. Add relations so that all lines are along the x, y, and z axes. Add an Equal relation to three of the lines so that the sketch defines a cube.

5. Add a centerline connecting two opposite corners of the cube. Add a 4-inch dimension of this line, which will ensure that the atoms on the corners will touch the center atom. Add a point to the midpoint of the centerline, as shown in **Figure P6.7C**.

6. Close the sketch.

FIGURE P6.7B

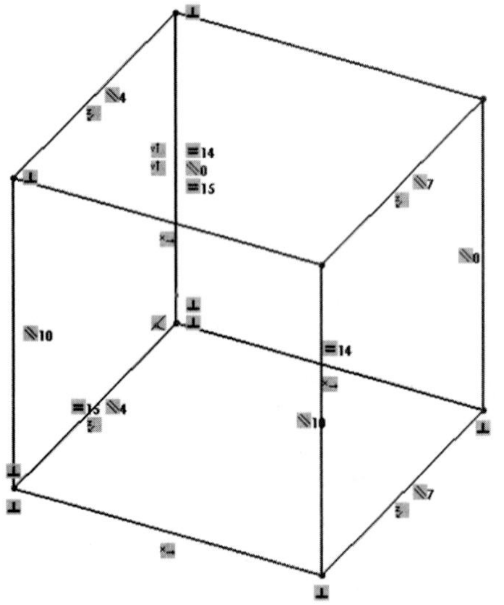

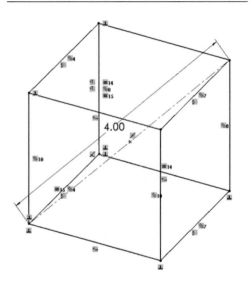

FIGURE P6.7C

FIGURE P6.7D

7. Insert nine atoms into the assembly. Turn on the display of the origins.

8. Add mates between the origin of each of the atoms and a corner or the center point of the 3-D sketch, as shown in **Figure P6.7D**.

9. Turn off the display of the origins, and hide the 3-D sketch.

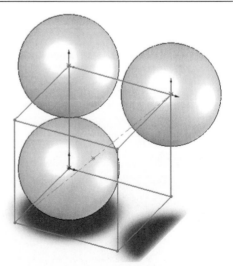

P6.8 The *packing factor* of a crystal structure quantifies how tightly packed the atoms of the structure are, and is defined as the volume of atoms contained within a *unit cell*, or basic building block of the crystal structure, divided by the total volume available within the cell. Find the packing factor of the body-centered cubic structure by following this procedure:

1. Cut away parts of the model created in Problem 6.7 to create a unit cell, as shown in **Figure P6.8**.

2. Use the Mass Properties Tool to find the volume of atoms within the unit cell.

3. Calculate the volume of a solid cube of the same dimensions as the unit cell.

4. Divide the volume of the atoms by the volume of the solid cube.

(Answer: 68%)

FIGURE P6.8

P6.9 Repeat Problem 6.7 for the *face-centered cubic* structure in **Figure P6.9A**. The 3-D sketch defining the atom positions is shown in **Figure P6.9B**. Note that a point must be added at the center of each of the six faces of the cube.

FIGURE P6.9A

FIGURE P6.9B

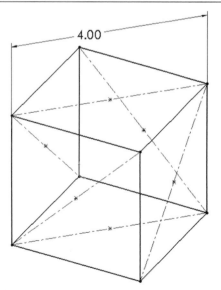

4.00

P6.10 Find the packing factor of the face-centered cubic structure model in P6.9. The unit cell is shown in **Figure P6.10**.

(Answer: 74%)

FIGURE P6.10

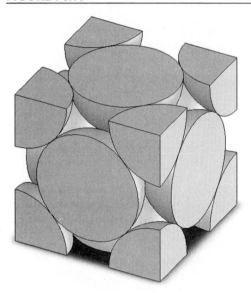

CHAPTER 7

Advanced Assembly Operations

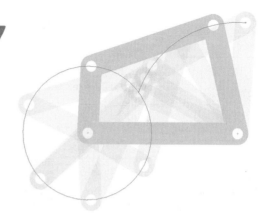

Introduction

In Chapter 6, the basic operations required to create a SolidWorks assembly were introduced. In this chapter, some advanced modeling, visualization, and analysis operations will be developed. The hatch sub-assembly and assembly models created in Chapter 6 will be used in the tutorials.

Chapter Objectives

In this chapter, you will:

- add assembly-level features to an assembly model,

- create an exploded view of an assembly model, and

- use the interference detection and collision detection features to analyze the assembly model.

7.1 ## Adding Features at the Assembly Level

In Chapter 6, assemblies were created from pre-existing part files. It is sometimes desirable to make modifications to the parts in the assemblies. In this section, the addition of features at the assembly level will be described.

FIGURE 7.1

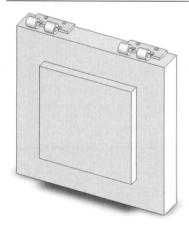

Open the assembly file entitled door.SLDASM created in Chapter 6, which is shown in Figure 7.1.

Based on our design intent, we would like to produce a hole in the hatch component corresponding to each of the four countersunk holes in the hinge component. Therefore, we will use the existing holes in the hinge to establish relations that precisely locate our new holes to match the holes in the hinge. The first step will be to create points on the top surface of the hatch where the holes will be added.

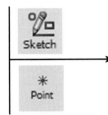

Switch to the Top View, and zoom in on one of the hinges. Select the top surface of the hatch, as shown in Figure 7.2. Open a sketch, and use the Point Tool from the Sketch group of the CommandManager to add points at the center of the holes in the hinge, as shown in Figure 7.3. (It may be necessary to hold the cursor momentarily over the perimeter of the hole to "wake up" its center mark.) Close the sketch.

FIGURE 7.2

FIGURE 7.3

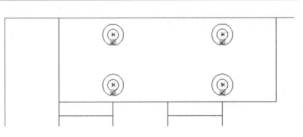

It will be easier to add the holes in the proper position if the hinge is hidden. Otherwise, the Hole Wizard may not find the proper surface to define the hole.

Right-click on the hinge in the FeatureManager, and select Hide, as shown in Figure 7.4.

The hinge is now hidden from view, as shown in Figure 7.5. The points of the sketch just created should be visible. If they are not, select View: Sketches from the main menu.

FIGURE 7.4

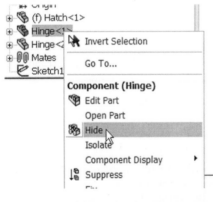

FIGURE 7.5

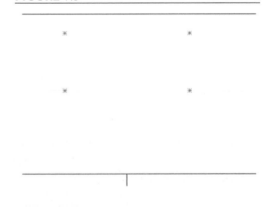

Select the Assemblies group of the CommandMana-ger. Click on the Features Tool, which reveals a menu of assembly-level features, as shown in Figure 7.6. Select the Hole Wizard.

Four *pilot holes* will be added to the hatch, matching the positions of the holes in the hinges. (Note: the holes in the hatch are drilled undersized to allow the screws to thread into the hatch.)

FIGURE 7.6

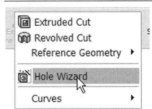

In the Hole Specification PropertyManager, with the Type tab selected, set the Hole Specification to plain hole, the Size to 7/64 (inches), the End Condition to Blind and the depth to 0.75 inches, as shown in Figure 7.7.

FIGURE 7.7

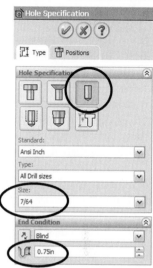

Click on the Positions tab in the PropertyManager, and the Hole Position PropertyManager will prompt you for the position of the holes. Click on each of the points created earlier, and click the check mark to create the holes, which are shown in Figure 7.8 (in wireframe mode).

Right-click on the hinge in the FeatureManager and select Show.

The holes added match the positions of the holes in the hinge, as shown in Figure 7.9.

Repeat the entire operation on the other hinge.

Right-click on each of the sketches defining the hole positions and select Hide.

Save the changes to the assembly by selecting File: Save.

FIGURE 7.8

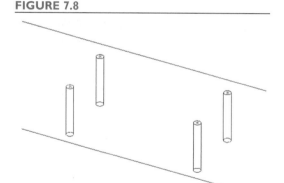

FIGURE 7.9

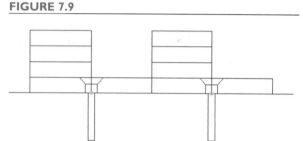

FIGURE 7.10

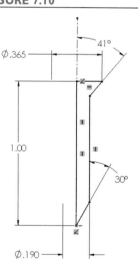

7.2   **Adding Fasteners to the Assembly**

We will now add wood screws to the assembly model. Commercial and educational licenses of SolidWorks have an add-in feature called SmartFasteners that can be used to intelligently insert appropriate mechanical fasteners into an assembly. Some limited-license SolidWorks products do not contain this feature, so we will create a wood screw part model for this exercise.

Open a new part. On a new sketch in the front plane, sketch and dimension the geometry shown in Figure 7.10 (dimensions are inches).

DESIGN INTENT | Part-Level and Assembly-Level Features

Since the holes that we are adding in the tutorial affect only the hatch part, we could have added them to the part file. Instead, we have added them at the assembly level, and the holes do not appear in the part model (verify this by opening the hatch file after adding one or more of the holes to the assembly). There are two types of features: *part-level* features, and *assembly-level* features. Where we apply the features should reflect the actual manufacturing and assembly processes. For example, if the holes are predrilled into the hatch before the assembly with the hinges, then the holes should be added to the part model and are considered part-level features. If the holes are added after placing the hinge on the hatch and using the hinge's holes to locate the

drilled holes in the hatch, then these are assembly-level features.

The difference between part-level and assembly-level features is especially important when creating detailed drawings. In this example, the part drawings would contain all information needed to manufacture and/or inspect the hinge and hatch parts. The assembly drawing would show which parts make up the assembly (in a *Bill of Materials*), and would contain only the dimensions necessary to assemble them. In this case, the dimensions to locate the hinges and the hole definitions would be defined on the assembly drawing (we will learn how to make an assembly drawing in Chapter 8).

FIGURE 7.11

Revolve the sketch 360 degrees to create the screw body, as shown in Figure 7.11.

Open a sketch on the screw head and sketch a rectangle centered at the origin. The rectangle should extend beyond the edges of the screw, and should be 0.055 inches tall, as shown in Figure 7.12. Extrude a cut 0.040 inches deep to create the slot in the screw head, as shown in Figure 7.13. Save this part file as "screw."

FIGURE 7.12

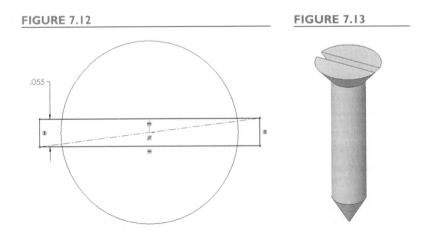

.055

FIGURE 7.13

Switch back to the door assembly. Expand the definition of the first hinge in the FeatureManager, and click on the first hole created in the hinge. This will highlight the hole, as shown in Figure 7.14.

FIGURE 7.14

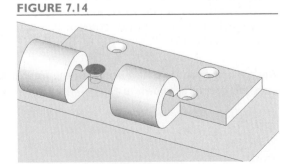

By placing our first screw in the first hole created, we can use the pattern that was previously defined for the holes to place the other screws, rather than placing them one at a time or defining a new pattern.

FIGURE 7.15

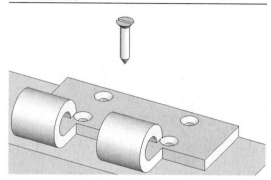

Insert a screw into the assembly, placing it approximately in the position shown in Figure 7.15.

Select the Mate Tool. Select the conical surface of the screw head, as shown in Figure 7.16. Select the conical face of the first hole in the hinge, as shown in Figure 7.17.

FIGURE 7.16

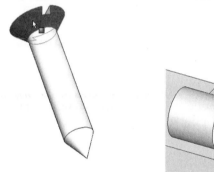

FIGURE 7.17

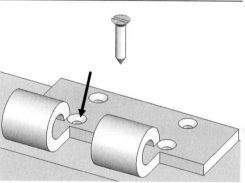

By default, a concentric mate will be created. However, we can override the default to create a coincident mate. Adding a coincident mate to the two conical surfaces will completely locate the screw in the hole.

FIGURE 7.18

In the Mate PropertyManager, change the type of mate to Coincident, as shown in Figure 7.18. Click the check mark to apply the mate, and click the check mark again to close the Mate PropertyManager.

The screw is shown in its final position in **Figure 7.19**. Rather than add the remaining screws individually, we will create a pattern.

FIGURE 7.19

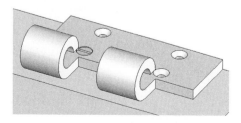

Since the pattern of the screws will follow that of the holes in the hinges, we will use that pattern to create a *feature-driven* pattern.

FIGURE 7.20

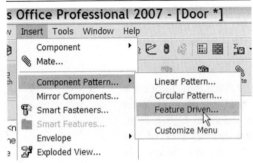

From the main menu, select **Insert: Component Pattern: Feature Driven**, as shown in Figure 7.20. Select the screw as the component to be patterned. For the Driving Feature, click on one of the holes in the hinges, as shown in Figure 7.21.

FIGURE 7.21

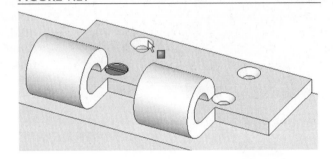

FIGURE 7.22

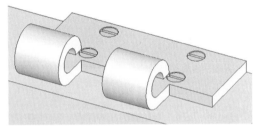

Click the check mark to complete the pattern, which is shown in Figure 7.22.

The screws in their holes are shown in Figure 7.23 in wireframe mode. Note that the screws are larger in diameter than the pilot holes in the hatch.

FIGURE 7.23

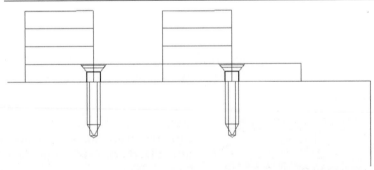

Repeat for the other hinge, as shown in Figure 7.24. Save the changes to the assembly.

FIGURE 7.24

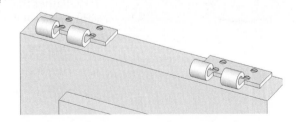

7.3   **Creating an Exploded View**

Exploded views are often used to visualize assemblies. In this section, an exploded view of the door assembly will be created.

Select the Exploded View Tool from the Assembly group of the CommandManager. ◄

Click on each of the screws to select them. If you accidentlly select one of the hinges, click on it again to cancel its selection.

FIGURE 7.25

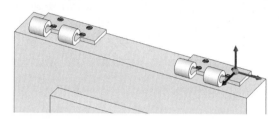

These components will appear in the Settings box in the PropertyManager. A manipulator handle will appear in the model window, as shown in **Figure 7.25**. This allows for "drag and drop" explosion of assembly components.

FIGURE 7.26

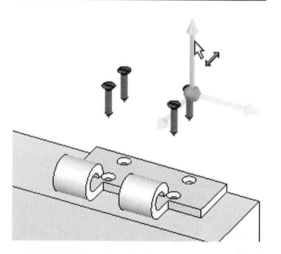

Click and hold on the manipulator handle that points in the Y direction, and drag the fasteners up to the desired location, as shown in Figure 7.26. Release the mouse button to place the components.

Note that this explosion step, denoted Explode Step 1, now appears in the Explode Steps box of the PropertyManager, as shown in **Figure 7.27**. We can make modifications to this step by using the PropertyManager entries.

FIGURE 7.27

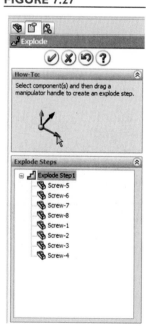

FIGURE 7.28

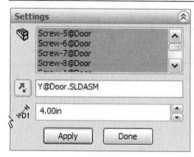

Double-click on Explode Step I in the Explode Steps box of the PropertyManager to select it. Change the distance to 4 inches, as shown in Figure 7.28. Click Apply to change the distance, and click Done to end Explode Step I.

The Explode PropertyManager should be open on the screen. The Settings box should be highlighted in pink, prompting for the selection of components to explode.

DESIGN INTENT   Manufacturing Considerations

The placement of the holes in the hatch and the hinges can be accomplished in one of three ways, and each way simulates a different approach to the manufacturing of the door assembly. First, the holes could be added to the hatch at the part level, just as they are in the hinge part. In this method, at the final assembly step, the hatch and the hinges would be received with the holes in place. The hinges would be aligned with the holes in the hatch, and the fasteners inserted. In this case, the holes would be classified as part-level features. In the second method, neither the hinge nor the hatch would have holes before arriving at the assembly step, where the holes would be classified as assembly-level features.

In the third method, the hatch would be received without holes, and the hinges received with the holes pre-drilled. The holes in the hatch would be drilled to match the holes in the hinges. This is the method modeled in the tutorial. In this case, we have combined a part-level feature (the holes in the hinges) with assembly-level features (the holes in the hatch). Although the final assembly would look the same regardless of which method is chosen, the definition of where the holes are added can be an important consideration in the actual manufacturing process, and the method used to create the solid model should represent the actual manufacturing steps.

Click and hold on the manipulator handle that points in the Y direction, and drag the hinges up to the desired location, as shown in Figure 7.29. Release the mouse button to place the components.

Double-click on the entry in the Explode Steps box of the PropertyManager to select it. Change the distance to 2 inches, as shown in Figure 7.30. Click Apply to change the distance, and click Done to end the explode step.

FIGURE 7.29

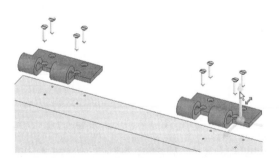

FIGURE 7.30

Click the check mark to complete the exploded view. Save the modified assembly.

Now that the exploded view has been defined, you may toggle between the exploded and collapsed views at any time.

In the FeatureManager, right-click on the name of the door assembly. Select Collapse (Figure 7.31).

FIGURE 7.31

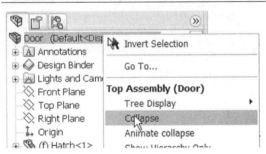

The exploded view will be toggled to the collapsed view.

Right-click on the name again, and select Explode, as shown in Figure 7.32.

This will toggle the display back to the exploded state.

The assembly steps can still be modified at any time.

FIGURE 7.32

From the top of the FeatureManager, select the Configuration-Manager tab (Figure 7.33).

The ConfigurationManager will appear.

Expand the entries in the ConfigurationManager so that the defined Explode Steps will appear.

FIGURE 7.33

Right-click on one of the Explode Step entries, and select Edit Feature, as shown in Figure 7.34.

The Explode PropertyManager will appear. The entries can be modified, and new steps can be added if desired.

Experiment with changes if you desire. Undo any changes you made, and save the assembly, which will be used in the creation of an assembly drawing in Chapter 7.

Sketch lines can be added to the exploded view to show how the parts fit together. Although they are not really necessary for a simple assembly such as our door, they can be very helpful in more complex assemblies.

FIGURE 7.34

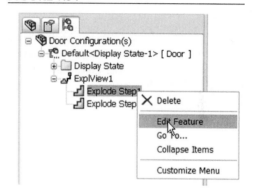

FIGURE 7.35

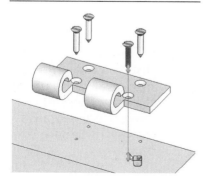

Select the Explode Line Sketch Tool from the Assembly group of the Command-Manager.

A 3-D sketch will be opened.

Click on the cylindrical face of one of the fasteners near the bottom of the fastener. Then click on the edge of the corresponding hole in the hatch, as shown in Figure 7.35. Click the right mouse button (OK) to create the sketch line.

FIGURE 7.36

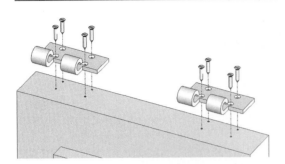

Repeat for the other fasteners, as shown in Figure
7.36. Close the sketch to complete the operation.

The 3-D sketch containing the explode lines is
stored in the ConfigurationManager with the associated exploded configuration, as shown in **Figure
7.37**.

FIGURE 7.37

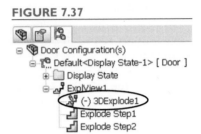

**Close the assembly window, without saving the
last changes made.**

7.4 Detecting Interferences and Collisions

In the assembly mode, the SolidWorks program has the ability to check for interferences between components. It does this by determining locations where solid
volumes overlap. This tutorial will demonstrate these capabilities.

FIGURE 7.38

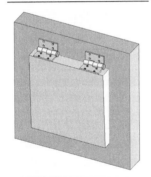

**Open the file "hatch assembly.SLDASM" created in Chapter 6. Click and
drag on the hatch to rotate it into the approximate position shown in**
Figure **7.38. Press the esc key to deselect the hatch.**

In doing this, we have intentionally introduced an interference between
the door and the frame.

From the main menu, select Tools: Interference Detection.

The PropertyManager shows the parts for which interference is to be
analyzed. By default, the entire assembly is selected.

FIGURE 7.39

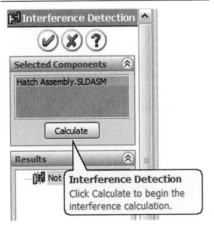

**Click the calculate button to commence interference
detection (**Figure **7.39).**

FIGURE 7.40

In the PropertyManager,
the interference between
the frame and hatch is
identified, as shown in
Figure 7.40. Note that the
first item shown is the
overlap of the door and
the frame. The other interferences detected are the
screws in their undersized
holes.

Click the X in the PropertyManager to end interference detection.

FIGURE 7.41

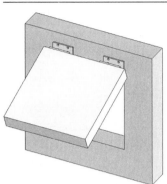

Although we have seen that components in an assembly can be moved by simply clicking and dragging them, the Move Component Tool allows collision detection to be incorporated into part movements.

Move Component

Click and drag the hatch to the approximate position shown in Figure 7.41.

Select the Move Component Tool from the Assembly group of the CommandManager. In the PropertyManager, check Collision Detection and Stop at collision. Under Advanced Options, select Highlight faces and Sound, as shown in Figure 7.42.

FIGURE 7.42

Move the hatch toward the frame until it stops, as shown in Figure 7.43.

Note that when the hatch and frame faces touch, the faces are highlighted and a tone signifies a collision.

Now drag the hatch upward as far as possible, as shown in Figure 7.44.

The movement stops when the hinges collide, as shown in the right view of **Figure 7.45**.

Click the check mark or hit the esc key to deselect the Move Component Tool, and close the file.

FIGURE 7.43

FIGURE 7.44

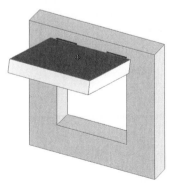

FIGURE 7.45

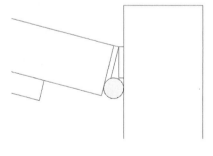

PROBLEMS

P7.1   Import the part model created in Problem P6.1 into a new assembly. Import a socket-head cap screw from Chapter 4 into the assembly. Right-click on the cap screw and select properties. Select the 101 configuration. Add mates to locate the cap screw, and define a linear pattern to place cap screws in the other holes.

FIGURE P7.1

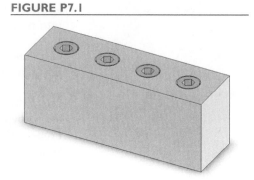

P7.2   Create an exploded view of the assembly created in **Figure P7.1**.

FIGURE P7.2

P7.3   Create an assembly from the frame part and two hinges, as shown in **Figure P7.3A**. The hinges should be located as shown in **Figure P7.3B**. Add 7/64 holes (0.75 inch deep) to the frame, aligned with the holes in the hinges, and insert screws to attach the hinges to the frame.

FIGURE P7.3A   **FIGURE P7.3B**

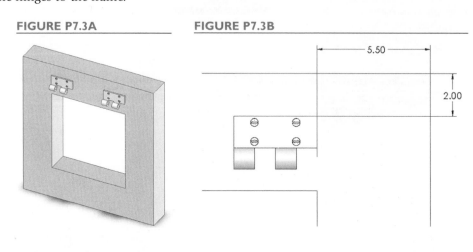

P7.4 Create a new hatch assembly, using the door assembly from Chapter 7, the frame/hinge assembly from P7.3, and two pins.

FIGURE P7.4

P7.5 Create an exploded view of the flagpole assembly model created in Problem P6.3

FIGURE P7.5

P7.6 Create an exploded view of the hinge model created in Problem P6.2.

FIGURE P7.6

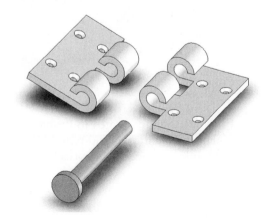

P7.7 Add an angular dimension between the faces of the hinges in the hinge assembly model, as shown in **Figure P7.7**. Use the Move Component Tool with collision detection to move the hinge into its limiting positions. What is the total angle through which the hinge can be rotated?

(Answer: 284 degrees)

FIGURE P7.7

46.40°

P7.8 Create an exploded view of the pulley assembly model created in Problem P6.4.

FIGURE P7.8

P7.9 Open the flagpole assembly created in Problem P6.3. Modify the diameter of the pole component to 2.00 inches, and rebuild the assembly. Use the Interference Detection Tool to locate the interferences between the components in the rebuilt assembly.

CHAPTER 8

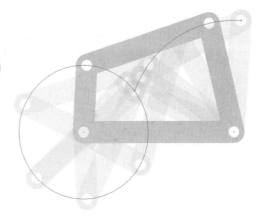

Creating Assembly Drawings

Introduction

In Chapters 6 and 7, the development of solid models of complex assemblies from SolidWorks part files was described. In this chapter, the documentation of these assemblies through the use of 2-D assembly drawings will be introduced.

Chapter Objectives

In this chapter, you will:

- create a 2-D assembly drawing,

- incorporate an exploded view into an assembly drawing,

- generate a Bill of Materials, and

- explore the associativity between part models, assembly models, and assembly drawings.

8.1 Creating an Assembly Drawing

In this section, an assembly drawing of the door assembly created in Chapter 6 and modified in Chapter 7 will be produced.

Open the assembly file "door.SLDASM" (modified in Chapter 7). Make sure that the assembly is in the "collapsed" configuration. Select File: New from the main menu, and choose Drawing from the template choices.

Select the sheet format that you created in Chapter 2, as shown in Figure 8.1, if desired. If you prefer a blank drawing sheet, select A-Landscape and clear the "Display sheet format" box.

FIGURE 8.1

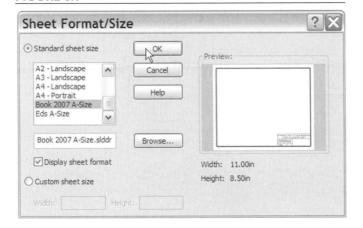

211

Select the Standard 3 View Tool from the Drawings group of the CommandManager. In the PropertyManager click on the assembly name ("door") to select it. Click the check mark.

Three standard drawing views will be displayed, as shown in **Figure 8.2**. (If necessary, turn off the display of origins by selecting View: Origins from the main menu.) If your drawing views show hidden lines, select each view and click on the Wireframe Tool (hidden edges removed). Typically, hidden lines are not displayed on assembly drawings.

FIGURE 8.2

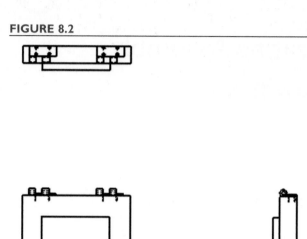

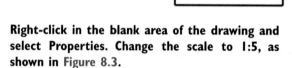

Right-click in the blank area of the drawing and select Properties. Change the scale to 1:5, as shown in Figure 8.3.

We will now add dimensions to the drawing. For an assembly drawing, we want to show only the dimensions associated with assembly-level features and operations.

FIGURE 8.3

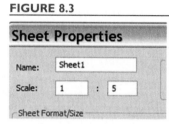

Select the top view, as shown in Figure 8.4. From the main menu, select Insert: Model Items.

FIGURE 8.4

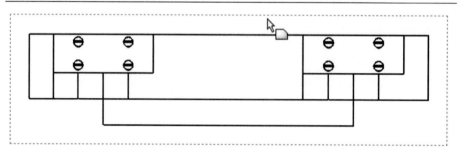

In the Model Items PropertyManager, select Only assembly from the Source Menu, as shown in Figure 8.5. Click the check mark to complete the operation.

The dimensions related to the placement of the hinges are imported, as shown in Figure 8.6. You may need to drag them into the positions shown.

FIGURE 8.5

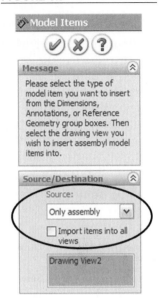

FIGURE 8.6

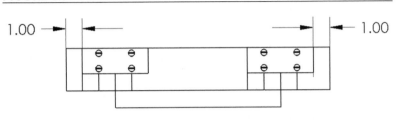

Although it is not necessary to show both dimensions, we will see later that we can adjust the locations of the hinges by changing these dimensions on the drawing. Since the two hinges were placed in the assembly separately, the two 1-inch dimensions are not related. Note that if we wanted to add an equation to the assembly model, then only one of the dimensions would be needed.

8.2 Adding an Exploded View

FIGURE 8.7

In Chapter 7, an exploded view of the door assembly was created. This exploded view can be easily added to the drawing.

Select the Model View Tool from the Drawings group of the CommandManager.

The door assembly should be selected by default in the PropertyManager. If it is not, select it. Click the Next arrow, as shown in Figure 8.7.

DESIGN INTENT | Assembly-Level Dimensions

When importing dimensions into our assembly drawing, we selected the option labeled "Only Assembly," as opposed to "Entire Model." As a result, we imported dimensions associated only with assembly-level features. If the other option had been chosen, then the dimensions defining the components would have been imported as well. These dimensions could be edited, resulting in changes to the part files.

Including component dimensions in an assembly drawing is not usually recommended. One reason is that the components are defined in separate drawings, so adding the dimensions to the assembly drawings is redundant. Another reason is that a component may be used in multiple assemblies, so editing a component at the assembly level may produce unexpected changes to other assemblies.

FIGURE 8.8

The PropertyManager will now contain a list of available orientations associated with the door assembly.

Select Single View, and check the Trimetric View, as shown in Figure 8.8. Scroll down in the PropertyManager, and select Wireframe (without hidden lines) as the display type, and check the "Use sheet scale" option, as shown in Figure 8.9.

Click on the location in the drawing window where the exploded trimetric view will appear, as shown in Figure 8.10.

With the new view selected, select More Properties from the PropertyManager.

FIGURE 8.9

FIGURE 8.10

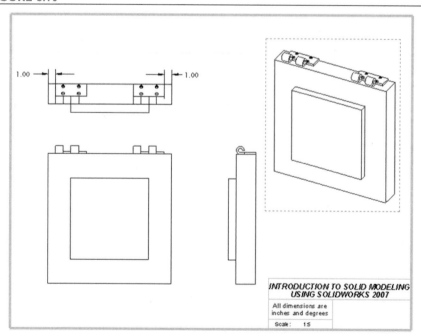

The Drawing View Properties dialog box will appear.

Check the "Show in exploded state" box to change the currently selected view to an exploded view (Figure 8.11), and click OK.

FIGURE 8.11

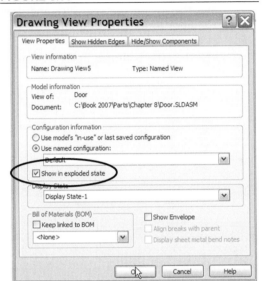

The exploded view will now appear in the drawing window, as shown in **Figure 8.12**.

We will now add a note regarding the placement of the holes in the hatch.

Select the Note Tool from the Annotations group of the CommandManager.

Click on the edge of one of the holes in the exploded view. This will create a leader for the note, as shown in Figure 8.13.

FIGURE 8.12

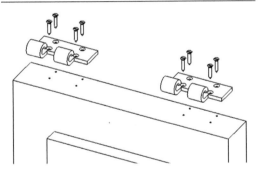

FIGURE 8.13

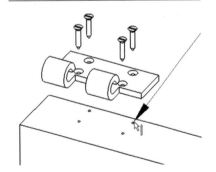

Click on the approximate location of the note, as shown in Figure 8.14.

FIGURE 8.14

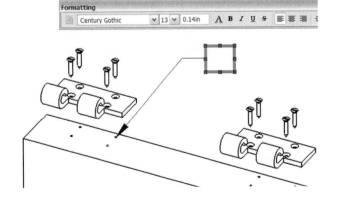

FIGURE 8.15

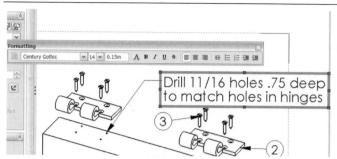

If desired, change the font type and size. Enter the text shown in Figure 8.15.

Click in the drawing window to place the note, and then press the esc key to end the Note command. Click and drag the note to its final position.

The drawing is shown in Figure 8.16.

FIGURE 8.16

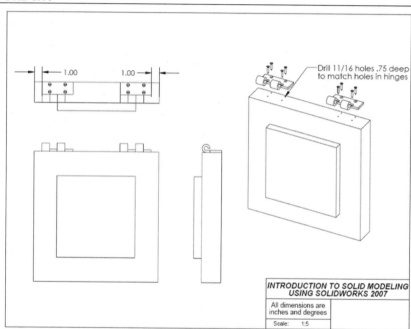

8.3   Creating a Bill of Materials

FIGURE 8.17

It is often desirable to generate a parts list, or Bill of Materials (BOM), associated with an assembly. The SolidWorks program can automatically create this list from an assembly file.

Select any of the drawing views. From the main menu, select Insert: Tables: Bill of Materials, as shown in Figure 8.17.

Accept the default selections listed in the PropertyManager, and click the check mark (Figure 8.18).

Click anywhere in the drawing to place the Bill of Materials, as shown in Figure 8.19.

FIGURE 8.18

FIGURE 8.19

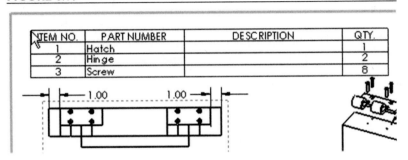

The Bill of Materials, listing all parts in the assembly by name, along with the quantity and a description column (blank), will appear.

Right-click in the DESCRIPTION column, and select Delete: Column, as shown in Figure 8.20.

Click in any cell of the table. Select Table Format from the PropertyManager, as shown in Figure 8.21. Uncheck the "Use document font" box and click the Font button. Edit the font type and size as desired. Also, click on the Center Justify and Middle Justify icons, as shown in Figure 8.22.

FIGURE 8.20

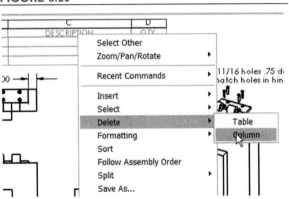

Click and drag on column boundaries to adjust column widths, as shown in Figure 8.23.

FIGURE 8.21   FIGURE 8.22

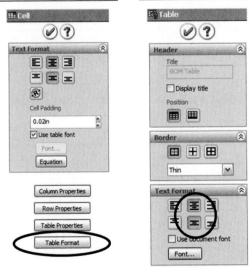

FIGURE 8.23

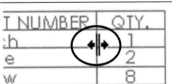

Most companies use the part number, rather than a name, as the file name of a component or assembly. Therefore, the column displaying the file name is labeled "PART NUMBER." Since we have saved files with descriptive names rather than part numbers, we can change the heading in the Bill of Materials.

FIGURE 8.24

FIGURE 8.25

Click on the Part Number cell, and select Column Properties from the Property-Manager, as shown in Figure 8.24.

Edit the Title box to read PART NAME, as shown in Figure 8.25, and click the check mark.

To change the row height, click and drag the cursor over the entire table to select all cells, right click and select Formatting: Row Height, as shown in Figure 8.26.

FIGURE 8.26

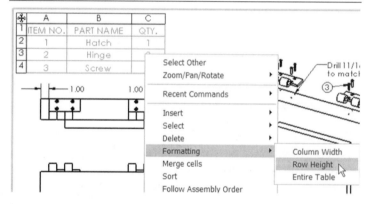

Click and drag the move icon in the upper left corner of the Bill of Materials to the position desired, as shown in Figure 8.27.

Our drawing is almost complete, but the item numbers in the Bill of Materials are not linked with the components in the drawing. We will add "balloons" with part numbers to the drawing.

FIGURE 8.27

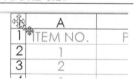

Select the exploded Trimetric View. Select the AutoBalloon Tool from the Annotations group of the CommandManager.

Balloons will be added to the view, as shown in **Figure 8.28**. The appearance of the balloons can be changed from the PropertyManager.

FIGURE 8.28

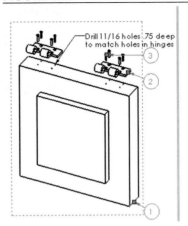

FIGURE 8.29

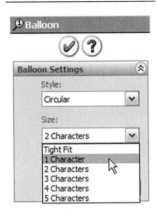

In the PropertyManager, select I Character from the Size pull-down menu, as shown in **Figure 8.29**. **Click the check mark to close the PropertyManager.**

Click and drag the part numbers to relocate the balloons as desired. Move the drawing views to the desired locations, and add the title with the Note Tool from the Annotations Group of the CommandManager. The completed drawing is shown in Figure 8.30.

FIGURE 8.30

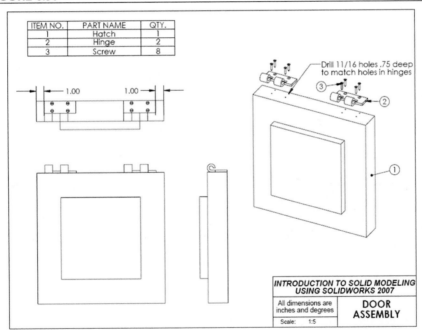

Save the drawing with the file name "door," and close it.

Note that the drawing file has the extension .SLDDRW.

8.4 Investigating Associativity

As with part drawings, assembly drawings maintain *associativity* with the assembly models used to create them; the drawing dimensions are linked to the model dimensions. Changes to assembly drawings will propagate to the assembly models; however, since only assembly-level dimensions are shown on assembly drawings, the part files will be unchanged. On the other hand, since assembly models are composed of part models, changes to part files will propagate to the assembly level and thus to the assembly drawing. In this section, this associativity will be demonstrated.

Open the door assembly file (door.SLDASM), the hatch part file (hatch.SLDPRT), and the door drawing file (door.SLDDRW). From the main menu, select Windows: Tile Horizontally to display all three windows at once, as shown in Figure 8.31.

FIGURE 8.31

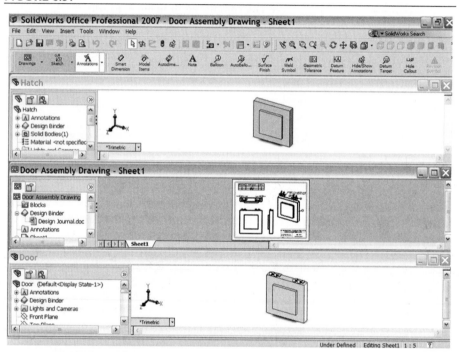

FIGURE 8.32

In the drawing window, zoom in on the top view. Double-click on each of the 1-inch dimensions locating the hinges, and change the values to 3 inches. Click the Rebuild Tool, and the hinges will be displayed in the positions shown in Figure 8.32.

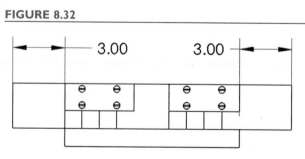

FIGURE 8.33

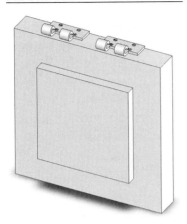

Click in the assembly window, and the assembly will be updated, as shown in Figure 8.33.

If you click in the part window, the hatch part will be unchanged.

We will change the hinge-location dimensions back to 1 inch from the assembly window.

In the assembly window, right-click on Annotations in the FeatureManager, as shown in Figure 8.34. Click on Show Feature Dimensions, and the dimensions will be displayed.

Double-click on each of the 3-inch dimensions and change them to 1 inch each. Rebuild the assembly, as shown in Figure 8.35.

FIGURE 8.34

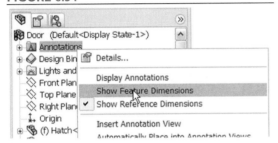

FIGURE 8.35

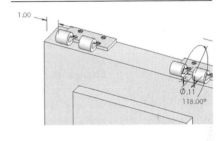

If you click in the drawing window, you will see the drawing update to the new dimensions.

We will now see how a change to a part propagates to the assembly and the assembly drawing.

FIGURE 8.36

In the part window, double-click Extrude2 in the FeatureManager, as shown in Figure 8.36.

The dimensions associated with this feature (the raised portion of the hatch) will be displayed.

Double-click on the 1-inch dimension, and change it to 3 inches. Rebuild the model.

FIGURE 8.37

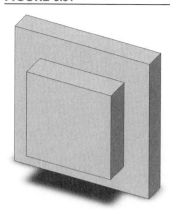

The updated model is shown in **Figure** 8.37.

Click in the assembly window. The message shown in Figure 8.38 **will appear, letting you know that a component of the assembly has been changed. Click Yes to rebuild the assembly, or wait for the timer to expire.**

FIGURE 8.38

SolidWorks 2007 (Automatically dismissing in 8 sec...

Models contained within the assembly have changed. Would you like to rebuild the assembly now?

Yes   No

☐ Don't tell me again in this session

FIGURE 8.39

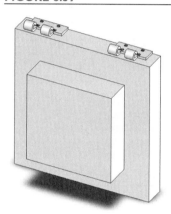

The result is shown in **Figure** 8.39.

Click in the drawing window.

The assembly drawing will show the modified component, as shown in **Figure** 8.40.

Change the dimension back to 1 inch in the part window.

We will now change the name of the hatch component. Suppose that there are several other hatch sizes available, and so we want to give the 16-inch hatch a distinctive name.

FIGURE 8.40

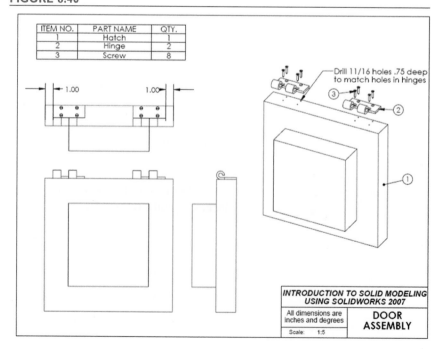

ITEM NO.	PART NAME	QTY.
1	Hatch	1
2	Hinge	2
3	Screw	8

Drill 11/16 holes .75 deep to match holes in hinges

INTRODUCTION TO SOLID MODELING USING SOLIDWORKS 2007

All dimensions are inches and degrees

DOOR ASSEMBLY

Scale: 1:5

In the part window, select File: Save As from the main menu. The message displayed in Figure 8.41 will be displayed.

FIGURE 8.41

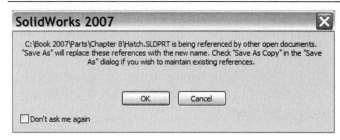

This message is warning you that the part you are about to rename is used in assemblies. If you are creating a copy to use elsewhere, then you will want to use the "Save as copy" option when saving the file. This will maintain the old file as the one that is used in the existing assemblies. If the "Save as copy" box is left unchecked, then the newly created file (with the new file name) will replace the old file in the assemblies. We will use the latter option, since we want the new file name to be used in our assembly.

Click OK to close the message box. In the Save As box, save the file with the file name Hatch16. Leave the "Save as copy" box unchecked. Click Save.

In the assembly window, notice that the new file name is referenced in the FeatureManager (**Figure 8.42**).

Switch to the drawing window, and rebuild the drawing.

Note that the part name of the hatch has changed in the Bill of Materials (**Figure 8.43**).

FIGURE 8.42

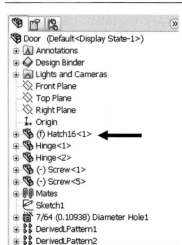

FIGURE 8.43

ITEM NO.	PART NAME	QTY.
1	Hatch16	1
2	Hinge	2
3	Screw	8

Close all of the windows. It is not necessary to save the changes.

PROBLEMS

P8.1 Create an assembly drawing, complete with exploded view and bill of materials, for the hinge assembly created in Problem P6.2.

FIGURE P8.1

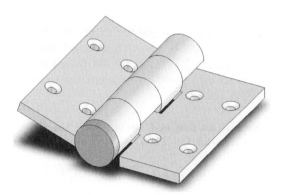

P8.2 Create an assembly drawing, complete with exploded view and bill of materials, for the flagpole assembly created in Problem P6.3.

FIGURE P8.2

P8.3 Create an assembly drawing, complete with exploded view and bill of materials, for the shaft assembly created in Problem P6.4.

FIGURE P8.3

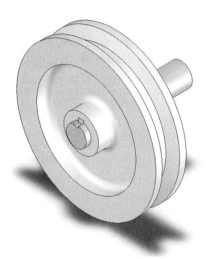

P8.4 Create an assembly drawing, complete with bill of materials, for the frame assembly created in Problem P6.5.

FIGURE P8.4

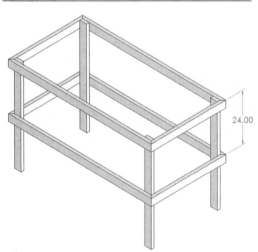

P8.5   Create an assembly drawing, complete with exploded view and bill of
materials, for the frame-and-hinge assembly created in Problem P7.3.

FIGURE P8.5

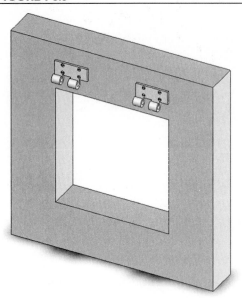

PART TWO

Applications of SolidWorks®

CHAPTER 9

Using SolidWorks for the Generation of 2-D Layouts

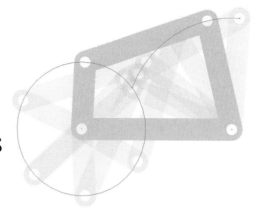

Introduction

Earlier we learned to create 2-D drawings from solid parts and assemblies. For some tasks, however, working directly in the 2-D environment is preferred. For example, floor plans and site drawings, plant equipment layouts, and electrical schematic drawings are usually created in 2-D. The SolidWorks program can be used for these applications, and the ease of changing dimensions allows multiple configurations to be quickly evaluated.

9.1 A Simple Floor Plan Layout

In this exercise, we will prepare a layout drawing of a simple quality assurance lab for a manufacturing shop. The following items need to be placed in the lab:

- A tensile test machine, with a rectangular "footprint" of 4 feet wide by 3 feet deep
- An inspection bench, 8 feet by 3 feet
- A desk, 5 feet by 30 inches
- Three cabinets for storing measuring tools and fixtures, each 4 feet wide by 2 feet deep, with doors that swing outward

Chapter Objectives

In this chapter, you will:

- choose and set the scale for a 2-D layout,

- use a unit system of feet and inches,

- create a floor plan and learn how to modify the layout to evaluate alternate configurations,

- expand your knowledge of using relations with 2-D entities, and

- calculate the areas, centroid locations, and moments of inertias of 2-D areas.

FIGURE 9.1

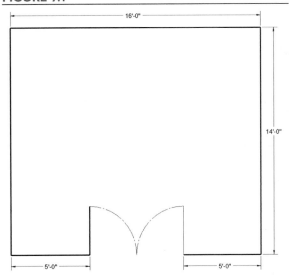

Parts will be brought in bins that are 4 feet square, so there will need to be room for one parts bin. The room that has been proposed for the lab is shown in **Figure 9.1**. We would like to prepare a layout drawing to show how the equipment should be placed in the room.

Begin by opening a new drawing in SolidWorks. When prompted to select a sheet format, pick A-Landscape as the paper size, and make sure the "Display sheet format" box is unchecked, as shown in Figure 9.2. Click OK. If the Model View dialog appears in the PropertyManager, clear the box labeled "Start command when creating new drawing," and click the x to end the Model View command.

FIGURE 9.2

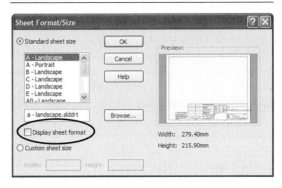

When we import parts into drawings, an appropriate scale is automatically set. When preparing a 2-D layout, we must specify the scale. To make the room fill most of the paper, we can set the scale at 1 inch equals 2 feet. Thus, the 14-foot dimension will appear as 7 inches on the drawing.

Right-click anywhere in the drawing area, and select Properties. Set the scale to 1:24, as shown in Figure 9.3. Click OK.

FIGURE 9.3

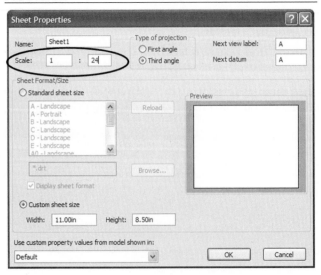

We can use units of feet, inches, or mixed feet and inches for this layout. We will use mixed feet and inches.

Select Tools: Options from the menu. Under the Document Properties tab, click on Units. Select Custom as the unit system, and feet & inches from the pull-down menu of length units. Set the decimal places to zero, as shown in Figure 9.4. **Click OK.**

Select the Rectangle Tool from the Sketch group of the CommandManager, and drag out a rectangle. Dimension the sides of the rectangle, as shown in Figure 9.5. **When entering the dimensions as feet, include the foot symbol (') after the number. Otherwise, the dimension units default to inches.**

If sketch relation icons do not appear on the drawing, select View: Sketch Relations from the main menu.

FIGURE 9.4

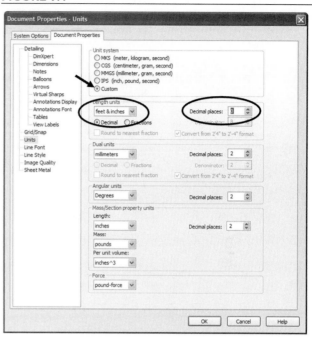

FIGURE 9.5

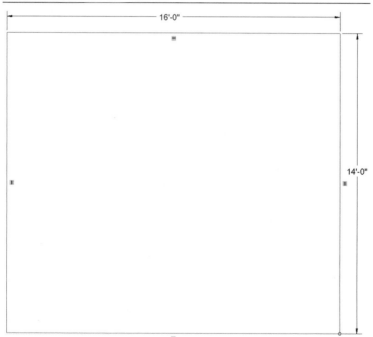

FIGURE 9.6

With the Dimension Tool turned off, click and drag on one corner of the rectangle until the shape is centered on the sheet. Then select Fix in the PropertyManager to fix the point on the sheet, as shown in Figure 9.6.

Delete the bottom line and replace it with the two lines shown in Figure 9.7. Dimension each of the new lines, and add a collinear relation to the lines.

FIGURE 9.7

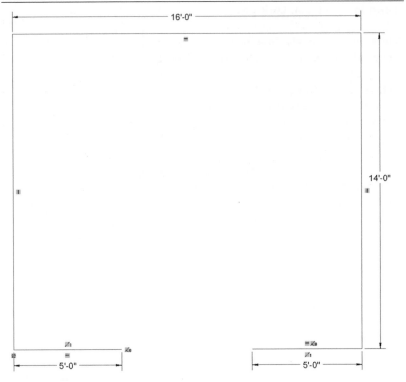

The drawing should be fully defined.

There are several ways that the doors and the arcs that represent their swing paths can be drawn and dimensioned. The method here uses relations to define the geometry.

FIGURE 9.8

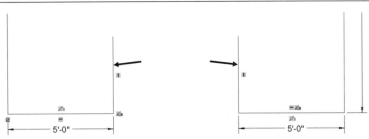

Draw the vertical lines as shown in Figure 9.8.

Select the Centerpoint Arc Tool from the Sketch group of the CommandManager. ←

This tool allows you to construct an arc by picking the center of the arc and then the two endpoints.

FIGURE 9.9

Move the cursor directly over the intersection of one of the vertical lines and the adjacent horizontal line, as shown in Figure 9.9. Click once on the intersection to set the center point of the arc. Click again on the other end of the vertical line, as shown in Figure 9.10, to set the starting point of the arc. Now drag an arc approximately 90 degrees, as shown in Figure 9.11, and click to finish the construction of the arc.

Check the "For construction" box in the PropertyManager.

FIGURE 9.10

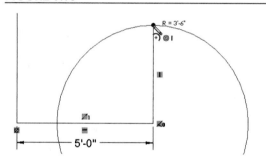

FIGURE 9.11

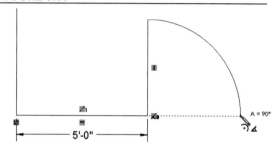

Repeat for the other door, as shown in Figure 9.12.

Select the endpoints of the arcs, as shown in Figure 9.13.

FIGURE 9.12

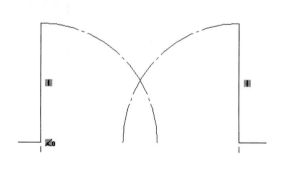

FIGURE 9.13

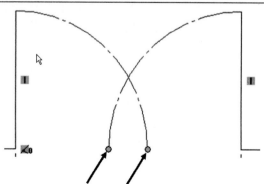

In the PropertyManager, click Merge, which joins the two points, as shown in Figure 9.14. Select both arcs, and add Equal and Tangent relations. The arcs will now appear as shown in Figure 9.15.

FIGURE 9.14

FIGURE 9.15

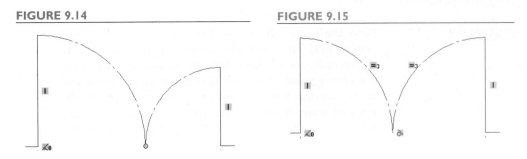

The drawing should once again be fully defined.

In order to make the outer walls and doors stand out, we will make those lines thicker. For this, we will use the Line Format toolbar.

FIGURE 9.16

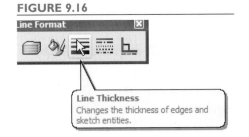

Right-click in the toolbar area. Click on Line Format. Select the lines representing the walls and doors. In the Line Format toolbar, select the Line Thickness Tool, as shown in Figure 9.16, and pick a thicker line than the default. Click the check mark in the PropertyManager to apply the selected line thickness.

The walls and doors now stand out from the dimension and construction lines, as shown in Figure 9.17.

FIGURE 9.17

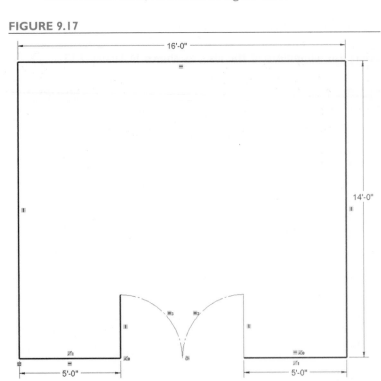

We will now place the tensile test machine in the room.

Draw a rectangle somewhere in the room, and dimension it as 4 feet by 3 feet, as shown in Figure 9.18.

FIGURE 9.18

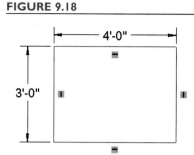

The dimensions that we added are not necessary to show in the drawing, but are required to set the size of the machine's footprint. We can hide the dimensions so they do not show, but still control the size of the rectangle.

Turn off the Smart Dimension Tool. Right-click on one of the dimensions and select Hide, as shown in Figure 9.19. Repeat for the other dimension.

FIGURE 9.19

The rectangle is fully defined except for its position on the drawing. By clicking and dragging on one of the corners, you can move it.

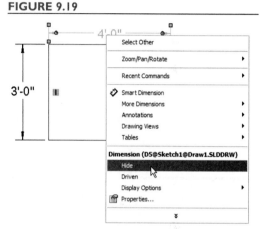

Click and drag a corner of the rectangle until it is placed near the upper-right corner of the room, as shown in Figure 9.20.

Note: if you drag a corner until it contacts another point or a line, as shown in Figure 9.21, then a relation is automatically created with that entity, and you will be unable to move the rectangle away from the entity. If you desire to do so, then click on the coincident icon and delete it.

FIGURE 9.20

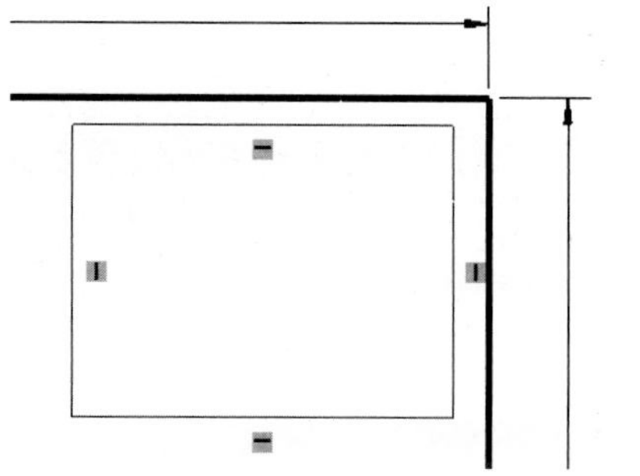

FIGURE 9.21

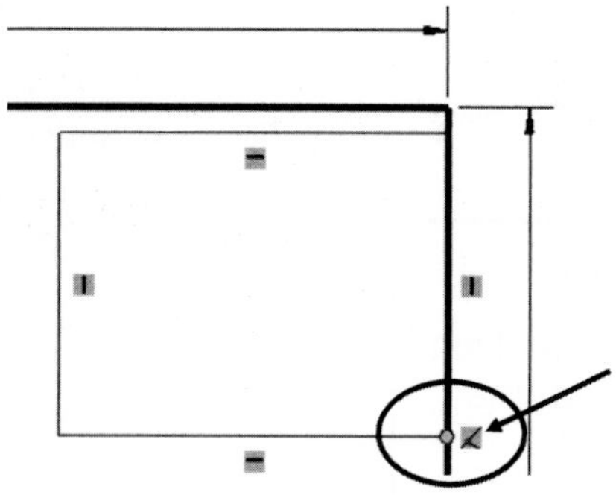

While it is not necessary to fix the rectangle in place, doing so is a good idea in that it will make the drawing fully defined if all other required dimensions and relations are present. If you fix the position of the rectangle and the status bar reports that the drawing is still underdefined, then you will probably want to check existing dimensions and relations to see why.

Click on a corner of the rectangle to select that point and display its properties in the PropertyManager. Click Fix to fix that point, and close the PropertyManager. Hit esc to deselect the point.

The drawing should now be fully defined. We will now label the rectangle as the location of the tensile test machine.

Select the Note Tool from the Annotations group of the CommandManager. Click at the approximate location of the note, near the new rectangle.

Set the desired font, size and alignment (centered), as shown in Figure 9.22. Type "Tensile Test Machine" in the text box.

FIGURE 9.22

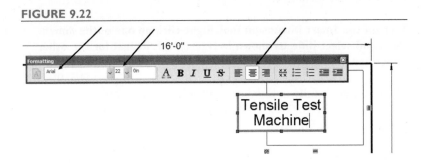

Click anywhere outside of the note box, and then esc to end the note creation.

(If you want to place the same note in another location, then you can click the note down in multiple locations before using the esc key to end the process.)

Click and drag the note to its final position, as shown in Figure 9.23.

If you want the note font changed for the entire drawing, do so from Tools: Options: Document Properties: Annotations Font: Note from the main menu, as shown in Figure 9.24.

FIGURE 9.23

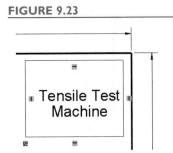

FIGURE 9.24

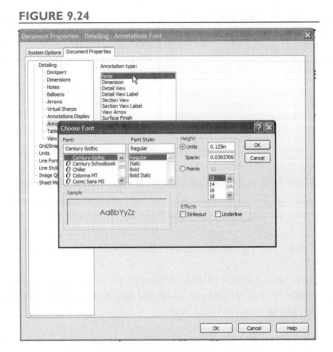

FIGURE 9.25

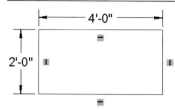

FIGURE 9.26

FIGURE 9.29

Add the first of the cabinets by drawing and dimensioning the rectangle as shown in Figure 9.25. Hide the dimensions.

After drawing the cabinet and moving its location around, you may decide that turning the cabinet 90 degrees will allow it to fit into the space better. The easiest way to do this is simply to switch the values of the dimensions. This will require showing and editing the currently hidden dimensions.

Select View: Hide/Show Annotations from the main menu, as shown in Figure 9.26. The hidden dimensions will be shown in gray. Click on each dimension that you want to show, as shown in Figure 9.27. Select Hide/Show Annotations again or esc to return to the editing mode. Change the cabinet dimensions as shown in Figure 9.28.

FIGURE 9.27   **FIGURE 9.28**

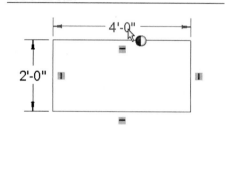

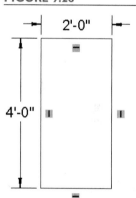

To hide the dimensions again, we can either right-click on each and select Hide, as we did earlier, or to hide several dimensions at once, we can use either Hide/Show Annotations from the menu or the Hide/Show Annotations Tool.

Select the Hide/Show Annotations Tool. Click on each dimension to be hidden. Dimensions selected will be shown in gray. Press the esc key to return to the editing mode, and the selected dimensions will be hidden.

Add a note identifying the cabinet. If desired, rotate the text 90 degrees by clearing the "Use document font" box and changing the angle in the Property-Manager, as shown in Figure 9.29. Click the check mark.

Add the other two cabinets. Dimension, locate, and label them, as shown in Figure 9.30.

FIGURE 9.30

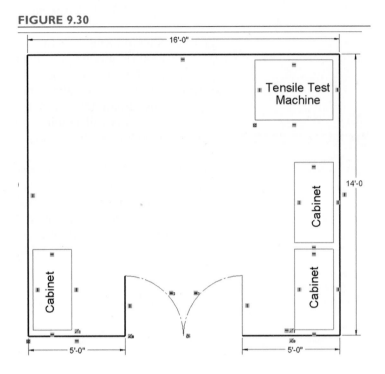

Note that if you want to use Copy and Paste to add the cabinets, then the dimensions defining their sizes must also be copied, or else the cabinets will change size when dragged into a new position. Hidden dimensions cannot be copied, so you must first unhide the dimensions before using Copy and Paste commands.

Add and dimension rectangles representing the inspection bench and desk, as shown in Figure 9.31.

FIGURE 9.31

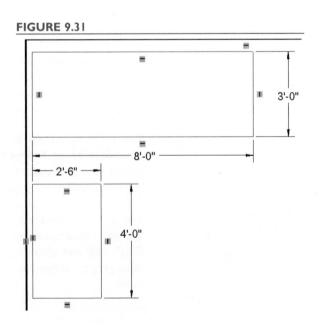

Label the inspection bench and desk. Add and label the 4-foot-square parts bin, with the lines representing it shown as construction lines. Fix all of the entities in position so that the drawing is fully defined. Hide the dimensions defining the bench, desk, and parts bin. The finished drawing is shown in Figure 9.32. Note that the sketch relation icons are not shown when the drawing is printed.

FIGURE 9.32

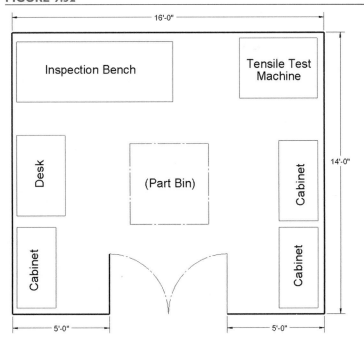

Finally, suppose that we wish to rotate the tensile test machine 45 degrees to give the operator better access to the machine. To do so, it will be necessary to delete some of the relations created automatically when the rectangle was drawn, and to add some new relations to maintain the rectangular shape and orient the rectangle properly.

Click on the Fixed icon, as shown in Figure 9.33. Delete it. Delete the horizontal and vertical relations from the four lines defining the machine position. Add parallel relations between each of the pairs of opposite sides, as shown in Figure 9.34. Select two adjacent sides, and add a perpendicular relation, as shown in Figure 9.35.

FIGURE 9.33   FIGURE 9.34   FIGURE 9.35

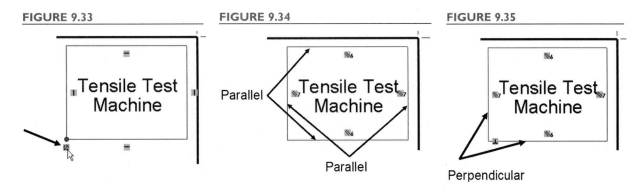

The addition of these relations defines the shape as a rectangle, but the removal of the horizontal and vertical relations allows it to be rotated. The hidden dimensions still apply to the rectangle, and fix its size.

FIGURE 9.36

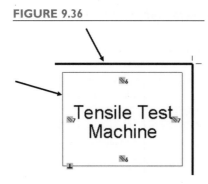

Select the Smart Dimension Tool. Select one of the vertical lines of the rectangle and then a horizontal wall, as shown in Figure 9.36.

This will create an angular dimension between the lines, as shown in Figure 9.37. Change the dimensions to 135 degrees, reflecting a rotation of 45 degrees, as shown in Figure 9.38.

FIGURE 9.37   **FIGURE 9.38**

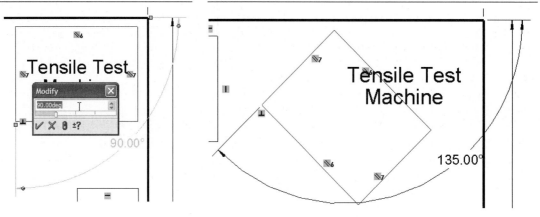

Rotate the text labeling the machine –45 degrees, as shown in Figure 9.39.

Hide the angular dimension, drag it into position, and fix one of the corner points.

FIGURE 9.39

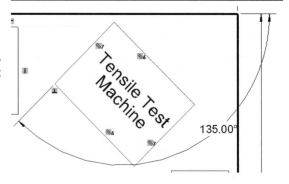

FUTURE STUDY

Industrial Engineering

In this example, we created a floor plan to see if the proposed lab space would accommodate the equipment required for the lab. Consider the challenge of planning the layout of a manufacturing plant with hundreds of thousands of square feet of floor space and hundreds of machines. If not well planned, the operations of the plant will be crippled by inefficiencies in the ways that raw materials and parts move through the plant. Efficient plant layout is one of the functions of industrial engineers.

Industrial engineers perform many other functions toward the goal of improving operations. These functions might include monitoring and improving the quality of finished products, streamlining material handling and product flow, or redesigning work cells for better efficiency.

While the word "industrial" refers to the manufacturing environment where industrial

engineers have traditionally worked, the skills of industrial engineers are now being widely used in service sector businesses as well. For example, many hospitals use industrial engineers to help improve quality and efficiency. Package-delivery companies, facing monumental logistics challenges associated with delivering packages worldwide under extreme time pressure, also use the services of industrial engineers.

Industrial engineers also are involved with product design, usually from the standpoint of *ergonomics*, the consideration of human characteristics and limitations in the design of products. In this area, there is overlap with the functions of the industrial designer.

Most engineering students in other disciplines take some coursework in industrial engineering topics. These topics could include engineering economy, quality control, project management, and ergonomic design.

The drawing is now complete, as shown in **Figure 9.40**. Dimensions can be added to precisely place the objects in the room, if required. (It will be necessary to delete the fixed relations of the points if these dimensions are to be added.)

FIGURE 9.40

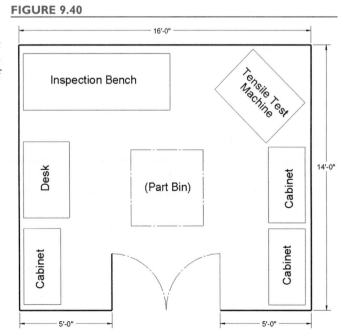

9.2 Finding the Properties of 2-D Shapes

The SolidWorks program can be used to determine the properties of areas. For example, the areas of complex shapes can be determined, and the locations of *centroids* and the values of *moments of inertia* of areas can be computed.

9.2.1 Calculating the Area of a Shape

Consider the building lot shown in **Figure 9.41**. Suppose that we want to find the acreage of this lot. The first step is to draw the lot. In order to fit the drawing on an 8-1/2 x 11 inch sheet, the minimum scale factor possible will be 1320 inches (110 feet) divided by 8.5 inches = 155. We will use a scale factor of 1:200.

Open a new drawing. Choose an A-Landscape paper size without a sheet format displayed. Set the drawing scale to 1:200 and draw and dimension the lot shown in Figure 9.41. Fix one corner of the lot, and the drawing should be fully defined.

FIGURE 9.41

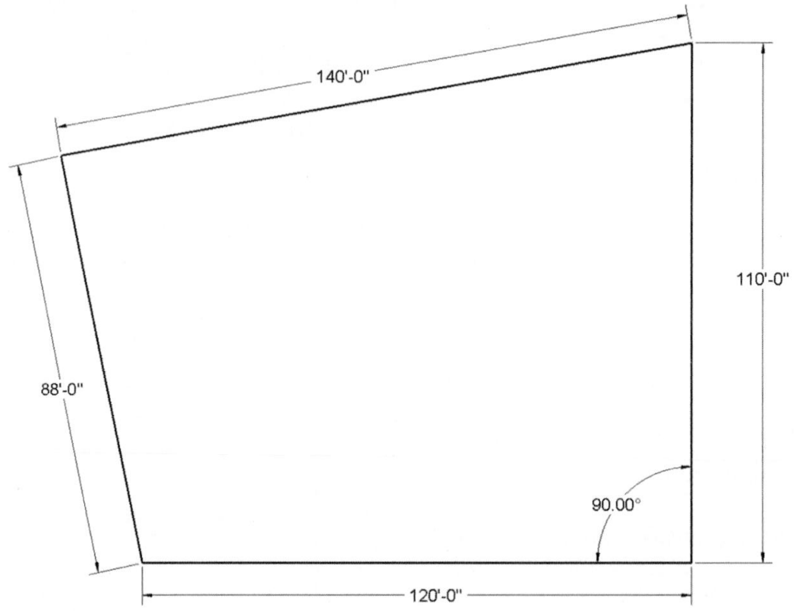

140'-0"

110'-0"

88'-0"

90.00°

120'-0"

FIGURE 9.42

Press the esc key to deselect any points or lines. Select Tools: Section Properties from the main menu. Click the Options button, and set the units to feet and the number of decimal places to 6, as shown in Figure 9.42. Click OK.

The area will be displayed in the units selected, in this case square feet. However, the area displayed will be that of the *drawing* area, not the actual area. Since the area of the drawing in square feet will be small, a large number of decimal places will be needed for accuracy.

The area displayed is 0.318910 square feet, as shown in **Figure 9.43**. To determine the area of the lot, the calculated area must be adjusted to account for the scale. Since area has the units of length squared, the calculated area must be multiplied by the scale factor squared:

$$\text{Area} = (0.318910 \text{ ft.}^2)(200^2) = 12{,}756 \text{ ft.}^2$$

To convert to acres, the conversion factor of 43,560 ft.^{2}/acre must be applied:

$$\text{Area} = (12{,}756 \text{ ft.}^2)/(43{,}560 \text{ ft.}^2/\text{acre}) = 0.29 \text{ acres}$$

FIGURE 9.43

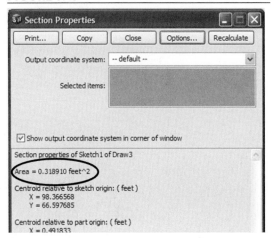

9.2.2 Calculating the Section Properties of a Shape

In mechanics of materials, it is often necessary to compute the moment of inertia of the cross-section of a structural member. For simple shapes, such as a rectangle or circle, easy formulas can be used for this computation. For compound shapes, such as a T-beam constructed from two rectangular shapes, the calculations are lengthier.

FIGURE 9.44

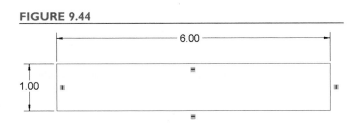

Open a new drawing. Choose A-Landscape paper without a sheet format displayed. Draw and dimension a rectangle, as shown in Figure 9.44.

FIGURE 9.45

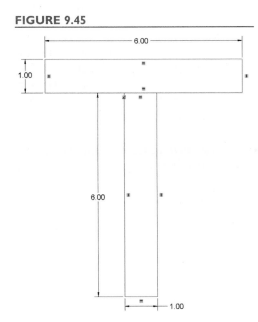

Add and dimension the second rectangle shown in **Figure 9.45**, making sure to snap the first point of the new rectangle to the edge of the first rectangle.

FIGURE 9.46

To center the second rectangle relative to the first, we could add a dimension. A better way is to add the centerlines shown in Figure 9.46, and add an Equal relation between them.

To compute the area or moments of inertia of the shape, it is not necessary to locate the drawing on the page. However, if we want to know the location of the centroidal axes, then we need to set a point at a known location.

Select the lower-left point of the second rectangle, as shown in Figure 9.47.

FIGURE 9.47

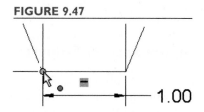

FIGURE 9.48

In the PropertyManager, set the coordinates of the point to x = 5 and y = 1, as shown in Figure 9.48.

In drawings, the lower-left corner of the page is the origin of the x-y coordinate system.

Select Tools: Section Properties from the main menu. A message will be displayed that the sketch has intersecting contours. Close the Section Properties dialog box.

The properties can be computed only for a sketch or drawing containing a single, closed contour.

FIGURE 9.49

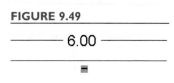
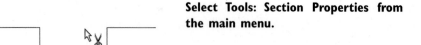

Select the Trim Entities Tool from the Sketch group of the CommandManager. Trim away the overlapping portions of both rectangles, as shown in Figure 9.49.

Select Tools: Section Properties from the main menu.

FUTURE STUDY

Mechanics of Materials

The study of mechanics of materials involves determining *stresses, strains,* and *deformations* in bodies subjected to various loadings. Stress is the force per unit area acting on a point in a body, and the calculation of stress is necessary to predict failure of a structure. Strain is a measure of geometrical changes within a body. Stress and strain are related by properties of the material used. Deformations are related to strains in the body. While strain applies at a given point, deformation is the dimensional change of the entire body. For example, consider a 1 x 6 inch wooden plank resting on sawhorses near its ends. If the *span* of this beam is 6 feet, and a 175-pound man stands in the middle, how much will the plank move downward?

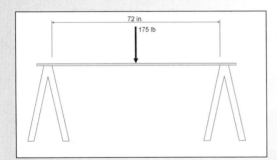

Using mechanics of materials concepts, it can be determined that the deflection of such a beam is:

$$\delta = \frac{PL^3}{48EI}$$

where:

P = force = 175 lb.

L = span = 72 in.

E = *modulus* of the material. A typical value for wood = 1,500,000 lb/in.[2]

I = moment of inertia of the cross-section

For a rectangular shape, the moment of inertia is:

$$I = \frac{1}{12}\,bh^3$$

So for our plank, with base b = 6 inches and height h = 1 inch, I = 0.50 in.[4], and the deflection = 1.81 inches. If we could carefully place the plank so that it is resting on the 1-inch edge, then the values of b and h are switched. The moment of inertia increases to 18 in.[4] and the deflection reduces to 0.05 inches. Therefore, the *bending stiffness* of the plank has increased by a factor of 36 by changing its orientation. The moment of inertia is increased by moving material to the greatest possible distance away from the *centroidal axis* (the axis passing through the centroid, or center of area, of the section). With wood construction, this is done by aligning the members appropriately, as with floor beams that are placed with their long dimensions perpendicular to the floor. In steel construction, wide-flange beams maximize bending stiffness by placing most of the material in the flanges, as far from the centroidal axis as possible.

When complex shapes are used, calculation of the moment of inertia can be cumbersome. First, the centroid must be located, and then the moments of inertia of simple regions of the shape must be calculated and adjusted for their distances away from the centroidal axis. Finally, the moments of inertia of the individual regions are summed.

The Section Properties Tool can be a useful tool for calculating and/or checking the value of moment of inertia.

FIGURE 9.50

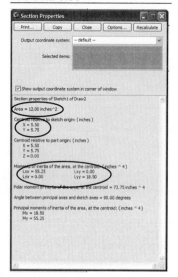

The section properties are displayed, as shown in **Figure 9.50**.

There are two principal moments of inertia calculated. The moment labeled "Lxx" is the moment of inertia about an axis through the centroid of the cross-section, parallel to the X axis. The location of this axis is given by the Y coordinate of the centroid, 5.75 inches. Since a point at the bottom of the section was set at Y = 1 inch, the axis is 4.75 inches above the bottom of the section, as shown in **Figure 9.51**. The moment of inertia about this axis is 55.25 in.[4]. The other principal moment of inertia is about the axis shown in **Figure 9.52**. The value of the moment of inertia about this axis is 18.50 in.[4].

FIGURE 9.51

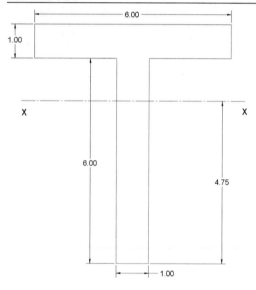

FIGURE 9.52

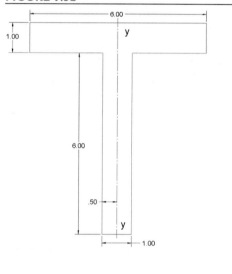

P9.1 Place the items from section 9.1 into the space shown here, which includes two 18-inch-square columns.

FIGURE P9.1

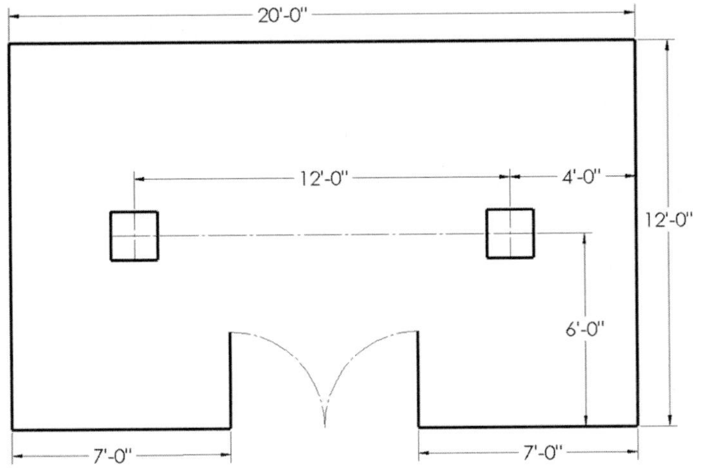

P9.2 Sketch a floor plan of your room or apartment, showing the locations of furniture.

P9.3 A builder desires to construct a house on the irregular lot shown here. The desired house will be rectangular in shape, 55 feet by 40 feet, with the front of the house 55 feet wide. The front of the house is to be parallel to the street. If local regulations require that there be 10 feet between property lines and any point on the house, can the proposed house be built on the lot?

FIGURE P9.3

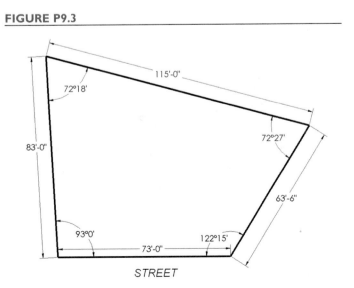

Note: Three of the angular dimensions will be driven dimensions, since the length of all sides and one angle defines the lot shape. However, when property is surveyed, all lengths and angles are measured. Trigonometry is then used to ensure that the dimensions are consistent to within a certain tolerance. This method allows for incorrectly measured or recorded lengths and angles to be detected. The angles are measured in degrees and minutes (1 minute = 1/60 degree).

Hint: Use the offset entities tool to offset the property lines 10 feet inward. You can then check to see if the house plan fits within the offset lines.

P9.4   Find the number of square feet in the lot described in P9.3.

(Answer: 6506 ft.²)

P9.5   Find the location of the centroid and the principal moments of inertia of the channel shape shown here. Make a sketch showing the locations of the centroidal axes.

FIGURE P9.5

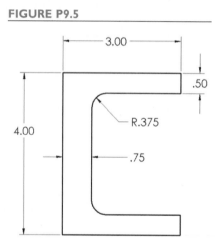

P9.6   a) Fiber-reinforced composite plates are often made by stacking up
layers of material with the fibers oriented in specified directions.
Consider a 6-inch by 12-inch rectangular plate that is to be made up
of two layers with fibers oriented at +30 degrees relative to the long
axis of the plate, and two layers with fibers oriented at –30 degrees,
as illustrated in **Figure P9.6A**. If the fiber-reinforced material comes
on a roll that is 24 inches wide, with the fibers oriented along the
length of the roll, determine the length L that is required for a
rectangular portion of material from which the four required layers
can be cut (see the example in **Figure P9.6B**). Since the material is
expensive, try to place the layers in a manner that reduces the
amount of scrap. Calculate the percentage of material that will be
scrap.

FIGURE P9.6A   **FIGURE P9.6B**

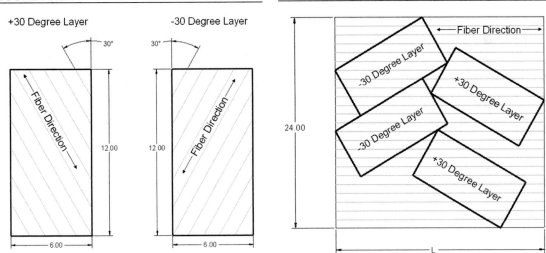

   b) Suppose you are asked to evaluate a suggestion that the material be
cut into rectangular sections from which two complete plates can be
made (that is, four +30 layers and four –30 layers can be cut from
the rectangular section). Can you develop a cutting pattern that will
reduce the scrap percentage calculated in part a?

CHAPTER 10

Application of SolidWorks to Vector Mechanics

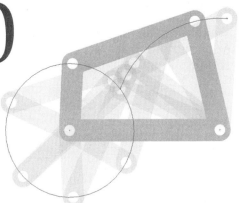

Introduction

Many engineering problems involve the manipulation of *vectors*. A vector is a representation of a quantity that is defined by both a magnitude and a direction, as opposed to a scalar quantity that can be defined by a magnitude only. For example, the speed of an object is a scalar quantity, while velocity is defined by both the speed and the direction of the object's motion, and therefore is a vector quantity. The SolidWorks 2-D drawing environment allows for easy graphical solution of vector problems.

10.1 Vector Addition

Consider the two forces acting on the hook as shown in **Figure 10.1**. We would like to find the resultant force, that is, a single force that affects the hook in an equivalent manner to the two forces. The resultant force is the vector sum of the two vectors **A** and **B**. (Vector quantities are usually denoted by bold type or by a bar or arrow over the symbol: **A** or $\bar{A}$ or $\vec{A}$.)

FIGURE 10.1

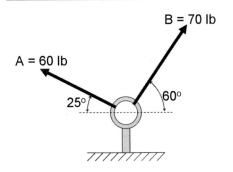

B = 70 lb

A = 60 lb

25° 60°

FIGURE 10.2

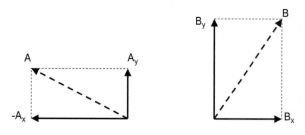

Analytically, the vectors can be added by adding the *components* of the two vectors. If we define an x-y coordinate system, then each vector can be broken into its x and y components, as shown in **Figure 10.2**.

The components of the resultant vector **R** are found by adding the components of **A** and **B**:

	x component	y component
A	$-60 \cos (25°) = -54.38$ lb.	$60 \sin (25°) = 25.36$ lb.
B	$70 \cos (60°) = 35.00$ lb.	$70 \sin (60°) = 60.62$ lb.
R	-19.38 lb.	85.98 lb.

From the components, the magnitude and direction of **R** can be determined (**see Figure 10.3**):

$$R = \sqrt{(19.38)^2 + (85.98)^2} = 88.14 \text{ lb.}$$

$$\theta = \tan^{-1} \left(\frac{85.98}{19.38} \right) = 77.3 \text{ deg}$$

FIGURE 10.3

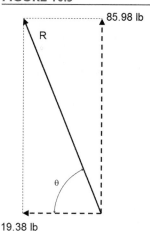

10.2 Vector Addition with SolidWorks

Open a new drawing. Choose A-Landscape as the paper size, with the "Display sheet format" box unchecked.

FIGURE 10.4

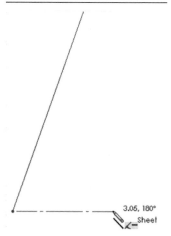

We must now choose scales: one for the magnitude of the vectors and another for the drawing. The vectors must be drawn to scale so that the length is proportional to its magnitude. If we choose to let 1 inch represent 10 pounds of force, then our two vectors will be 6 and 7 inches long. To fit onto our 8-1/2 x 11 inch drawing, it will probably be necessary to draw the vectors at one-half scale.

Right-click anywhere in the drawing area, and select Properties from the pop-up menu. Change the scale to 1:2.

(The default scale is defined in the template selected when creating the drawing.)

Select the Line Tool, and drag out a diagonal line to represent the first vector. From the starting point of the first vector, drag out a horizontal centerline, as shown in Figure 10.4.

If desired, you can show sketch relations by selecting View: Sketch Relations from the main menu.

Dimension the length of the vector line as 7 inches, and the angle between the vector line and the horizontal centerline as 60 degrees, as shown in Figure 10.5.

To add vectors graphically, we set them "tip-to-tail." That is, the second vector starts at the end of the first vector.

FIGURE 10.5

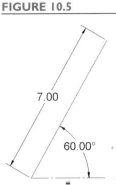

FIGURE 10.6

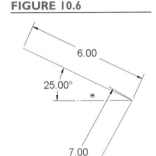

Draw the second vector line diagonally from the end of the first vector. (Be sure not to align this vector line with any of the dashed lines that appear. Doing so will add a constraint to the line that will have to be deleted before the vector's magnitude and direction can be defined.) Add another horizontal construction line, and add the 6-inch and 25-degree dimensions as shown in Figure 10.6.

The resultant vector extends from the starting point of the first vector to the ending point of the second vector.

Add the line representing the resultant vector, as shown in Figure 10.7, snapping to the endpoints.

Add another horizontal centerline, and add the dimensions for the length and orientation angle of the resultant vector. When you add these dimensions, you will get a message that adding this dimension will make the drawing over-dimensioned, and asking if you want to make the dimension driven or leave it as driving (Figure 10.8). Click OK to make each dimension driven.

FIGURE 10.7

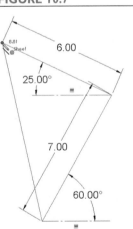

FIGURE 10.8

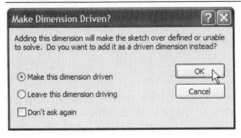

A driving dimension is one that helps control the size and position of the drawing or sketch entities, while a driven dimension does not.

FIGURE 10.9

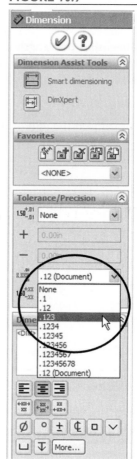

FIGURE 10.10

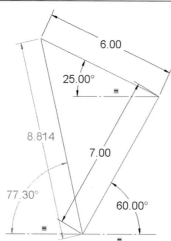

If the length of the resultant vector is not given to 3 decimal places, select that dimension and choose .123 from the pull-down menu in the PropertyManager, as shown in Figure 10.9.

The completed drawing is shown in Figure 10.10. The length of the resultant vector is 8.814 inches, corresponding to a magnitude of 88.14 pounds. This value and the angle of 77.3 degrees relative to the horizontal agree with the results found analytically.

10.3 Modifying the Vector Addition Drawing

The drawing just created is fine for calculating the magnitude and direction of the resultant vector, but visually is not clear. Vectors are usually shown with arrowheads to indicate their directions, and the line format of the vector lines can be changed to make them stand out from the construction and dimension lines. Also, the dimensions of the resultant vector can be shown differently to make them stand out from the input dimensions. We will modify the drawing to make it more understandable, and to allow easy modifications of the input quantities.

For this exercise we will use the Formatting and Line Format toolbars.

Right-click on any open toolbar. If they are not already displayed, click on Formatting and Line Format to display those toolbars.

We will first add arrowheads to the vectors. We will use a simple arrowhead: a single line segment.

FIGURE 10.11

Add a line to the end of the 7-inch vector line. Add a length dimension of 1 inch and angular dimension of 20 degrees, as shown in Figure 10.11.

Select both the vector line and the arrowhead line. From the Line Format toolbar, click on the Line Thickness Tool, as shown in **Figure 10.12**, and choose a thicker line style. If desired, change the color of the lines, using the Brush Tool to the left of the Line Thickness Tool.

FIGURE 10.12

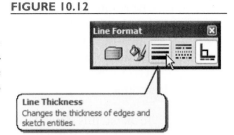

These lines now stand out, as shown in **Figure 10.13**.

Hide the I-inch and 20-degree dimensions, as shown in **Figure 10.14**.

FIGURE 10.13

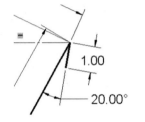

FIGURE 10.14

Add and dimension arrowhead lines to the other vector lines. Hide the dimensions, and change the line thicknesses and colors, if desired, of the vector and arrowhead lines (**Figure 10.15**).

FIGURE 10.15

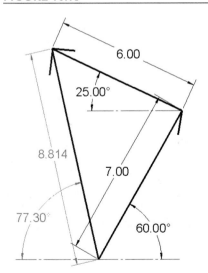

Use a different color for the resultant vector to make it stand out from the other vectors.

Modify the text of the dimensions by selecting them and changing the point sizes from the Formatting toolbar. Make the dimension text associated with the resultant vector larger than those of the other vectors. You can also make these text items bold by clicking the "B" Tool on the Formatting toolbar, as shown in **Figure 10.16**. To change the default color of the driven dimensions from grey to black, select **Tools: Options** from the main menu. Under the **System Properties** tab, select **Colors**, and change the color of **Dimensions, Non Imported (Driven)** to black.

FIGURE 10.16

FIGURE 10.17

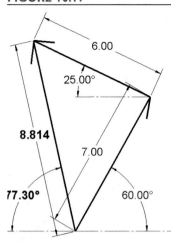

The completed vector drawing is shown in **Figure 10.17**.

One of the main benefits of using the SolidWorks program to add vectors is that the vector drawing can be easily modified to solve different problems. We will use our drawing to add a different pair of vectors.

To make this drawing more useable, define the orientation of the vectors from a common reference: the +x direction.

Delete the 25- and 77.3-degree dimensions and associated reference lines. Add new construction lines and dimensions as shown in Figure 10.18. Add the 155-degree dimension first so that the 102.7-degree dimension is the driven one.

FIGURE 10.18

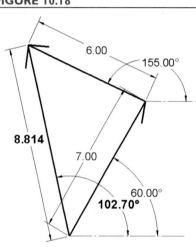

Dimensions can be changed from driven to driving or from driving to driven by right-clicking on the dimension and checking or un-checking Driven. Of course, if too many dimensions are driving, the drawing will be over-defined.

Let's use this drawing to add the two vectors shown in **Figure 10.19**.

FIGURE 10.19

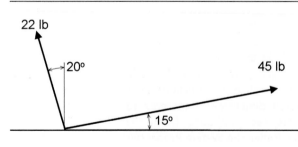

We will let 1 inch equal 1 pound for the vector's scale.

Change the dimensions of the input vectors to 22 inches and 110 degrees (from the horizontal) for the first vector, and 45 inches and 15 degrees for the second vector.

Of course, the drawing now extends beyond the edges of the sheet.

Right-click anywhere within the sheet borders, and select Properties. Set the scale to 1:5.

In the dialog box that appears, leave the check boxes as shown in Figure 10.20 and click OK.

FIGURE 10.20

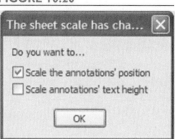

This will allow the relative position of the dimension to stay the same, without changing the size of the text.

Drag the drawing into the sheet boundaries, and drag the dimensions into desired positions, as shown in Figure 10.21.

FIGURE 10.21

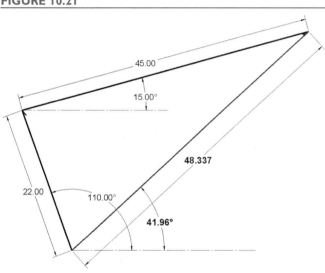

The resultant vector has a magnitude of 48.3 pounds, and is oriented at 42 degrees counterclockwise (CCW) from the x axis.

10.4 Further Solution of Vector Equations

In the previous example, two vectors were added to find the resultant vector's magnitude and direction. In a vector equation, any two unknowns (magnitudes and/or directions) can be determined. The following examples illustrate this concept.

FIGURE 10.22

A small plane can travel at an airspeed of 300 miles per hour. The flight path is to be at a heading of 15 degrees. (Heading is the angular direction measured CW from due North.) The wind is blowing from the WNW, as shown in Figure 10.22, at 60 mph. Find the plane's ground speed and the direction of the plane's travel relative to the air.

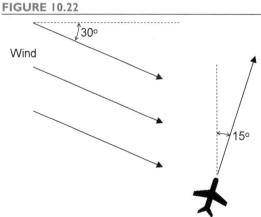

The vector equation for this problem is:

$$\vec{V}_{plane} = \vec{V}_{air} + \vec{V}_{plane/air}$$

where:

$\vec{V}_{plane}$ = absolute velocity of the plane (ground speed)—magnitude unknown and direction known

$\vec{V}_{air}$ = wind velocity—magnitude and direction known

$\vec{V}_{plane/air}$ = velocity of the plane relative to the air (airspeed)—magnitude known and direction unknown

Open a new A-size drawing and set the drawing scale to 1:50. We will let 1 inch equal 1 mile per hour.

FIGURE 10.23

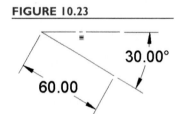

Begin by drawing and dimensioning the vector representing the wind speed, as shown in Figure 10.23, near the bottom of the sheet.

It is helpful when we are dragging vectors together later to have a point fixed on the drawing.

Select the starting point of the first vector and click on the Fix icon in the PropertyManager.

If you need to move this point later, click on the point and the Fix relation will be listed in the PropertyManager. Select this relation and use the delete key to remove it. The point can then be dragged to a new location.

FIGURE 10.24

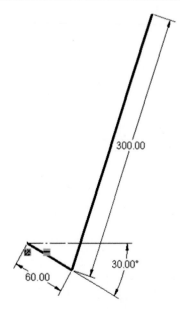

Add the airspeed vector of 300 mph at an arbitrary angle, as shown in Figure 10.24.

Add the resultant (ground speed) vector at 15 degrees from vertical. The length is unknown, but make the line long enough so that the airspeed vector will intersect it when rotated into position, as shown in Figure 10.25. If desired, change the color of the resultant vector line to make it easy to distinguish from the airspeed and wind vectors.

Click and drag the endpoint of the airspeed vector until it intersects with the ground speed vector (see Figure 10.26).

With the Trim Entities Tool, trim away the end of the ground speed vector, as shown in Figure 10.27. (Make sure that the Trim option is set as "Trim to closest.")

FIGURE 10.25

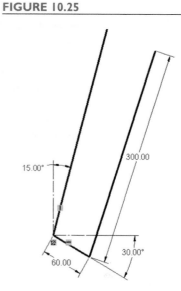

FIGURE 10.26

FIGURE 10.27

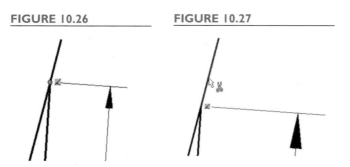

Add dimensions for the ground speed magnitude and the direction of the airspeed, as shown in Figure 10.28.

FIGURE 10.28

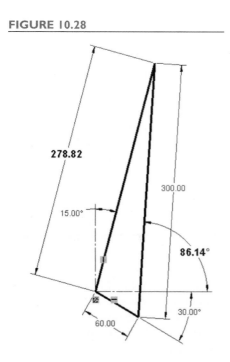

The result is that the ground speed is 279 miles per hour. Relative to the wind, the plane must fly about 4 degrees east of due north to achieve the desired course.

Variations of this problem can be easily solved by changing the input quantities. For example, consider the case where the wind is blowing from due west at 70 mph.

Change the dimensions defining the wind speed vector, as shown in Figure 10.29.

Figure 10.29 shows the resulting vector equation. The ground speed is now 310 miles per hour, as the wind contributes to the east-to-west component of the plane's travel.

FIGURE 10.29

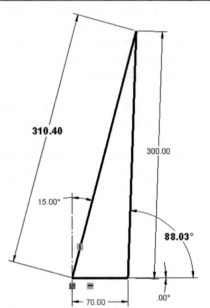

10.5 Kinematic Sketch of a Simple Mechanism

In Chapter 11, we will look at the application of the SolidWorks program to model mechanisms, with assemblies of 3-D component parts. Often, the first step in the design of a mechanism is the preparation of a *kinematic sketch*, a 2-D drawing showing simplified representations of the members. For example, a four-bar linkage, which is a common mechanism used in many machines, can be represented by four lines, as shown in **Figure 10.30**.

FIGURE 10.30

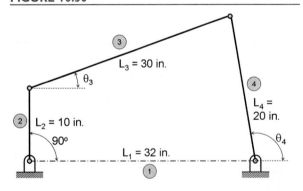

In a *kinematic analysis*, the velocities and accelerations of the links and points are calculated, based on the velocity and acceleration of the driving link. For example, if Link 2 is connected to a motor and rotated about its pivot point at a constant velocity, the angular velocities and accelerations of the other two moving links and the translational velocities and accelerations of points on those links can be calculated. The accelerations are important because force is proportional to acceleration. If the accelerations are known, the forces acting on the members and joints can be calculated. (Note: Although there are only three moving members, this mechanism is referred to as a four-bar linkage because it is connected to a fixed or ground link, which is usually called Link 1.)

The first step in any kinematic analysis is a *position analysis*. For a given position of the driving link (the angular position of Link 2, 90° in the example), the positions of the other links must be calculated. Obviously, these positions can be calculated using trigonometry. For many mechanisms, a position analysis using trigonometry is surprisingly complex. A graphical solution is often utilized. The SolidWorks program is an excellent tool for graphical position analyses, in that dimensions can be easily changed and the effects on the rest of the linkage can be determined.

FIGURE 10.31

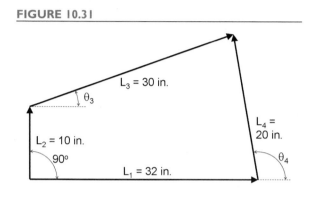

L_3 = 30 in.

θ_3

L_2 = 10 in.

90°

L_1 = 32 in.

$L_4 =$ 20 in.

θ_4

The links are often represented by vectors, as shown in **Figure 10.31**. In this case, all of the vector magnitudes (lengths) are known, as well as two of the vector angles (Link 1 is horizontal, and we will be performing the analysis for a given orientation of Link 2, the driving link). Therefore, we can solve the vector equation for the two unknown quantities, the angles θ_3 and θ_4.

Open a new A-size drawing, and set the scale to 1:5.

Draw three lines at arbitrary orientations, as shown in Figure 10.32, without adding vertical, horizontal, or perpendicular relations.

Select the three lines, and increase their thicknesses from the Line Format toolbar.

Add a centerline representing Link 1, and add a Horizontal relation to this line, as shown in Figure 10.33.

FIGURE 10.32

FIGURE 10.33

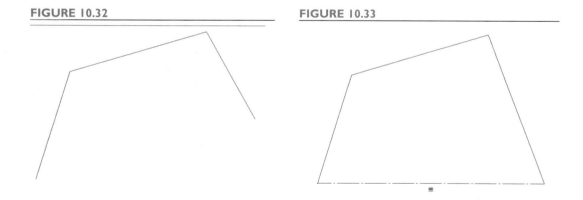

FIGURE 10.34

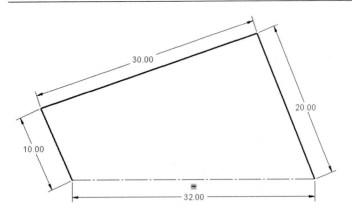

Add length dimensions, as shown in Figure 10.34. Be sure to add dimensions oriented with the links, not horizontal or vertical dimensions.

Add the angular dimension between Links 1 and 2, setting it to 90 degrees, as shown in Figure 10.35. Add a Fix relation to one of the points on Link 1.

FIGURE 10.35

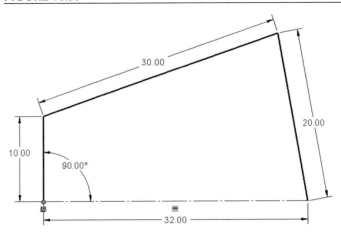

Note that although both points on Link 1 are fixed, the 32-inch distance and horizontal relation cause one point to be fully defined when the point at the opposite end is fixed. Therefore, adding a Fix relation to both points would result in the drawing being overdefined.

FIGURE 10.36

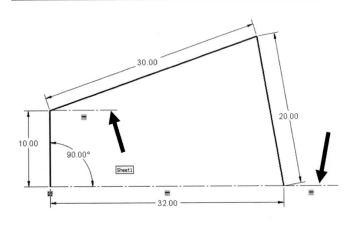

Add horizontal centerlines from which the angular positions of Links 3 and 4 will be measured, as shown in Figure 10.36.

Add an angular dimension between Link 3 and the adjacent horizontal centerline. A box will appear with the message that this dimension will overdefine the drawing. Select OK to make the dimension driven, as shown in Figure 10.37.

Add an angular driven dimension defining the position of Link 4. Right-click on each of these dimensions and select Display Options: Show Parentheses, as shown in Figure 10.38.

FIGURE 10.37

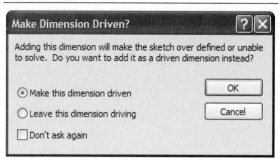

FIGURE 10.38

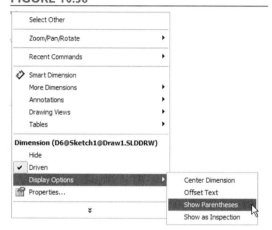

When driven dimensions are shown with parentheses, as shown in **Figure 10.39**, it makes clear that these dimensions do not control the position of the mechanism. Double-clicking on these driven dimensions will not allow their values to be edited.

While the angular dimensions found from **Figure 10.39** could be easily found with any 2-D CAD system, the advantages of the SolidWorks drawing environment is seen when multiple configurations of the mechanisms are to be found. For example, if we need to find θ_3 and θ_4 for a value of $\theta_2 = 45$ degrees, we need to change only that dimension.

FIGURE 10.39

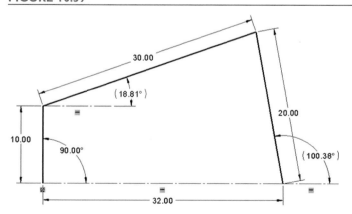

FIGURE 10.40

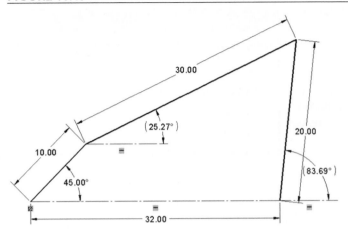

Double-click on the 90-degree dimension and change its value to 45 degrees.

Notice that the driven dimensions θ_3 and θ_4 are updated accordingly, as shown in **Figure 10.40**.

A driving dimension can be changed to a driven dimension by right-clicking and selecting Properties, and then checking the Driven box, as shown in **Figure 10.41**.

Change the 45-degree dimension to Driven.

We can now click and drag the endpoint of Link 2, as shown in **Figure 10.42**, to investigate the range of possible motions. This mechanism is classified as a *crank-rocker* because one of the members that pivots about a fixed point can rotate 360 degrees (a crank), while the other member that pivots about a fixed point oscillates back and forth (a rocker). We notice that as the crank, Link 2, revolves, there are two positions for which Link 4, the rocker, is vertical. If we want to determine the positions of the crank for which this condition applies, then we need to make θ_4 a driving dimension.

FIGURE 10.41

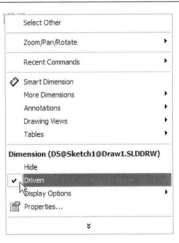

FIGURE 10.42

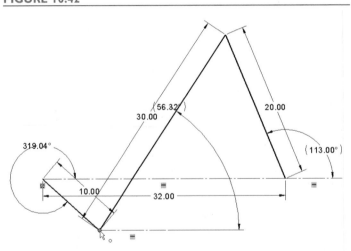

Drag one of the links until Link 4 is almost vertical, as shown in Figure 10.43.

Right-click on the dimension defining the angular position of Link 4 and clear the Driven box. Change the dimension to 90 degrees.

FIGURE 10.43

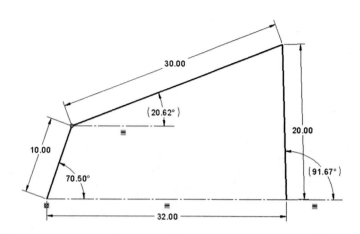

We see in **Figure 10.44** that θ_2 equal to 66.23 degrees results in Link 4 being vertical.

When dragging Link 2 through its full range of motion, we found that there are two configurations for which Link 4 is vertical.

FIGURE 10.44

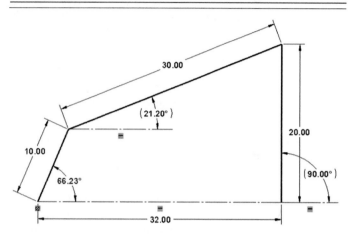

Set the 90° angle defining Link 4 to Driven. Drag the mechanism to approximately the position shown in Figure 10.45, and set the dimension back to Driving. Set the dimension to 90 degrees.

We see that $\theta_2 = 357.8$ degrees (or −2.2 degrees) is another solution for which the rocker is vertical.

We can now examine the effect of changing the length of one of the links.

FIGURE 10.45

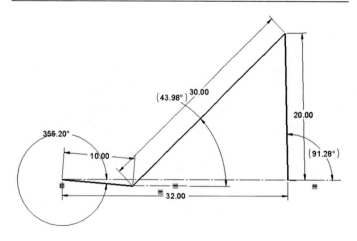

FIGURE 10.46

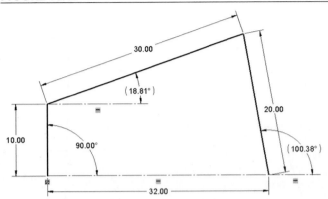

Set the mechanism back to its original position, with θ_2 as the driving dimension and θ_4 as a driven dimension, as shown in Figure 10.46.

Double-click the 30-inch dimension and change its value to 20 inches, as shown in Figure 10.47.

Change the 90-degree dimension to 150 degrees.

FIGURE 10.47

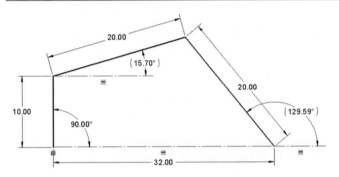

Note that the position of the links remains unchanged. This is because the position we have entered is not possible. The "No Solution Found" message in the status bar, as well as the color-coded highlights of the geometric conflicts, indicate this, as shown in **Figure 10.48**. To understand why the position is invalid, we can drag the links to determine their range of motion.

FIGURE 10.48

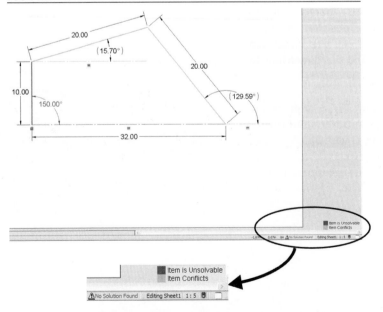

Set the 150-degree dimension to Driven, and drag the endpoint of Link 2 as far as possible in the counterclockwise direction, as shown in Figure 10.49.

FIGURE 10.49

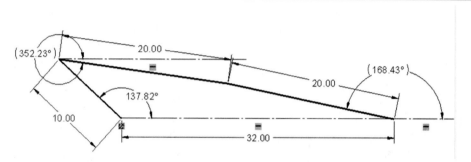

We find that when θ_2 reaches about 138 degrees, Links 3 and 4 are aligned, preventing Link 2 from rotating further. This condition defines a *toggle position* of the mechanism. The mechanism is called a *double-rocker*, since neither link that pivots around a fixed point can rotate 360 degrees.

To find the precise location of the toggle position, a relation between Links 3 and 4 can be added.

Select Links 3 and 4, and add a collinear relation. The value of θ_2 shown in Figure 10.50, 138.05 degrees, defines the toggle position.

FIGURE 10.50

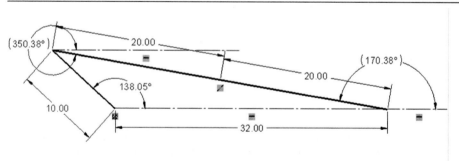

A second toggle position exists at $\theta_2 = -138.05$ degrees.

If you want to move the mechanism, it is necessary to either click on the collinear relation icon on the drawing and press the delete key, select either Link 3 or Link 4 and delete the collinear relation from the PropertyManager, or use the Undo key to remove the relation.

PROBLEMS

P10.1-10.4 Find the vector **C**, which is the sum of vectors **A** and **B**, graphically. Check your results by adding the x and y components of the vectors. All angles are measured CCW from the +x axis, as shown in **Figure P10.1**.

FIGURE P10.1

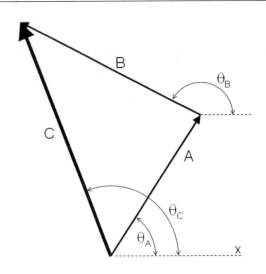

	Vector **A**		Vector **B**	
	Magnitude	Angle	Magnitude	Angle
p10.1	300 lb.	45°	150 lb.	90°
p10.2	10 m/s	0°	15 m/s	270°
p10.3	50 N	−10°	70 N	80°
p10.4	5 ft./s²	120°	4 ft./s²	300°

P10.5-10.8 Consider the vector equation **A** + **B** = **C**. Graphically find the unknown quantities for each set of vectors. All angles are measured CCW from the +x axis.

	Vector **A**		Vector **B**		Vector **C**	
	Magnitude	Angle	Magnitude	Angle	Magnitude	Angle
	A	θ_A	B	θ_B	C	θ_C
p10.5	200 lb.	25°	?	160°	300 lb.	?
p10.6	?	?	22 m/s	90°	36 m/s	78°
p10.7	?	130°	?	95°	50 N	110°
p10.8	8 ft./s²	112°	5 ft./s²	?	?	88°

P10.9 The mechanism illustrated here is called an *offset slider-crank.*

As Link 2, the crank, rotates, Link 4, the slider, moves back and forth along a horizontal line. The distance L_3 is the horizontal distance from the pivot point of the crank to the pin joint between the connector, Link 3, and the slider. Link 1 is the ground, and the distance L_1 is the offset distance.

Construct a layout drawing of the mechanism, with L_1 = 30 mm, L_2 = 50 mm, and L_3 = 150 mm.

a. Find L_4 and θ_3 for a crank angle θ_2 = 45 degrees
[Answers: 170.4 mm, 25.8 degrees)
b. Find L_4 for values of θ_2 of 0, 90, 180, and 270 degrees.
c. Find the minimum and maximum possible values of L_4, and the corresponding crank angles.

FIGURE P10.9

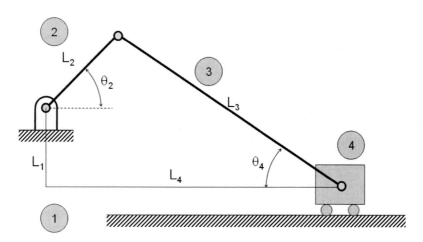

CHAPTER 11

Using SolidWorks in the Design and Analysis of Mechanisms

Introduction

A *mechanism* is an assemblage of *links* and *joints* that are connected together to achieve a desired motion task. The *links* provide the mechanical structure of the mechanism, while the *joints* provide the ability for the mechanism to move. Some typical kinds of mechanisms used by mechanical engineers are shown in **Figure 11.1**.

FIGURE 11.1

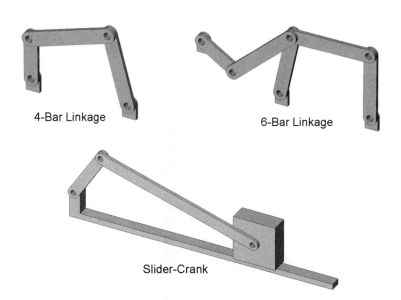

4-Bar Linkage

6-Bar Linkage

Slider-Crank

The ways in which we can connect links with joints and provide a mechanism with the ability to move are seemingly endless! Also, the links can take on any shape and size we desire, and the motion may change in complicated and seemingly unpredictable ways as we modify the links. The design of a mechanism may seem like a daunting task.

Chapter Objectives

In this chapter, you will:

- learn some basic terminology associated with mechanism design,

- use the assembly modeling techniques learned in Chapter 6 to develop a working model of a mechanism,

- perform a motion simulation of a mechanism, and

- export a motion simulation as a video file.

Computer-aided design (CAD) packages have become valuable tools in the design and analysis of mechanisms. The ability for the design engineer to adjust the size, shape, and interconnectivity of links and joints and quickly assess the impact on the mechanism has accelerated the design cycle of mechanisms. The SolidWorks program, with its ability to represent geometric constraints between structural components using assembly mates, is ideally suited to the design and virtual prototyping of complex mechanisms.

The remainder of this chapter will be devoted to the use of the SolidWorks program in the design of mechanisms through a case study involving the design of a *four-bar linkage*.

11.1 Approaching Mechanism Design with SolidWorks Assemblies

Consider the *four-bar linkage*, a classic mechanism used in engineering, shown in **Figure 11.2**.

It consists of three structural *links*, connected to each other and to fixed pivot points by *pin joints* that allow for rotating motion between the links. Though it only has three physical links, it is called a *four-bar linkage* because there is an implied fourth structural link (or *bar*) that connects the fixed ground points, as shown in **Figure 11.3**.

FIGURE 11.2

FIGURE 11.3

While the choice of a four-bar linkage as our preliminary design solution is an important step, the *parametric design problem* of selecting the appropriate link lengths and ground pivot locations to give us the desired motion is a difficult engineering task. We will develop a SolidWorks model to aid in this parametric design phase.

The features that we will employ are the *assembly* capabilities. The development of assembly models and the definition of assembly mates were covered in Chapter 6. Mated assemblies are an ideal tool for use in mechanism design, since the *joints* that provide the physical relationships between the *links* are analogous to the *mates* that define the geometric relationships between *parts*.

Think about two links connected by a pin joint, as shown in **Figure 11.4**.

FIGURE 11.4

The pin through the holes in the links allows for rotation between the links, giving a "scissors" action. The *mated assembly* representation of this type of link/joint assembly would involve two parts, with two mates serving the same geometric purpose as the pin joint in the physical linkage:

- The front face of one link is aligned with the back face of the other link using a *coincident mate*; this allows one link to "slide by" the other without any interferences between the surfaces.

- The hole in one link is aligned with the hole in the other link using a *concentric mate*; this keeps the holes aligned at their central axes.

By capturing the essential geometric constraints that underlie a *pin joint*, this sequence of two mates imparts the same motion capabilities to the solid model that are seen in the physical mechanism.

Using this simple two-link mechanism as a building block, complex mechanisms can be assembled and virtually tested. Mechanism motion can be tested and debugged without the need for physical prototypes to be constructed. The following section will step through the development of a model of a four-bar linkage.

11.2 Development of Part Models of Links

In this section, a step-by-step tutorial will lead you through the development of the part models required to make a "working" assembly model of a four-bar linkage. Four links, similar in shape but of different dimensions, will be constructed.

Open a new part, and select the Front Plane. Draw a rectangle and center it about the origin, as shown in Figure 11.5.

Select the Tangent Arc Tool. Click on a corner point of the rectangle, and drag the arc away from the rectangle, as shown in Figure 11.6.

FIGURE 11.5

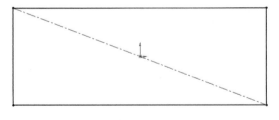

FIGURE 11.6

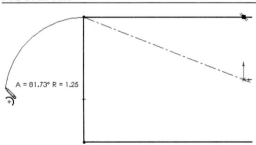

Drag the arc so that the endpoint snaps to the corresponding corner of the rectangle, as shown in Figure 11.7.

Draw a second tangent arc connecting the endpoints on the other end of the rectangle (Figure 11.8).

FIGURE 11.7   FIGURE 11.8

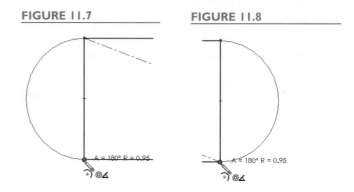

Use the Trim Entities Tool to remove the short sides of the rectangle, as shown in Figure 11.9. Add the dimensions shown in Figure 11.10.

FIGURE 11.9

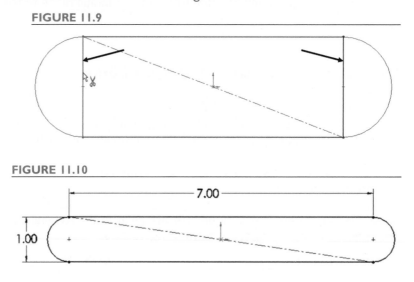

FIGURE 11.10

The sketch should be fully defined.

Extrude the sketch to a depth of 0.25 inches (Figure 11.11).

FIGURE 11.11

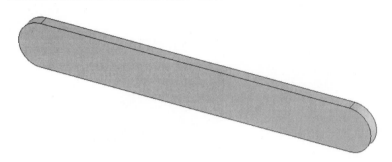

Select the front face of the part and choose the Circle Tool.

Two circles, concentric with the arcs at the ends of the link, will now be added. In order to activate the center points of the arcs as snap points, these features must first be "woken up."

"Wake up" one of the center marks by momentarily holding the cursor on the circular edge of the part (Figure 11.12).

FIGURE 11.12

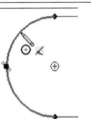

The center point of the arc will now be available as a snap point.

FIGURE 11.13

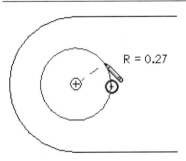

R = 0.27

Sketch a circle centered at this snap point, as shown in Figure 11.13. Repeat this process at the other end of the link. Press the esc key to turn off the Circle Tool. Select both circles, and add an Equal relation. Dimension one of the hole diameters as 0.50 inches, as shown in Figure 11.14.

The sketch should be fully defined.

Extrude a cut (type Through All) to create the holes.

FIGURE 11.14

⌀.50

The finished part is shown in **Figure 11.15**.

FIGURE 11.15

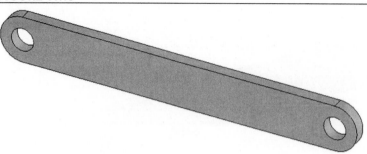

Save the part as "Link1."

The easiest way to create each of the other three links is to modify the length of the first part and save it with a different name. All dimensions except the length should be identical for the four links.

Double-click Extrude1 in the FeatureManager. The dimensions defining this feature will be displayed, as shown in Figure 11.16.

FIGURE 11.16

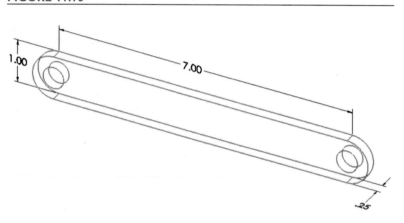

FIGURE 11.17

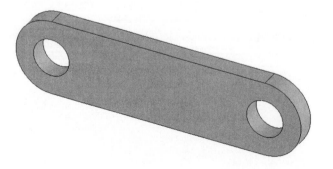

Double-click the 7-inch length and change it to 3 inches. Rebuild the model (Figure 11.17).

Choose File: Save As from the main menu. Save this part as "Link2."

Create the other two links, using the lengths as shown in Table 11.1, and save them using the names "Link3" and "Link4." Close the part window.

TABLE 11.1 Lengths of the Four Link Parts

	Length
Link1	7 in.
Link2	3 in.
Link3	5 in.
Link4	6 in.

11.3 Development of the Assembly Model of the Four-Bar Linkage

The part models developed in Section 11.2 will now be used to construct an assembly model of the four-bar linkage. It is this assembly model that will allow us to perform parametric design and simple motion analysis of the mechanism.

FIGURE 11.18

Open a new assembly. If the PropertyManager shown in Figure 11.18 does not appear, open it by selecting the Insert Component Tool from the Assembly group of the CommandManager. Select Browse, and select the file Link1. Click anywhere in the drawing space to place this part.

This first part will be fixed in space—note the "(f)" beside its name in the Design Tree. We refer to it as the "ground link" since all motion of the other links will be relative to this fixed link.

Select the Insert Component Tool. Browse to select the file Link2. Click to place Link2 in the approximate position shown in Figure 11.19.

FIGURE 11.19

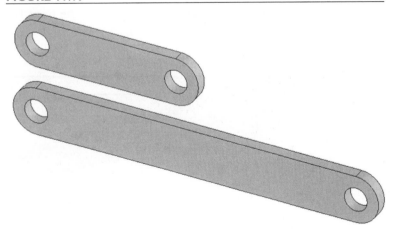

Note that you can click and drag Link2 to move it to a new position, as shown in
Figure 11.20.

FIGURE 11.20

A coincident mate aligning the faces of these links will be defined.

Press esc to cancel any selections made when moving Link2.

Select the Mate Tool to initiate a new mate.

The Mate PropertyManager will open.

**Using the Rotate View Tool, rotate the parts so that the back faces of the links
can be seen. Select the back face of Link2, as shown in Figure 11.21.**

FIGURE 11.21

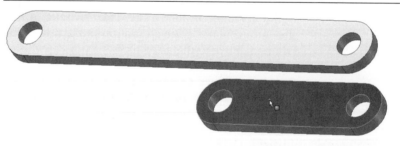

**Switch to the Trimetric View, and select the front face of Link1, as shown in Figure
11.22.**

FIGURE 11.22

Link2 will automatically move toward Link1 so that the selected faces show a coincident mate.

Click the check mark in the PropertyManager or the pop-up box to apply the mate.

A concentric mate between the holes must also be added to simulate the kinematic constraint of the pin joint.

Select the inside surfaces of the holes at the left end of the links (Figure 11.23).

A concentric mate will be previewed, as shown in Figure 11.24. Click the check mark to apply the mate. Click the check mark again to close the Mate PropertyManager.

FIGURE 11.23

FIGURE 11.24

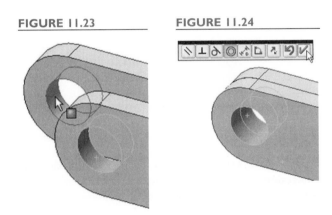

The kinematic constraints of the pin joint are now fully defined. Link2 is still free to move, as long as the movements do not violate the mates that we have placed on it. We can experiment to see the type of motion still allowed under the constraints we have imposed.

Click and drag on Link2. Confirm that you can rotate the link though a full 360 degrees. Leave Link2 in the approximate position shown in Figure 11.25.

Note that the only unconstrained motion is rotation about the mated hole, as if the links were pinned together.

FIGURE 11.25

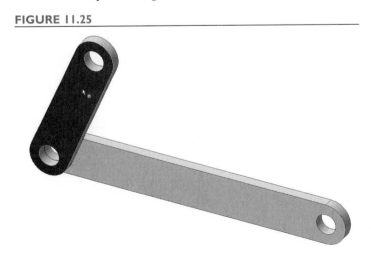

Select the Insert Component Tool. Select Link3 and place it into the assembly.

Select the Mate Tool.

In earlier chapters, we learned a shortcut method of selecting faces not visible from the current view orientation. We will use that technique to select the back face of Link3.

Move the cursor over Link3. Right-click, and pick Select Other, as shown in Figure 11.26.

FIGURE 11.26

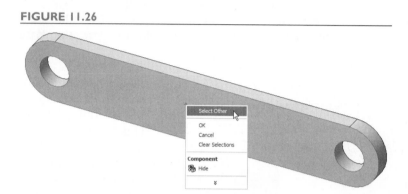

The back face of the link is highlighted, as shown in Figure 11.27. Click the left mouse button to accept the selection. Select the front face of Link1. A coincident mate will be previewed; click the check mark to accept the mate.

FIGURE 11.27

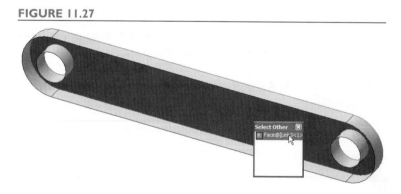

Add a concentric mate to the inner faces of corresponding holes in Link1 and Link3. Close the Mate PropertyManager.

Click and drag Link3 to the approximate position shown in Figure 11.28.

FIGURE 11.28

Insert Link4 into the assembly. Add three mates:

1. **A coincident mate between the back face of Link4 and the front face of either Link2 or Link3,**

2. **A concentric mate between the inner faces of the corresponding holes of Link2 and Link4, and**

3. **A concentric mate between the inner faces of the corresponding holes of Link3 and Link4.**

Note that only one coincident mate is required. The coincident mate between the back face of Link4 and the front face of one of the other links completely defines the z-direction location of Link4. If another coincident mate is added between the back face of Link4 and the front face of another link, the assembly will be over-constrained and simulation problems may result.

FIGURE 11.29

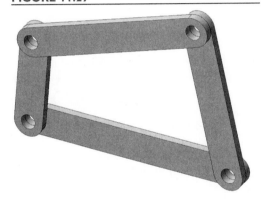

The completed assembly is shown in **Figure 11.29**.

While we can rotate Link2 manually, we can also add a simulated motor and animate the motion of the assembly.

Select the Simulation Tool from the Assembly group of the Command-Manager. Pick Rotary Motor from the pop-up menu, as shown in Figure 11.30.

Click on the front face of Link2, as shown in Figure 11.31. This places a motor driving Link2 around an axis perpendicular to the selected face.

FIGURE 11.30

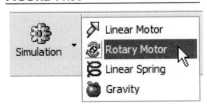

FIGURE 11.31

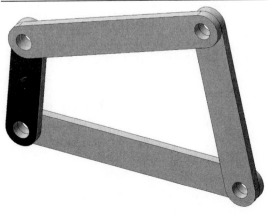

FIGURE 11.32

In the PropertyManager, the velocity of the motor can be set. Click the Numeric check box, and enter the velocity as 30.00 deg/s, as shown in Figure 11.32. Click the check mark to close the PropertyManager.

Select the Simulation Tool, and select Calculate Simulation from the pop-up menu, as shown in Figure 11.33.

The linkage will continuously rotate through its range of motion, as illustrated in Figure 11.34.

FIGURE 11.33

FIGURE 11.34

To end the simulation, select the Simulation Tool and Stop Record or Playback, as shown in Figure 11.35.

To place the links into the position in which they were assembled, select the Simulation Tool and choose Reset Components, as shown in Figure 11.36.

FIGURE 11.35

FIGURE 11.36

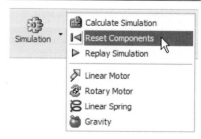

Save the assembly file using the filename "Linkage."

Machine Dynamics and Machine Design

In this chapter, we have examined a four-bar linkage and performed some simple motion analysis. If we were designing this mechanism for an engineering application, many more questions would remain:

- How fast will the output link oscillate, if we know the speed of the input link?

- What size motor would be required to drive the input link?

- How will we transmit the rotational power of the motor to the input link?

Providing the answers to these questions would generally require the expertise of a mechanical engineer. The analysis of link speeds and accelerations is classified as a kinematics problem; extending this analysis to the sizing of motors is classified as a kinetics problem. Most engineering programs include basic courses in physics and dynamics, which address the essentials of kinematic and kinetic analysis. However, because of the great emphasis in mechanical

engineering on applying these principles to mechanisms and machinery, many mechanical engineering programs include upper-level courses in the advanced application of kinematic and kinetic analysis. Such a course is often called a *machine dynamics* course, and may include the study not only of linkages, but also of the dynamics of gears, cams, and other mechanical devices.

The question of power transmission requires further insight beyond kinematic and kinetic analysis. The choice of transmission also requires the investigation of various alternatives, such as a geared transmission, a system of belts and pulleys, or a chain and sprocket drive. The selection and sizing of the appropriate transmission system requires knowledge not only of kinematic and kinetic analysis, but also of the application of stress analysis to the transmission components. This type of analysis is often covered in mechanical engineering programs in *machine components* or *machine design* courses.

The behavior of the assembly, with Link2 rotating through a full 360 degrees, is controlled by the relative lengths of the links. In particular, there will always be one link that can rotate fully (this link is called a "crank") if this equation is satisfied:

$$L + S < P + Q$$

where:

L = the length of the longest link
S = the length of the shortest length
P and Q = the length of the other two
   links.

For our linkage, L = 7 inches, S = 3 inches, and P and Q are 5 and 6 inches. Therefore, the condition above is satisfied, and at least one link (Link2) is a crank.

The SolidWorks program allows you to easily modify one of the links, and the associativity between parts and assemblies causes the changes you make to your parts to be reflected in the assembly. In fact, parts can be edited directly from the assembly window.

Double-click on Link4 in the modeling window. The dimensions associated with the part are displayed, as shown in Figure 11.37. Double-click the 6-inch dimension and change it to 4 inches. Rebuild the assembly.

FIGURE 11.37

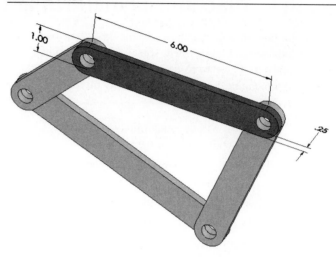

FIGURE 11.38

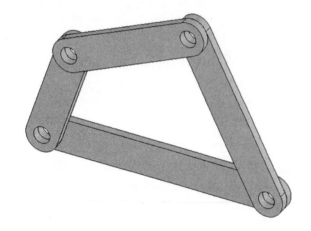

The modified assembly is shown in **Figure 11.38**. If we consider the equation discussed above, we find that L is still 7 inches, while S remains 3 inches. P and Q now equal 4 and 5 inches. Therefore, L + S is greater than P + Q, so the condition for a crank does not exist.

Select the Simulation Tool, and choose Calculate Simulation.

The linkage begins to move as before, but "locks up" when it reaches a certain point, as shown in **Figure 11.39**.

FIGURE 11.39

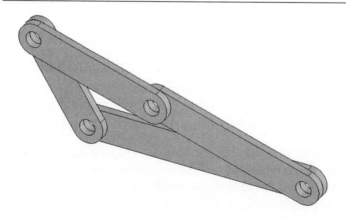

From the front view, we see that the motion has stopped when Link3 and Link4 are in alignment, as shown in **Figure 11.40**.

Reset the components. In the FeatureManager, right-click on the RotaryMotor (you may need to click the + sign next to the Simulation item to expand it), and choose Edit Feature, as shown in Figure 11.41. Click the Reverse Direction icon in the PropertyManager, as shown in Figure 11.42. Click the check mark to apply the change.

Run the Simulation.

FIGURE 11.40

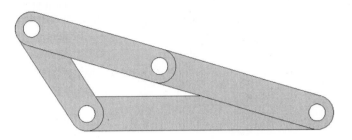

FIGURE 11.41

FIGURE 11.42

This time the linkage will lock up in the position shown in **Figure 11.43**.

The positions in which the mechanism "locks up" are called toggle positions. (Recall that in Chapter 10, we used 2-D layouts to determine the precise orientations of the toggle positions.) The presence of toggle positions may be undesirable, since they prevent full rotation of the input link. In other cases, they may be desirable, if the mechanism is to be used as a clamp or fixturing device.

FIGURE 11.43

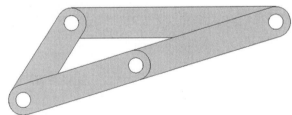

While we have looked at mechanisms for which L + S is less than P + Q (one link can rotate 360 degrees), and for which L + S is greater than P + Q (no link can rotate 360 degrees), it is logical to ask what will happen if L + S is exactly equal to P + Q.

FIGURE 11.44

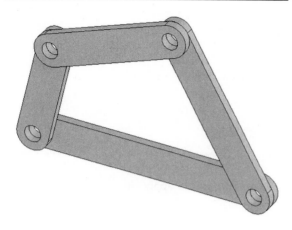

Click and drag Link2 into the approximate position shown in **Figure 11.44**.

Double-click Link4 to display its dimensions. Double-click the 4-inch length and change it to 5 inches. Rebuild the assembly.

The values of L and S remained unchanged at 7 and 3 inches, respectively. The values of P and Q are 5 inches each, so L + S = P + Q.

Run the simulation.

The motion of the linkage will appear unusual. If you watch it carefully, you will notice that for two complete *cycles* (360-degree rotations) of Link2, the motions of Link3 and Link4 are different from one cycle to the next. In **Figure 11.45**, positions from one cycle are shown, while in **Figure 11.46**, positions for the next cycle are shown.

FIGURE 11.45

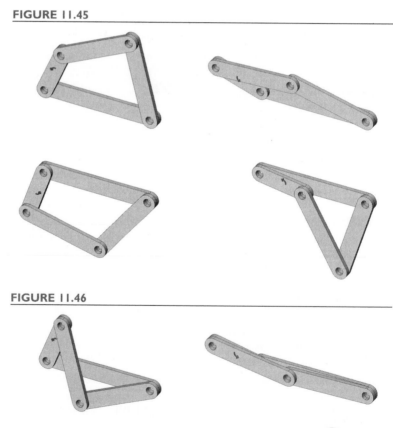

FIGURE 11.46

This mechanism is *unstable*. When the linkage passes through a certain point (when the links are all lying flat), there are two possible paths for the links to take. In a stable four-bar mechanism, the links can be assembled into either the open configuration (**Figure 11.47**) or the crossed configuration (**Figure 11.48**). Physically, the only way to change from one configuration to another is to remove the pin connecting two of the links, move the links to the other configuration, and replace the pin. The unstable mechanism switches from the open to the crossed configuration. When used in a real application to drive a moving component, the behavior of such a mechanism may be unpredictable.

Stop the simulation. Close the assembly window without saving the changes.

FIGURE 11.47   **FIGURE 11.48**

11.4 Using SolidWorks Animator

SolidWorks Animator is a powerful add-in that can be used to make video files (in the commonly-used standard AVI format) of various SolidWorks operations.   In this section, the use of SolidWorks Animator to make video files of simulations will be described.

FIGURE 11.49

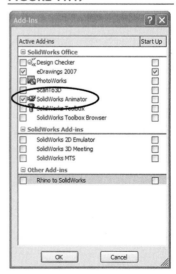

Open the assembly file Linkage.

This file should contain a saved simulation created in Section 11.3. We will create a video file of this simulation.

From the main menu, select Tools: Add-ins. Check the box to add the SolidWorks Animator add-in, as shown in Figure 11.49.

This will enable the ability to perform a video screen capture of our simulation.

FIGURE 11.50

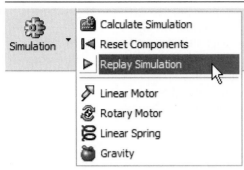

Click on the Simulation Tool. From the pop-up menu, select Replay Simulation, as shown in Figure 11.50.

The saved simulation will be replayed in the graphics window, and the Animation Controller will appear.

From the Animation Controller, click on the red button, as shown in Figure 11.51.

FIGURE 11.51

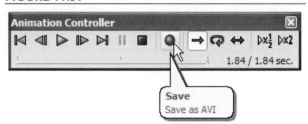

This will initiate the creation of the AVI file. The Save Animation to File dialog box will appear, as shown in **Figure 11.52**. This allows us to select the appropriate directory and filename for our video file. It also allows us to set the number of frames per second to be saved as we create our video file. More frames per second means a smoother-looking motion, but also a larger file size. For this application, we will accept the default value.

FIGURE 11.52

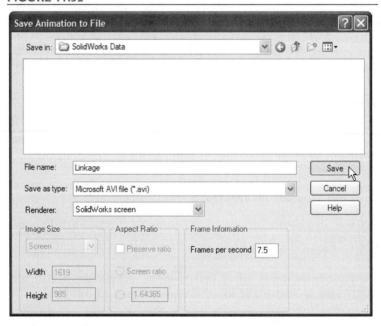

Browse to the appropriate file location, and click Save.

The Video Compression dialog box will appear, as shown in **Figure 11.53**. This dialog box allows us to select the image resolution of the video file. Higher-resolution images will result in larger file sizes. For this application, we will accept the default values for Compressor type and quality.

FIGURE 11.53

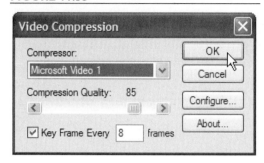

Click OK to close the Video Compression dialog box.

The simulation will be replayed again in the graphics window. While this is occurring, the video file will be written at the frames per second and compression level we specified.

The video file will be stored in the directory specified in the Save Animation to File dialog box, with the filename Linkage.avi. This file is a stand-alone video file; it is not linked in any way to your SolidWorks part or assembly files. As such, it can be sent to and viewed by anyone with standard video playback software, such as Windows Media Player or RealPlayer, and does not require access to the SolidWorks software or files. Remember, however, that all connectivity is lost; subsequent changes to your part/assembly files or simulation parameters will not affect this video file. If changes are desired, a new AVI file must be created.

PROBLEMS

P11.1   A type of mechanism used in engineering systems is the *slider-crank* (see **Figure P11.1A**). In the slider-crank, the input link (crank) rotates continuously through a full 360 degrees, while the output slider slides along a fixed surface. Among other things, the *slider-crank* is the working schematic for a single cylinder of an internal combustion engine. Create a working SolidWorks assembly model of this mechanism, using the dimensions shown in **Figure P11.1B**. The dimensions are mm. (Hint: The bottom of the slider is always coincident with the ground plane.)

FIGURE P11.1A

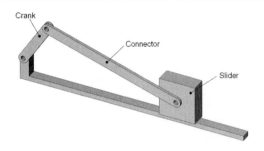

FIGURE P11.1B

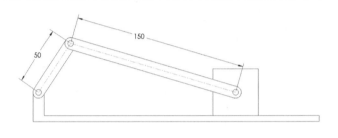

P11.2   The mechanism described in P11.1 can be modified by offsetting the pivot location of the crank from the path of the slider, creating an *offset slider-crank*, as shown in **Figure P11.2A**. This type of mechanism is sometimes called a *quick-return* mechanism, since the back-and-forth motion of the slider is different in one direction from the other. Create a working model of this mechanism, using the dimensions shown in **Figure P11.2B**. The dimensions are mm.

FIGURE P11.2A

FIGURE P11.2B

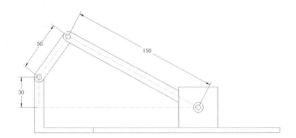

P11.3 Additional links can be added to a four-bar linkage to modify the motion of the links. A common engineering example is the *six-bar linkage*. **Figure P11.3A** shows a model of a six-bar linkage that simulates the operation of a car's windshield wipers. The Crank is attached to the wiper motor, which rotates at a constant speed. The lengths of the Crank and Connector 1, along with the attachment location to the blade, are selected so that the rotational motion of the wiper motor is converted to the desired oscillating motion of the first wiper blade. Connector 2 links the two blades together so that they move parallel to each other.

FIGURE P11.3A

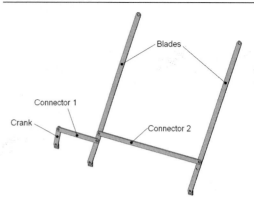

Model the components shown in **Figure P11.3B**, and assemble them into the mechanism, using the spacing of ground joints shown in **Figure P11.3C**.

FIGURE P11.3B

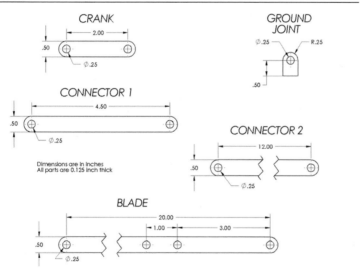

FIGURE P11.3C

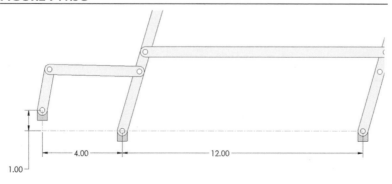

P11.4   In the 1700s, noted engineer James Watt devised and patented a mechanism for generating straight-line motion with a rotational input. In this mechanism, shown in **Figure P11.4A**, the center point of Link 3 will trace out a straight line in space as the input link (Link 2) rotates, as illustrated in **Figure P11.4B**. Originally designed for guiding the stroke in a steam engine piston, this mechanism is currently used to guide axle motion in automotive suspension applications[1]. Develop a working model of the *Watt Straight Line Mechanism*. Use a length of 8 inches for Links 2 and 4, and a length of 4 inches for Link 3. The distance between the fixed pivot points is 16 inches. (Note: This a considered a *double rocker mechanism*; the input link is *not* able to rotate through a full 360 degrees.)

FIGURE P11.4A

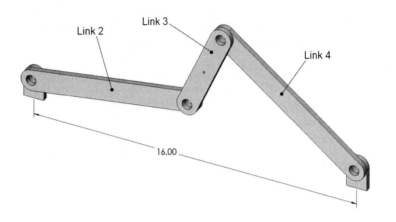

FIGURE P11.4B

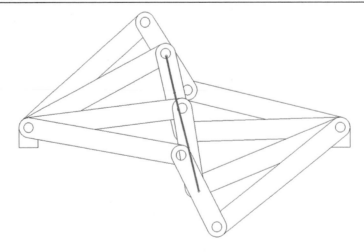

[1] Robert L. Norton, *Design of Machinery*, 2nd ed. (New York: McGraw-Hill, 1999).

P11.5   A *geneva mechanism*, which is illustrated in **Figure P11.5A**, is used to transform constant rotational motion into intermittent motion. Among other uses, this type of mechanism is used to control the motion of an *indexing table* in an assembly line. An indexing table will remain stationary for a period of time, and then rotate a fixed amount.

Model the components necessary to create a model of the geneva mechanism:

FIGURE P11.5A

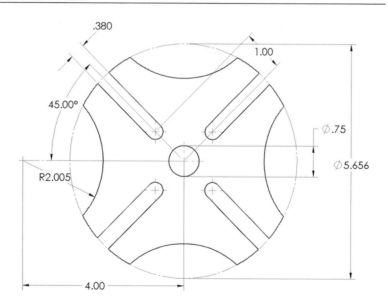

a.   The *geneva wheel*, as detailed in **Figure P11.5B** (thickness = 0.25 inches)

FIGURE P11.5B

b. The *locking disk*, as detailed in **Figure PI1.5C** (thickness = 0.25 inches)

FIGURE PI1.5C

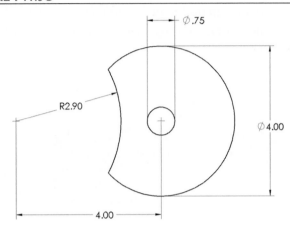

c. The *crank*, as detailed in **Figure PI1.5D** (thickness = 0.25 inches)

FIGURE PI1.5D

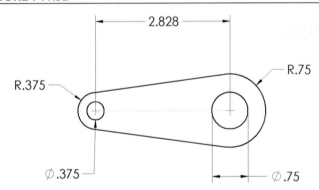

d. The *ground link*, as shown in **Figure PI1.5E** (thickness = 0.25 inches)

FIGURE PI1.5E

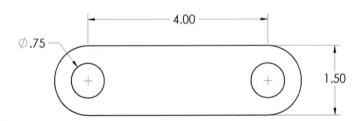

e. A cylindrical *shaft*, 0.75 inches in diameter by 2 inches long

f.   A cylindrical pin, 0.375 inches in diameter by 0.50 inches long.

Create the subassembly shown in **Figure P11.5F** from a shaft and the geneva wheel. Add mates so that the wheel is completely fixed relative to the shaft.

FIGURE P11.5F

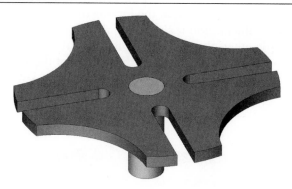

Create the subassembly shown in **Figure P11.5G** from a shaft, the crank, the pin, and the locking disk. Add mates so that the crank, pin, and disk are all completely fixed relative to the shaft.

FIGURE P11.5G

Create a new assembly with the ground link as the fixed component. Add the two subassemblies created above, and create mates so the shafts can rotate within the ground link. Add a rotary motor to the crank/locking disk assembly, and watch the motion, which is illustrated in **Figure P11.5H**.

Notes: Make sure that the initial orientation of the locking disk is such that one of the cutouts of the wheel is aligned so that the locking disk can be placed without interference. When the motion is simulated, the simulation may slow down slightly when the pin enters the slot of the wheel and the contact of the parts is recognized. If you replay the simulation, the motion of the assembly will be smooth.

FIGURE P11.5H

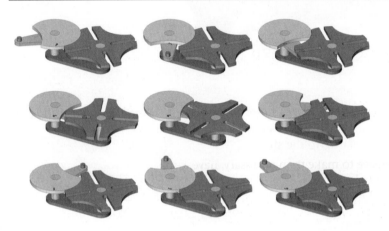

CHAPTER 12

The Use of SolidWorks as a Tool for Manufacturing: Mold Design and Sheet Metal Parts

Introduction

A design engineer must always consider the method of manufacture when designing any part. Failure to do so may result in part designs that are more expensive to make than necessary, have high scrap rates, or cannot be made at all.

Some manufacturing processes create unique challenges from a solid modeling standpoint. For example, when designing a mold, the shape of the part to be molded must be removed from the interior of the mold, usually with the dimensions adjusted to allow for shrinkage of the part during the cool-down portion of the molding cycle. Sheet metal parts are cut from flat material, and then bent into the final shape. Therefore, the part definition must include both the flat shape and the finished geometry. The SolidWorks program has specialized tools for working with molds and sheet metal parts.

Chapter Objectives

In this chapter, you will:

- create a cavity within a mold base,

- create and modify two mold halves that are linked to the mold base with a cavity,

- make a simple sheet metal part, and

- learn how to show a sheet metal part in either the flat or bent state.

12.1 A Simple Two-Part Mold

In this exercise, we will make a mold to produce a simple cylindrical part. We will begin by making the part itself.

Open a new part. Draw and dimension a 3-inch diameter circle in the Right Plane, centered at the origin. Extrude the circle using a midplane extrusion, as shown in Figure 12.1. Set the total depth of extrusion to 5 inches. Save this part with the file name "Cylinder." Do not close the part window.

The next step is to create a *mold base,* from which a cavity the shape of the part will be removed. The mold base must be large enough to completely enclose the part.

Open a new part. Draw and dimension a 4-inch by 6-inch rectangle in the Top Plane. Add a centerline between two opposite corners of the rectangle. Add a Midpoint relation between the centerline and the origin, as shown in Figure 12.2.

FIGURE 12.1

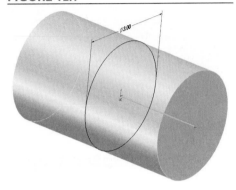

FIGURE 12.2

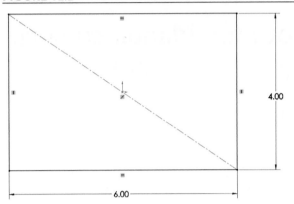

FIGURE 12.3

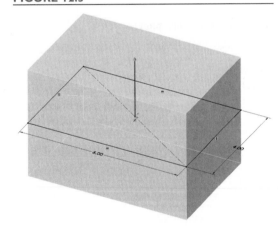

Extrude the rectangle with a midplane extrusion, as shown in Figure 12.3. Set the total depth of extrusion to be 4 inches. Save this part with the file name "Base." Do not close the part window.

We will now place the part within the mold base.

Select the Make Assembly Tool from the Standard toolbar, as shown in Figure 12.4. Click OK to accept the default assembly template.

FIGURE 12.4

A new assembly window will open, and the base will appear as the first component to be inserted. (Note: If the base part is not previewed in the graphics window, check the Graphics preview box under the Options tab of the PropertyManager.)

If the origin is not visible in the graphics area, select View: Origins from the main menu to display it.

Click on the origin of the assembly to place the base, as shown in Figure 12.5.

FIGURE 12.5

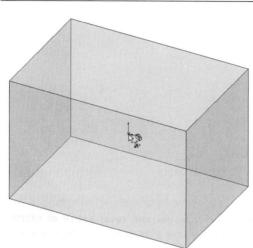

Note that placing the origin of the first component of an assembly at the origin of the assembly itself is not required, since the first component will be fixed and subsequent parts will be located relative to the first part. However, placing the first part in this manner is good practice, since the Front, Top, and Right Planes of the assembly can be used as mating entities.

Select the Insert Component Tool. Select the cylinder part from the list of open files, as shown in Figure 12.6, and click to place it in the assembly, as shown in Figure 12.7.

FIGURE 12.6

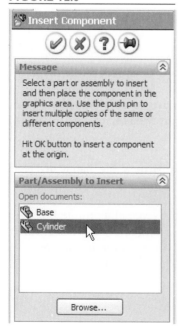

FIGURE 12.7

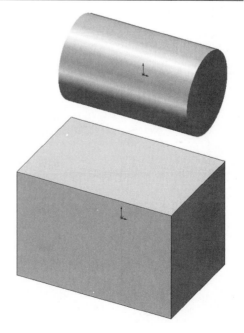

Select the Mate Tool.

In the FeatureManager, which flies out to the right of the PropertyManager, click on the + sign next to each of the parts to expand their definitions, if necessary. Select the Front Plane of each, as shown in Figure 12.8.

A preview of the resulting coincident mate is shown in **Figure 12.9**.

FIGURE 12.8

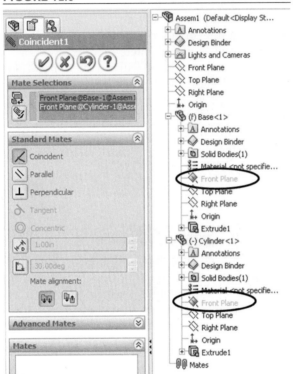

FIGURE 12.9

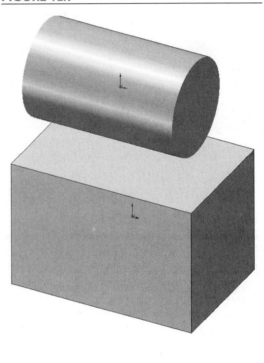

FIGURE 12.10

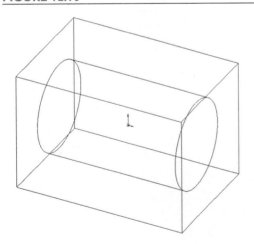

Click the check mark to complete the mate.

Repeat this procedure to mate the Top Planes, and then the Right Planes, of the base and cylinder.

Save this assembly with a file name of "Mold Assembly."

The cylinder is now centered within the base, as shown in the wireframe view of **Figure 12.10**. Rather than work in a wireframe mode, it is helpful to display the base as transparent.

FIGURE 12.11

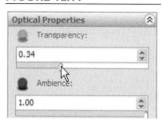

Click on the part name "Base" in the Feature-Manager to select it. Click the Edit Color Tool. Near the bottom of the PropertyManager, select the transparency slider bar, as shown in Figure 12.11. Move this bar to the right to display the base in varying degrees of transparency. Click the check mark to apply the desired transparency.

FIGURE 12.12

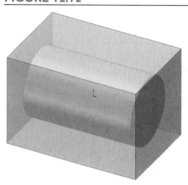

The cylinder can now be seen within the base, as shown in Figure 12.12.

We will now create the cavity. Since the cavity will be created in the base, the base must be selected for editing.

Select the base from the FeatureManager. Choose the Edit Component Tool from the Assembly group of the CommandManager. ←

From the main menu, select Insert: Molds: Cavity, as shown in Figure 12.13.

In the PropertyManager, select the Cylinder part from the FeatureManager as the component defining the cavity. Set the "Scale about" option to "Component Centroids" and the scale to 3%, as shown in Figure 12.14. Click the check mark to create the cavity. Click on the Edit Component Tool to end the editing of the base.

The scale factor causes the cavity to be larger than the finished part. Most molding materials shrink during cure or cooling, so the scale factor allows for that shrinkage.

The cavity can now be seen within the base, as shown in Figure 12.15. If you look closely, you can see that there are gaps between the edges of the part and the corresponding edges of the cavity, because of the shrink factor.

FIGURE 12.13

FIGURE 12.14

FIGURE 12.15

The base, which now includes the cavity, needs to be split into two halves. For this simple mold, the two halves will be identical, and so we could cut away half of the original base part. However, if the two mold halves will be different (as in the next exercise), then copies of the base must be made. This procedure of creating *derived parts* is illustrated here.

Select the Base from the FeatureManager. From the main menu, select File: Derive Component Part, as shown in Figure 12.16.

A new part window is opened, and a copy of the base (including the cavity), is created, as shown in **Figure 12.17**. The advantage of creating a derived part rather than simply saving a copy of the base part is that associativity is maintained. That is, if a change is made to the cylinder part, then the cavity in the assembly, the base, and the derived mold half part are all updated.

FIGURE 12.16

FIGURE 12.17

Select the front face of the new part. Select the Line Tool, and draw a line completely through the part, passing through the origin, as shown in Figure 12.18. Extrude a cut with a type of Through All, with the direction to cut arrow pointing up.

The resulting part is shown in Figure 12.19.

FIGURE 12.18

FIGURE 12.19

Save the part with a file name of "Mold Half."

To illustrate the associativity of the parts, open the cylinder file and change the diameter of the part from 3 to 2 inches. If you switch immediately to the mold half part, then no changes will be seen. However, if you switch to the mold assembly, then the cavity will be updated. Then, switching to the mold half will cause the change to be reflected, as shown in **Figure 12.20**.

Two of these mold halves can now be assembled, and mold-level features (fill and vent ports, alignment pins, etc.) can be added.

FIGURE 12.20

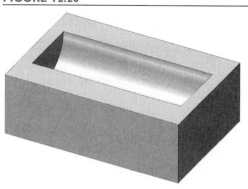

12.2 A Core-and-Cavity Mold

In this exercise, a two-piece mold for making the card holder from Chapter 5, shown in **Figure 12.21**, will be created. The shape of this part requires that the mold geometry consist of a *core* half (**Figure 12.22**), with features protruding outward from the parting line, and a *cavity* half (**Figure 12.23**), with features cut inward from the parting line.

FIGURE 12.21

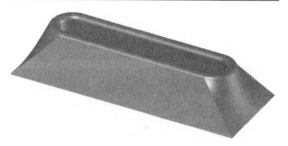

FIGURE 12.22

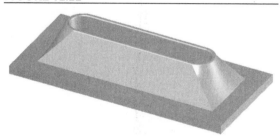

FIGURE 12.23

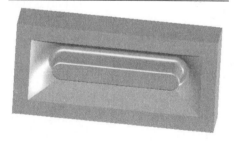

Our procedure will be similar to the one followed in the previous section. Since there are several files involved in this procedure, it is helpful to consider the process steps, which are illustrated in **Figure 12.24**. An interim assembly will be made from the mold base and part, so that the cavity can be placed in the mold base. From that assembly, copies of the mold base (with the cavity) will be derived. These copies will be modified to become the two mold halves. Finally, the two mold halves will be brought together into an assembly.

FIGURE 12.24

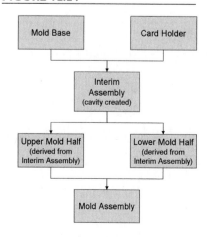

The first step of the process will be to create the mold base, which must be sized so that the card holder part fits completely within its boundaries.

Open a new part. In the Top Plane, draw and dimension a rectangle, as shown in Figure 12.25. Use a centerline and a Midpoint relation to center the rectangle about the origin.

FIGURE 12.25

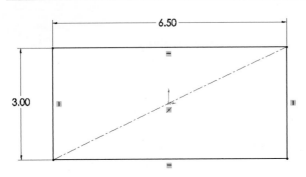

The dimensions shown are each 1 inch greater than the corresponding dimensions of the card holder, allowing for 1/2 inch clearance between the part and the mold edges.

The height of the mold base will be selected to allow for 1/4 inch above and below the part.

Extrude the rectangle upward a distance of 1.5 inches, as shown in Figure 12.26.

Choose the Edit Color Tool, and move the Transparency slider bar toward the right, as shown in Figure 12.27.

FIGURE 12.26

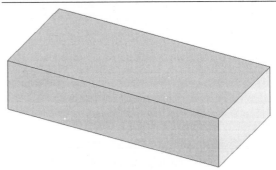

The transparent part is shown in Figure 12.28.

FIGURE 12.27

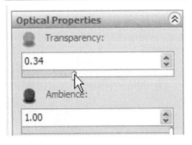

FIGURE 12.28

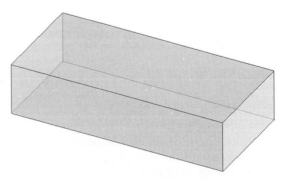

Save this part as "Mold Base."

Choose the Make Assembly Tool from the Standard toolbar. Insert the mold base into the assembly, aligning the two origins. Choose the Insert Component Tool and browse to locate the card holder part. Click to place it in the assembly in the approximate position shown in Figure 12.29.

We will now align the card holder with the mold base.

Rotate the view so that the bottom surfaces of the card holder and the mold base are visible, as shown in Figure 12.30.

FIGURE 12.29

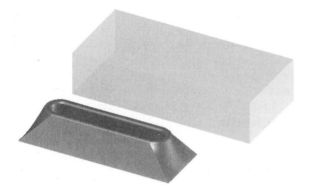

FIGURE 12.30

FIGURE 12.31

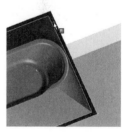

Choose the Mate Tool. Select the bottom surface of the card holder (Figure 12.31), and then the bottom surface of the mold base. A coincident relation will be previewed. Select the Distance Mate icon from the PropertyManager (Figure 12.32). Set the offset distance between the two surfaces to be 0.25 inches. If necessary, check the Flip Dimension box so that the bottom surface of the card holder is above the bottom surface of the mold base, as previewed in Figure 12.33. Click the check mark to apply the mate.

FIGURE 12.32

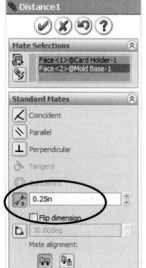

FIGURE 12.33

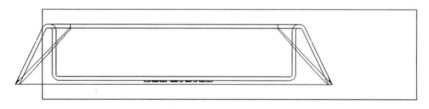

FIGURE 12.34

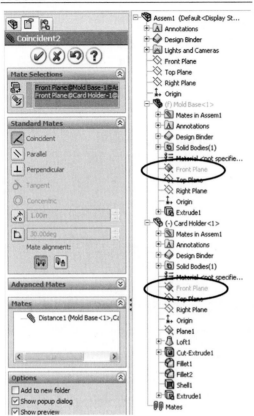

Select the Front Planes of the card holder and mold base, as shown in Figure 12.34. Add a coincident mate, as shown in Figure 12.35.

FIGURE 12.35

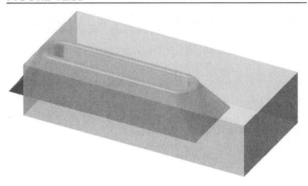

Add a coincident mate between the Right Planes of the card holder and mold base. Close the Mate PropertyManager.

The card holder is now placed within the mold base, as shown in Figure 12.36.

FIGURE 12.36

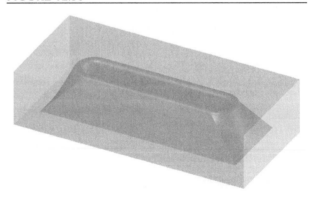

FIGURE 12.37

Save the assembly as "InterimMoldAssy."

Select the mold base from the FeatureManager. Choose the Edit Component Tool from the Assembly group of the CommandManager.

From the main menu, select Insert: Molds: Cavity. In the PropertyManager, select the card holder as the component defining the cavity. Set the "Scale about" option to Component Centroids and the scale to 1%, as shown in Figure 12.37. Click the check mark to create the cavity. Click the Edit Component Tool to end the editing of the mold base.

Select the mold base from the FeatureManager. From the main menu, select File: Derive Component Part.

A new part window is opened, and a copy of the mold base is created.

Display the part in the Wireframe mode, as shown in Figure 12.38.

We will now cut away the top portion of the mold to create the lower mold half. This cannot be done with a simple extruded cut, since that would also cut through the core feature that will form the underside of the card holder. Rather, we will perform two separate cutting operations to achieve the desired geometry.

Select the top surface of the part and choose the Sketch Tool from the Sketch group of the CommandManager to open a sketch. Select the four edges of the cavity shown in Figure 12.39. (Remember to use the ctrl key to select multiple entities.)

Select the Convert Entities Tool, which will create lines from the selected edges.

Extrude a cut with a type of "Up to Next." This will cut away the top of the mold, but only to the cavity, as shown in Figure 12.40.

FIGURE 12.38

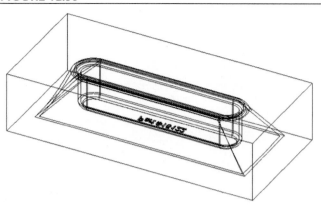

FIGURE 12.39

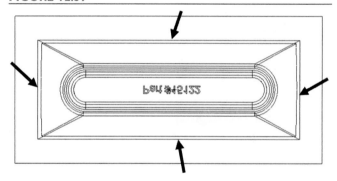

FIGURE 12.40

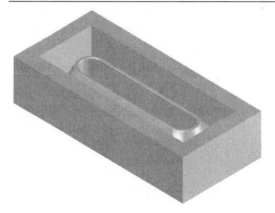

In order to cut away the material around the edges of the mold half, it is necessary to use a different type of cut: one that cuts down to the parting surface.

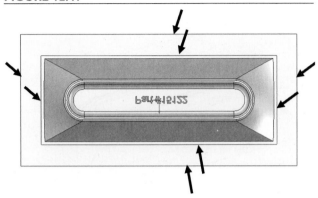

Open a new sketch on the top surface. Convert the eight edges shown in Figure 12.41 into lines, using the Convert Entities Tool.

Extrude a cut, with a type of "Up to Surface." For the surface, choose the bottom surface of the cavity, which corresponds to the parting line, as shown in Figure 12.42.

The completed mold half is shown in Figure 12.43.

FIGURE 12.42

FIGURE 12.43

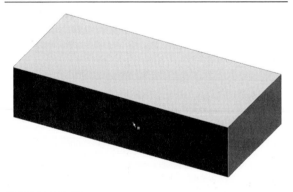

Save this part as "MoldHalf-Lower."

We will create the upper mold half.

Switch back to the assembly containing the mold base and the card holder (InterimMoldAssy). Select the mold base, and from the main menu, select File: Derive Component Part.

FIGURE 12.44

In the new part, select the front surface, as shown in Figure 12.44. Select the Line Tool from the Sketch group of the Command-Manager. Choose the wireframe display mode.

FIGURE 12.45

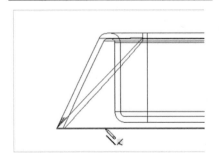

Without any mouse clicks, hold the cursor over the bottom edge of the cavity momentarily, as shown in Figure 12.45.

This will "wake up" the feature and allow the endpoint of the line to be aligned with this edge.

Move the cursor past the left of the mold base, aligned with the bottom edge of the cavity, as shown in Figure 12.46.

Click and drag a horizontal line across the mold base, as shown in Figure 12.47. Select the line just drawn and the point at the lower left of the cavity, and add a coincident relation. Select the Extruded Cut Tool from the Features group of the CommandManager.

FIGURE 12.46

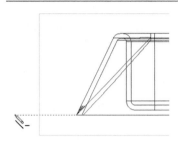

FIGURE 12.47

FIGURE 12.48

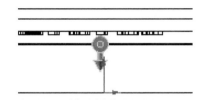

Since we are not using a closed sketch, we must define whether the material above or below the line is to be cut away.

Set the extrusion type as "Through All". Check the "Flip side to cut" box in the PropertyManager, so that the arrow indicating the part to be cut away is pointing down, as shown in Figure 12.48.

FIGURE 12.49

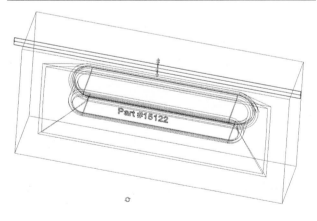

Before completing the cut, rotate the view orientation so that you can see the bottom of the mold, as shown in Figure 12.49. Click the check mark.

Since this cut will produce two separate solid bodies (the mold half and part of the core), you are prompted to identify which of the bodies you want to keep. In our case, we do not want to keep the core with the upper mold half. In the dialog box, checking the Selected bodies box allows you to choose which of the solid bodies you want to keep, and which will be deleted.

Choose the Selected bodies option. Check the box for Body 1 (the mold half) and clear the box for Body 2 (the core), as shown in Figure 12.50. The selected bodies are highlighted in green. Click OK to complete the cut.

FIGURE 12.50

The resulting part is shown in **Figure 12.51**.

Save this part as "MoldHalfUpper."

Open a new assembly. Insert the two mold halves, as shown in Figure 12.52. Make sure to place the first mold half at the origin of the assembly.

FIGURE 12.51

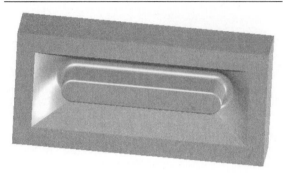

FIGURE 12.52

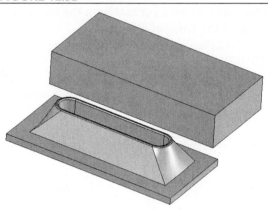

Add three mates to align the mold halves together, as shown in Figure 12.53.

Choose the Section View Tool from the View toolbar.

Click the check mark to accept the Front Plane as the section plane, as shown in Figure 12.54.

FIGURE 12.53

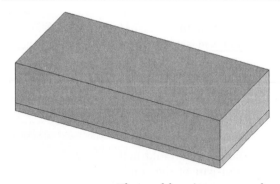

FIGURE 12.54

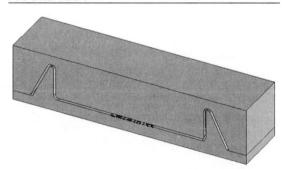

The mold cavity can now be clearly seen.

Save the file with the name "Mold Assembly."

Suppose that we now want to change the thickness of the molded part. Often, if a material change is specified, the thickness will need to be changed, since the flow of the material in the mold is a limiting factor on the thickness.

FUTURE STUDY

Materials and Processes

Our simple two-piece mold includes a cavity the shape of the finished part. If we created this mold for making a few prototype parts from a room-temperature curing material, such as polyurethane, then we could add holes for bolting the halves together, a hole for pouring in the material, and a vent hole, and our mold would be functional.

Most molds require many other features, however, and tooling design is an important function at any manufacturing company. If a plastic part is to be injection-molded, then the injection points and vent locations must be carefully designed so that the molten plastic fills the cavity completely. The plastic's melt and cooling temperatures and its resistance to flow must be considered when designing both the part and the mold. The tolerances required for the finished part might require that a filler be added to the material for dimensional stability. Ejector pins might need to be added to help remove the part from the mold. (Note that in our example, even though the part walls are tapered, the shrinkage of the part onto

the core will result in forces that will need to be overcome in order to remove the part from the lower mold half.) Since the plastic must be injected hot but allowed to cool before removal from the mold, cooling lines for circulating water are usually added to the mold halves.

Other materials have different processing requirements. Composite materials used for automotive materials are mostly compression molded, in which the raw material is placed between two mold halves and formed by applying pressure with a hydraulic press. Lower-quantity parts can be produced by resin transfer molding, in which dry fabric is placed in a mold and liquid resin is pumped in under low pressure.

Often the choice of a process depends on the quantity of parts to be made. A high-quality tool for injection molding can cost tens of thousands of dollars, but if this cost can be spread over 100,000 or 1,000,000 parts, then the fast cycle times resulting from a good mold design can result in significant cost savings.

Open the card holder part. Right-click on the shell feature in the FeatureManager. Select Edit Feature, and double the thickness, from 0.06 to 0.12 inches. Rebuild the model.

The modified part is shown in **Figure 12.55**.

Open, or switch to, the interim mold assembly, then the two mold halves, and finally the mold assembly. At every step, the models will be updated to reflect the new thickness.

FIGURE 12.55

FIGURE 12.56

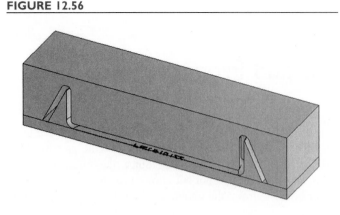

The updated mold assembly is shown in **Figure 12.56**. Of course, the mold we created is not usable without some way to get material into the mold. The manner in which this is done depends on the molding process, as discussed in the Future Study box. Many other features may also be required for the mold to be usable. Mold design is a very specialized field, combining mechanical design with material science. However, an essential part of any mold design is the creation of the mold cavity and the separation of the core and cavity mold parts, such as we have done in these exercises.

12.3   A Sheet Metal Part

In this exercise we will create the sheet metal part shown in **Figure 12.57**. The part can be shown in either the bent or flat state.

Open a new part. From the main menu, select Tools: Options: Document Properties: Units. Set the unit system to MMGS (millimeters), and the number of decimal places to zero for both the length and angular values.

FIGURE 12.57

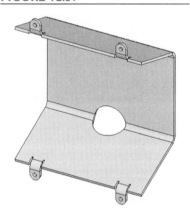

FIGURE 12.58

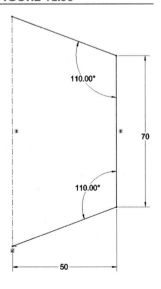

FIGURE 12.59

Select the Right Plane. Sketch and dimension the three lines shown in Figure 12.58. Use the vertical centerline to align the endpoints of the diagonal lines.

Note that we are not adding radii to the sharp corners. In sheet metal parts, *bends* are added as separate features to a part.

Select the Extruded Boss/Base Tool from the Features group of the CommandManager. Set the extrusion depth to 100 mm. Since the sketch is open, a thin-feature extrusion will be created. Set the thickness to 2 mm, as shown in Figure 12.59.

Change the directions of the extrusion and/or thickness if necessary so that the extrusion is to the left and the dimensions apply to the outside of the part, as shown in Figure 12.60.

FIGURE 12.60

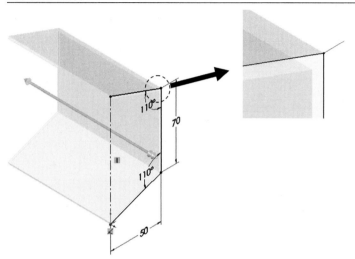

FIGURE 12.61

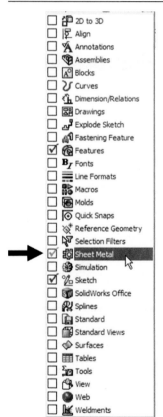

There are a number of tools that are specific to sheet metal parts. We can access these tools through the Sheet Metal toolbar or by adding the Sheet Metal Tools to the CommandManager. For new users, the CommandManager helps to distinguish the tools from one another, as the tool name is displayed along with the icon.

Right-click on the CommandManager and choose Customize CommandManager. In the list of tool groups that is displayed, click on Sheet Metal, as shown in Figure 12.61. Click away from the menu to close it.

The Sheet Metal Tools are now included in the CommandManager.

Select the Sheet Metal icon from near the left side of the CommandManager. Select the Insert Bends Tool.

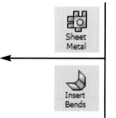

Select the middle face as the one that will remain flat during the bending, as shown in Figure 12.62. Set the radius to 4 mm, and set the K-factor to 0.50. Leave the auto relief checked with the type as Rectangular and the factor set to 0.50, as shown in Figure 12.63.

The resulting bent geometry is shown in Figure 12.64.

FIGURE 12.62

FIGURE 12.63

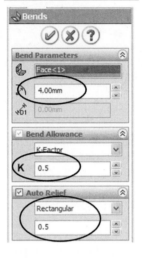

FIGURE 12.64

The K-factor is used in converting the bent geometry into the flat geometry. A K-factor of 0.5 means that the length of the flattened metal will be calculated based on the arc length at the midthickness of the metal. This is typical for relatively large bend radii. If extremely tight bends are desired, then the K-factor may need to be adjusted to get a better correlation between the flat geometry and bent geometry dimensions.

The FeatureManager now shows several new items, as shown in Figure 12.65. These new items include Sheet-Metal, where the bend radii, K-factor, and Auto Relief factors are defined, Flatten-Bends, where individual bends can be edited, and Process-Bends, which restores the bends when the part is rebuilt. The Flat-Pattern, which is shown as suppressed, contains the information to show the flattened configuration of the part.

FIGURE 12.65

The part can now be toggled between the flat and bent configurations using the Flatten Tool.

Click on the Flatten Tool to show the part in the flattened state, as shown in Figure 12.66.

FIGURE 12.66

Notice that the Flat-Pattern is now active in the FeatureManager. Expanding the Flat-Pattern shows the bend lines and individual bend properties, as shown in **Figure 12.67**.

Click the Flatten Tool again to display the part in the bent state.

FIGURE 12.67

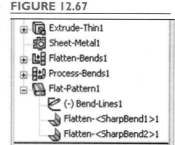

With the part in the bent configuration, the bends themselves can be suppressed with the No Bends Tool. This tool allows you to toggle between the state with sharp corners and the state with the bends shown.

To add the tabs, we need to create a new plane. Since the tabs are to allow the part to mount flush to another surface, the new plane needs to correspond to the front edge of the part.

Select Insert: Reference Geometry: Plane from the main menu or the Features group of the CommandManager. If there are any items already selected, clear them by right-clicking in any white space and selecting Clear Selections.

Select the edge shown in Figure 12.68, and then one of the front corner points, as shown in Figure 12.69. Click the check mark to create the plane.

FIGURE 12.68

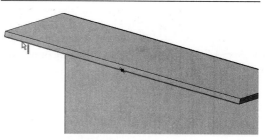

View the plane from the right view to make sure that it is in the correct location, as shown in **Figure 12.70**.

Select the new plane. Sketch and dimension the first tab, near the upper-left corner of the part, as shown in Figure 12.71. Make sure to add a line along the bottom of the tab so that a closed contour is created.

FIGURE 12.69

FIGURE 12.70

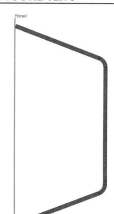

FIGURE 12.71

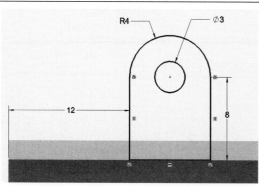

FIGURE 12.72

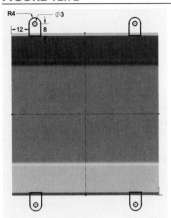

Add centerlines, snapping to midpoints on the edges. Use the Mirror Tool from the Sketch group of the CommandManager to place the other three tabs, as shown in Figure 12.72. To use the Mirror Tool, select all of the lines and arcs to be mirrored and the centerline that the entities are to be mirrored about, and then click the check mark.

Extrude the tabs toward the rear of the part. Check the "Link to thickness" box, shown in Figure 12.73, to set the thickness as the same value that was chosen when the part was defined as a Sheet Metal part. Click the check mark to complete the extrusion.

FIGURE 12.73

FIGURE 12.74

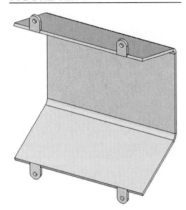

Note that the tabs have sharp corners rather than bends, as shown in Figure 12.74. This is because the tabs were added after the bends were added in the FeatureManager. Rather than define a new set of bends for the tabs, we can rearrange them in the FeatureManager. Plane1 must also be moved, since it must be defined before the tabs can be added.

Click with the left mouse button and hold on the new plane (Plane1) in the FeatureManager. Drag the cursor up until the arrow points between the Extrude-Thin1 and the Sheet-Metal1 definitions, as shown in Figure 12.75.

Release the mouse and Plane1 will now appear before Sheet Metal in the FeatureManager, as shown in Figure 12.76.

Now click and drag the tabs (Extrude1) to immediately after Plane1, as shown in Figure 12.77.

FIGURE 12.75

FIGURE 12.76

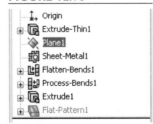

FIGURE 12.77

The tabs now appear with bends, as shown in **Figure 12.78**. The metal around the bends was cut per the Auto-Relief parameters set earlier. (The width of the cuts is 0.5 times the thickness, and the cuts extend 0.5 times the thickness beyond the end of the bends.)

The cut-out in the part must be added in the flattened state, so that it can be cut as a circle.

Drag the Rollback Bar to just below Flatten-Bends in the FeatureManager, as shown in Figure 12.79. On the front surface sketch and dimension the 25-mm circle as shown in Figure 12.80, using centerlines to place the circle.

FIGURE 12.78

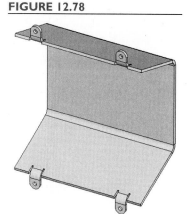

FIGURE 12.79

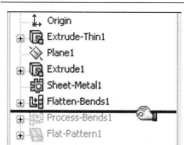

FIGURE 12.80

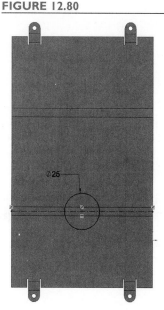

Cut the hole with a through-all extruded cut. Show the part in the bent shape by dragging the Rollback Bar to the end of the FeatureManager, as shown in Figure 12.81. The finished part appears in Figure 12.82.

FIGURE 12.81

FIGURE 12.82

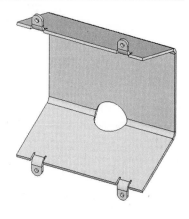

PROBLEMS

P12.1   Open the interim assembly of the mold base and card holder that was created in section 12.2 (**Figure P12.1**). Perform an interference detection on the assembly. How are the interferences found related to the shrinkage factor used to create the cavity?

FIGURE P12.1

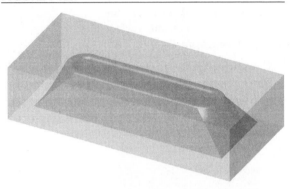

P12.2   Create a two-piece mold for the flange part of Chapter 1, allowing a 2% shrink factor. **Figure P12.2A** shows the lower mold half. Note that the material forming the holes is contained in the lower mold half. **Figure P12.2B** shows the upper mold half. Note that the chamfer feature is included in the upper mold half.

Hint: The easiest way to cut away material from the mold halves is to use *revolved cuts*. **Figure P12.2C** shows the sketch defining the "cutting tool" to be revolved around the centerline to create the lower mold half.

FIGURE P12.2A

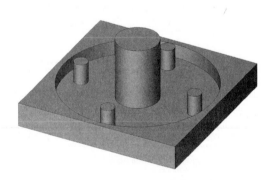

FIGURE P12.2B

FIGURE P12.2C

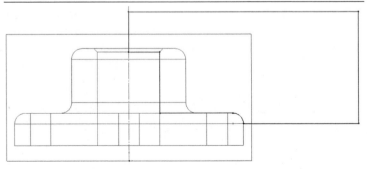

P12.3 Create an assembly of the two mold halves of P12.2 and the flange. Show a section view of the assembly, with the mold halves transparent, as shown in **Figure P12.3**.

FIGURE P12.3

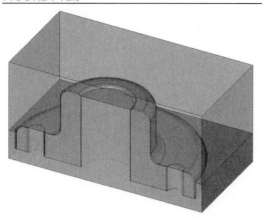

P12.4 Create a model of the sheet metal part shown in **Figure P12.4**. The metal thickness is 0.060 inches, and the bend radii are 0.125 inches. All dimensions shown are in inches.

FIGURE P12.4A

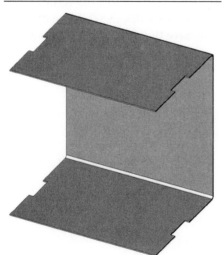

FIGURE P12.4B

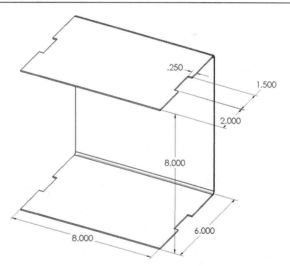

P12.5 Create a model of the sheet metal part shown in **Figure P12.5**. The metal thickness is 0.060 inches, and the bend radii are 0.125 inches. All dimensions shown are in inches.

FIGURE P12.5A

FIGURE P12.5B

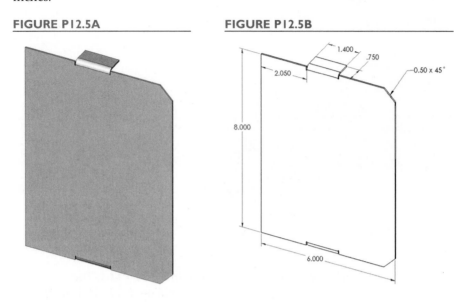

P12.6 Create the box shown from the parts created in exercises P12.4 and P12.5. Since the sides of the box are mirror images of each other, it will be necessary to have two different part files. Open the part created in P12.5, and select one of the vertical faces. Then select Insert: Mirror Part from the main menu. Click the check mark, and a new part file is created, linked to the original file. Save this file with a new name, and then assemble the three parts to form the box.

FIGURE P12.6

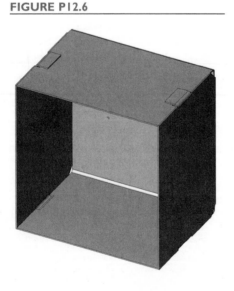

CHAPTER 13

The Use of SolidWorks to Accelerate the Product Development Cycle

Introduction

Any company that designs and/or manufacturers products has seen an increase in global competition over the past decades. To remain competitive, there is great pressure to develop new products. As a result, product models have shorter lives, and development costs are spread over a fewer number of units.

With these increased pressures, there has been a greater emphasis on improving and accelerating the development process. While different industries and companies have their own unique procedures, there are some activities that are typically a part of a modern product development cycle:

- Physical prototypes are used early and often.
- Computer analysis is used extensively to complement physical testing.
- Engineering functions are performed simultaneously as much as possible, necessitating better teamwork and data sharing.

Solid modeling is an important tool in the product development process. The solid model becomes the common database used for a variety of engineering functions. In this chapter, we will explore two of the most common uses of solid modeling in product design: rapid prototyping and finite element analysis. We will also consider the challenge of managing and controlling the data produced during the product development cycle.

Chapter Objectives

In this chapter, you will:

- be introduced to the most popular rapid prototyping processes,

- see how the stereolithography file is used to define a solid part,

- learn how to create a stereolithography file,

- be introduced to the capabilities and limitations of finite element analysis, and

- learn about Product Data Management software.

13.1 Rapid Prototyping

The introduction of solid modeling made possible a new industry called Rapid Prototyping (RP) or Solid Freeform Fabrication (SFF). Rapid prototyping refers to the creation of physical models directly from an electronic part file using an *additive* process. That is, the model is created by building it layer by layer rather than starting with a block and removing material to create the finished shape.

FIGURE 13.1

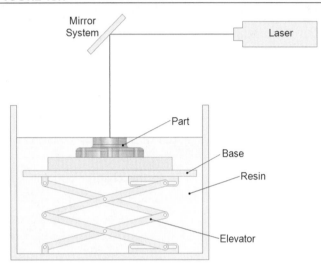

FIGURE 13.2

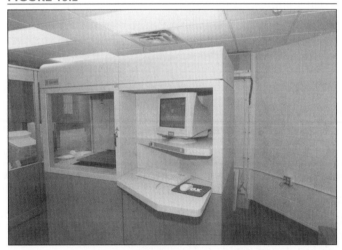

Paul Roberts; Milwaukee School of Engineering

The first commercial RP method to be introduced was stereolithography in 1987. In this process, a *photopolymer*, a liquid resin that cures under the application of certain wavelengths of light, is cured layer by layer by a precisely guided laser beam. The stereolithograhy process is illustrated in **Figure 13.1**. The part is submerged in a vat of photopolymer, supported on an elevator platform. The fabrication of each layer begins with the elevator lowering by the thickness of a layer, typically about 0.005 inches. The part is then covered by uncured resin. A mirror system directs the laser beam across the area to be cured for that particular cross-section. Laser power and the speed of the beam across the resin surface are controlled to ensure a complete cure of the resin while maximizing the speed of the process. When all of the layers are completed, which is typically several hours after the beginning of the build, the elevator lifts the essentially finished part out of the resin. Cleaning the part with a solvent and curing in a UV oven to complete the cure of the photopolymer are usually the only steps necessary to finish the part. A stereolithography machine is shown in **Figure 13.2**.

In the early 1990s, many new RP processes were commercialized. Among the most important was Selective Laser Sintering. In this process, plastic powder is *sintered*, or fused together, by the heat from a precisely guided laser beam. The advantage of this process is that many engineering plastics, including nylon and polycarbonate, can be used. Other processes that achieved commercial success included Laminated Object Manufacturing, a process that creates parts from layers of paper, and Fused Deposition Modeling, a process that can be thought of as precisely directing a fine hot-glue gun to build up a part.

The introduction of Fused Deposition Modeling was especially significant in that no laser or hazardous materials were required, allowing the machine to be placed in an office environment.

When RP was introduced, the available modeling materials had low strength and were extremely brittle. As a result, the only practical use of RP was to produce visual aids. This use was important, since the effective communication of complex designs can minimize errors in the interpretation. However, improvements in materials have allowed RP models to be used for many other functions. The Wohlers Report[1], an annual survey of the RP industry, found the uses of RP models in 2006 to be widely varied, and included:

Functional models	17.0%
Visual aids for engineering	13.5%
Patterns for prototype tooling	11.1%
Patterns for cast medal	10.9%
Fit and assembly	10.3%
Direct manufacturing	9.6%
Presentation models	9.0%
Tooling components	7.5%
Other	3.8%
Ergonomic studies	3.3%
Visual aids for toolmakers	2.7%
Requesting quotes	1.1%

The fact that an RP model can now be used in a functional prototype product or in tooling (which usually requires the longest lead time of all development activities) has increased the usefulness of RP greatly over the past few years.

One of the biggest obstacles to increased use of RP has been cost. The systems described above range in cost from about $100,000 to well over $500,000. When the costs of maintenance, materials, and a trained operator are added, the costs of producing even a small RP model can be in the hundreds of dollars. Also, even *rapid* prototyping systems can be too slow at times. An engineer who has an idea for a new design concept in the afternoon and a design meeting the next morning probably will not be able to have a physical model in time for the meeting.

A new generation of RP machines has focused on lower costs and higher speeds, with some sacrifices made to accuracy and durability. The combination of low-cost materials and inexpensive off-the-shelf printing technology results in a fast and affordable (these machines cost about $30,000 or less) prototyping process.

Most domestic RP machines accept as input a type of file called a stereolithography (.stl) file. The structure of an .stl file is quite simple: the surfaces of a solid model are broken into a series of triangles, the simplest planar area. Each triangle is defined by four parameters: the coordinates of each of the three corners, and a *normal vector* that points away from the part, identifying which of the two faces of the triangle represents the outer surface of the part.

---

[1]*Wohlers Report 2006, Rapid Prototyping, Tooling & Manufacturing State of the Industry Annual Worldwide Progress Report* (Fort Collins, CO: Terry T. Wohlers, Wohlers Associates, Inc.; wohlersassociates.com).

To illustrate how an .stl file defines a solid part, consider the simple part shown in **Figure 13.3**. Since this part has only flat, rectangular surfaces, two triangles can exactly define each surface, as shown in **Figure 13.4**. Since the part has six surfaces, the part can be described by 12 triangles.

To illustrate how an .stl file is created for a part with curved surfaces, consider the flange part modeled in Chapter 1, which is shown in **Figure 13.5**.

FIGURE 13.3

FIGURE 13.4

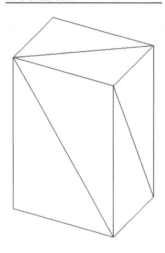

FIGURE 13.5

FIGURE 13.6

To create an .stl file from a SolidWorks part, select File: Save As from the main menu and select STL as the type of file from the pull-down menu, as shown in **Figure 13.6**.

FIGURE 13.7

Before saving the file, select the Options button. This opens the Export Options dialog box, and allows you to adjust the resolution of the .stl file, as shown in **Figure 13.7**. If the Preview option is selected, then the triangles of the .stl file are shown displayed in the part window.

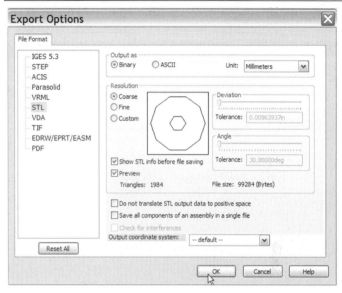

The triangles created for a resolution set to Coarse are shown in **Figure 13.8**. Note the rough approximation of the fillets by the triangles.

The number of triangles created and the file size are displayed in the Export dialog box. For the Coarse resolution, 1984 triangles are used, and the size of the .stl file is 99 kb.

If the resolution is changed to Fine, then many more triangles are added to the curved surfaces, resulting in a smoother approximation of the actual shape, as shown in **Figure 13.9**. In this example, 5512 triangles are created, resulting in a file size of 276 kb. This file size is small enough to be easily transferred by e-mail or temporary storage media.

FIGURE 13.8   **FIGURE 13.9**

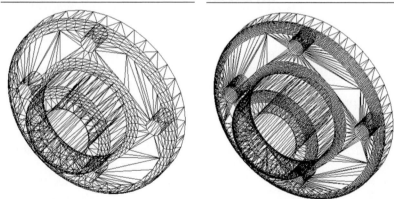

Usually, the Fine quality is sufficient. For parts where greater resolution is desired, the Custom quality can be selected, and the slider bars moved toward the right. The only trade-off for this higher quality is larger file sizes. However, since the transfer of large files via e-mail or Internet has become easier in recent years, file size is usually not a major problem.

When the .stl file is received by the RP machine, the file is "sliced" into cross-sections by machine-specific software. If the part contour is curved, then the surface finish will include "stair-stepping," as illustrated in **Figure 13.10**. Some RP machines allow the layer thickness to be adjusted, but, of course, thinner layers result in increased build times.

A model of the flange created by stereolithography is shown in **Figure 13.11**.

FIGURE 13.10

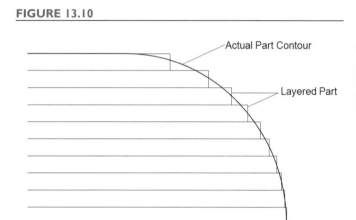

FIGURE 13.11

Paul Roberts; Milwaukee School of Engineering

13.2   Finite Element Analysis

Finite Element Analysis (FEA) is a method of predicting the response of a structure to loads by breaking the structure down into small pieces (*elements*). The locations where the elements come together are called *nodes*. Equations predicting the response of each element are then assembled into a series of simultaneous equations. Solution of this system of equations yields the displacements of the nodes. From these displacements, the *stresses* (forces per unit area) are calculated for each element. From the stresses, the factor of safety against failure of the structure can be predicted. The finite element method can also be applied to fluid flow analysis, heat transfer, and many other applications.

FIGURE 13.12

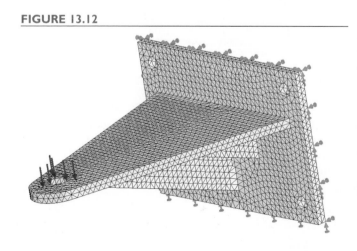

Solid modeling has enabled the increased usage of FEA, because it automates the task that in the past required the most time: creating the geometric model and the finite element mesh. A finite element mesh can be created from a solid model with only a few mouse clicks. **Figure 13.12** shows a mesh created from the bracket model of Chapter 3.

A 50-pound load will be applied to the end of the flange. After the mesh is created, the loads and *boundary conditions* are applied. Boundary conditions are the displacements controlled by external influences. For example, if we assume that the bolts attaching the bracket to the wall cause the back face of the bracket to be perfectly fixed, then we would apply corresponding constraints to the movements of the nodes on that face. The stresses resulting from the 50-pound load are shown as stress contours in **Figure 13.13**.

As FEA has become easier to use, it has also become easier to *misuse*. While the software takes care of the number-crunching, a knowledgeable engineer is required to set up analysis and interpret the results.

FIGURE 13.13

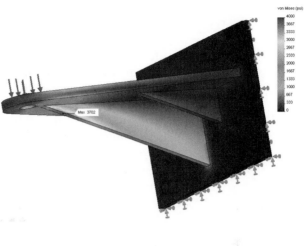

Among the common errors made by inexperienced users of FEA are:

- *Inappropriate choice of elements.* Solid modeling software with built-in FEA meshers allows a mesh of solid elements to be easily created from a solid model. However, in many cases solid elements are not the best choice. Relatively thin structures subjected to bending loads are usually better approximated with shell elements. A frame made up of welded structural members may require tens of thousands of solid elements to produce an acceptable grid, while a few beam elements will produce better results with substantially less calculation time.

- *Use of only linear behavior.* Linear analysis is based on the assumption that structural response varies linearly with loading. For example, the deflections and stresses of the bracket when loaded to 200 pounds are exactly double those produced by a 100-pound load. There are two types of nonlinearities possible, however. Geometric nonlinearity is present when the structure's stiffness is significantly different in the displaced configuration than it is in the original configuration. Material nonlinearity is present when the material is stressed beyond its yield point. When the material has yielded, it may not break, but will deflect further with little or no additional loading. Both of these nonlinearities require iterative solutions. That is, rather than applying all of the load at once, an increment of the load is applied and the equations are solved. The equations are then reformulated based on the results of the first solution, and solved again. This process is repeated until the solution is found. While this procedure requires much more processing time, it is necessary to obtain an accurate solution for many problems.

- *Inappropriate boundary conditions.* In the example of the analysis of the bracket, it was assumed that the back face of the bracket was fixed to a rigid wall. Is this a reasonable assumption? Maybe, but if the screws holding the bracket stretch slightly, then the top of the bracket will separate from the wall, placing more force on the bottom of the bracket. Most actual structural restraints are neither perfectly fixed nor perfectly free, requiring the engineer to use judgment in specifying the conditions to be placed on the model. In some cases, the analysis may be performed several times with different boundary conditions to obtain the limits of possible structural response.
- *Misinterpretation of results.* In **Figure 13.13**, the stresses displayed are the von Mises stresses. These stresses are calculated based on a specific failure criterion (the von Mises criterion) that is an excellent predictor of the yielding of ductile materials, but it may be inappropriate for predicting the failure of many materials.

These common errors are not presented to discourage the use of FEA, but rather to encourage the proper use of the method. An engineer should have a good understanding of mechanics of materials and at least an introduction to FEA theory before using FEA for any important application.

13.3   Product Data Management

We have mentioned earlier that solid modeling supports concurrent engineering, since many engineering functions can work from the same database (the solid model). Allowing multiple users to work on the same model or drawing, however, creates challenges, as well. How do companies manage their part files and drawings to control who can make changes?

Before answering this question, it is helpful to consider how companies managed paper drawings and other data before solid modeling was introduced. When a draftsman completed a drawing, it was checked and then went through a *release* process in which it was approved and signed off by various department representatives (design engineering, manufacturing engineering, safety, etc.). Copies were made and distributed, and then the released drawing was stored in a vault. Most medium-sized and large companies had a *configuration management* department that controlled the release process and subsequent changes. When a change was requested, a formal engineering change order process was followed. When the change was approved, it was amended to the drawing, or the drawing was modified and given a revision number, if the change was significant. It should be noted that many drawings would eventually have dozens of associated change orders, so managing this process was an important job. When a user of the drawing, say a stress analyst about to begin an FEA model, needed a copy, the configuration management department provided the latest version, including all change orders. Similarly, the Bill of Materials for each part was maintained and provided to the purchasing and manufacturing departments. In addition to controlling the drawing changes, the configuration management department would maintain *drawing trees* that showed how drawings related to each other.

A change in a part could affect an assembly at the next level. Other data might have been controlled but not necessarily linked to the drawings. For example, a stress analysis report might have been released and stored in the vault, but a person looking at the drawing would probably not know that the analysis had been done, or where to find it. Similarly, in industries where weight is important, mass property reports were produced, but usually not linked to drawings.

The introduction of solid modeling presented many new challenges to configuration management. Some of the features that make solid modeling so exciting to design engineers—associativity between parts, assemblies, and drawings, ability to use the solid model for many functions—could cause huge problems from a data management perspective. That is, one person could make a seemingly simple change to a component and that change would propagate throughout an entire assembly without the person being aware of its effect. Now that some companies model major systems with solid modeling, controlling who can make changes is vitally important.

Product Data Management (PDM) software is used to perform some of the tasks of the configuration management department, while streamlining communications between various departments. PDM entails two broad categories of functions:

- Data management, the control of documents (part files, drawings, stress reports, etc.), and
- Process management, the control of the way in which people create and modify the documents.

The data management function is similar to that of the paper-based configuration management department, except that the released drawings are now electronic files and are stored in a *virtual* vault instead of a physical vault. (Actually, backup tapes and disks of the virtual vault are often stored in a fire-proof physical vault.) Since the part and drawing information is stored in a relational database, immediate location and retrieval of files is possible. This helps to reduce redundancy, especially among standard components such as rings and fasteners. A design engineer who needs to specify a fastener can easily determine if there is already a similar fastener with a part number assigned in the system. If there is, then the purchasing department will not have an additional item to buy.

Process management is the control of active procedures: who generates the data and how the data are transferred from one group to another. One important feature of PDM systems is work history management. In a paper-based system, having old, outdated drawings around is an invitation for trouble, since they can be used by mistake. But by destroying old drawings, the history of the modifications made to that drawing can be easily lost as well. PDM software can track the change history of a part, an important function in Total Quality Management (TQM), while protecting against accidental usage.

What does the future hold? Most manufacturing companies implemented Manufacturing Resource Planning (MRP) systems long before PDM became popular. MRP systems allow the tracking of raw materials, work in progress, and finished inventory in the plant. The move to reduce inventories and adopt just-in-time raw materials deliveries necessitated the adoption of MRP systems. In many ways, implementing PDM to engineering functions is analogous to implementing MRP for manufacturing.

The logical next step, then, is to combine MRP and PDM systems into a single system referred to as Product Lifecycle Management (PLM) or Enterprise Resource Planning (ERP). As with any new large-scale system, implementation is expensive and time-consuming, and so these systems are not widely used in most industries.

A recent example of the complexity of engineering data and the challenges of managing that data is the delay announced in 2006 of the production of the Airbus 380 jumbo jet. Both Airbus and its competitor in the commercial aircraft market, Boeing, have suppliers around the world. Coordinating the work of these suppliers is a monumental challenge. On October 3, 2006, Airbus CEO Christian Streiff announced that delivery of the 550-seat A380 would be significantly delayed because of data translation problems between engineers in Germany, who were designing and building the wiring harness for the plane, and engineers in France, where the final assembly of the plane was taking place. As a result of the errors, the wiring harnesses would not fit correctly—a major problem for a plane with hundreds of miles of wiring. The problems were expected to cost Airbus over $6 billion dollars in profits.[2]

13.4   Some Final Thoughts

The widespread adoption of solid modeling has been part of a revolution in the way that products are designed and developed. As many companies have thrived with new technology, others that have not kept up have not been able to compete and have been forced to close. Although no one can predict the future, one thing seems certain: the pressure on companies to develop new products faster and better will not lessen.

On a more personal scale, the same concept has held true for many engineers. An engineer who is adverse to change and reluctant to learn new tools is at a great competitive disadvantage to his or her peers.

The good news is that most people who enter the engineering profession do so because they have the curiosity to want to learn new things. Keeping that curiosity alive will allow an engineer to have a rewarding career that is always fresh and interesting.

---

[2]"PLM: Boeing's Dream, Airbus' Nightmare," Mel Duvall and Doug Bartholomew, *Baseline*, February 1, 2007, Vol.I number 69, Ziff Davis Media.

INDEX

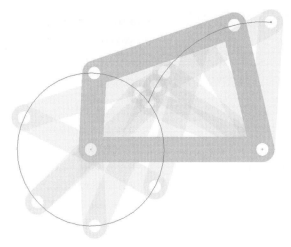